The Mirour of Mans Saluacioune

The Middle Ages
a series edited by
Edward Peters
Henry Charles Lea Professor
of Medieval History
University of Pennsylvania

The Mirour of Mans Saluacioun

A Middle English translation of
Speculum Humanae Salvationis

A critical edition of the fifteenth-century manuscript
illustrated from *Der Spiegel der menschen Behältnis*
Speyer: Drach, c. 1475

AVRIL HENRY

upp

University of Pennsylvania Press
Philadelphia

First published by Scolar Press, 1987

First published in the United States
by the University of Pennsylvania Press, 1987

Library of Congress
Cataloging-in-Publication Data
Speculum humanae salvationis. English,
Middle (ca. 1100–1500)
The mirour of mans saluacioune.

(The Middle Ages)
Text in Middle English; commentary
and notes in English.
Bibliography: p. 261
Includes indexes.
1. Bible—History of Biblical events—
Poetry. 2. Typology (Theology)—
Poetry. 3. Theology—Poetry.
I. Henry, Avril. II. Title. III. Series.
PR2085.M6 1987 871'.3 86–19364
ISBN 0–8122–8054–7

CONTENTS

LIST OF PLATES

ABBREVIATIONS

References to books and articles cited by author or title and date are found in full only in the Bibliography.

a(a).	article(s) (in references to Aquinas' *Summa Theologica*)
Abb.	Abbildung
absol.	absolute
add.	added
adj.	adjective
adv.	adverb
alt.	altered to to the lemma, or to the word following 'alt.'.
Apoc.	Apocalypse
art.	article (in grammatical context)
Bd.	Band
BP	*Biblia Pauperum*
CE	*College English*
can.	cancelled by being struck through
Cant.	Canticle of Canticles
cap.	capitulum
ch(s).	chapter(s)
Col.	Colossians
Comestor	Petrus Comestor *Historia Scholastica*
comp.	comparative
conj.	conjunction
Cor.	Corinthians
d.	deceased
Dan.	Daniel
dat.	dative
def.	definite
dem.	demonstrative
Deut.	Deuteronomy
Eccles.	Ecclesiastes
Ecclus.	Ecclesiasticus
EETS	Early English Text Society
Eph.	Ephesians
ES	Extra Series
Ex.	Exodus
Ezech.	Ezechiel
f(f).	folio(s)
gen.	genitive
Gen.	Genesis
Gesta	*Gesta Romanorum*
Heb.	Hebrews
imp.	imperative
impers.	impersonal
indef.	indefinite
indic.	indicative
ins.	inserted
interj.	interjection
interr.	interrogative

intr.	intransitive
Is.	Isaias
JB	*Jerusalem Bible*
JWCI	*Journal of the Warburg and Courtauld Institutes*
KC	Kathleen Colquhoun
L	the Latin (referring to the text of Lutz and Perdrizet's edition of *Speculum Humanae Salvationis*).
Lam.	Lamentations of Jeremias
Lev.	Leviticus
l(l).	line(s)
L-P	Lutz and Perdrizet
Mach.	Machabees
mar.	in the margin
Matt.	Matthew
ME	Middle English
MED	*Middle English Dictionary*
MET	Middle English Texts
MMS	*Mirour of Mans Saluacioune*
ModE	Modern English
MS(S)	manuscript(s)
n.	note *or* noun
NCE	*New Catholic Encyclopedia*
neg.	negative
nn.	notes
N.F.	Neue Folge
no.	number
nom.	nominative
N.S.	New Series
num.	numeral
Num.	Numbers
ODCC	*Oxford Dictionary of the Christian Church*
OE	Old English
OED	*Oxford English Dictionary*
o.er.	over erasure
ord.	ordinal
OS	Original Series
o.s.o.	otiose stroke over
over	written interlinearly over the lemma
o.i.e.l.	(over into extended link-lines); over and out into the margin where couplet-linking lines were extended to receive the early gloss.
Par.	Paralipomenon
para.	paragraph
pa.t.	past tense
pers.	personal
Pet.	Peter
PG	*Patrologia Graeca*, ed. Migne
Phil.	Philippians
PL	*Patrologia Latina*, ed. Migne
pl.	plural
Pl(s).	Plate(s)

PMLA	*Publications of the Modern Language Association of America*
poss.	possessive
ppl.a.	participial adjective
pr.	present
pr.p.	present participle
prep.	preposition
pron.	pronoun
Prov.	Proverbs
Ps.	Psalms
Pt	Part
q.	question (in references to Aquinas' *Summa Theologica*)
q.v.	quod vide–referring the reader to the Bibliography.
r	recto
refl.	reflexive
rel.	relative
RES	*Review of English Studies*
Rom.	Romans
rub.	in red (rubricated)
sb.	substantive
sec(s).	section(s)
sg.	singular
Ser.	Series
SHS	*Speculum Humanae Salvationis*
sig.	signature (used only of the 'pages' of the Biblia Pauperum)
ST	*Summa Theologica* (Aquinas)
subj.	subjunctive
subp.	cancelled by being subpuncted
sup.	superlative
s.v.	sub verbum
Tim.	Timothy
Tob.	Tobias
tr.	transitive
underl.	roughly underlined
u.r.	under rubrication
u.v.	(visible under) ultra-violet light
v.	verb
vbl.n.	verbal noun
Wis.	Wisdom
with ... mar.	related to (...) which is written in the margin
Zach.	Zacharias
|	marks the division between left-hand and right-hand marginalia
?	the material following is in doubt

ACKNOWLEDGEMENTS

My greatest debt is to Miss Christina Foyle and her husband Mr Batty, who repeatedly and unhesitatingly allowed me free access to the manuscript of the *Mirour* at Beeleigh Abbey, their home. They not only permitted me to study the manuscript, make the microfilm of it, return to check my transcription and take ultra-violet photographs of illegible portions, but gave me the use of a darkroom for the taking of beta-radiographs of its watermarks. In addition to all this, I was shown a great deal of personal kindness.

For the microfilming I am grateful to Mr J. Saunders, Head of the Photographic Unit of the University of Exeter, and for the subsequent ultra-violet work I thank Mr G. Bye, Head of the Photographic Unit of the University of Cambridge. The willing cooperation of photographers of their calibre, experienced in manuscript work, made a major contribution to the project. I am grateful to the University of Exeter for financing their work.

The book was prepared with the aid of computers and, more significantly, their programmers. The support of the Computer Unit of the University of Exeter has been expert and unflagging: in particular, I should like to acknowledge the patience and skill of Ms Migs Reynolds, Mrs Helen Ashdown, Mrs Jackie Beard and particularly of Mr Ivan Dixon, who wrote many clever programs to answer editorial questions. After he had embedded all the Lasercomp commands in my material, the book was printed in Garamond on the Oxford University Computing Service's Lasercomp: we owe a great debt to OUCS for its staff's steady willingness to deal with awkward problems and unreasonable requests, Ruth Glynn bearing most of the burden.

Mr John Lane and students of the Department of Typography and Visual Communication at the University of Reading made the design of this book a third-year project. It is a great pity that the demands made by time and money made it impossible to adopt their elegant solution to the problems of planning an attractive design within a fixed format.

To a number of colleagues I owe grateful thanks for their willingness to share their specialised knowledge: Professor R. Porter (n.531), Professor C. Holdsworth (n.913), Miss M. Dexter , Mrs A. Erskine, Professor E. Yates, Professor D. O'Connor, and Mr C. Skidmore, research student. For his unstinting help Mr Jack Osborne deserves a better description than that of research assistant: for many years now he has shown every sign of pleasure in solving conundrums, ferreting out references and translating from a bewildering variety of languages, showing the same remarkable zest for these tasks as he does for everything.

From the staff of five libraries I received the courteous and learned service for which they are renowned: the British Library, the Bodleian and Ashmolean Libraries, Cambridge University Library, and Exeter University Library, where my long-suffering colleagues deserve special mention.

For permission to reproduce a hundred and sixty-eight of the woodcuts from a splendid microfilm of their copy of Drach's edition of *Spiegel der menschen Behältnis* I am most grateful to the Bayerische Staatsbibliothek, Munich.

Dr Oliver Pickering and Dr Manfred Görlach, editors of the series Middle English Texts for which this book was prepared camera-ready, were most helpful. Unfortunately MET found the type-size dictated by format unacceptably small.

More intangible but equally valuable help came from my dear Father, as steadily supportive in this as in everything. He died suddenly on 18 January 1985, while this book was in the final stages of preparation. It is for him, nevertheless.

INTRODUCTION

SPECULUM HUMANAE SALVATIONIS (THE MIROUR OF MANS SALUACIOUNE)

STRUCTURE AND CONTENT

The *Mirour of Mans Saluacioune* (*MMS*) is an anonymous translation of *Speculum Humanae Salvationis* (*SHS*).[1] *SHS* was written at an unknown date (probably between 1310 and 1324)[2] by an unidentified author,[3] whose nation of origin is as uncertain as that of the book.[4] It may be lacking in credentials, but it was a best-seller, as is shown by its survival in at least three hundred and ninety-four fourteenth- and fifteenth- century manuscripts: an extraordinary number.[5] These are mostly in Latin, but are found also in German, French, Dutch, and Czech; one, the subject of this edition, is in English.[6] The geographical distribution of the text, even before 1350, was remarkable, covering an area bounded by Dortmund in the north, Prague in the east and Toledo in the south and west.[7] The popularity of *SHS* in the fifteenth century is further shown by the fact that it was among the earliest books to be printed from moveable type,[8] following hard on the blockbook *Biblia Pauperum* which influenced many of its woodcuts.[9]

---

1 The standard edition of *SHS* is by Lutz and Perdrizet (1907, 1909), hereafter referred to as L-P. (Full references are given only in the Bibliography, to which the reader is referred by 'see' and 'q.v.'.) The Middle Dutch manuscript version is edited by Daniels. The most recent work on *SHS* which I have been able to consult is Evelyn Silber's valuable unpublished dissertation (1982) which shows a refreshingly sceptical attitude to received opinion on date, authorship and provenance. I am indebted to Dr Silber for permission to use her material. Not yet published in the U.K. (May 1985) is the Wilsons' lavishly illustrated survey of the manuscripts and incunabula (1984 for 1985), which I have been able to consult briefly in a pre-publication copy. It reproduces all the woodcuts in the earliest printed *SHS*, briefly describing each. Though the authors knew Silber's article they were too early to use her thesis, extensively cited here.

2 Silber (1982:50-55) throws new light on the possible date. She doubts that the year of composition is indicated by the 1324 date which appears at the start of the Prohemia in two Italian copies of *SHS* (Paris, BN, MS lat.9584 part of which is Cambridge, Fitzwilliam Museum, MS 43-1950, and Paris, Arsenal, MS 593). This entry reads: ***Incipit prohemium cuiusdam nove compilationis edite sub anno domini millesimo ccc° 24° nomen vero auctoris humilitate siletur. Sed titulus sive nomen operis est speculum humanae salvationis.*** The attempt by H. M. Thomas (1970 and 1975) to prove a post-1324 date from a supposed reference to the Beatific Vision controversy of A.D.1331-5 (ch.28/3055-65 in this edition) is inconclusive, *SHS* expressing conventional theology here. 'Ubi est Papa, ibi est Curia' (ch.28/3057), which he interpreted as a quotation from a gloss of A.D.1325, was shown by Baier (1977) to be a catchphrase of the late 13th century, which suggests this as a possible date for *SHS*. The mention of Aquinas (canonised 1323) among the Blessed signifies little since he had been regarded as a saint well before canonisation, his views being defended from 1286; it is therefore 'conceivable that the ***Speculum*** itself provides ground for a ***terminus post quem*** of 1286', though the range c.1310-1324 would seem more likely on manuscript evidence (Silber 1982:309).

3 Most of L-P's arguments (1907:245-9) for his having been a Dominican are discredited, though his Latin, his sources and his ***Prologus*** suggest a cleric (see Appendix). However, a strong Dominican bias is suggested by the fact that in the whole text only four contemporary saints are mentioned: Dominic, Francis (ch.37/3940-52), Peter Martyr (ch.41/4364), and Thomas Aquinas (ch.42/4464)—a major source for the author. Three of these are Dominican, and the exception, Francis, is mentioned only in the context of a vision by Dominic. Also discredited is the argument by H. M. Thomas (1970, and 1975:204-33) for Franciscan authorship. The theological culture of the day was dominated by Franciscans and Dominicans: Franciscan elements may thus be contemporary commonplaces. Appuhn's contention (1981:134-5) that the author was a member of the Teutonic Order is unproven. That the author was unlikely to have been Ludolf of Saxony was revealed by Bodenstedt (1944), whose support for Nicolas of Strasbourg as author is no more credible (Silber 1982:41-48).

4 Germany, Austria and perhaps Italy have been suggested as the places of origin (Silber 1982:55-58, 131, 311-12) where it is made clear that a possible origin in the university town of Bologna need not imply Italian authorship. *SHS* certainly became more widely distributed in northern Europe than in the south.

5 Silber (1982:Appendix One) lists MSS, updating L-P (1907:ix-xviii, 329-32) and Breitenbach (1930:5-43). In black and white facsimile are those edited by L-P (1909), and by Berenson and James (1926). The best facsimile, in full colour, is by Neumüller (1972). Appuhn (1981) publishes miniatures in colour, his little book offering very good value.

6 In the only edition hitherto published (Huth 1888) ME was ***invented*** to fill lacunae in the MS. Kathleen Colquhoun's unpublished M.A. dissertation (1964) contains in secs.IV,V discussions of the phonology and accidence of the translation. I am grateful to Mrs Helen Bishop (her present name) for permission to make use of her material in my introduction.

7 Silber (1982: map between 306, 307).

8 For early editions relevant to the present illustrations from Drach see n.58 below; for an account of Drach's importance as a printer and publisher see Geldner (1962).

9 For an outline study of blockbooks of the period see Hind (1935:I, ch.iv).

Clearly *SHS*, in common with the majority of medieval books, was not sold on its author's name. Neither did its appeal lie primarily in any originality. In his *Prologus*, the writer tells us that his work was 'compiled' (a largely accurate description, for the work is based on a collection of traditional ideas and images) to instruct both the laity and clergy.[10] Its title shows that it belongs to a very large genre of medieval works forming 'guides' to various subjects: there are, for example, Mirrors of the World, of the Church, of the Virgin, of Christ.[11] Part of its original attraction was no doubt that it served as a *summa* or compendium, acting like a handbook. But though orthodox theologically, *SHS* is in other ways sometimes innovatory: a number of new images and devotional themes find their earliest expression in it. Even when the images and stories used are familiar, their application is often imaginative.[12] This interesting combination of 'ancient and modern' may account for the author's suggestion in his Prologus that preachers use *SHS* as a source-book for sermons, and for his provision of a summary of chapter-contents so that those unable to afford the whole book may buy only the summary, and if they know the stories mentioned, use it as an *aide-mémoire*.

It is easy to imagine how a well-built and satisfying sermon might be made out of any one of its chapters. Consider, for example, the very varied material of ch.28, which deals with Christ's descent into so-called 'Hell' (the event mentioned in the Apostles' Creed). The opening section is rather dryly theological. We are told that Hell is quadripartite, only one portion of it being a place of punishment for the damned. Three of its portions accommodate the saved: unbaptised children, those in the cleansing pains of Purgatory, and 'saints of the Old Law'–the souls of those unredeemed until the coming of Jesus. Christ's visit to these last is then compared with three earlier occasions on which comfort was brought to prisoners. All three comparisons are far from dry. They offer vivid moral stories in themselves, each illustrating the innocent endurance of hardship. First is the dramatic account of the three youths thrown into their persecutor's furnace, their faith and flesh protected by an angel sent *into the oven* among the flames. Second is the tale of the prophet Daniel imprisoned but unharmed in the den of lions (*The seven lyons takenynge the noumbre of feendes alle*), his food air-lifted to him by the reluctant Habacuc, whom an angel carried in by his hair.[13] Third is the strange (and rare) story of the Ostrich's offspring, trapped inside a glass vessel until freed by the parent's application of a serpent's blood known to dissolve glass.

The chapter offers a good mix of intellectual, emotional and arresting approaches to its subject. In addition to their intrinsic interest, the three parallels are examples of protection or release from pain, hunger and isolation, and so act as imaginative glosses on the nature of temporary separation from God and its joyful cessation. All three examples also carry traditional meanings associating the saving figure with Christ. The angel in the furnace represents Christ's immunity in the midst of Hell's evil;[14] Daniel's survival presages Christ's coming Resurrection;[15] the saving serpent's blood is that of Christ crucified, for like Moses' brazen serpent he was 'lifted up in the desert'.[16] This is all good material for meditation on the life hereafter: on the relation between merit and reward, on the justice and mercy of God, and on the power of the atonement. Whether or not the book was ever used for public instruction, it clearly offers material for private prayer.

---

10 The original author's interesting *Prologus*, in which he describes his aims and methods, has no equivalent in the ME, in which the Prohemium or Summary of Chapters occurs immediately before the main text.

11 *Specula* listed in the bibliography include those by Vincent of Beauvais, by the so-called Honorius of Autun, by Conrad of Saxony, and a 15th-century Dutch Life of Christ edited by Beuken and Marrow (1979), as well as Caxton's *Mirrour of the World*–the earliest English translation of an encyclopedia. For an account of medieval *Specula* see Bradley (1954) Grabes (1982) and Silber (1982:1-3). The image, deriving ultimately from I Cor. xiii 12 and James i 23-24, developed under the influence of Augustine's comparison of Scripture to a mirror (*PL* XXXII 57, *PL* XXXVI 248, XXXVII 1338), picked up in Alcuin (*PL* CI 616) and in Bernard (*PL* CLXXXIV 788).

12 Examples are Adam and Eve mourning Abel (ch.26), the ostrich saving its young (ch.28) and several Marian images: the conquest of Satan by the Virgin (ch.30), the Virgin visiting the sites of her son's life (ch.35), and interceding for man in St Dominic's vision (chs.37, 38).

13 All Biblical names and quotations are taken from a modern-spelling version of the Douay-Rheims translation of the Vulgate (see *Holy Bible*).

14 In the *Biblia Pauperum* (sig.m) the scene appears on a page devoted to images suggesting the Trinity, and the angel signifies the unity of the Trinity.

15 As in the *Biblia Pauperum*, sig..l.; the scene is for this reason common even in the 4th-century art of the catacombs.

16 John iii 14-16; the parallel is illustrated in the *Biblia Pauperum*, sig..e..

This example of a chapter's potential as material for meditation gives a foretaste of the interior 'typological' structure of most of the work: ancient prefigurations or analogues (types) of events throw light on events from the New Testament or its apocrypha (antitypes). A modern reader is perhaps most likely to turn to *MMS* as a handbook of this kind of medieval imagery, both visual and verbal. It is the only fully typological and iconographical text which exists in a Middle English version. The typological aspect of the work needs to be seen in the context of its overall shape. Most of its building blocks are traditional. The main early sources are the Bible and the apocryphal gospels. The most important later ones are the *Historia Scholastica* of Petrus Comestor (who died c.1179), and two which provide a significant *terminus post quem*: Jacobus de Voragine's *Legenda Aurea*, written in the 1260s, and St Thomas Aquinas' *Summa Theologica*, unfinished at his death in 1274 but officially made the basis of Dominican teaching in 1278.[17] *SHS*'s highly formal structure is typical of many devotional and didactic medieval works (the best known example is perhaps the *Summa* itself).[18] Indeed, if the typological infrastructure is ignored for a moment, the work's contents, as they appear in a simplified summary, seem to be entirely predictable. In its fullest, unabridged form (which unless otherwise stated is the form followed by *MMS*) it consists of:[19]

PROLOGUS: 100 lines explaining the author's aims and methods, including an interesting warning that typological parallels may sometimes seem shocking. (This beguiling section, absent from *MMS*, is given in modern English in the Appendix to this edition.)

PROHEMIUM or Table of Chapters (introduced and concluded by two brief passages also absent from *MMS*, and so also included in the Appendix).

CHAPTERS 1-42, each of 100 lines, each chapter composed of four events and four associated illustrations. In the most general sense, *SHS* is an outline of the major events in history which bear on salvation. The inclusiveness of this subject-matter, extending from the Creation to beyond Apocalypse, is similar to that displayed in the English medieval Mystery Cycles (on which it may have had some influence),[20] or the *Cursor Mundi*. The first two chapters are not typological: they give the eight essential background events from Genesis: the fall of Lucifer, the creation of Eve, the marriage of Adam and Eve and the divine prohibition of the Tree (as one scene), the deception of Eve by Satan, the Fall, the expulsion from Paradise, Adam and Eve's life of labour, and Noe's ark (the latter present as the great Old Testament symbol of judgement and salvation itself). The main body of the work, chs. 3-42, is typological: it presents the life of the Virgin, embedded in which is the life, death, resurrection and ascension of Christ, then Pentecost followed by the Last Judgement, Hell and Heaven. Each main scene is presented as foreshadowed by three events.

CHAPTERS 43-45, each of 208 lines. The method here is not typological. Each chapter begins with a 26-line preamble composed of a brief introduction (4-8 lines) and a 'tale' (18-22 lines) told respectively by a hermit, a friar and a cleric, to whom visions of the subsequent events are attributed. These events are presented as devotions related to the seven canonical Hours; in each chapter the preamble is followed by a 182-line set of Hours, each of 26 lines (20 lines and a 6-line prayer): the Seven Stations of the Passion, The Seven Sorrows of the Virgin, The Seven Joys of the Virgin.[21]

In the roughly contemporary *Le Pèlerinage de la vie humaine* written by Guillaume de Deguileville in 1330, the Pilgrim whose life-journey is the subject of the poem carries a staff crowned by a large

17 Silber (1982:55). The sources are described in L-P (1907:287-322) and Colquhoun (1964:15).

18 Another appropriate example, devotional rather than didactic, is the *Meditations on the Life of Christ* (q.v.). Some examples in ME include the *Ancrene Riwle* (see Dobson), Dan Michel's *Ayenbite of Inwit*, also *Dives and Pauper*, *The Orcherd of Syon*; see also n.21.

19 Silber (1982:53-54, 62-66) challenges L-P's and Breitenbach's belief that *SHS* grew from 34 to 45 chapters: she sees the rare shorter versions as abridgements rather than examples of the original form. In particular, the three final chapters, once considered a late addition, are now thought to be part of the original.

20 For typology in the Cycles see Vriend (1928), Woolf (1957), Williams (1968), Leiter (1969) and Meyers (1975).

21 Since the first two chapters are a non-typological prelude, and the last three chapters non-typological formal meditations, the bulk of the book can be seen as composed of forty chapters–as is the whole *Biblia Pauperum* in its fullest popular form. Could there be an association with the 40 days of Lent?

knob, with a smaller one under it. The lower knob is a light-emitting jewel which is also the Virgin. The upper one is a mirror, which is also Christ. In this mirror the Pilgrim can always see the New Jerusalem, the Everlasting City of the next world.[22] The mirror is his goal, and insofar as it is Christ it is his guide. Our text has much in common with this mirror. The greater part of the work (chs.7-33) is concerned with the life of Christ: it is in this sense a predictable model or guide. But in addition to this legendary and historical material, it also offers a less familiar vision of a timeless reality, for within the overall structure already described it is built on the typological mode apparent in ch.28 (the Descent into Hell) discussed above.

TYPOLOGY

Since I have considered typology in some detail elsewhere,[23] it is perhaps sufficient here simply to describe it in outline.[24] Each of the forty main chapters (3-42) consists of a leading event (usually from the New Testament) followed by three events (usually from the Old Testament, but also from the New, and sometimes from other sources) which are symbolically related to it. The relationships are commonly traditional, but are not fixed: for example the drowning of Pharao in the Red Sea, which is a type of Baptism in earlier typology, is a type of the Last Judgement here (ch.41c). The structure is intended to reflect a divine plan in which the past and the material world together form a kind of 'book'. Correctly read, this book gives us understanding of a higher, divinely-conceived pattern than is apparent at the merely historical or literal level: it enables us to glimpse a reflected truth 'as through a glass, in a dark manner'.[25] Visual and verbal juxtaposition of the main event (antitype) with three of its prefigurations or foreshadowings or explanatory analogues (types) reveals hidden meanings inherent in all four events. By means of this truly 'reflective' method, history is viewed in terms of its hidden relationship to the Incarnation: we momentarily see creation as if from God's point of view, from which space and time fit into a timeless pattern.

The imaginative habit of interpreting the present or future in terms of the past was strong even among the Jews. The Gospels often refer to an event occurring 'that the scripture might be fulfilled'. The intention expressed in 'that' (a purposive 'in order that') is of course an intention in the eternal mind of God that is being realised. For example, John xix 37 tells us that the side of the dead Christ was opened to fulfil Zacharias' Messianic prophecy: 'They shall look on him whom they pierced'.[26]

The relationships perceived in what may be called 'comparative' typology are more complex than those created by the mere fulfilment of prophecy. Christ himself used the comparative technique. He made a somewhat enigmatic equation between himself and the serpent of which Moses made an image (I have already mentioned the passage in discussion of the Ostrich's freeing of her young).[27] He also compared his coming death and resurrection to Jonas' three days in the fish.[28] It is interesting that neither of these images is simple: each provokes thought by a certain unexpectedness or obscurity. It seems strange to compare Christ with an idol-like image of a poisonous reptile, or with a reluctant and self-obsessed minor prophet: we begin to see why the author warned his own audience against finding some of his typological comparisons shocking. It is a little surprising that the author felt it necessary to warn his readers, for interpretation of New Testament events in terms of Old Testament prefigurations is found in the earliest Biblical commentators (such as Tertullian), and by the twelfth century the typological mode had become a major factor in Christian literature and art. Its importance is suggested in Alan of Lille's well-known verse:

22 Guillaume de Deguileville, ed. Henry, ll.1868-85, 1999-2043.

23 Introduction to *Biblia Pauperum*.

24 Typology is lucidly described by Auerbach (1938), by Mâle (1961), by P. Block, 'Typologie' in Kirschbaum (1968-1976:IV,395-403) and by Silber (1982:14-17).

25 I Cor. xiii 12.

26 Zach. xii 10; other examples are John xix 24 (quoting Ps. xxi 19), 36 (quoting Exod. xii 46, Num. ix 12).

27 See n.15 above.

28 Matt. xii 40; the implications are fully discussed in *Biblia Pauperum* (ed. Henry), sigs. .g., .i..

Omnis mundi creatura,
Quasi liber, et pictura
Nobis est, in speculum,
Nostrae vitae, nostrae sortis,
Nostri status, nostrae mortis
Fidele signaculum[29]

('The whole world of creation is like a book or picture to us: an indicator, for the believer, of our life, our lot, our condition, our death, as in a mirror.') One of its finest expressions in the art of the time is the great ambo of Nicholas of Verdun; its powerful panels, which once covered the sides of a pulpit, often provide precedents for images in the *SHS*.[30] The sequence of twelfth- and thirteenth-century typological windows in Canterbury Cathedral perhaps offers the best example of the mode surviving in Britain.[31] By the thirteenth century a corpus of ancient correspondences between the two Testaments was embodied in the *Biblia Pauperum*. In the fourteenth century the number of such texts increased, and we find *SHS* and then Ulrich of Lilienfeld's enormous *Concordantia Caritatis*, the major examples among several typological books.[32] This wide and complex tradition has to be taken account of when dealing with *MMS*.

THE USE OF TYPOLOGY IN *SHS/MMS*

The types presented in *SHS* (and so *MMS*) relate to the main scenes in several different ways. Sometimes they simply recall actual events associated with the antitype, extending the narrative rather than the meaning. For example, in ch.13, as the author himself remarks, the three types of the Temptation of Christ echo three stages in his resistance: to gluttony (Daniel's conquest of Bel and the Dragon), pride (David's slaying of Golias) and avarice (David's destruction of the lion and bear–used because *thas two beestis betakened auarice ... In thaire gredy ravynne reving Dauid his shepe*). In ch.15, the Entry into Jerusalem, the types again reflect events immediately surrounding the main narrative (and again the author draws attention to his method, at 1707-10): Jeremias' lamentation over Jerusalem prefigures Christ's weeping over the city; David's acclamation after killing Golias prefigures the triumphal Entry itself (though not without irony, for the nature of Christ's achievement is misunderstood by the crowd); Heliodorus beaten and expelled from the Temple presages Christ's expulsion of money-changers from the same Temple, his first major act after entering the city.[33]

The author shows a wide choice of types. As already observed, they are not always from the Old Testament. On several occasions they are Christ's own parables. In ch.40b,c the twin parables of the wasted talents and the foolish virgins, which Christ relates about the Last Judgement, hold their biblical meaning. However, in ch.22c the parable of the murdered heir of the vineyard is used, with skilful modification of its original purpose, as a type of the Carrying of the Cross; in ch.33c the parable of the lost sheep, again by a subtle modification of its original use, becomes a type of the Ascension (in which God takes mankind's nature back to heaven); in ch.35c the tale of the lost drachma is turned, with brilliant originality, into a type of an equally original antitype: the Virgin's visiting of the sites hallowed by her son. Types are also drawn from outside the Bible, especially from associated narratives such as Petrus Comestor's *Historia Scholastica*, or Jacobus de Voragine's *Golden Legend*.

Typological juxtapositions often invite the imagination to do more than draw simple parallels. There is great variety in the use of the more complex method. Superficial parallels may serve to point an instructive contrast: Jesus is, as he himself said, *greater* than Jonas. In ch.16, the priest Melchisedech brings bread and wine to Abraham. The food prefigures the Last Supper, which was

---

29 *PL* CCX 579 and *The Oxford Book of Medieval Latin Verse* have *in speculum*; sometimes the reading *et speculum* is found.

30 For example the 'sea of brass ' (ch.12). After a 14th-century fire, the ambo was removed from the front of its pulpit, extended and reshaped into its present 'triptych' form. It is reproduced only in black and white by Röhrig, but splendid colour transparencies are available from the monastery at Klosterneuburg.

31 See Caviness (1977) for a reconstruction of the original sequence and meaning of these windows.

32 See James (1851) for an outline of the *Concordantia*. The whole text is unpublished, though in 1972 Neumüller reported as in progress a facsimile edition for the same series as his *SHS*.

33 Noted by Silber (1982:13).

not, like Melchisedech's offering, a gift after manifest victory, but a prelude to apparent defeat. The manna which in ch.16 also prefigures the eucharist differs from it precisely because as Christ said: "Your fathers did eat manna in the desert: and are dead. This is the bread which cometh down from heaven: that if any man eat of it, he may not die."[34]

The three types in a *SHS* chapter often give us three quite different perspectives on the main scene. For example in ch.11, the apocryphal fall of the idols as the infant Jesus is carried into Egypt is prefigured by two other breakings and one building. The building is the (apocryphal) account of the Egyptians' earlier construction of a statue of a virgin and child in response to a prophecy of the coming overthrow of their gods in the fall of idols–a placatory gesture to a god apparently more powerful than theirs. This is a rare causal relationship between antitype and type. The fall of the idols is then prefigured by the legendary story of the boy Moses' breaking of Pharao's idol-bearing crown (the woodcut shows his eating of live coals offered to him like sweets–his acceptance of them proving his inexperienced immaturity, and so the absence of any political motive in his breaking of the crown). Moses' action is simultaneously 'meant' (by God, signifying the child's coming power over Pharao and idolatry) and 'accidental', insofar as it was performed by a clumsy child. We think of the Egyptian idols, which fell in the mere presence of the infant Jesus, and we consider that his coming ordeal will be undertaken with the full consent of his godhead and manhood. The account of Moses' breaking of the crown is skilfully followed by recall of his birth and survival, included because it is itself a standard parallel to the Flight into Egypt–both children escaping a massacre of boy-children by an insecure tyrant. Typological relevance has taken precedence over chronological narrative. The third type is not from legend but from one of the great prophetic books, Daniel. Nabugodonosor's weird dream is of a statue broken into its component, incompatible parts by a stone which fell unquarried from a mountain (an image of the Virgin Birth, the stone being 'uncut by human hand'), and subsequently grew into a mountain itself. Daniel interprets the vision as the kingdoms of earth superseded by the Kingdom of God. All three types suggest the supremacy of the Kingdom of God over earthly powers. Taking us from an infancy, through a boyhood to the powerful maturity implied in the stone become a mountain, they offer a prophecy fulfilled, a parallel action from the apocryphal life of one of Jesus' main types, Moses, and a future foretold. Using time past, time parallel and time future, they make us think about the paradox of God as a child, and of his ultimate stature as a man.

The types of the Ascension (ch.33) show that Jesus has come, laboured and gone. Jacob's ladder makes a link between heaven and earth, for angels descend it. The parable of the lost sheep recalls Christ's ministry, while also suggesting his journey from his heavenly home to seek out lost mankind and take him 'home'. Elias' fiery chariot taking him heavenwards shows us his mantle falling on Eliseus, as Christ's going made way for the grace of the Holy Spirit shortly to descend on the Apostles. The chapter as a whole is as much about movement in space as in time.

The mind is constantly invited to perceive more patterns than are explicit in the text. In ch.21 the Crowning with Thorns is prefigured by scenes suggesting first that Christ suffered humiliation on three levels: as mankind's lover (Darius mocked by his concubine), as a surrogate for man, whose sin deserved his humiliation (as David admitted that it was God's will he be stoned by Semei) and as God's envoy (as David's messenger was abused by Amon).

Sometimes great delight is taken in spinning ideas round minor details of a type. In ch.12 the twelve oxen supporting the Temple laver are equated with the twelve apostles bearing the burden of bringing the sacrament of baptism to the world, and the mirrors hung round it represent the examination of conscience necessary before adult baptism.[35] Another sacrament receives attention in the Entry into Jerusalem (ch.15). The Entry is seen (1741-54 in *MMS*) as an allegory of Christ attracted to an honest soul: the soul running out to meet him is Contrition, the hosannas of the crowd are Confession, the palms carried and laid down are Satisfaction (even the clothes laid down

34 John vi 49-50.

35 Silber (1982:11-12).

being alms, and the flowers virtues or deeds of charity). This brief treatment of the three parts of the sacrament of penance has great charm: the allegory carries within it many of the human implications of penitence which are also presented, however differently, in *The Parson's Tale*.

The same pleasure in focussing on minor elements is apparent in ch. 20c. Joseph is put into the well, and there is a long list of parallels and contrasts between him and Jesus, for example:

Joseph's cote fro his nekke rechid til his helis behynde
Bot fro Cristis crovne to his too was none hele for to fynde.

The author enjoys lists like this. In ch. 25 (Christ dead on the Cross) the third type is Evilmerodach: his legendary chopping up of his father takes only four lines, but is followed at 2751-802 by a chant-like list of ways in which sinners re-torture Christ, e.g:

And thas er*e* saide to depart to thaym Cristis clothinges
Who p*re*sumes for to destruye, robbe or ref neghburgh thinges,
And Jh*esu* Crist w*ith* Judas kissis he tresovnously
Who þ*at* his neghburgh gloses for to begile hym sleghly. (2771-74)

That the list is not wholly in the historical order of Christ's sufferings gives a possibly deliberate effect of fragmentation, in contrast to other, orderly rehearsals of the Passion, as at ch. 30a, ch. 35a.

The details picked out are often interpreted in terms of familiar groups of precepts or graces. In ch. 4 the popular image of the Jesse Tree is expanded beyond its usual signifying of Mary's birth, its parts being interpreted as the Gifts of the Spirit; in ch. 10, which is about Mary's (unnecessary) adherence to the Law in her Purification, no less than three such examples occur: the Ten Commandments which are in the Ark of the Covenant are listed (1217-44), the Ark's four rings are compared to the Four Cardinal Virtues (1253-56), and the seven branches of the Temple candelabra are the Seven Works of Mercy (1261-68).

NARRATIVE METHOD

Rather unexpectedly, one of the chief pleasures in reading *SHS* is to find how often the writer works with freedom within his seemingly rigid framework. The actual 'narrative' technique sets up a kind of counterpoint against the expectation of regularity created by the apparently rigid overall structure. This freedom shows itself in several ways. One is his habit of retaining narrative coherence in the Passion sequence by introducing summary accounts of essential events which are not accounted for in the antitypes and their illustrations. These usually, but not inevitably, occur at the beginning of chapters. Ch. 17 is about the falling back of Christ's persecutors at his arrest, but before this is described we are reminded (1907-18) of how Judas left the Last Supper to betray his Lord. Ch. 19, ostensibly devoted to the Mocking and Buffeting, begins with an event which ought strictly to be described as part of the Betrayal and Arrest, in the previous chapter: the cutting off of Malchus' ear by Peter. It is included at this point because of a legendary identification of one of the buffeters with this Malchus. Before the Flagellation (ch. 20), the writer recalls the trial of Christ before Pilate, then Herod and then Pilate again, and finally Christ's symbolic clothing in first red and then white before being stripped for flogging. Pilate's washing of his hands, the release of Barabbas and the dream of Pilate's wife are then given at the opening of ch. 22 (2407-36) before the Carrying of the Cross which is its theme. Simon of Cyrene's enforced assistance with the Carrying of the Cross is illustrated in ch. 22, but his tale is told at the start of ch. 23, followed by the offering of vinegar and gall (which in Matt. xxvii 34 may be interpreted as occurring before the Crucifixion) and only then by the Nailing to the Cross which is the main subject. The most extraordinary example is probably in ch. 34/3607-44 where Pentecost is preceded by the longest speech given to Christ in the whole work: a tissue of quotations which introduce and explain Pentecost itself, and act as a kind of farewell since at Pentecost his place on earth is taken by the Holy Spirit.

SHS often includes material which is, strictly speaking, outside its narrative or typological pattern, though it is always relevant in other ways. The types themselves are, as we have seen, sometimes parables: but parables are also used in this 'extra-typological' way. Ch. 3 is devoted to the

Conception of Mary by her mother; the first type is preceded by a 40-line retelling of the parable of the Good Samaritan, the parable being used (as it is in *Piers Plowman*, see Explanatory Note 510) as an allegory of God's pity on wounded mankind, to whom he therefore sends Mary to bear his Son.

Sometimes additional elements serve a more overtly didactic purpose. The teaching method can be very simple: in ch.12, the Baptism of Christ, the author signals a minor detour by his *and* nota *are we go ferthere*, and gives at 1419-32 an account of the three baptisms (of water, fire, blood), and the formal requirements for valid baptism. The aim may be a plain moral one: in ch.15/1790-1804 the cleansing of the temple from money-changers leads the author to warn his readers against all forms of usury (the passage is one of the rare ones where we seem to hear him addressing a religious community):

"Ȝe shalle none vsure take, nor alle sup*er*haboundaunce."
O brether*e*, haldes fast in mynde thir*e* wordes for alle chaunce;
Bot more reuth is, fulle many named Cristen men todaye
Mantilles swilk man*ere* vsure als sleghly als eu*er* thai may,
Whilk will noght lone purely for Gods dileccioune,
Bot for gift or s*er*uice, fauo*ur* or p*ro*mocioune.

A moral about our attitude not to the living but the dead is made in ch.31/3315-24, where the release of souls from one part of 'Hell' –Limbo–leads the writer to advise haste in praying for those in another–Purgatory.

At other times more esoteric theological concepts are detailed. Mention has already been made of the account in ch.28 of the four-part division of Hell: this is an essential theological background to correct understanding of the patriarchs' release from Limbo, for we must not confuse their state with that of the damned, or those suffering purgation, or those with only limited access to the vision of God. In teaching us about the truly damned (ch.41a) the author uses not the catalogue of horrors we expect in an account of Hell proper, but an indirect method: 4319-46 describe instead the glorified body's remarkable properties, technically called 'clarity, impassibility, subtlety, agility'–the gifts lost by the damned–while 4355-68 describe the sufferings of martyrs which are as nothing in comparison with the least pain of Hell.

On still other occasions, the author teaches by appealing not to his reader's head but to his heart. Two passages on the joys of heaven show a method in complete contrast to the one just described: a rational, didactic tone is replaced by repetitive, chant-like lists of attributes. Ch.33/3593-6 gives an (entirely conventional) rehearsal of similes for celestial joy:

And if the welkyn and the werld war*e* turnyd to p*ar*chemyn white,
Men myght noght the leest joye of hevene on it fulle write,
And thogh alle watres ware enke it shuld be thorgh wastid
Ar*e* be it the leest joye of heven war*e* descryvid. (3593-96)

and similar joys are listed again in ch.42/4406-66, the lines repeatedly beginning *There...*, *There....*:

Ther*e* bes p*er*petual hele w*ith*out alle man*ere* sekenesse,
Ther*e* shal be strengh stably w*ith*out alle werynesse.

These sustained celebrations may seem naive to the modern mind unlikely to pick up the liturgical, litany-like connotations of this method. More immediately appealing are the moments when the writer draws on the emotional power of vivid, familiar images such as the Worm of Conscience (ch.41/4368-74), or Christ treading the winepress alone (ch.39/4232-36) or, in an extended popular metaphor, Christ as knight in armour (ch.39/139-64).

Freedom is also displayed in the refusal of the writer to fix a constant length for any of the four sections of a chapter. The reader has to be alert, for sometimes the antitype is described with extreme brevity, and that on the most surprising occasions. Chs.24 and 25 both treat of the Crucifixion: the first presents Christ alive, and all we hear is:

> Here fylows howe he his deth forshewed figuratifly;

the second presents Christ dead, and all we have is:

> Here nowe howe thay hym scorned maliciouusly.
> It suffized noght the Jewes of Crist the cruwelle sleeyng,
> Bot thay after þat he ware dede reioyst in hym scorneyng.

The horror of the Crucifixion is most powerfully conveyed not here but in ch.27 (which is the Entombment) as part of the first type, the Mourning of Abner by David, because that story raises the question of recognising the true worth of a dead man, just as witness to the importance of Christ's death was given by darkness and earthquake, the rending of the Temple veil and rising of the dead. On the other hand, an antitype may be described at length: ch.19 has forty-four lines (2117-60) on the Mocking and Buffeting.

None of the aims identified here is unusual. The varied elements from which the author built his Mirror are mostly traditional, even commonplace. But the way he fits them into a strong framework without doing violence either to it or to them has its own kind of appeal. The strong framework is always apparent, not least in its underpinning of recurrent prayer, the mode adopted at the end of each chapter and seven times in every set of the Hours which form the last three sections.

THE TRANSLATOR

In his *Prologus* the author says that he has used a simple style or method (*dictamen*) in order to be understood by uneducated as well as educated men. Such claims are, of course, no more necessarily true than the notorious remark made by Chaucer's patronising eagle who, after a rhetorical *tour de force* observes: *Lo, so I can / Lewedly to a lewed man / Speke....*[36] But the Latin is demonstrably unpretentious (in comparison, say, with the elaborate rhetoric of St Bernard) as a few lines from ch.36 (the equivalent of 3859-72) will show.[37] It is in rhymed prose couplets of very varied 'metre'. The author is stitching together various lines from the Song of Songs:

> Quod videntes, angeli admirantes stupebant,
> Et prae admiratione invicem quaerentes, dicebant:
> "Quae est ista, quae ascendit de deserto, deliciis affluens,
> Innixa super dilectum suum tanquam sponsa blandiens?"
> Ad haec respondens Maria, sponsa Filii Dei vera:
> "Inveni, inquit, quem quaesivit et diligit anima mea;
> Tenebo eum, nec unquam dimittam eum,
> Tanquam Sponsum, tanquam Filium, tanquam Patrem meum.
> Osculetur me osculo oris sui,
> Ut possim perpetuo ejus dulcedine frui;
> Laeva ejus sub capite meo,
> Ut possim sempter vivere et laetari cum eo;
> Et dextra illius amplexabitur me,
> Quia secura sum quod me nunquam repellet a se."

About the translator we know very little. Substitution of St Benedict for St Dominic at 250 suggests his Order. The unremarkable mixed dialect of the text shows northern elements which may indicate his origins.[38] Vestiges of alliterative technique may imply a post alliterative revival

---

36 *House of Fame* (Chaucer, ed. Robinson 1957:290/856-66).

37 L-P (1907:75/55-68).

38 Brix (1900:119-24) tentatively concludes that the dialect is of the north midlands. Colquhoun (1964:35-47) notes various northern and north-east midland characteristics, such as OE *o* + *g* appearing in *slayne* rhyming with *aȝeyne* at 175-76. The computer reveals how common in the text are some of her other examples. OE *e* appears as *i* in *wriche* at 1541, 2945, 4743 (and see 2570, 2785, 3389, 3965, 4269, 4628, 4866, 4931), in *briste* at 1013, 2920 (see also 1328, 4881), in *rist* at 611, 4882, 4996. OE *a* is retained in *thase* at 20, 1421, 1422, and in 34 other places; in *slade* at 1252, 1498, 3846; in *vprase* at 227, 3046; in *Gast* at 567, and on 48 other occasions (but *Gayst* at 235, *Gost* at 1423); in *Haly/haly* at 200, 235, and on 93 other occasions (but *Holy/holy* at 910, 2761, 3494, 3942). OE *ā* + *w* appears as *aw/av* in *avne* at 167, *awen* at 1582 and on 25 other occasions; *awne* at 310, 1296, 2212; in *knawe* at 504, and on 14 other occasions; in *saule/sawle* at 310, 1742, 1819, 3008 and 214 as well as on 47 other occasions (but *soule* at 812, 3007, *sowle* at 3208); in *slawe* at 482, in *snawe* at 1833, 3433. OE *o* appears as *o* but also as northern *u*: *blode* occurs 37 times, *blude* 12 times, *gude* 102 times, *gode* 3 times. OE *ēō* sometimes appears as *o*, as in *ȝode* at 1476, 1912, 1921. OE palatal *c* sometimes appears as *k*, as in *swilk* at 314 and on 60 other occasions, *ilk* at 24, and on 31 other occasions, *mykel/mikelle/mykil* at 2283, and on 22 other occasions. OE initial *hw*, usually *wh* (as in *whalle/whallis* 2998, 2999, 3462, 3467) appears as *qw* in *qwall* at 229.

date.[39] Some two per cent of his lines show possible echoes of it, as in *O man, be warre on this of wikked wommans glosing*. The paper is A.D.1429, so the translator (whose manuscript might have lain behind the one edited here) may have been working in the late fourteenth or early fifteenth century.[40] He uses a line usually of six stresses, occasionally with a disconcerting number of syllables. The translation has been condemned for this irregularity, and for being so literal as to mangle English syntax.[41] However, the frequency of such infelicities has been exaggerated: the Middle English reads lucidly most of the time. The translator will also treat his source freely on occasions.[42] He can be neatly inventive in imagery where the demands of rhyme require it, adding trenchant little images. For example, *Ostende filium tuum, quem expectamus et quaerimus* becomes in ch.8/1011-12 *Shewe us ... / Thi Son wham we abide and seke als foghil the day*, and *Sed quando vinum sanguinis sui in cruce Regi coelesti est oblatum* becomes in ch.8/1050 *Bot wyne of Cristis blode pressed in the Crosses horn*, and *Vel posset per aquas coeli vos omnes delere* becomes in ch.17/1941 *Or be watres of the heven with bekenynge of his hande / Drown ȝow* ....[43] As Colquhoun usefully observed, his vocabulary is surprising too, showing some sixty words (usually but not always Latinisms) which are unique to this text, or recorded in it for the first time, or only later. Examples are 3592 *absinthe*, 3339 *adiutorie*, 277 *appensioune*, 118 *colaphiȝed*, 4985 *conclose*, 42 *condignely*, 2183 *condolent*, 4740 *consolatrice*, 4318 *defourmable*, 1009 *dominatour*.[44]

The clumsiness which does occur seems to be due not to overliteralness but to twisting of ME syntax and word-order to bring words into rhyming positions–a freedom that echoes the Latin original. The resulting obscurities receive clarification in the Notes: for example at 666 where in *Be erthly thinges, hevenly gifs intellecte knawynge* subject and object are transposed, and at 3327 *The Sonday tofore the mornyng fro death rysyn, the mydnyght* where literal adherence to the Latin line itself is not responsible: *Media autem nocte, die dominico, quando a morte resurrexit.*

It is a mistake to read this translation as if it were 'poetry'. It is best read as what it is, rhythmic rhyme in an unpretentious style which does not attempt the formal framework of strict metre and alliteration. It should be compared with, say, the *Metrical Life of Christ*, *The Metrical Version of Mandeville's Travels*, or (more similar in rhythm) *The South English Legendary* or *The South English Nativity of Mary and Christ* (q.v.).

The fragmentary postscript at the end of the manuscript (p.226 below) seems to be an apology by the translator: Colquhoun (who misread it in places) assumed it to be his comment on his own work. The writer speaks of closely following *my wyser*, which is presumably a reference to 'a person more learned than myself'. The gloss on the 'postscript' seems to apply to the Latin: *the Auctour toke more hede to fede the sowles hert þan to soften þe bodely ere*. The Latin author's attention was not on verbal music: he tried to reach the *sowles hert* through the rational, recollective, associative, creative faculties (which Langland embodied in Imaginatyf) engaged by his construct and its content. The translator did not try to improve on this purpose.

DESCRIPTION OF THE MANUSCRIPT

CONTENTS

Prohemium (summary of chapters only) [f.1[r]]; The Miroure of Mans Saluacioune [f.5[r]]; Index [f.62[r]]–a limited and idiosyncratic subject index. The scribe left blank the bottom of f.57[r], all ff.57[v] and 58[r] and the top of f.58[v], to receive material missing from or illegible in his exemplar.

COLLATION

This runs a-c[16] (bix wanting) d[20] (d18, 19, 20 wanting). The binding is too tight to allow sight

39 Line 359, cited Colquhoun (1964:68-69), who mentions 94 such lines. Examples are ll.301, 1130, 1195, 2485, 2757, 4623, 5017.

40 I am grateful to Mrs Audrey Erskine for her confirmation that the hand is of this period (notwithstanding *OED*'s acceptance of 1450, and *MED*'s improbable 1500).

41 Colquhoun (1964:58-59) gives examples, but some are of normal ME. Brix (1900:23) found about two hundred literally translated lines.

42 Examples are at 364, 427, 3603, detailed in the Explanatory Notes.

43 L-P (1907:18/46, 18/84, 36/37) and Brix cited Colquhoun (1964:62-63).

44 Such words are identified in the Glossary below. Colquhoun (1964:70-75) and her later article under her married name (Helen Bishop, 1972) need modification in the light of more recent volumes of the *MED*. She found twenty-two words recorded first at a later date, but *MED* records possibly earlier examples of *mercyfullenesse* and *mysbegetyn*. She also found thirty-nine unrecorded words, but eleven of these can be discounted: for *geme* see *OED yeme*; *laccere* in *neuer the laccere* is a variant form of a common comp., not a rare n.; *gobbettinale* should read *gobbettmale* and is under *MED gobetmele* with several earlier examples; *lusaunt* is *MED*'s *lucent*, cited for A.D.1449, though this text is not mentioned; *gloȝaunt*, *inmersioune* (*MED immersionne*), *inmodraunce* (*MED immoderaunce*) and *inprovise* (*MED improvise*), *numularies*, *payentee*, *prefiguraunce*, are now recorded in *MED* (up to *propugnacle*) though only in this text.

of the MS's construction, which is revealed only by the catchwords, signatures and distribution of watermarks (one to each sheet). Number of extant leaves: 64.

Signatures occur as follows, those absent from the first half of quires being victims of cropping: 8^{r} *avi{ij}*, 17^{r} *b{j}*, 18^{r} *bij*, 19^{r} *biij*, 20^{r} *biv*, 21^{r} *bv*, 22^{r} *bvj*, 23^{r} *bvij*, 24^{r} *bviij*, bix wanting, 32^{r} *cj*, 33^{r} *cij*, 34^{r} *ciij*, 35^{r} *ciiij*, 36^{r} *cv*, 37^{r} *cvj*, 48^{r} *dj*, 49^{r} *d{ij}*, 50^{r} *diij*, 51^{r} *diiij*, 52^{r} *dv*, 53^{r} *dv{j}*, 54^{r} *dvij* u.v., 55^{r} *dvi{ij}*, 56^{r} *dix*, 57^{r} *dx*.

CATCHWORDS
f.16^{v} O gude Jh*es*u
f.31^{v} O gude Jhesus
f.47^{v} The Aungell felle

PAGINATION AND FOLIATION
Modern pencil pagination appears at the top of each page. Modern foliation under the bottom left-hand corner of the text, just under the first word of the last line on each recto, correctly numbers all extant folios. This is the foliation referred to throughout this edition. Medieval foliation in the top corners is unreliable. It is correct up to what it calls f.44 (clearly showing that f.25 is missing). Thereafter it breaks down: the number 45 is given to two consecutive folios; the numbering remains one out up to and including 54, then 55 and 56 are both numbered 56. After what it calls 58, no folios are marked in this medieval hand.

PAPER
The manuscript is in folio. The paper is apparently of uniform stock, showing a pair of eight-point Suns (or, according to Zonghi's clasşification, Stars) watermarks which closely resemble Zhongi no.1408, from the ancient paper-mills of Fabriano, near Ancona in Italy. It is dated near 1429 if Augusto Zonghi is correct in saying that the paper used for documents in the Fabriano archive was 'used in the year in which it was made' (p.60). It is not possible to be quite certain of the uniformity, since in spite of the paper's thinness the marks are often very ill-defined, and it was not possible to take beta-radiographs of them all. Marks occur on the following folios, a query indicating that identification of a Sun/Star was not possible, an asterisk indicating that a beta-radiograph was taken: 1, 3, 4*, 5?, 6, 9, 10?, 15, 18, 19, 25, 26, 27, 28, 31, 32, 34, 35, 38, 40*, 42, 43?, 46?, 48*, 50, 52, 55, 57, 59, 61, 62*, 64*. The missing folio once before f.25 would have borne a mark.

Disturbed colour as well as chain and laid lines show that skilful repair with medieval paper was made to the upper corners of ff.41-64 inclusive, before the rebinding in brown leather by Bedford. Under u.v., faint words or lines of Latin are occasionally visible on the repairs.

HAND
The main hand is of the early fifteenth century, a date *c.*1429 being suggested by the watermark evidence. F.64, giving the Latin for a passage for which a space was left in the text, is in a different, contemporary hand, similar to that of the main corrector. Ff.62^{r}-63^{r}, the ME Index, are in a third contemporary hand which uses the double *a*, and also appears in marginalia, etc.

INK
Brown, leaving an orange stain when faded.

RUBRICATION
Strokes in most initial letters of lines and elsewhere in marginalia; alternate couplet-linking lines; underlining of some marginalia; occasionally the enlarged chapter initials; sometimes marginalia themselves; once (f.54^{v}) the running chapter number at the foot of the pages.

PROVENANCE
Remarks on f.4^{v} (see below) show that in about 1570 the manuscript belonged to a certain Thomas Cowper (variously spelled), who was, f.58^{r} tantalisingly tells us, 'off kylbury'. The next clear knowledge we have of ownership is that it belonged to Huth, who died in 1910. It was sold at

Sotheby's on 1 July 1918 to the bookseller Bailey, and in 1946 and 1947 was offered for sale by Martin Breslauer in his catalogues 60, 62, at six hundred pounds. It was bought by Mr W. A. Foyle, and has been at his daughter's home, Beeleigh Abbey near Maldon in Essex, since his death in 1963.

ANNOTATIONS

The couplet-linking lines are often over interlinear comments, suggesting that the latter are commonly scribal, and at f.12^{r}/13-14, f.14^{r}/7-8 and f.18^{r}/11-12 the linking-lines are extended to enclose annotations that obtrude into the right margin. Couplet-linking lines (in red) appear also in the postscript, f.63^{v}.

Sometimes marginalia apparently in the same hand were clearly written at different stages in the annotation of the manuscript. For example, on f.16^{r} (l.1222) the marginal note was written first, then the numbers of the ten commandments running down the page, for *ij* by the second commandment could not be written in line with *j*, *iij*, etc., but had to go to the right of the marginal note in the way. A later layer of still early annotation is apparent on f.24^{v}/9-10 where the marginal note *no*ta *Cristis mekenesse* has, in another hand, *nota* above and *bene* below it.

Included here are some mere pen-trials which unless deciphered may tease the reader with the promise of a signature or other significant annotation. Annotations which seem to relate to the text are given in the Critical Apparatus. Some are hard to place with certainty: for example, the unintelligible marginal note on f.8^{v} is given here, but it may be a comment on the text; on the other hand, at l.331 *benedicta est* (which is in the brown ink hand described among the later hands below) is given in the Critical Apparatus since it seems likely to be a comment on the text.

In the list below, occasions on which the name of Thomas Cowper appears are listed first in folio order, together with any clearly associated additions. These are followed by four mentions of a 'Thomas' who may or may not be Cowper. Thereafter, items are simply listed in folio order.

F.4^{v}, in the space at the end of the Summary of Chapters, are various remarks in two hands, one using grey, one brown ink, the former occasionally cancelled by the latter, which uses a distinctive '-rr-'. First comes a largely illegible line in the slightly later brown ink:

... *hl* ... *my* ... *d my lord gode[s] Amen* ...;

under this is the first entry in grey ink, partly cancelled in brown:

Iste liber Pertenet here it well in mynd
ad thomam Cowper | tow justice so bynd[45]
~~*ad vincula*~~ *[.....]*[46] *he in*[47] *hym brynge*
Ad Vitam eternam to þe euerlastynge kynge. Amen ;

above and partly obscuring the start of this last line is something illegible in brown ink:

... *ee me* ... [? *noght*] *my* ...;

under it in brown ink, another largely illegible and nonsensical line:

Ego [? *linquor*] *non derigetur in terram*;[48]

next in grey ink:

flodom feild was in þe yere of our lord god a thowsand | & fyue hundreth & xiiij & þat ys seine threscore | yere saue thoy |[49]

above this last line in brown ink:

nota bene

and under it, again in brown:

Nota *bene thomas cop | th thomas copperre* [? *on*] *thi |*

followed by a clumsy copy, in the same brown ink, of part of the last line on the next page:

whilk ete for hoege;[50]

---

45 Perhaps *bynd* began as *bryng*.

46 The word after *vincula* is illegible owing to cancellation and blotting. *Justicie* or *Legis* would make sense, but the first letter seems to be *d*.

47 The words *he in* should possibly read *hem*.

48 If this refers to the verse, the subject may be justice, i.e. 'I [?...] it is never relaxed on earth'. However, this line may be a continuation of the last (illegible) line in brown ink, or a comment on the battle of Flodden below.

49 (This means that the comment was written in 1571 (1514 + 57)–though Flodden was of course in 1513 by modern reckoning.)

50 This hand and ink produced a similar copy of the same words and *noght* under the original line at the foot of f.5^{r}, and the two marginalia on that folio.

f.5^{r} also shows part of the same last line copied below:

whilk ete for hoe... noghtt [sic]

and in the margin, again in the same ink:

my God

f.7^{r} also shows part of its last line copied twice in this hand:

And heled this rob... | And heled this r...;

f.34^{v} also shows, in a different hand (which perhaps wrote the line on f.64^{r} that mentions 'pet*er* kychynman');

*Whoy mayd thys worke þat dyd thomas Cowpp*er *þat good Clarke*;[51]

f.47^{v} at the foot, in the brown ink of f.4^{v}, a very faint:

*Good Th Cowpp*er;

f.53^{r}, at the foot, in the ink and hand of the lines on f.52^{v} mentioning 'thomas wylkynson*e*' (see below):

*pray for þe soulle of Thomas cowpp*ere;

f.55^{v}, upside down at the foot:

*Thomas Cowpp*er;

f.63^{r} has another passage in the grey ink and hand of f.4^{v}:

*Who some eu*er *on me doy loke |*
I am Thomas Cowper booke |
yff perchaunce ye doy me fynd |
I pray you hartyly be so kynd |
þat ye will wittsafe to take þe payne |
*Doy restore me toy my mast*er *agayne |*;

f.63^{v}, after the postscript paragraph commenting on the plain translation, in the brown ink of f.4^{v}:

[? *Nom*ine *domini*] *Thomas copperr*;

under it in the same hand and grey ink which appears on f.4^{v}:

*Thomas Cowp*er *ane Thys boke |*
*God send hym eu*er *more good luke |*;

then come two lines in the brown ink hand with the distinctive '-rr-' again:

who mayd thys wirke þat *dyd thomas cowp*er *| þe parysse clark parrysse clarke |*;

f.64^{v} is the second page of the Latin text written at the end of the manuscript to represent the ME section for which blanks were left on ff.58^{r}-59^{v}. The top left-hand corner of the text is faded, and must have been so for some time, for over it is written in black ink:

*Thomas Cowp*er.

Four times the name 'Thomas', which might belong to Thomas Cowper or Thomas Wylkynson (see f.52^{v} below) appears alone:

f.43^{r}, in the right-hand margin, in black ink:

Thomas

and at the bottom, almost upside down:

Thos

f.48^{v} in the left-hand margin:

thos

f.63^{v} has:

Thomam

and some way above it, in the same hand:

Sapiencye.

F.8^{v}, by the text describing the powers of the parts of the Jesse Tree, the irritatingly unintelligible:

[? *Peto te*] or [? *Petoten*] or [? *Potetem* (for *Potentem*)].

---

51 The 16th-century claim to have 'made' this 'work' (a claim repeated on f.63^{v}), must refer to the sentence making the claim; cf. similar statements made by Thomas Wylkynson on f.52^{v}.

F.10^{v} has pen-trials in the top right-hand margin:

gfedcba.

F.17^{v}, at the foot:

Mayde.

F.38^{r}, by the text's mention of the Cross as a supporting staff, a contemporary crowned tau-cross on a 3-stepped, partly rubricated plinth (a Cross Calvary) saying:

In / hoc / vince /.[52]

F.43^{r} shows two possibly related full crosses, without the motto, the one at the foot of the page with the base sketched separately.

F.44^{r}'s penultimate line and first word of the last line are copied below:

*A womman has hevynesse til hir*e *childyng be done / Bot*

f.47^{v} has the first word of the last line copied below:

May.

F.49^{v} the top left-hand margin has *l... my* erased, and in the right-hand margin are two 8-like flourishes, one very faint, which resemble similar devices in the bottom margin of ff.16^{v}, 31^{v}. At the foot of the page:

Henry þe *viii by* þe *grace.*

F.51^{r} has an illegible erased line at the foot of the page.

F.52^{v} shows a few scribbled words ... *may* ... followed by:

Whoy mayd thys worke þat *dyd thomas wylkynson*e þat *good clar{ke}.*

F.57^{v}, left blank for some missing text, has four lines of pen-trial numbers in the hand which on f.49^{v} mentions 'Henry þe viii', and in another hand the tantalisingly illegible:

In [? *Heuenend*] ... *my lord and god haue marcye oppon us / misorabylye .....er & onn my* [? *sonn*].[53]

F.58^{v}, in a similarly blank space, a partly illegible, potentially important line, which u.v. reveals:

*will*i*am Copor es off kylbury in [? bech Enn] wyll*i*am banbred off.*[54]

F.60^{v} twice has in the margin:

myn.

F.62^{r}, in a gap in the index, has:

the fadere.

F.62^{v}, in a gap in the Index has:

flodome feld was in þe *yere off our lord a thowsand / v hundred & .xiiii anno* domini *1519*

and, copied in a different hand above an entry in the Index:

The porte close

and the last line of the left-hand column copied below:

Maries offryng to the Temple v.

F.64^{r}, in the space at the end of the Index has:

for asse [? *alse*] *myche ?\ase/ pet*er *kychynman.*

F.64^{v} bears many pen-trial numbers like those on f.57^{v}.

EDITORIAL PROCEDURE

TEXTUAL DIVISIONS

In an attempt to clarify the formal structure of the text, modern equivalents are found for scribal markings of sections. In chs.3-42 inclusive the start of each of the three Types in a chapter is indicated in the margin by ¶a,b,c; the eight main events in chs.1-2 are similarly marked (with ¶a-h) although they are not Types. In chs.43-45 inclusive the start of each of the 'tales' before each set of Hours is marked in the margin by §; the Hours themselves (seven in each chapter) are marked in the margin by †.

TRANSCRIPTION

Medieval capitalisation and punctuation are silently modernised. Word division is modernised except where there is an argument against it, as for example in the case of *an other*e, which is left as

52 Burke's *Peerage* has, under 'Arran' *In hoc signe vinces* (derived from Constantine's dream of the Battle of the Milvian Bridge), and observes that crosses are used for charges on bearings of the families who use this motto. The earliest example cited is 1628 (Burke of Glinsk, an Anglo-Norman family).

53 KC saw the last four words as the name *Conningham*, but the first letter is certainly not a *C*, more resembling a *Q* if it is not *&*; the last four letters of the whole are very ambiguous, but there is no *h* among them.

54 Two trial *g*s below this make it unlikely that *Enn* is *Eng*.

two words since some form of *ane othere* occurs eleven times (as at l.1190). The scribe's practice of suffixing intensitive *to* to *al* (*OED all* adv.) instead of prefixing it to the following word, is not retained: his *alto drawe* thus becomes *al to-drawe*. Some of these may in fact represent *alto* adv. + v. His habit of suffixing *-n* to form negatives (as in *schen had* for 'she did not have') is modified, so that if the negative element is abbreviated, it now prefixes the verb (809 *sche nhad*). If the negative element is complete (*ne*) it is treated as a separate word (957 *hene shuld* becomes *he ne shuld*, 1013 *Whyne wolde* becomes *Why ne wolde*, and the same has happened at 1104 *we ne falle*, 1119 *thay ne*, 1212 *sho ne shuld*, 1529 *war ne Godde*).

The scribe does not distinguish ȝ from z: in the interests of clarity z is used in the text where appropriate. The same is true of þ (thorn) and y. Scribal use of u/v and i/j is retained, though the functions of the latter are normalised in the capital forms.

Virgules are ignored; they usually mark cesuras but are unpredictable, sometimes occuring more than once in a line (790 *Neu*er *fell* / *to sharp* / *nor bitter*e / *bot*), and sometimes being inexplicable (1582 *And with is awen swerd hym* / *slewe Godde of bataile helpinge*). Editorial emendations are enclosed in square brackets ([ ]). Material which is missing or obscured on the manuscript is enclosed in curly brackets ({}). The exception to this rule is found in lines or passages wholly in italics: these portions are missing from the manuscript and have been replaced with a ModE translation from Lutz and Perdrizet's Latin, in order to retain the overall sense of the text. Scribal insertions are in funnels (\/).

Expansion is indicated by the use of italics. The usual variety and ambiguity of abbreviation marks is found. As a general rule, final flourishes on *d*, *p*, have been ignored, as have strokes through *l*, *h*, though there are exceptions: the stroke through *l* is taken to indicate an omitted vowel at *singu*l*e*r*e* at 61, 226, 590, and at 879 *singu*l*ere*, 3430 *g*l*orified*, 4468 *g*l*orie*, 4472 *g*l*orie*, 3499 *angu*l*e*r*e*, as is the stroke through *h* in the marginal note at 1842, which has *h*e*rbe*.

Expansion of final flourishes on *n* and *r* presented difficulty: in both cases some expansions may have been included which were not the scribe's intention. The flourish on *n* is not expanded except where curving back over the letter it is somewhat extended after *-oun* (-io*un*) or *-on* (-o*un*). Sometimes a clear 'dotted circumflex' over *n* has been expanded as *u* (e.g. *sou*n at 934, 987). The same abbreviation mark is sometimes expanded to *-er* where it occurs on a medial nasal, as at 388 *man*ere. It sometimes occurs after two minims which represent not *n* but *u*, when it is also expanded to *er*, as at 84 *ou*er, 173 *moreou*er.

The final flourish on *r* is always expanded to -re, as its use is ambiguous. Computer analysis of all the text's forms of words so ending reveals that a significant number (forty-three) appear elsewhere in the text in full only in the *-re* form: ten of these are syllabic. For example, *noumbre* appears twelve times in full, as well as with a final flourished *-r*, and other syllabic examples are *candelabre* (in full at 1261 etc.), *chaumbre* (in full at 3177 etc.), *-clustre* (in full at 143 etc.), *delyure* (in full at 1860), *maugre* (in full at 346, etc.). A marked majority of forms support the expansion of flourished *-r* to -re. For example, *angul*er*e* (3490, 3494, 3496, 3499) appears in full at 3485; *answ*er*e* (2672, 3246, 4931) appears in full at 1925, 2294; *b*er*e* (453, 628) appears in full thirty-nine times (14, 34, 90, etc.); *d*er*e* appears abbreviated twice, but in full thirty-nine times (188, 304 etc.)–and there are thirty-nine similar examples of unambiguous scribal precedent for expansion of final flourished *-r* to *-re*.

The evidence is, however, not consistent. Some words showing the ambiguous flourish occur in full with both *-re* and *-r* endings: *brethere* and *brothir*, *floure* ten times but *flour* twice, *manere* thirty but *maner* three times; less conveniently we have *childere* once but *childer* twice, and *modere* once but *moder* twice. Sometimes the evidence seems to be more firmly against expansion of the flourish: *hire* occurs three times but *hir* sixteen.

The same is true in the case of seven words which sometimes show the final flourished *-r*, but appear in full only in the *-r* form: *ayer*, *fader*/*fadir*, *fynder*, *leddir*, *martir*, *rather*, *soper*.

A distinct group is formed by those words which appear rarely with the ambiguous final *-r* flourish, by far their commonest form ending with the abbreviation indicating *-ur* or *-ir*. In these cases, expansion of the final flourish on *-r* seems particularly suspect, though in some cases precedent for it in unabbreviated forms occurs. Five are particularly noteworthy: *after* occurs only twice, but *aft*er eighty-three times; *doghter* occurs not at all, but *doght*er twenty-five times; *honoure* once, but *hono*ur thirty-one times; *neuer(e)* does not occur, but *neu*er is found one hundred and twenty-one times; *ouer(e)* is not found, but *ou*er occurs fifty times. At least the reader has been warned.

Quite often large, careless horizontal strokes over words or groups of letters have been ignored, for example at 1459 *sevenfolde*, 1464 *heven*, 1465 *when*, but where the stroke is controlled or otherwise deliberate, or takes the form of a dotted circumflex, it may be expanded to *n*, as at 45 *son*n*es*, 46 *so*n*ne*, 97 *So*n*nonday*, 307 *Ma*n*nes*, 632, 1054 *ma*n*nes*, 356 *sy*n*ne*, 825 *wa*n*nhope*, 1053 *bry*n*nyng*, etc., or to *-ne* as at 365 *o*nne, or to *u* as at 201, 539 *a*u*ngel*, 202 *lyo*u*ns*, 207 *lyo*u*ne* (rhyming with *doune*), 1328, 1329, 1347 *coro*u*ne* (found in full at 1367, rhyming with *doune*.) etc.–depending, where possible, on precedents offered elsewhere in the text.

Although *þ*^{e} is simply given as *þ*e, *þ*^{u} is expanded to *þ*ou.

Ampersand is so transcribed. Chi is transcribed as *C* (not *Ch*), rho as *r*. *Jhu*, *Jhs* are expanded to *Jh*esu, *Jh*esu*s*, forms used in full by the scribe.

Contemporary corrections and insertions are, with very few exceptions, incorporated in the text (and noted in the critical apparatus), since it is impossible accurately to distinguish between scribal corrections and those of the corrector whose annotation (*corr.*) so often appears in the margins of the manuscript.

CRITICAL APPARATUS

Marginalia are cited after a lemma where the scribe or commentator has related his comment to specific words in the text by means of linking symbols. Where such links are absent, marginalia are cited after a reference to the line nearest to their position.

If it is obvious that a hand other than the scribe's appears, it is noted as 'hand^{2}'. This is used without further distinction for any roughly contemporary hand not found under the work of the rubricator (as is the corrector's hand, which may be that of the scribe). Obviously later hands are indicated by 'later hand'. Other abbreviations are explained in the List of Abbreviations.

L-P (1907:237) state that in their text *Amen* at the end of each of the first forty-two chapters should be reinstated, as an integral part of the two-line prayers which end each chapter. I have relegated all occurrences of final *Amen* to the critical apparatus, for a number of reasons. Such examples of *Amen* are (logically enough) always outside the couplet-linking lines; they are sometimes apparently in the scribe's hand (at 1604, 1904, for example), but are more often in the hand, perhaps the scribe's, that wrote the interlinear glosses (which are often under rubrication). They do not seem to have been regarded by the scribe as part of the main text, at least when he first wrote. Indeed, they are absent until ch.13, and occasionally thereafter (chs.14, 15, 18, 19, 25, 27, 34, 36). Even in the last three chapters, which are in prayer mode throughout, they are sometimes missing: from Prime and Sext in ch.43, for example, and from the Sixth Sorrow in ch.44 (from which the ends of Sorrows One to Four are lost).

The red alternate couplet-linking lines, underlinings, capitals beginning sections, strokes over capitals beginning lines, paragraph marks etc., are not recorded in the text or critical apparatus, though the occasional decorated capitals are mentioned.

Here, as in the text, underlinings have been ignored: chapter headings and other minor headings are often carelessly and inconsistently underlined. Also ignored are the points sometimes containing numbers, as in *.ij.*, *.xiiij.*, etc.: they are used inconsistently and are often doubtful or cropped. Unattributed readings are those of the MS.

THIS EDITION: THE LAYOUT AND WOODCUTS

SHS is not exactly ***about*** the pictures which illustrate it: it does not refer the reader to them ('as we see in the picture'), much less offer any aesthetic comment on them. Indeed, the manuscript of *MMS* is unillustrated. However, illustrations do seem to have been an integral part of *SHS* in both its manuscript and printed forms. The author's mention, in his *Prologus*, of his use in *SHS* of 'books of the laity, that is, pictures' (*picturis*) suggests employment of actual rather than metaphorical images. A third of the surviving manuscripts are illustrated, and no doubt the omission of illustrations must often have been due not to preference but to the dictates of economy. In all the illustrated forms of *SHS*, no less than in the medieval illustrated aids to meditation already mentioned and in those like the *Cantica Canticorum*[55] or *Apocalypse*,[56] pictures are not merely decorative adjuncts to the text, they form an important part of the pattern of ideas presented to the reader. *SHS* has much the longer text, but its visual images are similarly meant to act as 'icons'. Indeed, the relationship between the pictures frequently offers another level of meaning. That the images could, like the text, stand alone is shown by the frequency with which they appear in art. The earliest and most important cycle derived from *SHS* is in the stained glass at Mulhouse. The influence of *SHS* was once seen in stained glass at St Alban's Abbey, and is still to be seen in that of King's College Chapel, Cambridge.[57] But before considering any of the pictures, it is important to understand what we are looking at.

In the technical language of the bibliographer the present edition is a bastard: in the more comfortable if less honest imagery of the antique dealer it is a marriage. The unillustrated English text was copied out shortly after 1429; the woodcuts here presented with it are German, c.1475. They are from an early edition of the German version, *Spiegel der menschen Behältnis*, printed in Speyer by Peter Drach the Elder.[58] To explain the reasons for this particular choice and for the present format (fifty lines of text facing two woodcuts) the printing history of *SHS* must be briefly described.

The finest woodcuts illustrating *SHS* are found in the four earliest editions (two in Latin, two in Dutch) printed c.1468-1479. However, these editions do not contain the full text which is found in the manuscripts: sixteen of the forty-five chapters are omitted, so their woodcuts could not be used.[59] These lovely books do however retain the usual manuscript format. This appears at first to be ideal: one chapter on each opening, its four pictures (antitype and three types) running across the top of the double-spread, the associated text underneath.

Unfortunately, the earliest editions' relationship between pictures and texts is not as logical as it appears. The individual texts relating to single pictures differ greatly in length (so that much of the text under the first picture may in fact relate to the second). In addition, the text of a chapter may spill over to the next opening. The result is that these beautiful books can be confusing. The small size of the present edition does not permit a rationalisation of the earliest format which would show four pictures and their related text all on a single opening, but it retains as logical a relationship between picture and text as possible. Each opening presents half a chapter, that is, two of the four pictures, and half the text (which for reasons just explained cannot always correspond exactly with the images).

The woodcuts are from the earliest suitable printed version of the complete text. The version which is actually earliest is unsuitable. Printed by Zainer (in German and Latin) at Augsburg c.1473, its

55 See *Cantica Canticorum* for a facsimile of a hand-coloured copy. Verougstraete-Marcq and Schoute analyse two styles and nine compositional schemes in the earliest printed *SHS*, and list those in the latter which are parallel with compositions in the blockbook ***Biblia Pauperum*** proposing (1975:378) that they are in the same hand. They also briefly compare ***Canticum Canticorum*** with the other two.

56 See Musper (1961) for a facsimile of a blockbook *Apocalypse* (together with a ***Biblia Pauperum*** purporting to be the true Edition I, but see Henry (1981)).

57 L-P (1907:287-323 and 1909) reproduce the important Mulhouse stained glass at Mulhouse, also discussed in Lutz (1906). James (1888-1891:64-69) describes the lost 15th-century glass from the St Alban's cloisters, and gives a transcript of their inscriptions from Bodleian MS Laud Misc. 797 (nos. XIX-XXI, XXIII-XXV show specific *SHS* influence). Wayment (1972: 5-8) gives an account of the Cambridge glass. These and other examples are cited by Silber (1982: 10-11 in the Notes).

58 The relevant printed editions are: G. Zainer, Augsburg c.1473, c.1476 in Latin/German (Schreiber V no.5273); Peter Drach, Speyer c.1475, c.1492 in German (Schreiber V nos.5276, 5279); Bernard Richel, Basel 1476, in German (Schreiber V no.5274). At least fourteen editions appeared by 1500. I have not found a reliable list of editions: variations appear in Guichard (1840), Muther (1884 trans. 1972), Naumann (1910), Hind (1935), Goff (1973), Wilson and Wilson (1984 for 1985).

59 The earliest printed editions described by Schreiber IV 114-34 lack chapters 25, 28-30, 33-39, 41-45. There are four editions: two Latin, two Dutch, made in the Low Countries (Hind I 1935:245-47). A. H. Stevenson, in his introduction to the reprint of Briquet's *Les Filigranes* (1968) dates the first (Latin) edition at about 1468, the last (Dutch) about 1479. Kloss gives a facsimile of the Dutch version. (Berjeau's so-called facsimile is an inaccurate copy, best avoided). These abridgements have even fewer chapters than the short MS version, which only lacks eleven chapters.

woodcuts lack the detail which is likely to form a large part of a modern reader's pleasure in the pictures, and they are an inappropriate 'landscape' shape.[60] In contrast, those of the German-only editions, printed by Drach and Richel, are a 'portrait' shape, full of delightful detail and with a vivid use of the woodcut medium. Of these two, the Drach woodcuts were chosen because, notwithstanding current critical opinion, I believe that his edition, not that printed in Basel by Richel in 1476, is the earlier.[61] The use of woodcuts in a style so markedly German was unavoidable: there is no English series of printed illustrations to the *Speculum*.[62]

In the two editions of the German-only *Spiegel* the form and 'narrative' line of *SHS* is completely lost among the other writings with which it is mingled: the Fifteen Signs of Judgement, Prophecies of Antichrist, Epistles and Gospels for Sundays and Feasts, additional stories and parables from the Old and New Testaments, all fully illustrated. In addition, woodcuts are simply embedded in this multiple text as they are mentioned (and sometimes more randomly than that): they are not arranged formally and symmetrically on openings, with the result that these books are even more confusing than the earliest editions. The hundred and sixty-eight woodcuts used in the present edition, though all those which illustrate the *Spiegel* proper, thus represent only a fraction of the two hundred and seventy-seven in the whole of Drach's edition.[63] The last three chapters–the Hours–are left unillustrated, for two reasons. They are not typological in mode, so the illustrations have never borne the same close relationship to the text as obtains in the rest of the work, and in Drach's edition several woodcuts illustrating them are repeats.

Now that we know what we are looking at, we can return to the woodcuts reproduced here. The pictures used were cut by at least three hands: compare, for example, the heavy shading by the main cutter in the designs for chs.2 and 3, with the much 'whiter', more formally composed designs in ch.41c,d and 42c,d and with the much cruder execution, by a third hand, in ch.12. The woodcuts have a long and varied history, yet to be told. Some designs are traceable to manuscripts; some show the influence of the 'Hausbuchmeister' once thought to have made them;[64] some derive from the earliest printed *SHS*, some from the blockbook *Biblia Pauperum*; a few may be original.[65] Like any medieval religious illustrations, these raise interesting questions about their function. They are certainly mnemonic in the general sense, helping the reader to hold in his mind pictures recalling the main sections of each chapter. In some cases, the composition of the designs for types echoes that of the antitype, no doubt with a specific mnemonic purpose: for example throughout ch.20 (the Flagellation), or in ch.24a,b where the shape of the Cross is repeated in Nebugodonosor's visionary tree (which at the top bears the nesting Pelican in Her Pride, the mother bird's shedding of her own blood for her young signifying Christ's voluntary death). This kind of echo occurs also in ch.29a,b, where Bananias is shown killing the lion in a posture like that of Christ subduing Satan. In ch.31/1,2 the mouth of Hell and the gate of Sodom similarly release those who are escaping. The woodcuts must also have functioned as 'punctuators', breaking up the great mass of the expanded *Spiegel* text into digestible pieces. Even in the present layout they perform these functions to some degree. The rarer images must have intrigued the reader, drawing his attention to the text; on the other hand, they must often have worked by virtue of their familiarity, indicating the content of the text before it was read. The operation of the illustrations is as varied as the text they animate. The present edition is the first to present the ME text together with the illustrations which give it life. Together, text and woodcuts act for us as a fascinating compendium of medieval imagery and devotional thought.

---

60 For Zainer's woodcuts for *SHS*, which in his version is interspersed with the *Speculum Sanctae Mariae*, see Schramm II (1920, repr. 1981). Kunze (1975:pls.60-64) reproduces four scenes from a coloured copy. William Morris (1895:444) offers a rare appreciation of the cuts in both Zainer editions, noting their 'decorative and story-telling quality'.

61 Henry *Oud Holland*, 99i (1985), 1-15.

62 For a survey of 15th-century English books see Duff (1917), and for roughly contemporary English woodcuts see Hodnett (1973). According to its editor, the earliest English book printed with (woodcut) illustrations is *Caxton's Mirrour of the World* (q.v.).

63 All the Drach woodcuts may be seen in Schramm XVI (1933, repr. 1981), and in Naumann (1910), who also offers a somewhat suspect study of them. The errors about them made in Muther's 1884 work are unfortunately uncorrected in the 1972 translation. The need for new work in the field may eventually be met by the relevant volumes of Hollstein.

64 Flechsig's theory that the Hausbuchmeister was to be identified with the main cutter in Drach's edition was overturned by both Naumann (1910) and Buchner (1927) but the misidentification persists even as late as Friedländer (1970:41,44). For the Hausbuchmeister (Meister vom Amsterdamer Kabinett) see Lehrs (1888:28-31, 1893, 1894 and 1908:1-164).

65 Examples resembling those in the earliest printed *SHS* are in chs.1ii, 1iii, 8iv, 12iv, 17iii, 31iii. See Henry, *Oud Holland* (1985) for a list of the thirty-six designs derived from the *Biblia Pauperum*.

SUMMARY

Capitulum i^{m}

The fall of Lucifer
The creation of Eve
The marriage of Adam and Eve
The temptation of Eve

Capitulum ij^{m}

The Fall
The expulsion from Paradise
Adam digs and Eve spins
Noe's Ark

Capitulum iij^{m}

The annunciation to Joachim: Anna's conception of Mary
King Astiages' dream of his daughter
A garden enclosed, a sealed fountain
Balaam, who will prophesy the rising of Mary, beats his beast

Capitulum iiij^{m}

The birth of the Virgin
A stem shall spring from the root of Jesse
The closed door signifies the Virgin
The Temple of Solomon signifies the Virgin

Capitulum v^{m}

The presentation of Mary at the Temple
The Golden Table in the Sand is offered in the temple of the sun
Jephte sacrifices his daughter
The Persian Queen in her hanging garden

Capitulum vi^{m}

The marriage of Mary and Joseph
The marriage of Zara and Tobias the younger
The tower called Baris signifies the Virgin
The tower of David and its thousand shields

Capitulum vij^{m}

The annunciation to Mary: "Hail, full of grace"
Moses sees the burning bush
Gideon's fleece: "The Lord is with you, bravest of men"
Rebecca gives water to Abraham's messenger Eliezer

Capitulum viii^{m}

The birth of Our Lord Jesus Christ
Pharoa's butler dreams of a vine
Aaron's rod blooms
The Sibyl sees a virgin with a boy

Capitulum ix^{m}

Three wise men give gifts
Three wise men see a new star in the East
Three strong men bring water to King David
The throne of Solomon

Capitulum x^{m}
The presentation of Jesus in The Temple
The Ark of the Testament signifies Mary
The lamp of the Temple of Solomon
The presentation of the infant Samuel

Capitulum xj^{m}
Jesus enters Egypt (and the idols fall)
The Egyptians made an image of the Virgin and Child
Moses breaks Pharoa's crown and eats embers
Nabugodonosor dreams of a statue

Capitulum xij^{m}
Jesus is baptised by John
The 'brazen sea' for entrants to The Temple
The leper Naaman is healed
The Jordan is dry during the crossing

Capitulum xiij^{m}
The temptation of Christ
Daniel destroys Bel and kills the dragon
David kills Golias
David kills the bear and lion

Capitulum xiiij^{m}
The penitent Magdalen in Simeon's house
The prayer of Manasses in captivity
The prodigal son returns
David, admonished for adultery, repents

Capitulum xv^{m}
The entry into Jerusalem: Christ weeps over the city
Jeremias laments over Jerusalem
David is acclaimed
Heliodorus is beaten

Capitulum xvi^{m}
The Last Supper
The manna in the desert
The Paschal lamb
Melchisedec brings bread and wine to Abraham

Capitulum xvij^{m}
Christ fells his enemies with a word
Samson fells a thousand with an ass's jawbone
Samgar kills six hundred with a ploughshare
David kills eight hundred in one attack

Capitulum xviij^{m}
The betrayal of Christ
Joab kills his brother Amasa
Saul returns David evil for good
Cain kills his brother Abel

Capitulum xix^{m}
Christ is mocked and beaten
Hur is smothered by spittle

Noe's nakedness is mocked, then covered
Samson, humiliated, destroys the house of the Philistines

Capitulum xx^{m}
The flagellation of Christ
Achior is bound to a tree by Holfernes' servants
Lamech is beaten by his wives
Job is beaten by his wife and a demon

Capitulum xxj^{m}
Christ is crowned with thorns
Apemen makes a fool of Darius
Semei curses David and stones him
Amon humiliates David's messenger

Capitulum xxij^{m}
Christ bears his Cross
Isaac carries the wood for his own sacrifice
The heir of the vineyard is killed
The scouts carry grapes on a stave

Capitulum xxiij^{m}
Christ prays for his torturers
Tubalcain's forge: the discovery of music
The martyrdom of Isaias
Moab sacrifices his son

Capitulum xxiiij^{m}
Christ alive on the Cross
Nabugodonosor dreams of a tree
Codrus sacrifices himself for his people
Killing the elephant, Eleazar is crushed by it

Capitulum xxv^{m}
The dead Christ's side is opened
Michol mocks David
Absolom is killed
Evilmerodach chops up his father

Capitulum xxvj^{m}
The deposition: Mary's sorrow
Jacob mourns his son Joseph
Adam and Eve mourn Abel
Noemy mourns the death of her sons

Capitulum xxvij^{m}
The entombment
David mourns Abner
Joseph is put into the well
Jonas is swallowed by the fish

Capitulum xxviij^{m}
Christ's descent into hell
Sidrach, Misach and Abdenago in the furnace
Daniel in the lions' den
The ostrich releases her young

Capitulum xxix^{m}
Christ conquers the devil
Banaias kills the lion
Samson kills the lion
Ayod kills Eglon

Capitulum xxx^{m}
The Virgin's compassion overcomes the devil
Judith kills Holfernes
Jahal pierces Sisara's temples
Thamar beheads Cyrus

Capitulum xxxj^{m}
The Holy Patriarchs are freed from Limbo
Moses releases the Israelites from Egypt
The freeing of Abraham from Ur of the Chaldees
The freeing of Lot from Sodom

Capitulum xxxij^{m}
The Resurrection of Christ
Samson carries away the gates of Gaza
Jonas emerges from the fish
The rejected stone becomes the corner-stone (key-stone)

Capitulum xxxiij^{m}
The Ascension
Jacob's Ladder
The lost sheep found
Elias' chariot

Capitulum xxxiv^{m}
Pentecost
The tower of Babel
Moses receives the Law
The widow's cruse of oil

Capitulum xxxv^{m}
The Virgin visits the places Jesus knew
Tobias' mother laments her son's absence
The tenth drachma is lost
Michol is married against her will

Capitulum xxxvj^{m}
The Virgin enthroned after her assumption
The Ark before which David harped
The woman clothed in the sun
Solomon places his mother by him

Capitulum xxxvij^{m}
SS Dominic and Francis see the Virgin appease God
Abigael appeases David
The woman of Thecua reconciles David to Absolom
The woman of Abela throws Seba's head to Joab

Capitulum xxxviij^{m}
The Virgin as protectress
Tharbis defends Saba against Moses

A Theban woman kills Abimelech
Michol helps David to escape

Capitulum xxxix^{m}
Christ shows his wounds to The Father
Antipater shows his wounds to Caesar
The Virgin shows her breasts to her son
Esther pleads with her husband Assuerus

Capitulum xl^{m}
The Last Judgement
The parable of the talents
The parable of the wise and foolish virgins
The warning to Baltasar

Capitulum xlj^{m}
The damned
David punishes the city of Rabbath
Gideon's revenge on Socoth
The Red Sea overwhelms Pharao

Capitulum xlij^{m}
The blessed in heaven
Solomon in his glory
Assuerus' feast
Job's feast

Capitulum xliij^{m}
The hermit's Tale, and the Seven Hours: The Passion of Christ

Capitulum xliiij^{m}
The friar's Tale, and the Seven Hours: The Sorrows of the Virgin

Capitulum xlv^{m}
The priest's Tale, and the Seven Hours: The Joys of the Virgin

F.64[r]: the first of two pages (hand[2]) of the Latin passage for which there is no equivalent on ff.57[v]-58[v] (see p.214, n.4748).

scale cm 5

F.30r: the main scribe.

PROHEMIUM

In name of God almyghti, þe blyssed Trinitee
In o substaunce vntwynned and eure in persones thre,
And in Oure Laydis honour, hevenes souereyne qwene,
Þat most myne hert & hand gouerne if wele shall bene,
An for some of my freendes plesance in speciall,
And profit of Cresten folk vnlerned in generall,
And for increse of grace and also sawles mede,
Thenk I a buke translat–God lyking me to spede–
Fro Latyn of now late a compilacione.
"The Miroure" is named it "of Mannes Saluacione",
And in this bokes proheme be chapitles frist write I
The maters & the estories euerylkone by and by,
That who to studie þe proheme has grete lyst to asay,
Ful ethe in schort may he þe boke bere all away.

The fryst chapitle telles the fall of Lucyfere,
And to what honour Adam & his wife made were;

The secund of paradys lost for Godd maundement brekyng,
And of the exile of man the pynefull lang lastyng.
The fyrst two chapitles spekes of oure dampnacione,
Thas othere after tovches till oure saluacione.
Take hede in ilka chapitle the certein guyse es this,
That of the New Law forthemast a sothe reherced is
To whilk sothe suwyngly out of the Testament Olde
Thre stories ilk after other appliables shall be tolde
For to make feling prove of the forsaid sothfastnes
Be God schewed of olde tyme be figuratif lyknesse.

And than the thredde chapitle makes plenere mencioune
Of Oure gloryous Lady seintified concepcioune,
Als when þat God in erth liked man to be borne,
Be ry[ȝ]t nedes his modere most be sent hym toforne
Kyng Astiage & his doghter (and eke þe seled welle,
The gardyn close an\d/ Balaam sterre) figured how this befelle:
Till Astiage was shewed his doghter suld bryng furth a kyng,
To Joachim, his doghter suld bere a kyng, Lord of all thyng.
This sterre was in hire moders blissed wombe seintifide,
In stormes of this werldis see to ryght haven vs to guyde.

The ferthe chapitle telles of Oure Ladis natiuytee,
Figured in the ȝerd prophecide to spryng of þe rote of Jesse,
And be the shet\t/e ȝate shewed to the prophete Ezechie,
And be the Temple Salomon belded to God noblye;
For Oure Lady that come of the ligne of Jesse
The forsaid ȝate and Temple condignely shuld be. [f.1^{v}]

The fift chapitle vs telles Oure Ladys oblacioune
In the Temple, by thre figures of premonstracioune:
The sonnes borde, offered sometyme in the temple materiale,
Signed Oure Lady offerred in the Temple of the sonne eternale;

---

1 In...almyghti] *in another script.* 4 hert] i.e. myne intent *over*; hand] i.e. myne werk *over.* 11 þe proheme i.e. þe first wrod or the begynnyng *mar.* 15 j^{o} ca^{o} *mar.* 17 ij ca^{o} *mar.*; Godd] *? -es* maundement] ? *-es* 27 iij^{o} ca^{o} | De concepcione virginis gloriose *mar.* 30 ryȝt] ryst *subp. with* right *mar. hand²*. 33 kyng] i.e. syre *over.* 37 iiij^{o} ca^{o} | the birthe of Our Lady *mar.* 43 v^{to} ca^{o} How Our Lady was offerd in þe Temple *mar.*

And be the dogh*ter* of Jepte offred to God thogh indiscretly,
Was Mary fig*ur*ed, offred to God most *per*fittely.
Out of the garding suspensil beheld the qwhene of *Per*ce hir lande,
And Mary in Goddes Temple was eu*er* heven contemplande.

The syxte chapitle telles whi Oure Lady was wedded,
The whilk be thre exsamples was eke *pre*figured:
Be Sara, Raguels dogh*ter*, wedded vnto men seven
And ma\y/den neu*er* þ*e* lesse, be Godd*es* grace of hegh heven;
And be the tour*e* of Baris whilk was so verray stronge
That all the werld fro two men w*ith* force moght noght it fonge;
And als on Dauid toure wer*e* thovzand sheldes hanginge,
So wer*e* in Our*e* Lady Mary innou*m*brable vertus schinyng.

The sevent chapitle says how Our*e* Ladye was w*ith*‸childe,
Forshowed be thre fig*ur*es of þ*at* ma\y/den most mylde:
The brennyng busshe, & the flese bedewed be my*ra*cle sing*u*ler*e*,
Rebekka gaf at drynke til Abrahams camels & his messager*e*.

The eght chapitle tellis how Jh*es*u Cryst was borne,
And how þ*at* thre figures *por*tended it lange toforne:
The ȝerde of Aaron, the veigne of Pharaos boteller*e*,
A mayden be Sibille seen in \a/ *cer*cle of the sonne clere.

The nynte chapitle also tellis of the Ephiphanye
***Pre*figurd be the ster*re* þ*at* thre kynges of the Est come by,**
The stronge men þ*at* \fro/ Bedlem vnto Dauid thar*e* kyng
Broght watir*e*, & Salamons throne, thilk wonder*e* thing.

The teenth chapitle is how Our*e* Ladie to the Temple came
And offerd hir sonne Crist, Goddes verray Son and wysdame;
This *pre*figured the Testamentis Arche made be Besleel,
The golden candelabre & the offring to God of childe Samuel.

The ellevent chapitle how all the ydoles of Egypt ou*er*trw
When Marie and Joseph entred þ*at* same land wyth Jh*es*u.
This fortakned a virginis ymage w*ith* hir childe figurelly
Sette vp in Egipt sometyme be Jeremies *pro*phecie,
Be Phar\a/os coroune also þ*at* Moyses brast, & be the stone
Whilk al to-frushed the ymage w*ith*outen handes onone.

The twelft chapitle vs tellis how Crist was baptized,
Whilk thing be the brazen see was wele *pre*figured,
Be Naaman lepre þ*at* in flom Jordane heled wasse, [f.2r]
And be the same flvme drye whils Gods folk suld ou*er* passe.

The threttenth seith how the feende temptid Our Lord Jh*es*u,
And Crist in glutt*er*ye, in pryde and au*ar*yce the devil overthrwe.
The first victorye *pre*figured–full longe tofore–Daniell
That slewe the grete dragoun and distrued the godde Bell;
The secunde, the kyng Dauid when he Golias ouerthrwe;
The thrid, when he the lyone and the bere also slwe.

The fourtenth is how þ*at* Crist forgaf Mavdelen Marie,

---

49 garding] gardhing *(*h *subp.).* 51 vj^to ca^o Quom*odo* Maria fuit viro desponsata *mar.* 55 No*ta* de virg*in*itate *in the script of line 1, mar. hand²*. 59 vij^o ca^o {H}ow Our Ladie was wyth childe *mar.* 61 sing*u*ler*e*] ? singler*e* 63 viij^o ca^o Cristes birthe *mar.* 66 a] & *subp.* . 67 ix^o ca^o Of þ*e* Epiphanye *mar.* 71 x^o ca^o How Marie came to the temple *mar.* 75 xj^o ca^o How the ydols of Egypt fell *mar.* 81 xij^o ca^o How Crist was baptizede *mar.* 84 whils] i.e. filii Is*ra*el *over.* 85 xiij^o ca^o | How C*ri*st was tempted of the feende *mar.* 91 xiiij^o ca^o | Mavdelen was receyvid to mercy *mar.*

And forgiffes synners all þ*at* trewly m*er*cy will crye.
Loke this in Manasses þ*at* synned ou*er* the gravell of the see,
Whame God repentant delyvred out of captiuytee,
And in thilk pyest fader*e* till his fole-wastour*e* son,
In avotrer Dauid & manwheller*e* penaunce done.

In the fiftenth, how Crist on Palm So*n*nonday wept pitously,
How he was receyvid, & chaced out of the Temple m*ar*chands fiers[l]y.
The first was p*re*figured in the lamentacio*u*ne of Jeremye,
The second in hono*ur* gyven Dauid aft*er* the slaght*er* of Golie,
The thred, *id est* Crist flagellacio*u*ne, Helyodr*e* fig*ur*ed tofore
Þ*at* for the dispoillyng of God*es* Temple boght full sore.

The sextenth chapitle of Cristes soper makes mencio*u*ne
That in the manna had arst p*re*figuracio*u*ne,
And in the lambe paschal also done to the dede,
And in Melchisedek offryng til Abrah*a*m wyne & brede.

The sevententh, how Cryst enemys tofor him fell ilkone.
This fig*ur*ed Samson þ*at* slew a thouzand men in ane asse cheke bone,
And Sangar þ*at* w*ith* a plogh sokke of men sex hundreth slogh,
Eght hundreth Dauid in a birre, this is trew thing ynogh.

The eghtenth chapitle tellis of Judas & cosse & the *tr*ayto*ur*ye,
And how þ*at* Lord for luf was behated of Juerye.
This fig*ur*ed Joab þ*at* kyssed Amasay be tresoune,
And Saul Kyng p*er*suyng Dauid aȝeinst resoune;
Eke wikked Kayme p*re*fig*ur*ed this same thyng*e* wele ynogh
When he his brothir Abell causeles be enuye slogh.

The nynetenth sais how C*ris*tis visage hidde was dispisid,
Japed and all bespitted, scorned & colaphizid.
The mawmetiers vnto þ*e* ȝette calf of gold p*re*fig*ur*ed thes thinges,
Þ*at* choked to deth Vre þ*at* blamed thaym w*ith* thayr spittinges,
And Cham þ*at* scorned his fader*e* wikkydly lange toforne,
And the Philistiens whilk Samson blinded & loght to scorne.

The twentith chapitle tellis how C*ris*t was w*ith* scou*r*gis swongyn,
Figured in Achior Prince vntill a tree fast bonden, [f.2^{v}]
And be Lamech wham his two wyves sore to*ur*mentid,
For so two maner*e* folkes Our*e* Lord Jh*es*u Crist sore scourgid.
The payens bett him w*ith* scou*r*gis & w*ith* scharp ȝerd*es* eke,
The Juys stroke hym w*ith* reprowes and wikked tongis vnmeke;
And Job wham Satan stroke w*ith* bocchis fig*ur*id this,
To wham his wife rep*ro*vyng thareto did mykell amys.

In the on and twentyth capitle is how Crist was coroned,
Scorned & bespitted, and many a way dishono*ur*ed.
This Zorobabell schewed be Appimen the concubine,
That till a grete kyng didde oftsith both schame and pyne,
And Semei whilk þ*at* the kynge Dauid foully missaide,
And also w*ith* mire and stones & w*ith* stokkes on him laide.
Kynge Amon of Amonytes forschewed this thing also,
Doyng to Dauid messag*er*s for pece dispite and woo.

---

92 And] All *subp. with* And *u.r. mar.* 93 of the see] i.e. i*n*nou*m*brably *over.* 96 penaunce done] for both had mercye *over.* 97 xv^{to} ca^{o} | Touchand Palme Sounonday *mar.* 98 fiersly] fiersby. 103 xvj^{to} ca^{o} | of Cristis sopere *mar.* 107 xvij^{to} ca^{o} | How Cryst was taken *mar.* 111 xviij^{o} ca^{o} | of fals Judas *mar.* 117 xix^{o} ca^{o} | How Crist was bobbed *mar.* 123 xx^{mo} ca^{o} | Þhe Flagellacion of C*ri*st *mar.* 131 coroned] ? coro*u*ned; of Crist*es* coronyng wyth thorne | xxj^{o} ca^{o} *mar.*

The two and twentith how Crist the Crosse bare on his bak;
This beryng wodde for sacrifice p*re*fig*ur*ed Ysaak,
And the heyre of þ*e* vynȝerde casten out dispitusly,
And be the tylmen of þ*e* ȝerde slayne yvel & bitt*er*ly;
And the m*er*veillous grape-clustre was of þ*is* figuracioune
Whilk two men broght to desert out of the land of promissio*u*ne;
For so was Crist be two folke ledde out of Jer*usal*em creuwellye,
And putt to deth foullest in the mownt of Caluery.

The xxiii chapitle seith [h]ow Crist was na\y/led on Rode tree.
And p*ra*yed for his crucyfio*ur*s of his ineffable pitee.
Jubal, fynder of musik, fig*ur*ed this thing p*ro*perelye,
Finding in Tubalkaym hamers the tunes of melodye.
So Crist, as he was ruthfully hamerd apon the Croce,
Songe to his Fadir*e* of heven in a full swete voice:
So swete and faire was it, and full of all dulcoure,
Þ*at* it convertid thre thovzand men in þ*at* ilk one houre;
And Ysay this crucifixioune also p*re*figured,
Wham Manasses w*ith* a sawe of tree slew and dep*ar*tid.
It was prefigured by King [Moab] when he would sacrifice his son to the Lord
So that God should release his city from the siege.

In the four*e* & twentith er*e* thre thinges whilk be p*re*fig*ur*acio*u*ne
Portend of Our*e* Lord Jh*es*u the deth and his passioune:
The grete tree þ*at* Nabugodonosor see slepyng, as bukes telle,
Whilk Gods aungel him thoght co*m*manded dovne for to felle,
Bot the rote þ*er*of in erth to leve forthwyth he bede,
For thogh Cr*is*t wald be slayne, ȝit wolde he rise fro dede;
Secunde, Kynge Codrus fortakened Crist*es* deth fig*ur*atif,
Whilk for to sauve his folk o free will lost his lif;
Eleazar*e* be his avne deth the b\e/este to deth nuyed, [f.3^{r}]
So Crist, for he wald dye, oure deth foreur*e* destruyed.

The fyve and twentith chapitle tellis vs apertly how
Aft*er* his deth thes Juys scorned Oure Lord Jh*es*u.
This fig*ur*id Micholl þ*at* logh Dauid hir*e* lord to scorne
Playing before the Archa D*omi*ni when it was borne;
And moreou*er* scho lykned hym till harlots and ribavdes
Þ*at* naknes thaym tofor men to pleye and make thair*e* gavdes.
This fig*ur*ed Absolon þ*at* was w*ith* thre speres slane,
And aft*er* w*ith* Joab sqvyers swordes borne thurgh aȝeyne;
So Crist w*ith* thre diu*er*se sorowes was to*ur*mentid,
And ou*er* þ*at* w*ith* swordes of crewell tonges dishono*ur*yd.
Thus many folkes crucifies full oftsyth new and new–
Wittenes Seint Poule pistle–Our*e* sufferane Lord Jh*es*u;
And this [Ev]illmeradak, the kinge wikked, p*re*fig*ur*id
When he his fadirs body eft*er* deth vnherthid
And made it in gobbets kitt thre hundreth in one hovre,
And toke it till als many vovtours for to devovre.

The sex and twentith chapitle; of Our*e* Lady pitee
In old time openly was fortakened in fig*ur*es thre:

---

139 How Crist bare the Crosse | xxij^{o} ca^{o} *mar.* 147 How Cr*is*t was naled on the Crosse | xxiij^{o} ca^{o} *mar.* ; how] quomodo L, þow. 159 Of Cr*is*tis passioune | xxiiij^{o} ca^{o} *mar.* 167 nuyed] Nueyed *(1st* e *erased).* 169 xxv^{to} ca^{o} | How Crist was scorned dede *mar.* 181 Evillmeradak] willmeradak. 185 xxvi^{o} ca^{o} | How O*ur* Ladies doel on hir soune dede *mar.*

Frist, in Jacob sorowing so longe inconsolably
When he his dere sonnes cote see al to-rent and blody;
And eke Oure Ladis doele fig*ur*id Adam and Eue
Sorowing þ*er* sonnes deth ane hundreth ȝere, I leve–
And scho hir childres deth, þ*at* wald noght hatte "Neomy"
Bot bade to calle hire "Mara" (þ*at* is, "bitt*er*" or "sory").

The sevene and twentith tellis of the sepul*ture* of Jh*es*u
And of his modirs sorowyng, whilk all the werld myght rewe.
This fig*ur*ed Dauid the kyng tofor þ*at* many a ȝere,
With sorowe and wepyng teres fylowyng at Abners bere;
And Joseph put in the cisterne, also this fig*ur*id hee,
And Jonas þ*at* of a whall beswelowed was in the see.

In the eght and twentith chapitle is how Crist entred hell
To glad oure haly fadres in lymbo, as clerkes tell,
Also thre childer in the oven whilk the a*u*ngell kept fro hete,
And Daniell in þ*e* lake of lyo*u*ns þ*at* be Abacuc had mete,
And the struttio*u*ne w*ith* a wormes blode of desert somtyme wasse
Delyured hir briddes, be Salomon thanne closed w*ith*inne a glasse.

In the twenty and nynth is how the feend be Crist ou*er*come*n* wasse,
Whilk thing fig*ur*ed tofor the stronge man Bananyas
In the cisterne o tyme descending till a lyo*u*ne,
And onely with his staffe to deth he storke him doune; [f. 3v]
And also the lyon al to-rentte be Sampson,
And be Ayoth þ*at* styked ones the fatte Kinge Eglon.

The threttith is how Marie ou*er*came the feend vertuously,
And als our*e* modere gloriouse has venged vs on oure enmy;
For all þ*at* Our*e* Lord Jh*es*u soeffred in his passioune
Our*e* Ladie tholed in sawle be moderfull compassioune.
For als Crist be his passio*u*ne the feend endelesly ou*er*came,
Our*e* Ladie be hir compassio*u*ne be hym didde ryght the same;
And Judith eke fig*ur*ed this in the prince Olofern slayne,
And Jael þ*at* nayled Sisara thorgh his temples into the brayne;
Also be Qwen Thamar*e* þ*at* Cyrus heved ofbraid*e*,
And aft*er* in a fulle potte of mans blode scho it laide,
And said, "Thi thrust to shedde mans blode was neu*er* wery.
Spare noght, lat see, to drinke ynogh and be mery."

In the one and thretith, how Crist the seints out of hell delyvrid,
The Juys whilk passyng out of Egipt p*re*fig*ur*ed,
And Abrah*am* wham God delyvrid out of Vr*e* in Chaldee,
And Loth fro Sodoms sinkyng for his sing*u*ler*e* bo*u*ntee.

The two and thretith, how Crist fro dede to lyve vprase
Shewes, be Sampson*e* þ*at* ones struyed the ȝates of Gaze,
Be Jonas passing the thredde day out of the wombe of þ*e* qwall,
And be the reproved stone sett vp the cornar*e* of the wall.

The thre and threttith telles how Crist stegh vntill heven.
This takned Jacobs leddir, als bokes kan pleyner*e* neven;
Also the founden shepe broght home þ*at* arst was lorne,

187 sorowing] ? *-es* 193 xxvij° ca° | Off Crist gr*a*uyng *mar.* 199 xxviij° ca° | How Crist entred hell *mar.* 200 limbus i.e. a free pr*i*son in hell cald Abrah*a*m Bosme *mar.* 203 struttioune] i.e. a bridde *over.* 205 xxix° ca° | How Cr*i*st ou*er*come the fende *mar.* 210 styked] stryked *(r erased).* 211 How Oure Lady ou*er*come þe feend | xxx° ca° *mar.* 216 the same] i.e. ou*er*came him *over.* 217 Olofern] ? *-es* 219 Qwen] *subp. and can. with* Q *ins. and* Qwen *mar.* 223 xxxj° ca° *mar.* 225 sing*u*ler] ? singler 226 Off Cr*i*stes resurrecion | xxxij° ca° *mar.* 228 Sampson] ? -e Gaza] i.e. of þ*at* citee *over.* 229 Be] And *can. with* Be *u.r. mar.* 230 wall] i.e. of the Temple *over.* 231 xxxiij° ca° *mar.*

**And Elye þ*at* in a cart of fire to p*ar*adise was borne.
In the foure and threttith chapitle is of the Haly Gayst sendyng,
And sciens of all tonges to Crist disciples bringyng.
This takned the fyrst tonge departid so diu*er*sly,
And eke the Lawe also gyven in M*ou*nte Synay,
And to the wydowe of oyle the encrees & aboundaunce,
For all hir vessell voide, at Heliseus instaunce.**

**The fyve and threttith, Our*e* Ladies doel aft*er* Cr*is*tis ascens*iou*ne,
Figured be Toby wife in absence of hir*e* son,
And be the woman þ*at* soght the lost dra*m*me in hir*e* house,
And the doelefull Michol for hir bereft spouse.**

**The sex and threttith fig*ur*es the assumpcio*u*ne of O*ur* Ladie:
How Dauid broght Gods Arche vntil his house festivaylye,
And be the grete signe in heuen appering to Seinte John,
And be Salomon þ*at* sette his modir*e* in right halfe of his throne.**

**The seven and threttith, how Oure Ladie excused this werld to hir*e* son,
Als sometyme to Seinte Benet was shwed in avision,** [f.4r]
**When Oure Lord toward this werld shoke thre speres wrothly,
And Oure Ladie putt hir betwix and turned his ire to mercy.
This fig*ur*ed Nabals gude wife þ*at* Dauid ire amesid,
And the woman Theucuytes whilk Absolo*u*n til his fadir*e* plesed;
And this fig*ur*ed the woman in the citee Abela,
Breking the sege of Joab, gyven him the heved of Syba.**

**The eght and threttith is how Gods modir*e* is oure p*ro*tectrice
Ageyns Goddes ire, the fendes gildres and fraude of this werld nice.
The fyrst figured Tharbis þ*at* sauved Saba fro Moyses,
The secunde scho þ*at* Abimalech delyu*er*ed the to*ur* of Thebes,
The thredde p*re*fig*ur*ed Micol þ*at* lete out hire housebonde
At a window, and him sauved fro Sauls his enemy honde.**

**In the nyne and threttith chapitle is how Our*e* Lord Jhesus
Shewes to his Fadir his woundes, the moder*e* hir so*u*n for vs
Hir*e* hevenfull sucrish breestes, for synfull man prayng–
How suld oght be w*ith*seide vnto thus swete asking?
Shewing his woundes errys, this figured Antipater*e*,
And prayng for the Juys till Assure King, Ester*e*.**

**In the fouretith chapitle is of the day of dome than,
Whilk thing be p*ar*able figured thilk noble man
That toke his seru*au*nts, his gude & went in ferre regio*u*ne
And, taken the regne, came home and asked of tham reso*u*ne;
And the wise virgines þ*at* oele vnto the fole maydens denyed,
For thare none oyle of merecy to the dampned bes aspyed.
This takned also "Mane, techel, phares" scripsione,
That is for to say, noumbr*e*, weght and divisione;
For that dome salle be treted be noumbr*e* and appensio*u*ne
And ended of wikked fro the gude be eendeles remocio*u*ne.
The one and fourtith chapitle is of the \h/orrible payns of hell,
And þ*at* p*re*figured Dauid in slaght*er* of his enemyes fell,**

235 the sendyng of the Haly Gaist | xxxiiij° ca° *mar.* 241 Cristis ascens*iou*n | xxv° ca° *mar.* 242 Toby wife] i.e. Anna *over.* 245 O*ur* Ladies assumpcioune | xxxvj° ca° *mar.* 247 signe] *another word alt.*; John] ? Joha*n* 249 How O*ur* Ladie excused þ*e* werld | xxxvij° ca° *mar.* 253 wife] i.e. Abagael *over*; amesid] i.e. aȝeinst Nabal *over.* 254 Theucuytes] i.e. of þ*at* citee *over.* 256 Breking] ? A Breking 257 xxxviij° ca° | How Oure Ladie is o*ur* protectrice *mar.* 259 Tharbis] i.e. þ*at* woman *over*; Saba] i.e. þ*at* citee *over.* 263 xxxix° ca° | How Crist schewys his woundis and O*ur* Ladye hir breestes for mankynde *mar.* 266 errys] i.e. to Cesar Emp*erour* *over.* 268 Ester*e*] i.e. his wife *over.* 269 xl ca° | Of the day of dome *mar.* 274 thare none] i.e. at domesday *over*; aspyed] i.e. by Godde nor be his seints *over.* 275 scripsione] ? scripsio*u*ne *(2nd* s *o.er.)* 277 appensioune] i.e. be weght *over.* 279 xli° ca° | Of the payns of hell *mar.* 280 his...fell] i.e. of þ*e* citee of Rabath *over.*

For some were dismenbred w*ith* knyves, and some w*ith* sawes he suwe,
W*ith* cart*es* were some ou*er*gone and other he al to-druwe
And Gedeon figured this on men *þat* gave him scornes,
Wham he made al to-drawe w*ith* breres and w*ith* sharp thornes;
And Pharao with his grete ost this thing p*re*fig*ur*ed hee
Wham God ones al togider*e* drowned in the rede see.
So sall the dampned at the last, w*ith* alle the feends cruwell,
Be God wham þai displeysid be closed for eu*er* in hell.

The two and fourtith remembre the joye & the solace
That seints sall haue in heven tofor Gods worthi face. [f.4v]
This moght fulle wele fig*ure* of Salomon the storye,
Like whame we rede no man *þat* lyved in erthly glorie.
Also p*re*fig*ur*ed this the feest of Assuer*e* kyng:
We rede thar*e* made no moo a feest so longe lastyng.
The feestis shewed this also made be the childer*e* of Jope,
For of so many of othir*e* contynuyd we \ne/ rede, I hope.

The thre and fouretith tellis how is to eschuwe hell payne,
And how the joye of heven forlost salle com agayne.
If we desire the joye and think the payne to flee
Who will helpe Crist his Crosse to bere w*ith* him late see;
And how this Lord is holpen this hevy charge for to bere,
Loke in this ilk chapitle and fynde it clerely there.

The foure and fouretith comp*re*hendes seven sorows of Marie,
Tholed for hir one dere so*un* in erth full tendrely.

The fyve and fourtith & the last declares hir*e* swete joyes seven*e*,
In whilk of all this boke the werke is eendid even*e*. [f.5r]

283 him scornes] i.e. of the citee of Socoth *over*. 284 breres] brerers. 289 xlij ca° | Of the joye of heven *mar*. 297 How man shuld thank God at c*er*taine houres of the day | xliij° ca° *mar*. 303 Of seven sorows of Our*e* Ladye | xliiij° ca° *mar*.; fouretith] i.e. Chapitle *over*. 305 Of seven joyes of Our*e* Ladie | xlv^to ca° *mar*.; fourtith] i.e. Chapitle *over*.

The fall of Lucifer
Is. xiv 12-15; II Peter ii 4; Apoc. xii 7-9

The creation of Eve
Gen. ii 16-21

The Myroure of Ma*n*nes Kynde Saluacioune begynnes here,
In whilk man may his falle and hir*e* reparing lere,
And how God of his myght and his grete gudelynesse
Made man in saule for luf vntill his awne lyknesse,
And how the devile be fraude wroght our*e* dampnaci*ou*ne,
And eft God of his grace refo*ur*med vs to pard*ou*ne.
¶a Ageins his Creat*our* rose Lucyfere the cruwell,
And in a mo[m]ent fell he fro hegh heven vnto hell;
And God of his gudenesse wald make mankynde þ*er*fore
The falle of Lucifere and his for to restore.
Wharefore the envyous feend thoght make man to be shent,
And thorgh his sleght lede hym to breke Gods co*m*mandment.
And then this feend be fraude a s*er*pents kynde him chace,
Whilk ʒede vpright þ*at* tyme and bare a womans face,
In wham this wright of deth entred full wilyly,
And be word of þ*at* movth begilt the woman slely.
He thoght to tempe hir*e* firstc (in bokcs als ʒ*e* may see,
Halding Adam more warre, more wyse, more avysee).
Whils scho was fro the man come he to hire in hye,
For rather man fallis soelle than in gude companye,
And thus this wily feend, deceving Eue thus eth,
Broght in on all mankynde the rightwise dome of deth.
In Damacens feelde *nota* þ*at* God made man,
To p*ar*adys of delice and translatid him than.
¶b In p*ar*adys, als we rede, the woman to\ke/ hire makinge
Of one of Adames ribbes whils þ*at* he laye slepinge;
And thus above the man the woman had in thatte
Hono*ur* als be the place of hire makinge somwhatte,
Also scho was noght made, als man, of erthis slyme,
Bot of manes fleshe and bone, als God wald in that tyme.
¶c Noght of the fote, for that man shuld noght hir*e* despise,
Nor of the heved, for scho be pride shuld noght ou*er*rise,
Bot of the manes syde, als we rede, made was schee,
For helpe till hir*e* huseband and felowe þ*at* scho shuld bee;
And if this hono*ur* [yet] sho had kept in swete mekeness
Thare shuld neu*er* man o lyve hafe done woman distresse;
Bot for, trowinge the devel, sho wald be like to God,
Sho hase descerved forthi to soeffre of manes rod.
¶d The woman trowed the feend & noght the man, soth is,
Bot he till hire assented, alle wer*e* it maugre his.
That Adam shuld of the fruyte ete w*ith* hir instode Eue,
Whilk ete for hoege luf, þ*at* he shuld noght hir*e* greue. [f.5^{v}]
Salomon for wo*m*mans luf ano*ur*ned mavmetrye,
And novther*e* gods nor goddesses trowing tham more forthye,
And thus Adam for luf ete w*ith* dame Eue his wyve
Bot he ne hoped neuer*e* the more to be like God olyve.
The woman therefore sinned more than the man
Because she thought herself capable of being made like God;
And to the forsaid synne sho eked an other*e* full grete,
Hir*e* husband be glosinge when sho to sy*n*ne wald trete,

307 Ca^{m} j^{m} *mar.*; The] *(T with* IHC *and* M *inside it, rub.)*. 314 moment] monent. 331 benedicta sit *mar. hand*^{2}. 341 yet] þat. 344 rod] i.e. chastying *over*. 347 instode Eue] i.e. she praid incessably *over*.

The marriage of Adam and Eve
Gen. ii 22-24

The temptation of Eve
Gen. iii 1-6

For thogh the Bibles text ap*er*tely noght it write,
No doubt sho broght him inne w*ith* faging wordes white.
O man, be warr*e* in this of wikked wo*m*mans glosing,
If thow passe wele þ*at* paas holde it no little thing.
Adam, þ*at* noble man, loke, and the stronge Sampso*une*–
David, Gods hertes choise, loke, wisest Salomo*une*–
Sen thus stronge men and wise eschaped noght wo*m*mans arte,
If thov be nothing swilk, in tyme ware at thi parte.
And wham the feend to tempt on him dorst noght take on*ne*,
The wo*m*man, balder*e* then he, durst make hir*e* husband fo*n*n,
And thus the devel be fraude made Eue vntil hym falle:
Hir*e* husband sho so forthe, and all mankynde withalle;
And if man had alway kept Gods co*m*mandment
He ne had neu*er* felt of deth, nor of none other*e* to*ur*ment.
He ne shuld neu*er* hafe bene waike, nor felt of werynesse,
Nor neu*er* hafe felt a poynt of vnhelth, nor sekenesse.
W*ith*out weping and cry a man shuld hafe bene borne,
Nor neu*er* gronyng for charge the mother*e* hafe had þ*er*forne.
For neu*er* man shuld haue felt of tribulacioune,
Nor tholed brennyng of shame, nor ony confusioune.
His heres neu*er* hafe bene defe, his teth vneged evre,
His eghen neu*er* dy*m*me nor sovre, his fete hafe halted nevre,
Nor flode, cist*er*ne nor welle neu*er* man hafe drowned nor shent,
Be fire nor sonnes hete shuld nevre man haue bene brent.
No beest nor bridde cruwell shuld neu*er* on man hafe resed,
Nor wynd nor ayer*e* corrupt shuld neu*er* man hafe desesed,
Nor neu*er* man shuld hafe stryven, nor envye had till other*e*,
Bot eu*er*y man other*e* hafe luved right als his wombes brother*e*;
And to man shuld hafe bowed all erthly creature,
And evre shuld he hafe lived in joye w*ith*outen*e* cure,
And when that God had liked, man hafe passyd vnto heven,
This is no man*er*e doute, both body and sawle full even.
No man for p*ri*s of witte p*re*sume to seke at alle
Whi God angels and man made, wham he knewe to falle;
Why in the same way he wished to create the angels
Of whose fall he most certainly had foreknowledge;
Or whi God Pharaos hert wald in malice indure,
And Mavdelenes hert make soft, and be repentaunce pure; [f.6^r]
Whi Petre that thris forsoke God gaf grace to repayre,
And Judas als in his synne whi he lete disespayre;
Whi one thefe on the crosse God lightned w*ith* his grace,
And inspired noght þ*at* oþ*er* all in o tyme and place;
Why one synner*e* God drawes, an other*e* he drawes noght–
Be he man nevre so wise, of him this be noght soght.
For swilk werkes of trewe God, and many other*e* inscrutable,
Passes all man*er*e thinge to whilk mans witte is able.
And of swilk questiones Poule has answerd thus shortly:
"God wham hym lest indures, of wham hym lest has m*er*cy."

---

358 M*agis*tr*e* historiar*um* *mar.* 359 womans glosing] for gude wo*m*mans glosing is to p*ro*fit & hat more p*ro*perly chericing and to þ*at* other*e* touchis noght *over and into mar.* 364 thi parte] i.e. to kanwe glosing fro chericing *o.i.e.l.* 389 no*ta* *mar.* 393 indure] i.e. harden *over.* 404 Ro. ix° Exodi xxxiij° miserebor cui voluere *mar.*

The Fall
Gen. iii 6

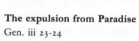

The expulsion from Paradise
Gen. iii 23-24

¶e In forsaide thinges herd we what hono*ure* to man God shope;
Now fylovs it for till here how man hymself forshope.
When man was in honour*e* of God toke he none hede
Bot rose ageyns his Lord and had of pride no drede.
¶f Out cast was he þ*er*fore fro p*a*radys of delyce
Vnto the sorowfull vale of this lewed werld and nice.
The hono*ur* that hym was takin, for he sett it at noght
Sithen has he fonden*e* disese, vnthreft, meschef and thoght.
¶g Fro he lost p*a*radise, that swete and joyouse stede,
Come he to swilk a place whar*e* he boght dere his brede–
Vnto this wily werld, full fals and fulle of fraude,
Heghting to many \one/ gude and paying tham w*ith* a gavde.
It heghtis a man lange lif: loke wher*e* this be a jape,
For, come the dedes howr*e*, he shall no point eschape.
Vnto the body heghts it hele be lange lastyngnesse,
And clethis both body and sawle in p*er*petuell seekenesse.
It heghts divers richesse, hye welth, and grete hono*ur*,
And filles a man at eende with rotynnesse and feto*ur*;
And thogh sometyme be gude the werld make man to fayne,
Alle nys bot indurable at eende, passing and vayne;
Nor werldely gude may noght o ȝere thi life p*ro*loigne
In c*er*tein point of the deth, nor o moment assoigne.
Loke, at thi*n* eende, thi gude (of the gifs hoege force)
Vnneths graunts the a shete to hile thi vilist corce.
The werld be right men may likne til a boxtree,
Of whilk the fruyt is sovre, the flowr*e* fair*e* to thyn eghe.
So semes full wonder*e* fair*e* the werldes delectacio*u*ne,
Of whilk the fruyt at the last is eendeles dampnacio*u*ne.
Als is this werld full like vnto the traytour*e* Judas,
Be whas kissing Our*e* Lord Jhesus betrayed was.
Swilk signe this vntrewe werld gyves to the devils of hell,
Als didde the traytoure Judas to Cristis foos cruwell: [f.6v]
"Wham that I kisse," says it (honour*e* and welth gyvynge)
"Take ȝ*e* hym–that–to ȝow to to*ur*ment ay lastynge."
Bot richesse er*e* noght ay to mans dampnacio*u*ne,
Bo[t] helps full many a man to thar*e* saluacio*u*ne;
For to Nabugodonosor the kyng saide Danyel
"Whith almouse bye thi synne and wyn thi sawles hele",
For God hates noght the riche, hymself eu*er* almyghty,
If thai wele vse thare gude, als taght his so*un* Thoby:
"If thow grete richesse weeld, of gift be aboundande".
If thow hafe lesse, study to dele part w*ith* glad hande.
Nor mete nor drinke files noght bot thair*e* vse vndiscrete,
Nor in fair*e* clething synne if the hert be to God swete:
For ilk man aft*er* his state may honest clething bere,
Als wham God makes a kynge besemes no sekke to were,
Nor husbandmen awe noght clothis to were of sylke.
Than eury man als his estate askis late him were swilk;
And thogh ilk man hafe leve to ber*e* his state dewly,
Hym nedes wele to be warr*e* of excesse besily.

405 Ca[m] ij[m] *mar.*; In...we] *in another script.* 410 Vnto] *followed by* to *can. and subp.* 416 gavde] i.e. a jape *over.* 427 thi] *o.s.o. erased.* 440 Bot] Bo. 441 Danyel iiij[to] *mar.*

Adam digs and Eve spins
Gen. iii 17-19

Noe's Ark
Gen. vi 5-viii 22

For if mesure be dette to kepe in eury thing,
Nede mot it be to blame dampned excesse in to bryng;
Than sithen be slithing gudes the werld wold vs betrayse,
Shape we to overcom hym thorgh mesure be all ways.
Thar*e* had neu*er* maide man bene tuyllyd in this bataille,
If man had dwelt alway in p*ar*adys w*ith*out faille:
Thar*e* \had/ he bene alway and neu*er* hafe felt disese,
And her*e* passis noght ane howre bot something hym displese.
Now haves hym in awayte his aperte enemy,
Now castis his feint freende to jape hym cou*er*tly;
Sometymes diseses man a migge or els a flee,
A flegh or than a worme, thogh it full little bee.
Be right is man inpu*n*gned w*ith* elementz and w*ith* beestes,
When he be pride wald breke his Creatoures hestes.
Whilom p*ri*kkes erth the man w*ith* breres & w*ith* thornes,
Sometyme is he to-rentt w*ith* beestis teth or thair*e* hornes;
Sometyme man is bewrappid in tempest or in flode,
Robbers slees on the see or woundes men for thair*e* gode.
The ayer corrumpes men and causes oft pestilence,
Briddes w*ith* beek or clowes done to men*ne* oft offence;
Till asshe wastes the fire of men both bone and flesshe,
And smoke dos to mans eghen oftsith grete hevinesse.
In p*ar*adys shuld neu*er* men til other*e* hafe bene enemys;
Who myght fynde here o freend war*e* full *gra*ycious and wis. [f.7^{r}]
Whils men hafe here estate, grete richesse and hono*ur*,
He shalle fynd freendes ynowe his cause for to fauo*ur*;
Bot if the state and gude passe ou*er* and tham w*ith*drawe,
Full many þ*at* semed his freendis at nede will be full slawe.
A trewe freend sall be knawen in grete adu*er*sitee,
If he wil till ane eend take than full part with thee;
Than who will for his freend advento*ur* hymself & his,
Men hald be reson rounde grete charitee in hym is.
Bot our*e* gude Lord Jh*es*u had more of charitee
When he for his enemys wald dye on Rodes tree,
For we wer*e* Gods enemys, dampned *per*petuelly,
And he has vs delyvred be his innoumbrable m*er*cy.
¶h Ther*e* myght no man eschu til entre helles p*ri*soune,
Fro whilk for til eschape suffized no mans resoune,
To-whills God of m*er*cy and of comfort at alle,
Of his benigne grace behelde oure forsaide falle,
And thoght vs to delyvre be his Sonne God olyve,
Gyving hir*e*of takenyng be a braunche of olyve
Broght to folk be a dowue in Noe shippe encloos,
For sawles fro helles lymbe shuld passe, maugr*e* thair*e* foos;
And thus noght to then closed in archa Noe oonely,
Bot als til all this werld takenyd that olyve m*er*cy.
This same thing was forshewed be many a fair*e* figure,
Als bisy reders may fynde seking in Haly Scripture.
Now, gude Jh*es*u, gif vs in Haly Scripture to lere,
Thi charitee for to knawe and kepe whils we lyve here.

483 Of a trewe freend *mar*. 496 Ge. viij^{o} | j figura *mar*. 500 The Lymbe was the free p*ri*soune i*n* hell callid Abrah*a*m Bosme in whilk wer*e* haly faders & other*e* of the Ald Law þ*at* shuld be redemyd be Crist *mar*.

The annunciation to Joachim: Anna's conception of Mary
Voragine V 99-101

King Astiages' dream of his daughter
Comestor 1470

If we the guyse will witte of our*e* saluaci*oune*,
Remembre we alder-fyrst Oure Ladies concepci*oune*;
For when Crist wald be man, *our* myscheif to restore,
His modres gen*er*acione mot nedesly come tofore,
More clerely whilk to knawe, lo her*e* of Haly Writte
A parable, how Jh*esu* Crist sometyme p*re*figu*re*d itte.
Ther*e* went a man sometyme fro Jer*usale*m descendande,
And in desert co*mm*yng he fell in theves hande.
His gudes fro hym bereft, sore wounded then left thay
Vnnethes hym halfe olyve, and than ȝede on thair*e* way.
A prest and eft a dekene come by passing furth than,
Bot noyther*e* of tham myght hele this ilke sore wounded man.
At the last a Samaritene had pitee, þ*at* come negh by,
And heled this robbed man of his woundes gudely; [f.7v]
And if it had noght befallen to come this Samaritene,
Thilk wounded man had neu*er* bene helid, without wene.
In this p*ar*able mankynde is shewed be figu*re* apert
Fro p*ar*adys of delice out cast in this desert,
Spoilled of the gudes of grace gyven hym of Gods gudenesse,
And smyten w*ith* a sore wounde of eendeles dedelynesse;
The whilk als halfe-way dede full lange lay soryly,
And was dede als in sawle, alle lyvyd it bodyly;
To wham nor preest nor dekne moght gyfe saluaci*oun*e
Nor make repare till heven penaunce nor circumcisi*ou*ne.
Than come this Samaritene and rewed this wounded man,
And bande his woundes togider*e* and helyd hym gudely than.
Samaritene, "kepere" thus mich is it to say,
Be whame swete Jh*esu* Crist wele vnderstand we may;
Ne had this keper*e* comen in this werld to be borne,
Elles had alle mankinde w*ith*out eend hafe bene lorne;
Wharefore love we and blisse forevre Our*e* Lord Jhesu,
That on this half-dede man come in this werld to rewe,
And when this Lord wald come eftyr*e* hys trewest hete,
Forthi sent he tofore his modyr*e*, þ*at* virgyne swete,
And his a*un*gell to telle hir*e* clere concepcioune,
Hir*e* name, and in his mynde hyr*e* ete*r*ne s*ein*tificacioune.
This is þ*at* Ladye swete, eu*er* mayden meek and mylde,
Be wham come all our*e* hele in Jh*esu* Crist hir*e* childe,
And wham God be figu*re* wald oftsith p*re*ostende,
And be p*ro*ph*et*es oracles till his freendes commende.
¶a The kinge Astiages a m*er*veillous visi*ou*ne sawe:
Out of his doght*er*s wombe a fulle fair*e* vigne to growe,
Whilk with braunche, flovre & fruyt spred it so largely
That his revme ovre & ou*er* it obumbred haly.
Than clerkes gon hym telle, wham he sperid of this thing,
That of his doght*er* shuld come a fulle grete worthi king;
And sho broght forth King Cyre, whilk of his grete bo*un*tee
Efter*e* delyvred the Juys fro Babiloyns captivytee.
Litteraly haf ȝe herde this dreme and what it ment,
Now lyes moreovre to knawe þ*er*of the mistik intent.

505 ca^{m} iij^{m} *mar.*; Iff...saluacioune] *in another script.* 506 Remembre] *3rd minim of 2nd* m *ins.* 539 Luc. j^{o} *mar.* 543 preostende] i.e. shewe tofore *over.* 545 j figura Daniel xiij^{o} *mar.* 546 Astiages *mar.*

A garden enclosed, a sealed fountain
Cant. iv 12

Balaam, who will prophesy the rising of Mary, beats his beast
Num. xxii 1-xxiv 17

Till Astiage was shewed his doght*er* shuld bere a king;
To Joachym, his doght*er* to bere the Lord of alle thing.
Cyrus delyvred the Juys fro Babiloyns captyvitee,
And Crist Kyng has vs reft out of the devils poustee.
The doghter*e* of Astiage p*re*figu*re*d Oure Ladye,
Of whas wombe sprange the vigne þ*at* alle o*ure* hele come by. [f.8[r]]
Blissed be thow, mayden mylde, doght*er* of the sou*er*ayne king,
Above both rose and lyllye candent and redoling.
Blissed be the sacred bode of thi concepcioune,
Whilk was the forme daweny*ng* of our*e* saluacio*u*ne.
Blissed be the Fader God þ*at* wald vs of the sese,
And hono*ur* to God the Sonne þ*at* the to moder*e* chese.
Blissed be the Haly Gast þ*at* blissed hir*e* longe toforne,
Ar*e* hir*e* blissed fader*e* and moder*e* shewed hir*e* to this werld borne.
¶b Of this doght*er* sometyme sange Salomon mistikly,
That in hir*e* moder*e* wombe God wold hir*e* seintify,
For a gardin enclose he lykned hir*e* vntoo,
And till a seled welle; this the reso*u*ne, loo:
For in hir moders wombe whils this virgine was shette,
On hir*e* the Haly Gast his speciell blissing yette,
And merkid hir*e* w*ith* the seale of the Haly Trinitee,
That neu*er* thing that warre synne shuld haue in hir*e* entree.
Forsoth, Marye, thowe ert gardin of alle swettenesse,
And welle of sawles witt, eu*er* flowyng in fulnesse;
¶c Also the Hali Gast, O Marye, heght the vs
When be the p*ro*ph*et*es movth Balaam he saide right thus:
"Thare sall of Jacob spryng a sterne of mykell light,"
P*or*tending Marye to be Gods chosen celle full bryght.
This Balaam thoght to hynder Gods folk be werying,
Bot the gloryous Haly Gast to*ur*ned it alle to blissing
Whareby the Haly Gast shewed be p*re*figu*ra*cioune
That the malison of our*e* for-moder*e* shuld torne to benediccio*u*ne,
And be a mayden clennest this *gra*ce shuld vs befalle,
Whas birth p*re*figured vs a sterne bright ovre other*e* alle.
This is blissed Marye of the see the ladere,
Amanges the wawes tempestuouses leder*e* and help sing*u*ler*e*,
Without wham we may noght this wawishe see ou*er*passe,
Nor hevenyshe haven rocovre, þ*at* be our*e* synne lost wasse;
Wharefore thus be a sterne God takned the byrth of Marye
For he til heven be hir*e* wald bring vs m*er*cyfully.
To hym that gave this st\e/rne be joye eu*er* newe and newe,
Be wham this sees wodenesse we may passe and eschewe.
O man, whatevre it be, disespaire neu*er* for thi synne;
Repent, and be this sterne thow may forgifnes wynne.
Con fest on it thyn eghe, what p*er*ile so evre thow doute,
[It] wil the hile and guyde, and trewly bring the oute.
This sterne in his disese Theople se and besoght,
And sho of hir*e* gudenesse till haven of hele hym broght. [f.8[v]]
Gyf vs so to behald this sterne, O gude Jhesu,
Þ*at* we the to displese be hir*e* mowe evre eschewe.

---

569 j fig*ura* *mar.* 571 Can*ticorum* iiij[to] *mar.* 581 Num*eri* xxiiij[to] | iij[a] figura *mar.* 582 Balaam Num*eri* xxij[o] *mar.* 583 folk] *with* i.e. of Israel *above the line.* 600 It] Iit.

The birth of the Virgin
Voragine V 101

A stem shall spring from the root of Jesse
Is. xi 1-2

The passed chapitle has tald Our*e* Ladyes anunciaci*oune*
Nowe fylows it for to here hir*e* birth and gen*er*aci*oune*.
¶a The ligne of Our*e* Ladye come of Dauid and Jesse,
Of wham thus lange tofore p*ro*phizide Isay, witte ȝ*e*:
"Of Jesse rote a ȝerd in tyme to come sall springe,
Out of that rote a floure vprightis ascendinge;
The sevenfold Haly Gast apon this flour*e* salle rist."
Thus saide this haly man, hereof ȝ*e* may be trest.
The ȝerd is Our*e* Ladye w*ith* fruyt be hevenysh dewe,
The floure hir*e* sonne þ*at* sho vnto this werld shall shewe.
In this floure err*e* to fynde medicynes full gode seven,
Takened be seven giftes of the Haly Gast full even.
T*u*ouching, savo*ur* and fruyte, thir*e* er*e* the forthmast three:
Colour*e*, leves and juys, and tast the sevent to bee.
To sawles the whilk err*e* seek er*e* medicynal thir*e* seven thinges,
Ageins seven dedely synnes whilk tham vnto hell bringes.
Thorgh touching of this floure, of p*ri*de swages bolnyng,
And man be gift of drede haves of hymself knawing.
Who thinkes for bolnyng pride how touched was Lucyfere,
He ma[t]es hym, and begynnes of God to have a fere,
For sith God wald noght thole Lucifers and aungels pride,
Wele lesse wille he thole man in p*ri*de by hym abide:
For thay had graces of whilk thair*e* pride thai myght pike out,
Bot stinking man nothing whar*e*of to ber*e* hym stout.
An hard envious hert this floures smell makes soft,
And the gift of pitee stires to compassione oft:
For of no manes disese has pitee the envious,
Bo[t] eu*er*y ma*n*nes woo rewes the misericordous.
Who takes this smelle (þ*at* is of Crist ensample þ*er*fore)
Of ilk man in disese compassi*oune* haves evre more,
And als Crist, wepes he with tham he sees weping,
In bodye or than in sawle when tham ales anything.
The fruyt of this swete floure of ire vndos woodnesse,
Als teches the gift of science to lyve in gudelynesse.
Ȝe see ane ireous man has no discrecioune,
Forthi he ne haldes no revle of resonable conu*er*sacioune.
The gift of science is mylde, homely and avisee, [f.9^r]
And techis to lyve at ryst w*ith* folk of alle degree.
The fruyt of Cristes werkes to suy who getes grace
To lyve may he noght faille duwly in eu*er*y place.
This floures colour*e* destruyes of accide the p*ar*alesye,
And be the swete gift of force a man is strengthid noblye,
That he no payne may fele, nor have drede of labo*ur*,
Of this floure Crist on Crosse behalding the colo*ur*:
And for seghen grapes blude the olyphaunt waxis felle,
To vices, seghen Crist blude, vs aght be more cruwelle.
This floures colo*ur* who than behaldes devoutly
For Crist*es* luf aght hym labo*ur* and thole alle thing gladly.
The leves chaces, of this flo*ur*, of auerice the ydropicye,
And so gift of counseil slees thrist of covetye.

---

605 Ca^m iiij^tu*m* *mar.* 609 j^a fig*ura* *mar.* 617 Tuouching] j *over*; savour] ij *over*; fruyt] iij *over*. 618 Colour*e*] iiij *over*; leves] v *over*; juys] vi *over*; tast] vii *over*. 621 j touching | vij giftes of the Hali Gast *mar.* 622 drede] i.e. of God *over*. 623 Ageins pride | j drede of Godde *mar.* 624 He mates him] He makes him (Humiliat se L). 626 *erasure mar.* 629 ij^o smelle | ij the gift of pitee *mar.* 632 ageins envye *mar.*; Bot] Bo. 637 iij^o the fruyt | iij the gift of science *mar.* 638 no*ta* *mar.* 639 ageins ire *mar.* 642 alle degree] alle gude degree *(*gude *subp.) and* i.e. w*ith* yvell and gude *over*. 645 iiij^to the colo*ur* ageines accide | iiij the gift of force *mar.*; of accidie] i.e. of sleuth *over*. 653 v the gift {of} counseille | v the leves ageynes covetize *mar.*

The closed door signifies the Virgin
Ezech. xliv 2

The Temple of Solomon signifies the Virgin
III Kings vi

Ther*e* leves er*e* Cristis wordes and his doct*ri*ne, teching
To dispise werdely gudes and lufe eu*er*lasting thing.
What man þ*at* this teching haves grace to keep duwely,
He p*ro*ves in him to dwelle the spirit of counseil trewly,
And swilk men haf no joye of richesse temporellye,
Bot swilk gude als God sendis, to part w*ith* hym frely.
This floures juys of glutt*er*ye voides replecioune,
And gift of intellecte gives sp*iri*tuelle cognicioune.
For juice is green, which clears the sight,
And by the gift of intellect Christ invites us to knowledge of heavenly things.
The gloton knawes erthlinesse, and vnknawes hevenly thing;
Be erthly thinges, hevenly gifs intellecte knawyng,
Als seyng the sonne so clere or a delitable floure
We knawe full fair*e* and swete is God thair*e* creatoure.
This floures tast makes baiske of luxure the delite;
The gift of sapience gifs of erthly lustis despite,
For who ones haf tasted the Haly Gastis swetnesse,
All man*er* werldely lust shal hym thinke bitt*er*nesse:
Als honye voides the tast of other*e* mete naturell,
So touching the Haly Gast cesses alle lust carnell.
O ingent magnytude, Lord, blissed mot thow be
Of thyn hidde swetlynesse to tham þ*at* dredes the,
Also the ʒerde of Jesse shewes wethin Marye was borne.
¶b Bot howe þ*at* ʒerde florist shewes in thilk ʒate sporne:
Ezechiel this ʒate cloos in his spirit see he,
That nevre w*ith*outen eend for thing shuld opned be,
For onely God hymself wald by it cloosed passe,
P*or*tending Cristis birth þ*at* aft*er* so m*er*veillous wasse. [f.9v]
Take this who take it may, Crist of Our*e* Ladye was borne,
Vnlike alle othir*e* men aft*er* his birth and toforne.
No wonder*e* at open dore a man passe on his gate,
And bot it is m*er*veille and more to passe thorgh spered ʒate.
¶c A Temple made Salomo*un* also to Godde noblye,
In whilk was p*re*figured the birth of Our*e* Ladye.
This Temple of Salomon had on it pynacles thre,
Be whilk the triforme auriole of Marye takened may be.
The first þ*at* sho fande \first/ is of virginitee,
Þ*at* oþ*er* of martirdome in sawle whilk soeffred shee,
The thredde is of precho*urs* and of doctour*es* hyeghnesse,
For sho was of apostles and of ewangelistes maistresse.
This Temple of marbre white was made vppe alle bedene,
Ennournyd w*ith* golde withinne, þ*er* moght none more be clene.
So was this virgine, white be purest chastitee,
With golde ou*er*cledde w*ith*inne of p*er*fite charitee.
O how is faire and clere gen*er*acioune of chastitee!
O Marye, charitable & chast eu*er*more mot thow wele be!
In the Temple was als a leddre be whilk to clyme vpward:
In Marie godhede enclos for our*e* ascensioune to hevenward.
Thorgh hir*e* meritz gif vs, O pie and gude Jhesu,
To thi joye til ascende, þ*at* evre is newe and newe.

---

661 vi[te] the gift of intellectee | vi[o] the juys ageines glutt*er*ye *mar.* 669 vij the gift of sapience | vij[o] the tast ageynes luxure *mar.* 677 ij figure *mar.* 687 iij figure *mar.* 696 moght] most *alt.* moght.

The presentation of Mary at the Temple
Voragine V 101-2

The Golden Table in the Sand is offered in the temple of the sun
Valerius Bk. IV ch. i, ext. 7

This chapitle last toforn told of \Our*e*/ Ladies bering;
In this fylows to here in the Temple of hir*e* offering.
Sho was broght to the Temple at age of fulle thre ȝere
To s*er*ue almyghty God and lettrure for to lere.
¶a The sonnes borde in the sande p*re*figu*re*d hir*e* oblaci*ou*ne,
Of whilk whi it heght so take her*e* shorttely res*ou*ne:
Fisshers kest in the see thair*e* nettis apon a day–
A table of fulle fyne gulde, this m*er*veille, vpp drugh thay;
This table, als stories telle, was riche and p*re*ciouse
Til eu*er*y mans thinking, and hogely speciouse.
By thilk see stode a temple beelded apon the sond,
Whilk in name of the sonne folk wyrshipt of þ*at* lond.
In thilk temple þ*at* borde was offred festivalye
Vnto god of the sonne, whilk ther*e* was hon*our*d heghlye,
And thus thorghout the werld, hold ȝ*e* this soth or fable,
Was it cald co*m*monly "In the sonde, the sonnes table":
And for thilk temple was sette in swilk place gravely
(Als ȝ*e* wote sonde to be) had it the name þ*er*by.
Be this table of the sonne was p*re*figu*re*d Marye [f.10^{r}]
To Godde the verray sonne offred full p*re*ciouselye.
The forsaid table was offred vnto to the sonne mat*er*ialle:
Our*e* Ladye vnto the Temple of the sonne et*er*nalle.
To se the sonne table fulle many a man list hadde,
And for Our*e* Ladies birth both aungels & men were gladde.
Of a full pure matere was made the sonnes table:
Marie was body and sawle to Godd p*er*fitely placable;
And be the table of the sonne Marye was takenyd fair*e*,
For to the table of hevene be hir*e* have we repaire,
For God Son Jh*es*u Crist bare vs þ*at* mayden gude,
Þ*at* fedes vs p*re*ciously w*ith* his fleshe and his blude.
Blissed be þ*at* joyouse table in heven and in erth here,
Be wham is vs this mete gyven Gods salutere.
Hir*e* fadir*e* and modir*e* be blissed, whilk broght hir*e* forth in kynde,
And offrid hir*e* for mans hele to God w*ith* haly mynde.
¶b In the Old Lawe rede we none his doght*er* þ*at* to God offride,
Sauf Jepte þ*at* sacrifide his and to wrange deth hir*e* dide.
Jepte his doght*er* to God offred vndiscretly,
Bot Joachym and Anne thair*e* doght*er* offred to God p*er*fitly;
For thair*e* doght*er* wald thai noght nor slee no sacrifye,
Bot offred hir*e* vnto Godde, to s*er*ue hym qwhikke swetlye.
Jepte made an avowe whilk haly doct*our*s reproves:
Our*e* Ladie made hir*e* avowe whilke God and man aproves.
The doght*er* of Jepte bewept to be a virgine dede:
Marie fande first the avowe of gloriouse maydenhede.
That aft*er* hir*e* shuld no childe of hir*e* leve wepped shee,
For Crist moght noght be borne of hir*e* posteritee;
An that þ*at* sho wept sore to be, thus vnhappy,
Marye it fande sely, selyer*e* and most sely.
Aft*er* victorie was she offrid als for lovyng,
Bot Marie was offrid tofore the victorie whilk was co*m*myng.

705 Ca^{m} v^{tu}*m* *mar.* 709 j figu*re* *mar.* 711 Maist*er* of Histories *mar.* 722 þ*er*by] *with* i.e. mensa solis in sabulo *mar.* 726 et*er*nalle] et*er*naile *alt.* 736 salutere] i.e. Gods sonne *over.* 739 ij figu*re* Judic. xj^{o} *mar.* 749 shee] i.e. þ*e* doght*er* of Jepte *over.* 750 posteritee] i.e. of hir*e* ligne descendant *over.* 751 sho] i.e. the doght*er* of Jepte *mar.* 753 she] i.e. of Jepte *over.*

Jephte sacrifices his daughter
Judges xi 31-39

The Persian Queen in her hanging garden
Comestor 1453

Jeptes doght*er* was offred for enemys temporele,
Our*e* Ladye for victorie of enemys spirituele.
She myght s*er*ue God no more *þat* in hyr*e* offring thus st\e/revid.
Bot Marie, aft*er* she was offrid, eu*er*more vnto God s*er*uid;
¶c And howe this Ladie hir*e* shope to s*er*ue God hir*e* lif-while
Was be the gardin fig*ur*ed sometyme cald suspensile,
Whilk made a king of Percy in hoege heght, \als/ rede we,
In whilk standyng his wife moght behald hir*e* contree.
Be whilk the contemplatif life was takenid of Our*e* Ladie,
For sho the contree of heven beheld evre besilye, [f.10^v]
And to devocioune evre and contemplacioune
Was sho gyven, and nevre ydel nor werldly vpp*e* nor doune.
To wirke or haly redyng gaf sho hir*e* bisylye,
Or contemplant was sho, or p*ra*yand devoutlye;
In ympnis or psalmodye was hir*e* songe jubilynge,
And in devout p*ra*yer*e* fulle oft swetely wepynge.
For hele of alle mankynde p*ra*yid sho w*ith*out stinting,
Reding contynuelly Script*ur*es of Crist co*m*myng;
And of Crists birth in erth when sho fand oght, for fayne
Sho halsed and kissed swetely and oft redde it aȝeine;
And when *þat* othir*e* virgines home fro the Temple went
Ther*e* to dwelle stil w*ith* Godde was eu*er*more hir*e* intent.
To studie in Gods lawes list eu*er* *þat* mayden bright,
And to rede and reherce p*ro*fited sho day & nyght.
If sho se oght vnclene in Gods Temple, *þat* weshe she,
And bisy how thinges amisse myght best amendid be.
She ne had neu*er* joye for slepe til ones hir*e* heved lay doune
Bot asking ful lawefulle nede of hyest discrecioune;
And thogh sho more or lesse slept sometyme bodily,
Neu*er* the lesse hir*e* sawle w*ith*inne woke than fulle halily.
Þat is that in his songes of hir*e* wrote Salomon:
"I slepe and myne hert wakes," menyng of hir*e* p*er*son.
So gudely wys was sche, so chast in swete mekenes,
That hir*e* lyf was ensample til all folk of gudenes.
Hire speche was lawe and soft, souleyn and fulle discrete,
Neu*er* fell to sharp nor bitter*e*, bot hevenly zucrish swete.
Nor pore nor fieble man dispised she neu*er* be signe,
Bot in speche and hailsing all folk held hir*e* benigne.
Sho was ou*er*, craft to telle, humble, pie and devoute,
To fulfille Gods wille all gyven and vnderloute.
Haly Script*ur*es and p*ro*phecies knew sho most felyngly,
Teching the Haly Gast ou*er* all oþ*er* clerely.
Sho kest neu*er* eghe on man to fest on hym hyr*e* sight,
Nor hir*e* nekke nor hir*e* fro*u*nt vsed sho to bere vppright.
Her*e* eghen donwards til erth amanges men bare sho ay;
Hir*e* hert vpwards on heven*e* was festined nyght & day.
In short, what tonge may telle in p*ri*se, or hert may mene,
Baldely be songen and saide of this swete virgine shene.
O gude Jh*es*u, graunte vs so luf this mayden*e* here
Þat bring vs to ȝow both in joie ete*r*ne and clere. [f.11^r]

757 She] i.e. Jeptes doght*er* *over*. 759 Ladie] i.e. Marie *over*; iij fig*ur*e *mar*. 763 no*ta* *mar*. 785 Cant. v *mar*. 793 pie] i.e. m*er*cifull *over*. 797 Of Our*e* Ladies port *mar*.

The marriage of Mary and Joseph
Matt. i 18; Comestor 1538-39

The marriage of Zara and Tobias the younger
Tob. iii 7-16

Off the last chapitle tofore herde ȝe Our*e* Ladies offring;
In this suys it to here the cause of hir*e* spousing.
Whi Crist his modir*e* wold wer*e* wedded vntil a ma*n*n
Ther*e*of clerks in thair*e* bokes eght causes assigne ca*n*n:
Frist, þ*at* sche nhad noght be hoped grete be fornicacio*u*ne
And als ane avoutresse demed to dampnacio*u*ne;
Secund, mans p*re*sence and help God gaf hir*e* to solace,
For hir*e* sat noght go soule wagrand fro place to place;
The thridde, to jape the feend of Cristes incarnacio*u*ne,
Þ*at* he shuld hope come of man hir*e* virginele concepcioune;
The fierth, for Maries wittenesse more of hir*e* chastitee
Was of hir*e* husband to trowe than of othir*e* in degree;
The fift, for that the ligne of Crists genologie
Shuld to Joseph descend, the husband of Marye,
For Haly Script*ur*es vses noght be wyves, þ*at* er*e* female,
To rekken genologie, bot aft*er* thair*e* husbandes male;
The sext, þ*at* matrimoigne shuld be for haly approved,
Nor of no man dispised als yvel, nor be reproved;
The sevent, þ*at* virginitee in mat*ri*moigne wer*e* able
To kepe, so þ*at* it be to both the p*ar*ties greable;
The eghtend, þ*at* wedded folk of wa*n*nhope shuld noght be,
Trowing the stat sauvable of onely virginitee–
For til approve ilk state wele kept come Crist Jhesu,
Ther*e*fore was his moder*e* virgyne, wife and wydev.
And thogh thir*e* thre estates be p*ro*ved gude and haly,
Ȝit bere thai difference amanges thaym hoegely:
For mat*ri*moigne gude and seint approved is for to be,
Maner*e*, tyme and intent, who may kepe wele thir*e* thre,
For better*e* than mat*ri*moigne is wydowes chastitee,
Bot best is the clennes of maydenhede in degree.
To wedlake trewly kept is aght the fruyt threttisme,
And to wydows sexty, to virgines full centisme.
The metalle of auricalke is knawen a p*re*ciouse thing,
Silver*e* more p*re*ciouse, gold alder-most passing.
The day-sterne is full bright, bot more bright is the mone,
The sonne brightest of alle, this may man p*er*ceve sone.
This werldes joye semes swete, bot swett*er* is paradyse;
Swettest the joye of heven inno*u*mbrable passing wise.
And thogh maydenhed excelle and be best for clennesse,
It nys noght worth bot it be kept w*ith* hertis holenesse: [f.11v]
For who þ*at* maydenhede kepe in flesh, and noght in wille,
Þ*at* thai have auriole et*er*ne of maydenhede is no skille;
And who is mayden in hert, and forlayne violently,
Leses none auriole, bot dubled gets it þ*er*by.
One shalle thai have, no dout, for herts virginitee,
A mede ou*er* for the force to thaym done thair*e* mavgree;
And the auriole forlost be hertis corrupcioune
May be recou*er*ed here thorght bisy contricio*u*ne.
Bot who ones in thair*e* fleshe is corrumpt wilfully,
Thar*e* auriole be nevre restored for any penau[n]ce *sur*ely;

805 Ca^{m} vj^{tum} *mar.* 809 j cause *mar.*; sche nhad] schen had. 811 ij cause *mar.* 813 the thredde cause *mar.* 815 the fierth cause *mar.* 817 the fift cause *mar.* 821 The sext cause *mar.* 823 The sevent cause *mar.* 825 The eghend cause *mar.* 829 Virginitas *rub. mar. different script.* 831 no*ta* de virginitate be*ne* *mar.* 832 Nota bene *mar.* 836 centisme] i.e. ane hundreth fald *o.i.e.l.* 850 force] i.e. pyne and passioune *over.* 852 Of the auriole lost nota *mar.* 854 penaunce] *2nd* n *a minim short.*

The tower called Baris signifies the Virgin
Comestor 1527

The tower of David and its thousand shields
Cant. iv 4

¶a And thogh Marie was joynte vnto man be spovsing,
Ʒit dwelt sho body and sawle in maydenhede eu*er*lasting,
And with Raguelis doght*er* Sara moght sho wele say:
"My sawle haf I clene kept fro alle concupiscence ay."
Sara to seven husbandis was wedded, thus it befelle,
And clene mayden alle þ*at* tyme, als Haly Writt can ʒow telle:
Be stronger*e* reso*u*ne than, myght Marye be ones wedded
And eu*er* w*ith*outen eend dwelle virgine vnwemmyd.
If Sara fro seven husbandes kept the feend Asmodee,
Why ne moght his moder*e* fro oone Godde kepe, be his poustee?
For wheneu*er* Seint Josep loked on thilk virgyns flour*e*,
Se he of hir*e* to sprede ane hoege divyne splendo*ure*:
Forthi durst he nevre more on eghe cast on hir*e* face
Bot in fulle hoege reu*er*ence and when it felle be some case.
Thre nyghts chastitee kept Sara and Thobye,
Bot virgines alle thair*e* lyve wer*e* Josep and Marye.
Josep virgyn was borne of Dauid p*ro*geny,
And be Gods wille conioint als keper*e* to Marie:
Noght þ*at* Gods special choise neded vnder*e* warde to be,
Bot that for suspecioune of men shuld kepe hir*e* hee,
For sho had to keper*e* sou*er*eyn God and verray,
Þ*at* fro alle man*er*e incurs of enemys kept hir*e* ay.
¶b O keper*e* had sho fro heven, an other*e* for to make twoo
In erth honest and trewe: sho ne had nede to no moo;
Wharefore this mayden*e* mylde thus sing*u*lere, of gude fame,
Is likned vnto the tour*e* of Baris þ*at* beres name,
Whilk toure moght wele be kept be two men defending
Fro all man*er*e men [þat] in this werld be lyving.
¶c So stronge and invincible was this virgine Marye
Wham God kept with his grace allway so tendrely, [f.12^r]
Withinne the walle of v*er*tues so s*ur*ely hir*e* closing
Þ*at* neu*er* none enemys fraude moght turn hir*e* to letting.
Whar*e*fore likned is hir*e* lyve to Dauid toure so stout,
On whilk a thovzand sheldes honge in compas about.
The sheldes er*e* swete studies and werkes vertuouse
Be whilk garnyst hir*e* lif this virgine gloriouse,
Þ*at* so fer*re* ou*er* all other*e* hir*e* lothed alle foule delite
That neu*er* fondyng of synne myght o spotte in hir*e* smyte:
Noght onely in hir*e*self voiding temptacioune*s*,
Bot be bemes als in other*e* of hir*e* infusioune*s*;
For alle wer*re* sho sothly the gudeliest of wymmen,
Ʒit moght neu*er* none be synne desire hir*e* of all men,
For swilk vertue divine bemed of hir*e* excellence
Þ*at* whoevre hir*e* behelde it qwenchid his concupiscens–
For als cip*re*sses smelle drives s*er*pents out of place,
So, p*re*sent Marie, lux*ur*es fledde thorgh hir*e* special grace;
And als flowring the vigne s*er*pents may noght abide,
So neu*er* foule concupiscence moght dwelle Marie beside.
O gude Jhesu, gif vs alle foule thoghtes to flee,
And our*e* herts with thi grace fille, for thi grete bountee.

---

856 maydenhede] ? maydene*h*ede 857 Thobie iij *mar.* 858 concupiscence] i.e. flesshly lustis *over.* 859 j fig*ur*e *mar.* 863 Asmodee] *(1st* e *o.er.)* 864 oone] i.e. husband *over.* 869 Of the virginitee of Marie & Joseph *mar.* 878 Baris *mar.* 879 ij figure *mar.* 882 þat] þhat. 898 concupiscens] i.e. the vnhonest lust *over.* 899 The nat*ur*e of cip*re*sse *mar.* 901 The nat*ure* of þ*e* vigne *mar.* 903 corr. *mar.*

The annunciation to Mary: "Hail, full of grace"
Luke i 26-38

Moses sees the burning bush
Ex. iii 2-14

Tofore of Oure Ladye herde 3e the swete wedding;
Now fylowes it for til here hire mirable conceyving.
When \in/ Jerusalem Joseph had taken Marie in spouse,
To Nazareth was sho had home vntil hire parentes house;
And whils Josep for thinges of wedding was bisy,
Conceyvid, vnwitting hym, of the Holy Gast Marye.
Trow nat þat Gabriel fand hire without clausure
To wham, without hire Godde, neuer sauoured creature.
Sho went neuer out to spye, like Dyna, the newe aray,
Nor dalied to homely with men, like Thamar, on the way,
Nor noght like Sara onely to man whilk covettid nevre,
Bot like the soliter[e] Judith fasting and praying evre.
Wharefore when hire with childe Josep perseyuyd and se,
With full grete dred of hert til hymself thus thoght he:
"Inpossible is þat this woman be fornicatrice,
So seint, abstynent and chaste, and hatere of alle vice.
Of mete nor drinke was sho neuer yhit diliciouse,
Neuer wont to hoppe ne daunce, nor renne fro house til house.
To convers in publike hase sho fledde all hire lif,
Halsing solitarie estat and pure contemplatif. [f.12^{v}]
Alle manere werldely joye dispising, and solace,
Brynnyng als gold in fyre to stand with God in grace.
Fro childhode in the Temple has sho dwelt God serving,
Þat neuer to man of lyve was sho sene once drawing;
And now sen sho come home to fadere and modere here,
Euer in hire chambre enclos, in fasting and in prayere,
Whareof shuld sho conceyue this grauidacioune,
Þat in this werld to synne gaf neuer occasioune?
Perauntre filled is in hire Ysayes prophecy:
'A mayden shalle conceyue and bere a soun sothly.'
Maybe of Jacob sede this virgyne is the same
Wham sometyme in a sterne prenuncyd Balaam,
Likyng the Haly Gast in this wise lange toforne
To shewe of a virgyne þat God Son shuld be borne.
Also this mayden be grace thilk 3erde flouryng may be
Prophecid to springe are this out of the rote of Jesse.
Perhaps this is the virgin of whom is to be born Christ
Who, it is said, will be born from the seed of David, son of Jesse.
In hire may noght be rette bot vertuouse honoure,
Wharefor certein this is modere of the Saveoure.
I am vndigne with hire of conuersacioune,
Wharefore gude is I flee of sposailles completioune.
In auntre suspeccione badde the folke take ellis þerby,
Me nedes fro hire presence withdrawe me prively."
Als Josep with Marye to dwelle dred in this wise,
So was Seint John afeerd to Jhesu Crist baptize.
To come noght in his house to Crist prayed centurio,
And Petre hym prayed o tyme out of his shippe to goo.
The womman Sunamyte dredde the cohabitacioune of Elye,
And Josep the cohabitacione of Gods modere Marye.

---

905 Ca^{m} vij^{m} *mar.* 911 clausure] i.e. wauerand in the strete *over.* 913 Gen. xxxiiij^{o} *mar.*; Dyna] i.e. Jacob doghter *over.* 915 Gen. xxxviij^{o} *mar.*; Sara] i.e. Raguels doghter *over.* 916 Judith viij^{o} *mar.* solitere] soliters. 923 publike] i.e. in comon place *over.* 934 Ysaye vij^{o} *mar.* 936 Numeri xxiiij^{o} *mar.* 949 Math. j^{o} *mar.* 950 John] ? Johan 951 Math. iij^{o} *mar.* 952 Luc. vij^{o} *mar.*

Gideon's fleece: "The Lord is with you, bravest of men"
Judges vi 36-40

Rebecca gives water to Abraham's messenger Eliezer
Gen. xxiv

And when þ*at* Josep of hir*e* thus hoege reu*er*ent drede hadde,
Gods aungel come hym to, to make his hert be sadde,
Bidding he ne shuld noght dout his spouse for to take than,
So grete of the Haly Gast, and neu*er* of erthly man.
¶a This concepcioune mirable of thilk swete virgyne ȝynge
Was shewed to Moyses sometyme in a grene bushe brennyng.
The busshe in flawme of fyre lost noght the grennesse,
Marye conceyved a son, evre virgine neu*er* the lesse.
God was hymself w*ith*inne the brynnyng busshe forsayde,
The same þ*at* in the wombe dwelt of this purest mayde.
God come doune in the busshe for the lib*er*acioune
Of Jewes, and in Marie for our*e* redempcioune. [f.13r]
To bringe Jewes fro Egipt in the busshe descendid he,
And in this virgines wombe fro helle to make vs fre,
And when this Lord wald be incarnat amange men
Alle one Mary chese he ouer*e* alle erthly wymmen.
¶b In Gedeones flece was this shewed figuratively,
Whilk men rede with dewe wette of heven m*er*veillousely,
For thilk flece be itself wete of this hevenyshe dewe,
The drie erthe ferre about had noght þ*er*of a drewe:
So of this dewe dyvine was onely filled Marye,
None oþ*er* of all this werld þ*er*to founden worthie.
"Ful many a doght*er* has gedrid," thus says the Boke, "rychesse,"
Bot ou*er* alle oþ*er* Marie be infinite excesse.
Of some signe in the flece to God Gedeon prayid,
Wher*e* Israel folke þ*at* tyme shuld be hym be delyvrid.
The weking of that wolle flece signed lib*er*acioune:
Marie this wise w*ith* child takned our*e* redempcioune.
This flece of Gedeon is blissid virgine Marie,
Of whilk make hym a cote Crist wald of his m*er*cye,
For in the cote be cledde wald he of our*e* freelte,
To cleth vs in the stole of eendles felicitee.
Gedeons flece to\ke/ dewe nothing blemyst the wolle;
Marie conceyved a so*u*n, virgine eure at the fulle.
Gedeon wronge out the dewe war*e*of a conke filled was:
Marie bare vs a son þ*at* filled this werld w*ith* grace.
¶c This swete concepc*iou*ne was broght be Gabriell,
Fig*ur*ed in Abrahams child and Rebecca Batuell.
Abraham sent Eliezer*e* to seke some virgine gudely
Til his sonne Ysaac a wif to be worthi:
Rebecca to Eliezer*e* asking a drinke it gave,
And he chaze hir*e* in spouse his lordis son for to have.
So sent the Fader*e* of heven to this werld Gabriel,
To seke for his dere So*u*n a moder*e* and virgine lele,
And he virgine Marie meke ou*er* alle oþ*er* fande,
That gaf, hym asking, a drinke, til his bòde consentande:
Rebecca ministred a drinke to message and camelle;
Marie till aungels and men opned of lif the welle.
O gud Jh*es*u, gif vs thin incarnacio*u*ne luf here,
Þ*at* in the welle of all lif we be eu*er* parcenere.

---

956 Luc. j° *mar.* 959 j figure *mar.* 968 virgines] *?* virgenes *alt.* virgines 971 ij figure Judic. vj^to *mar.* 977 Pr*ouer*. the last *mar.* 989 iij figure *mar.* 991 *979 is marked to begin the figure*; concepc*iou*ne] i.e. of Crist *over.* 992 child] i.e. his seruand *over*; Batuell] i.e. Batuel doghter *over.* 993 Eliezer] i.e. his servant *over.* 997 Luc. j° *mar.*

The birth of Our Lord Jesus Christ
Luke ii 1-7

Pharoah's butler dreams of a vine
Gen. xl 1-15

Herd in this pas tofore of Cristes concepcioune,
Now here of his manhede the seint gen*er*acioune, [f.13^{v}]
The whilk noght aunegels alon desired lange for to se,
Bot faders abode, and oft cryed "Lord, when shalle this be?
Send forth thi lambe, O Lorde of erth dominat*our*,
Thi light, thi sothfastnesse, God of ete*r*ne hono*ur*;
Shewe vs thi face fulle fair*e*, and sauf err*e* we for ay,
Thi Son wham we abide and seke als foghil the day,
Why ne wolde he brist the hevens and in this werld descende
And his folk fro thralledom*e* of alle the devels defende?
Bowe doune, right Lord, thyne hevenys, & til vs sauve descende,
Of thyne hoge maiestee, and thi right hande extende.
Haf nowe, Lord, mynde of alle thyne olde m*er*cyfullenesse;
Come refe vs fro the poustee of eu*er*lasting derknesse.
Come, Lord, þ*at* thi p*ro*phets be fonden lele and verray,
Thyne heghtis and thair*e* fig*ur*es be fulfilled in thair*e* day.
Come Lord, right sone, and hast and tary noght thi gudenesse:
Relese thi folkes trespasse, and take our*e* blode & flesshe.
No man suffises vs nor aungel til vnthralle;
Come thow þ*er*fore thyself, O Lord þ*at* made vs alle!"
At the last, m*er*cyfull God take our*e* hvmanitee
For to destruye of man the olde captivitee.
He þ*at* sometyme saide, "Me repents to haf made ma*n*n"
Liked to be inc*ar*nat, man to delyvre than.
¶a This was figured tofore be the botler*e* of Pharao*un*
Whilk dremed, in p*ri*soune shet\t/e, of his deliuriso*un*.
Hym thoght out of the grounde a vigne sprange hym tofore,
Whilk spredd it in thre bra*u*nches be p*ro*cesse more and more.
Thilk vigne broght noght furth grapes at ones in o moment,
Bo\t/ first lef and than flowres and grapes succedent;
He p*re*ssed in Pharaos cuppe þ*at* he held in his hande
Grapes, and offred his lord als he vsed toforhande.
Aft*er* of this dreme herd he swilk int*er*pretacioune
Þ*at* passed bot dayes thre to be qwite of p*ri*soune.
Of this dreme haf ȝ*e* herd the cas historiale;
Here nowe, if it ȝow like, the menyng spirituale.
Tofore that Oure Saveour*e* toke our*e* hvmanitee,
Mankynde had suffred lange reuthfulle captivitee.
At last a vigne, Jhesus, sprange of the erth, Marie,
Havyng in hym thre braunches, thre thinges wonderfullie:
For Crist in hym had fleshe and sawle and deitee,
Whilk thre thinges hafe destruyd all our*e* captivitee,
Or els thre p*er*sones thir*e* braunches ern in the Trinitee,
Whilk vs of priso*un*e has qwite of alle the feendes poustee; [f.14^{r}]
Bot noght mankind delivred onene þ*at* Crist was borne,
Bot wyne of Cristis blode p*re*ssed in the Crosses horne.
The thredde day aft*er* this wyne was pressed in passioune,
Than was mankind fre, qwite out of the feendis prisoune.
This wyne the King of heven enebried fulle swetely
When he ma*n*nes gilt þ*er*fore wald relese so freely.

1005 Ca^{m} viij^{m} *mar.* 1009 Ysaye xvj^{o} *mar.* 1025 hvmanitee] *(*u *alt.* v*).* 1027 Gen. vj^{to} *mar.* 1028 incarnat] *?* inc*arn*aat *alt.* 1029 j fig*ure* *mar.* 1031 Gen. xl^{o} *mar.* 1034 succedent] i.e. fylowing *over.* 1047 braunches] *a minim short.* 1049 Bot] Boght *(*-ght *subp. and can.).* 1051 passioune] i.e. of Crist *over.*

Aaron's rod blooms
Num. xvii

The Sibyl sees a virgin with a boy
Voragine I 27

The same wyne has vs left God, of his grete m*er*cy,
Eu*er*y day to be offred in the autier*e* mistikly
Vnto the hegh King of heven, for this werldis offence,
For ilk day it offendis þ*at* Lordis maiestee inmense.
Blissed be þ*at* Saveour*e* and his clemence divine,
In whilk is vs betaken thus helefulle medicyne;
And blissed be eu*er*more þ*at* virgine gloriouse,
Bering this vigne of wyne thus wele enebriouse.
When Crist was borne, the vignes floryshed of Engaddy,
To shew þ*at* Crist figured was comen than c*er*teinly.
Blissed be Our*e* Savio*urs* Crist joyouse natiuitee,
Of whilk til aungels and men comes alle vtilitee:
Be it fro feendis myght is mankind delivrid,
And be the same aungelkinde is gudely restorid.
¶b Of Cristis birth nowe herde the swete vtilitee,
Her*e* we þ*er*of forwardis the man*er*e and qualitee.
The man*er* þ*er*of figured Aarons ȝerde almandine,
Þ*at* florisshed and fruyt broght forth be souleine v*er*tue divine,
For to m*er*ueile þ*at* ȝerde contr*e*natu*r*ely burgeonde thar*e*,
So Marie of natu*r*es ordre m*er*veillously hir*e* son bare.
Aarons ȝerde fructified w*ith*out plantacio*u*ne:
Marie bare vs a son w*ith*out mans co*m*mixtioune.
The ȝerdes flour*e* shewed Aaron worthi vnto p*re*sthede,
And Marie childing bare vs a sou*er*ein preste in dede.
In the almondes shelle was hidde a swete nuclee:
In the shelle of Cristis flesshe was hidde his deitee.
In Aarons ȝerde we fynde of braunches the grennesse,
The swettnes of the floure, of fruyt plentivousnesse;
So is in Marie fonden eu*er* grene virginitee,
Of pitee the swettnes, pleinesse of s\a/intite;
¶c And Crist shewed noght his birth vnto the Jewes onely,
Bot to the payens also, of his aboundant m*er*cy:
For he come noght in erth ones for the Jewes sake,
Bot for his grace wald sprede all men sauf for to make.
Thir*e* tymes, Octovian was lord ou*er* alle the werld, rede we,
Wharefore the Romayns hym p*ro*fred hono*ur* of deitee, [f.14^v]
Of whilk thing he counseild w*ith* Sibille the p*ro*phetesse,
Wher*e* in this werld shuld eure man passe hym in gretenesse.
A sercle of gold at Rome aboute the sonnebeme sawe she
Thilk day þ*at* Crist was borne in the land of Judee;
Als in that cercle sho se the fairest mayden sitting,
A fair*e* son ou*er* alle oþ*er* in hir*e* swete armys halsing.
To the emp*er*oure Octavian thilk Sibille shewed that thing,
And saide ou*er* his estate þ*at* day was borne a king.
O myght of the King of kinges ou*er* alle þ*at* beres poustee,
Þ*at* has delivred mankind fro the feendis captivitee!
Augustus Caesar feared the power of this king,
And refused to allow men to consider or call him god.
Jh*es*u, gif vs thi birth til hono*ur* w*ith* myght and mayne,
Þ*at* in the devels thraldom*e* we ne falle neu*er* more aȝeine.

1056 mistikly] i.e. of the secre\t/e ordena*u*nce of Godde *o.i.e.l.* 1059 clemence] i.e. pitee *over.* 1063 Eccl*es*iastica historia *mar.* 1066 vtilitee] i.e. the profit *over.* 1070 almandine] for it bare almondes *over*; ij figure *mar.* 1079 nuclee] i.e. a kirnelle *over.* 1084 saintite] seintete *(1st e can.)*. 1085 iij fig*ure* *mar.* 1088 Thi. ij Pet. iij^o *mar.* 1104 corr. *mar.*

Three wise men give gifts
Matt. ii 11-12

Three wise men see a new star in the East
Matt. ii 1-10

The passed chapitle declared Cristis gen*er*acioune;
In this nowe is til here of the kinges oblacioune.
¶a Thilk day þ*at* Jh*es*u Crist was borne vs in Bethleeme,
Thre kinges se in the Est a sterne of fulle grete leeme,
In whilk newe sterne thai see a knave childe fair*e* and hulde;
Aboven his heved apiered a bright crosse of fyne gulde.
Fro thence herd thai a voice vntil thaim thre saying,
"Goos to Judee and thair*e* shalle ȝ*e* fynde a newe kinge."
To that lande went thays kinges alle thre fulle hastyly;
Hevens Kinge fande thi thar*e* borne, and offred til hym gudely.
¶b Thir*e* thre kinges be thre stronge men had p*re*fig*ur*ing,
Þ*at* broght fro Bethlemes cist*er*ne wat*er* to Dauid Kinge.
The boldenesse of thir*e* thre stronge was p*ra*ysed fulle mykil þ*er*by;
The come and offring of thir*e* thre kinges is loved hyeghly.
The thre stronge, of thar*e* foos thay ne hadde no man*er*e awe
To passe thorghout thair*e* ost the watir*e* thar*e* for to drawe.
Herodes pouwer*e* ryght so thir*e* thre kinges dred nothing,
Bot boldly Judee entrant, askid of o newe king.
Jaspar*e*, Balthasar, Melchor the thre kinges heght þ*at* day:
The thre stronge Bananyas, [Sobokay], Abasay.
The thre stronge at Bethleme feched wat*er* of the cist*er*ne:
The thre kinges come to Bethleme for wat*er* of grace et*er*ne.
The thre stronge wat*er* drew vpp out of a cist*er*ne t*er*restre:
The thre kinges toke wat*er* of grace of the botteller*e* celestre.
The cist*er*ne in Bethleme be this wayes fig*ur*ed even
In Bethleme þ*at* shuld be borne the buttelle*re* of hyest heven,
Whilk shuld byrle wat*er* of grace til ilk man wele thrysty
And freely gif wat*er* of grace to thaim þ*at* may noght by. [f.15^{r}]
Kyng Dauid, the watir*e* broght, offrid to Godde lovyng,
Þ*at* gaf hym so stronge men to do þ*at* mayst*er*fulle thyng:
Cryst lord of heven and erth toke exultacioune
Signed be thir*e* thre kynges co*m*myng of payens conu*er*sioune.
Dauid semed noght haf thristed wat*er*, bot his men*nes* v*er*tue:
Ryght so our*e* turnyng til hele thristed Our*e* Lord Jhesue.
The thre stronge to Bethlem went in fulle littel space:
So come thre kynges of the Est thidir*e* sone thorgh Gods grace.
Who askis how þ*at* this thing thus schort tyme myght befalle,
To Crist borne was nothing, say, inpossible at alle,
For he þ*at* broght Abakuc sodenley fro Jude to Babilone
Moght brynge thre kinges of the Est into Judee onone.
Thir*e* kinges did at Bethlem to Crist fulle meeke reu*er*ence,
And offrid hym devoutly gold, mirre and encence.
¶c The fig*ure* of this new king, and of his oblacioune,
Was in the kyngdome forshewed of the wise Kyng Salomo*u*ne:
For Salomone King a child ȝit thogh wysest was he,
And Godde childe made, als wise als arst in Trinitee.
Kyng Salomon sat in the throne of yvoir*e* fair*e* & clene
The whilk alle ou*er* was cledde w*ith* gold fynest and shene.
Alle kinges of erth to see King Salomon had bry*n*nyng,
And broght hym p*re*ciouse giftes and latsomest to fynd,

1105 Ca^{m} ix^{m} *mar.* 1107 j fig*ure* *mar.*; Thilk] *1102 is marked to begin the first figure.* 1115 ij figure *mar.* 1116 iij^{o} Reg. xxiij^{o} *mar.* 1123 The names of the three kinges *mar.* 1124 Sokobay] Sobokay. 1143 Daniel xiiij^{o} *mar.* 1147 iij fig*ure* *mar.* 1149 Reg. x^{o} *mar.* 1152 fynest] *(*y *o.er.).* 1153 bry*n*nyng] i.e. desire *over.*

Three strong men bring water to King David
II Kings xxiii 15-17

The throne of Solomon
III Kings x 18-20

Bot the Whene of Saba hym broght gyftes so many & slike
Þat in Jerusalem tofore warre neuer arst sene thaym like.
The throne of Salomon verray is the blissid mayden Marye,
In whilk satt Jhesus Crist, eterne verray Sophie.
This reuerent throne was made of alle there fynest trezore:
That is, of fynest gold and aldere-whittest yvore.
The yvore for his candoure and his coldnesse, witt ȝe,
Takenes virginele clennesse of hevenysh chaystytee.
Yvore a rede coloure takes vpp when it is olde:
Right so longe chastitee for martirdome is tolde;
And for golde in valoure passes euery metalle
It takenes charitee, the modere of vertues alle.
Thus Marie is cald yvoire for virginele chastitee,
And ouercledde alle with golde for perfitest charite.
Lord, gudely to maydenhede conioignes charitee,
Without whilk pleses nothing to God virginitee:
For als the vnbrynnyng laumpe a thef dredes nothing,
No mare the devil maydenhode, charitee in it failling.
Salomones throne was with sex greces exaltate,
And Marie superexcellis of all seints the state– [f.15^v]
Of patriarkes and prophetes and posteles dignitee,
Of martirs and confessoures and virgines in degree–
Or Salomones throne had greces sex, als I saide toforne,
For after the sex eages of the warlde was Marie borne.
Twelve leonceux ouer sex greces Salomones throne exourned,
And Marie als hevens qwhene the twelue aposteles anourned;
Or twelue leonceux of the throne whare notable embelissours
For þat the patriarks twelve ware Maries progenitours;
And two grete lyouns the throne of King Salomon vp bare:
Two tables of the commandments dowbly in Oure Lady sawle ware.
The top of this throne was curved,
Because Mary was completely clean, and without any dirty corner.
Two handes stablisshid the throne, one on othere parte,
For the Fadere and the Haly Gast fro Marie shalle neuer departe.
This throne verray Salomon made til hymself so clene
Þat neuer in no kynges aght was swilk ane oþer werke sene,
Wharefore the kynges swilk giftes toke with thaym for offring
Als to this lordfulle childe shuld seme be most sittyng.
Golde is a real gift for his grete nobletee,
Be whilk þai shewed the child a king verray to be.
Encense is oblacioune, ȝe wote, is sacerdotale,
And this child was a prest þat neuer hadde his egale.
In auncien tyme with mirre dede bodies biried were:
Crist, king and prest, for manne wald in this werld dye here.
Than aght vs offre to Crist golde of dileccioune,
Sithen he for vs bare payne of bitterest passioune,
Encense of devoute laude and of graces thanking,
And mirre of compassioune of his deth recoreding.
O gude Jhesu, gif vs so tendre of thi paynes be
In heven þat we descerve euermore the for to se.

1158 verray] *(*e *overwritten)*; sophie] i.e. hevenly wisdome *over*. 1163 nota *mar*. 1166 *over erased line*. 1173 exaltate] i.e. reisid *over*. 1174 superexcellis] i.e. highly passes *over* 1179 exourned] i.e. enbeliced outwardes *over*. 1186 dowbly] i.e. in thoght and dede *over*. 1189 throne] i.e. of Our Lady *over*; Salomon] i.e. Cristus *over*. 1193 Golde *mar*. 1195 Encense *mar*.; sacerdotale] i.e. fallyng to presthode *over*. 1196 egale] i.e. his pere *over*. 1197 Mirre *mar*. 1199 of] and *subp. and* of *ins*.; delecciounel i.e. of lufe *over*.

The presentation of Jesus in The Temple
Luke ii 22-39

The Ark of the Testament signifies Mary
Ex. xxv 10-16

In the chapitle tofore was of thre kynges offring;
Nowe fylowes it in the Temple of Cristis p*re*senting.
Our*e* Ladie the fourtied day of Cristis natiuitee
Of hir*e* purificacioune did the solempnitee;
Bot sho ne had nothing nede of purificacioune,
Þ*at* neu*er* conceyvid hir*e* son of ma*n*nes co*m*mixtioune,
Bot wold be purified to be of the Lawe executrice,
Þ*at* sho ne shuld noght be demed of the Lawe p*re*uaricatrice,
F[or] breker*e* of Gods lawe was sho noght c*er*teinly,
Bot alle þ*at* was þ*er*inne kept sho fulle bisily.
¶a The Arke of Gods Testament p*re*figu*re*d hir*e* þar*e*fore,
In whilk the p*re*ceptis of his Lawe warr*e* shette, both lesse & more.
In this Arke war*e* two tables of Moyses alle of stone
In whilk the x co*m*mandements war*e* writen ilkone by one, [f.16r]
The whilk for p*ro*fite of reders I write als þay war*e* thair*e*,
And ovre w*ith* a short glose I thynk thaym to declare.
The first, loke thowe ne be gods alien wirchiphing;
Þ*at* is, wirshippe trewe Godde and ou*er* hym luf nothing.
The secunde, thow shalle noght in vayne thi Lord God name take:
Þ*at* is, thov shalle no blaspheme nor othe in his name vnduely make.
The thredde is haf gude mynde thi haly day to seintifie:
Þ*at* is, do no vnleffulle werkes in it, nor synne noght dedely.
The ferth is fader*e* and moder*e* hono*ur* dewely obeiant,
Pitee and necessaries to thaym in savle & body ministrant.
The fift, slee noght in dede, in worde nor wikked ymaginacio*u*ne,
In help, consent, ensaumple nor any occasioune.
The sext, lecherye do none in dede, thoght nor spekyng,
No\r/ in thi jurisdiccio*u*ne be no swilk thing suffring.
Loke thov stele noght, the sevent, other mens thing to the drawyng,
Nor mawgree wham þ*at* it awe be sleghtes mysvsing.
The eghten is fals wittnesse aȝeins thi neghburgh þ*o*u ne saye:
Þ*at* is, alle leghes and wikked sleghtis and detraccioune flee aye.
The nynt, house & feeld of thi neghburgh to wilne eschew freely
(Til his disese or harme it knawyng specially).
The tenth, mayden nor knave wilne noght, nor wif fro hir*e* husband.
The forther*e* p*re*cept of vnmovable, this of movable vnderstand:
Thir*e* two last p*re*ceptes semes to discorde in nothing
Bot that thai of inmobles and mobles makes desseu*er*yng.
And alle the forsaide p*re*ceptes kept Marie bisyly,
Wharefore the Testamentis Arke p*re*figu*re*d hir*e* resonably.
This same Arke als contened the boke of the Olde Testament,
And Marie the bokes of Haly Writte herd in haliest entent.
In the Arke was Arones ȝerde whilk florisshed, a\l/s is made mynde,
And Marie wombe flovred & broght forth fruyt salut*er* to mankynde.
In the Arke was *vrna aurea* w*ith* manna cald aungels brede:
Of Marie come manna of heven þ*at* sauues fro eendles dede.
The Testamentis Arke of sethim, a tree inputr*i*ble, was made,
And Marie in rotynnesse ne poudr*e* neu*er* aft*er* hir*e* dede slade.
The Arke had in the sydes four*e* ringes of golde be tale:
In Marie war*e* four*e* vertues whilk men calle cardinale,

1205 Ca^m x^m *mar.* 1211 executrice] i.e. fylower *over.* 1212 Levi. xij° *mar.*; p*re*uaricatrice] i.e. breker *over.* 1213 For] Fro. 1215 j fig*ure* Archa Testamenti *mar.* 1221 n*ota* | j *mar.* 1222 Exposic*i*oune of the x co*m*mandements Deut*er*. vj° Exo*di* xxj° et Leuit. xix° *mar.*; ij *mar.* 1225 n*ota* | iij *mar.* 1227 n*ota* | iiij *mar.* 1229 n*ota* | v *mar.* 1231 n*ota* | vi *mar.* 1232 Nor] *(*r *a letter can. and subp. and another* r *ins.).* 1233 n*ota* | vij *mar.* 1234 wham] thaym *subp. and* wham *ins.* 1235 n*ota* | viij *mar.* 1237 n*ota* | ix *mar.* 1242 Arke] *followed by er.* 1239 n*ota* | x *mar.* 1252 slade] i.e. descendid noght to corruptioune *o.i.e.l.* 1254 vertues cardinale *mar.*

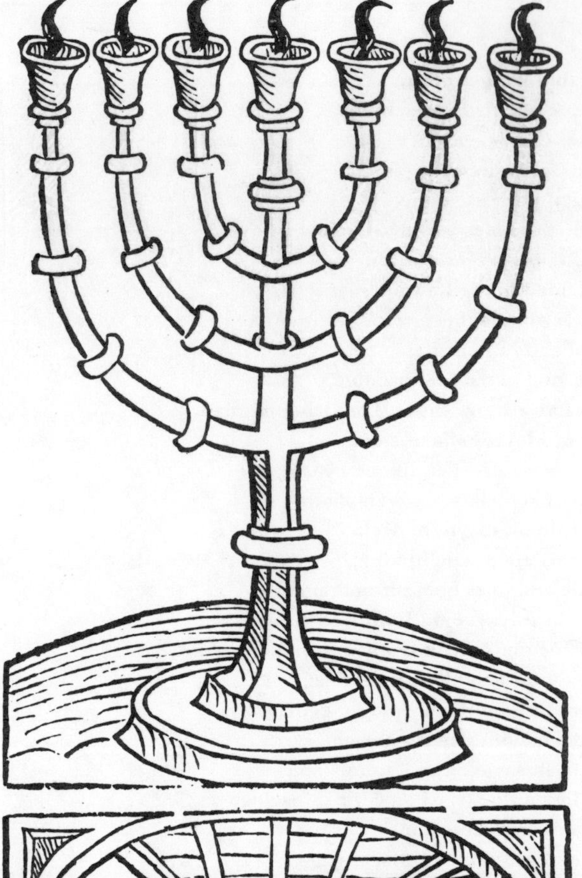

The lamp of the Temple of Solomon
Ex. xxv 31-40; Num. viii 2-4

The presentation of the infant Samuel
I Kings i 5-28

Þ*at* ere temp*er*aunce, p*ru*dence, force and the ferth justice,
The rotes of alle vertues for to destruye alle vice.
Thwo barres this Arke had eke be whilk it borne moght be,
Signifiant of God & man the double charitee.
The Arke withinne & w*ith*oute was alle ou*er* golde bygone,
And Marie withinne & w*ith*oute in alle gude vertues shone. [f.16v]
¶b **Als to the goldin candelabre was sho lykned forthi**
Whilk in the Temple of Jer*usale*m shone fulle nobly,
On whilk war*e* laumpes seven brynnyng fulle fair*e* standing,
The seven werkes of m*er*cye in Marie p*re*figuryng.
This ere: to hungry gif mete, and drink to pur*e* thristing,
The naked to cleth, and gedre to harbergh the nedy wagring,
Visit the seke, and p*ri*soners delivre and ou*er* thaym rewe,
Do graue dede mens bodies for Our*e* Lords luf Jhesu.
The werkes of m*er*cye no dout in Marie war*e* plen*er*ly,
Sen sho is moder*e* of pitee and qwene evre of mercy.
How shuld the moder*e* of m*er*cye the werkes of m*er*cye noght fille,
Or the candelabre fulle of divine fir*e* noght shyne be the same skille?
This Ladie is verray candelabre and C*ri*stis bright lanterne,
The laumpe brynnyng in fire of light sou*er*ayne sup*er*ne.
This virgine fulle of splend*our* and thorghout lumynouse
Is bright as som*er*es dawenyng and als the sonne radyouse.
Hir*e* bemes ou*er* alle the st*er*nes er*e* incomp*ar*abli bright:
Of this werldis nyght the mone is sho, and aungels light.
To this candelabre & hir*e* candele bere we devocioune
With light candels in the feest of hire purificacioune.
Marye to Godde in that feeste offrid a candel bright,
The whilk Seinte Symeon cald thus: "reuelacioune of folkes light".
Jh*es*u Crist, Marie son, is this candel brynnyng,
Be threfald matiers þ*at* ere founden in swilk a thyng:
For in the candel is fire, weke and wax, this thre–
In Crist warr*e* flesshe and sawle and verray divinitee.
This candele to God the Fader*e* was offrid for hele of man,
Be whilk the nyght of our*e* derknesse was lightned than.
¶c **Also the oblacioune of this gloriouse virgine candele**
Was sometyme p*re*figured in the haly child Samuele.
His moder*e* Anne was barayne & moght no childe bere,
Wharefor sho, God prayng, lete falle fulle many a ter*e*.
Till Anne gaf Godde a son ageynes alle nat*ur*el vse,
And above nat*ur*es vsage to Marie hir*e* so*u*n Jhesus.
Anna hir*e* son Samuel to Godde gaf in offring,
Bot Marie of hir*e* son to Godde his awne Fader*e* made gyving.
Sho offrid a son to be for the Jewes p*ro*pugnatour*e*:
Marie hir*e* son to be of alle this werld p*ro*tect*our*;
And of Jewes refused was after*e* the son of Anne,
And Marye son be thaym slayne, saklest þ*at* eu*er* was manne.
This thing be Symeon of Marie tofore p*ro*phecied was:
Þ*at* the swerde of hir*e* son shuld thorgh hir*e* sawle passe. [f.17r]
O gude Jhesu, in luf of thi presentacioune
Gif vs in hevenyssh Temple w*ith* thyn aungels to woune.

1261 Num*er*i viij Exodi xxv^to Parabil. iiij° *mar.*; *the start of the 2nd figure is unmarked.* 1264 The seven werk*es* of mercy *mar.* 1265 hungry] j *over*; drink] ij *over*. 1266 naked] iij *over*; harbergh] iiij *over*. 1267 Visit] v *over*; delivre] vi *over*. 1268 graue] vij *over*. 1272 The candelabre *mar.* 1283 Luc. ij *mar.* 1285 candele *mar.* 1289 iij figure *mar.* 1293 Regum j° *mar.* 1297 Sho] Anna *over*.

Jesus enters Egypt (and the idols fall)
Matt. ii 13-15; Comestor 1543 (Is. xix 1)

The Egyptians made an image of the Virgin and Child
Comestor 1440

ȝe haf herd her*e*tofore how Crist pr*e*sentid was;
How he fledde til Egipt nowe heris in this pas.
Josep, be the aungel warnid þ*at* Herod to slee Crist thoght,
With moder*e* and child onone til Egipt fleeyng he soght;
And when Crist and his moder*e* war*e* in thies contrees entrande,
All ymages of mawmetry ou*er*thruwe thorghout the lande,
Whilk thing to the Egipciens Jeremy had told to bee,
Tofore vnto þ*at* lande ledde in captivitee.
¶a For when the Egipciens herd Jeremy a p*ro*phett calle
Þai spired hym if in Egipt shuld any grete m*er*veilles falle.
He answerd a mayden shuld bere a son in tyme to co*m*me,
And than shuld the ydoles ouerthrawe thorgh Egipt alle & so*m*me,
And thai, demyng this childe ovre thair*e* gods till haf myght,
Treted what hono*ur* til hym for to do wer*e* best right.
A virgine w*ith* a fair*e* child didde thai make be entaylle
Hono*ur*yng it in thair*e* wise, thus sais the storie sanz faille.
Lange aft*er*, what this mote menc spird thaym King Tholome:
Thai saide thai hadde in p*ro*phecie þ*at* swilk a thing shuld be.
This p*ro*phecie was fullfillid in dede fulle verrayly,
When intil Egipt was entred Crist and his moder*e* Marie,
For alle the ymages in Egipt of ydoles ou*er*threw than,
Wharefore a mayden haf childede than demed ther*e* many a man.
¶b Als was this thing fig*ur*ed in Moyses and Pharaoune,
His coro*u*ne al to-bristing w*ith* the ymagie of godde Hamo*u*ne.
King Pharao did make his coro*u*ne of golde and perre nobly,
W*ith* the ymage of godde Hamo*u*ne þ*er*in wroght craftily.
Thai hadde p*ro*phecie þ*at* of the Jewes a knave child shuld be borne
Whilk shuld the Jewes delyvre, and Egipt be forlorne;
Wharefore the Jewes war*e* chargid þ*er* childer*e* in the flode cast
Þ*at* thus hym þ*at* thai dredde thai shulde slee at the last.
Her*e*fore to lyve in twynne thoght Amon & Jocabeth,
Als lever*e* to haf no childer*e* than bring tham forth to deth;
Bot Godde sent thaym his sonde to dwelle samne borde & bedde,
For thair*e*s shuld be thilk child whilk the Egipciens so dredde.
Jocabeth conceyved and bare a son fulle fair*e* and free,
And hidde hym in hir*e* hovse fulle p*ri*vely monethes three.
Aft*er*, when Jocabeth se sho moght no langer*e* hym hide,
Hym closid in a skeppette sho laide be the ryver*e* syde.
Termuth, Pharaos doght*er*, come by the ryver*e* þ*at* hovre,
And the childe founden adopte for son tille his honour*e*, [f.17^{v}]
Whaym sho gert calle Moyses and did hym norisshid to be,
And broght hym aft*er* on a tyme vnto the kyng for to see;
With whaym playing, his coro*u*ne toke he hym at the last,
And he doune to the erth kest it and alle to-brast.
A bysshopp of thair*e* mawments cryed thus when he this see:
"This is the childe whilk goddes shewed vs þ*at* slayne shuld bee"
And his swerde drawne to slee the childe for this doyng,
Some folkes saide þ*at* the thing was done of vnconnyng.
Qvhikke colys gaf thai the childe to part thair*e* threpe be skille:
Some kest he in his mouthe als it was Gods wille;

1305 {C}a^{m} xj^{m} *mar.* 1308 Math*e*i ij^{o} *mar.* 1311 j fig*ur*e *mar.* 1313 Historia Scolastica and i*n* the legende s*anct*or*um* on Cr*i*stenmesday *mar.* 1326 Maist*er* of the Stories *mar.* 1327 ij fig*ur*e *mar.* 1331 Thai] i.e. the Egipciens *over.* 1333 childer*e*] i.e. the males noght the females *over.* 1335 The names of Moyses fad*er* & his moders *mar.*; Amon] fader *over*; Jocabeth] the moder of Moyses *over.* 1337 Maist*er* Historiar*um* apon Exodi *mar.* 1344 adopte] i.e. chase be the lawe *over.* 1350 Magist*er* Histor*iarum* *mar.* 1353 threpe] i.e. debate *over.*

Moses breaks Pharoah's crown and eats embers
Comestor 1142-44

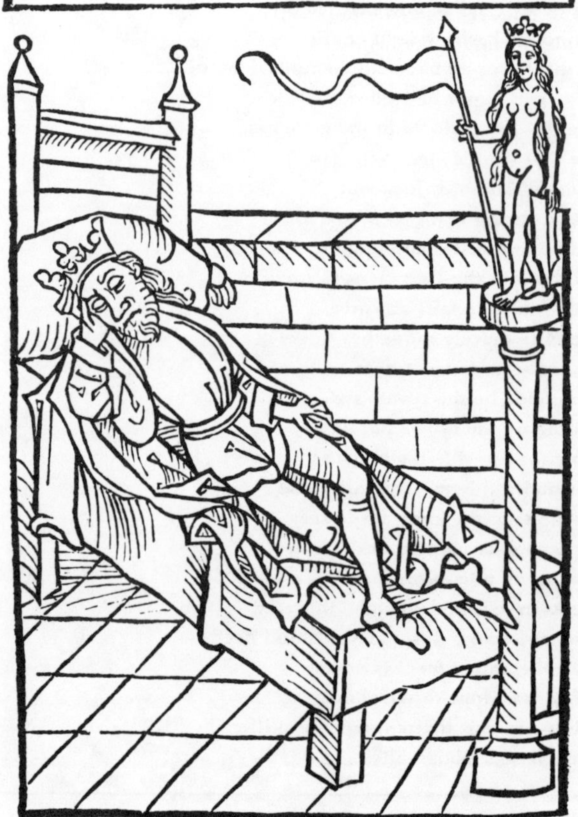

Nabugodonosor dreams of a statue
Dan. ii 31-35

And thus Moyses was sauued thorgh grace in his ȝonge age,
Þ*at* aft*er* delyvred the Jewes fro Egipciens s*er*uage.
And thinges þ*at* ȝe haf herd of this child Moyses nowe
Accordis in diu*er*se thinges vnto the childe swete Jhesewe,
For Pharao bad alle the Jewes þ*er* childer*e* male for to drovne,
And to drenche Moyses thaym w*ith* was his entencioune.
So Herod bad alle the childer*e* of Bethlem dede shuld be,
Þ*at* Crist childe shuld be slane amanges thaym thus kest he;
Bot als Godde sauued Moyses fro the handes \of/ Pharao,
So sauued he his Son Crist fro the swerde of Herod, loo.
For Israel out of Egipt to lede was borne Moyses,
And Crist borne to qwite man out of infernale disese.
Moyses the godde of Egipt to-brast with the coroune,
Crist alle þ*er* fals gods to-brast til noght and broght thaym doune.
¶c This ruyne of ydoles fig*ur*ed ane ymage fulle lange tofore
Seghen in his bedde sleping be Kyng Nabugodonosor.
This ymage heved and his nekke war*e* alle of gold fulle fyne,
The armys and brest of it war*e* thorghout argentyne;
This ymage wombe and the theghes war*e* alle togider*e* of brasse,
The leggis, als thoght the king, of yrnysshe matier*e*s wasse.
The feete some parte of erth the king thoght þ*at* shuld be,
Also some parte of yryn, als thoght his sleping ee.
Out of a hille a stone without mans hande was kytte,
And in the feet of the ymage or mawmet do*un* slathe itte,
Whilk stone þ*at* ymage grete in pouder*e* sone alle to-brast,
And aft*er* wax a mountaigne alder-most at the last.
This stone of Jh*es*u Crist gaf figuracioune,
Þ*at* toke mankynde in erthe for our*e* saluacioune.
This stone out of the mounteigne w*ith*out mans handis was shorne
For Crist was borne of Marie, virgine aft*er* als toforne.
This stone Crist in Egipt the ydoles eke alle to-brast,
Wher*e* thai ware silver*e* or gold: this is trevth hole and fast; [f.18r]
And mawmets of yryn and brasse ȝit brast he also thase,
With oþ*er* of erthe–ilkone Crist made turne til a maze.
In the remenbred ymage war*e* sene thir*e* maters alle,
And Crist made alle ydoles falle into pouder*e* fulle smalle.
That stone, the ymage to-broken*e*, in a grete mowntaigne grewe
For, cessing ydoles, the feith sprange thorgh the werld of Jh*es*u;
Or els the stone gruwe vpp in ane hille alder-moste
For Crist his enemy H\e/rod destruyde, for alle his boste.
Crist, callid out of Egipt, repaired in Jewerie thanne,
In eage and wisdo*u*me forthering tofor both God and manne;
And in a mountaigne so grete at the last thus growed he,
Þ*at* he filled heven and erthe w*ith* his inmensitee.
Who shalle this mountaigne clymbe, þ*at* is, who shalle Crist see,
Bot the innocent of his hande w*ith* hertis puritee?
He this shalle blissing take of Our*e* Lord almyghty,
And m*er*cy of his gude Godde his saluter*e* eendelesly.
O gude Jh*es*u, gif vs the \to/ serue w*ith* hert clene,
Þ*at* in the hille of thi blisse eu*er*more we mowe the sene.

1365 Israel] i.e. the childer of Isr*ae*l *over*. 1372 argentyne] i.e. of siluer *over*. 1380 wax] i.e. the stone *over*. 1389 maters] i.e. of golde and silver & e*tc*. *over*. 1394 Herod] (oe *alt*. e). 1395 Luc. ij *mar*. 1398 inmensitee] i.e. a thing þ*at* may noght be mesu*u*red *o.i.e.l.* 1399 Psalme xxiij *mar*. 1400 puritee] i.e. clennesse *over*.

Jesus is baptised by John
Matt. iii 13-17

The 'brazen sea' for entrants to The Temple
III Kings vii 23-27

In the last chapitle was tolde how Crist til Egipt was chacid;
Heres now in this howe John in Jordan*e* Crist baptizid.
When Our*e* Lord Jh*es*u Crist his trehtti*th* 3ere beganne
To Johan come he at the flvmme for to be baptized thanne:
Bot Crist to be baptized, wit wele, hadde he no nede
Sauf for mankyndes hele *þat* he it vnder3ede,
Þat water*e*, his sacrede body touchying, shuld vertue take
To man baptized in itte entree til hevens make.
¶a This was fig*ur*d tofore in thilk see of brasse
Whilk in the entree of the Temple of Jer*usale*m sette was,
In whilk the p*re*stes *þat* wolde in the Temple make entree
Had nede thaym for to washe, honest and clene to bee.
So in Gods Temple of heven entree who haue wille,
In baptisme be washed clene hym nedes, be like skille;
And *nota*, a*re* we go ferthere, *þat* the*re* bene baptismes thre:
Off flvmme, of flavme, of blode. Disseu*er* thaym thus shalle 3*e*:
Of flvmme thas whilk in wati*re* takes duwe inm*ers*ioune,
Of blode thas *þat* for Crist tholes martyrs passi*ou*ne,
Of flavme be the Haly Gost forsoth baptized is he
Þat p*ur*posed to baptisme and dyes a*re* it may be;
And if that man ou*er*lyve, hym suffizes noght the intent,
Bot of some man, if he may, the baptisme of wat*er* he hent:
Ne baptisme of blode nor marti*re* availles noght be this skille
Who may resceyue baptisme of wat*er*, and noght ne wille.
3e he*re* how necessarie is the baptesme of wat*er* \or/ flvmne [f.18v]
Who may it have and wilnes in Gods Temple for to come.
Baptesme of flvmme is doine only in wate*re* pure,
And noythe*re* in wyne nor mylke, nor in any othe*re* licou*re*.
The mare enen or the lauatorie the whilk was made of brasse
In whilk all man*ere* metallies be the fus*our*s 3ett was
Takened that wordes of baptesme may be in eu*ery* langage
So *þat* the wordes haf fo*ur*me aft*er* the trewe Kyrkes vsage:
And eu*ery* man the sacrament of baptesme may gif, loo,
If he it aft*er* Haly Kyrke haf trew entent to do,
And als twelue oxen of brasse bare vpp this brasen see,
So baptesme twelue apostles p*re*ched thorgh the werlde to bee;
Nor it nys noght to slide ou*er* *þat* *þis* mare enen was
Hild about w*ith* wymmens myrours of purest glas,
Þat folk in towards the Temple myght knawe, in thaym lokeing,
If any spotte or oght ellis wa*re* on thaym myssittying,
Whilk fig*ur*ed *þat* baptesme askes of conscience p*er*feccioune,
W*ith* displacens of all synne and hertly contrycioune.
*Þer*fore to some Pharisens Johan Baptist thus saide he
Whame w*ith*out contricioune to baptesme come he see:
"How shalle 3e flee the ire of the comyng juge, 3*e* neddre brode,
Taking baptesme without contricio*u*ne in 3*our* mode?"
¶b For he *þat* baptesme takes w*ith* hertis contricioune
Is clensid of alle his synnes be plen*er* remissioune.
In Naaman of Sy*re* was this shewed sometyme fig*ur*atifly,
Þat was lepre and clennsid in Jordan m*er*veillously.

1405 Ca^{m} xij^{m} *mar.* 1406 John] ? Joh*a*n 1409 *marked with a cross mar.* 1413 brasse] i.e. a lavatorie *over.* 1418 no*ta* *mar.* 1419 Off three manere Baptisme *mar.* 1429 or] of *subp.* 1433 j fig*ure* *mar.*; enen] a lauatorie *over.* 1435 iij Reg. vij^{o} *mar.* 1447 Johan] ? Joha*n*n 1449 Math. iij *mar.* 1453 iiij Reg. v^{to} *mar.*

The leper Naaman is healed
IV Kings v 1-14

The Jordan is dry during the crossing
Josue iii 14-17

This Naaman a payen was and nothing Godde he knewe,
Ȝit come he to seke hele of Gods p*r*oph*e*te Elisew.
He weshe hym, biding the p*r*oph*e*te, in flvmme Jordan seven sithe,
And was hole as a childe of alle his lepre thus swithe.
Helisev, be this sevenfolde in Jordanes water*e* wesheing,
P*re*figu*re*d of the seven dedely synnes in baptesme forgyving.
Naaman be Jordan was made fro lepre thorgh clene in body,
Bot foulest synners be baptesme er*e* made faire spirituelly
So þ*at* if, ar*e* thay synned eft, Godde ordeynd thair*e* deying,
Thai shulde passe vntille heven onone w*ith*out lettyng:
And this was takened when hevens war*e* opned ou*er* Crist anone,
When he in the flvmne Jordan had taken baptesme of John;
Wharefore whoso wille entre into the kyngdome of heven,
Nedes mot hym baptized be, als is forsaide fulle even–
¶c And in the passage of Jordan had p*re*figuracioune,
Entring the childer*e* of Isr*ae*l the land of p*ro*missioune [f.19r]
For first Jordan, the figu*re* of haly baptesme, thay passed,
Ar*e* thai war*e* in the lande of Gods p*ro*missioune entred.
Right so be baptesmes lauacr*e* mot ilk man have passing
Whilk to the verray lande of beheste desir*e*s to haue entring.
Archa Domini thorgh myddes Jordan was borne & ther*e* it stode,
And the folk with thair*e* bestaille drye-fote alle ou*er* it ȝode;
For on the over half the Arche the wat*er* no ferther*e* ranne,
Bot like ane hogest mountaigne it gadred togider*e* thanne,
And on the lawer*e* p*ar*tie the wat*er* ranne to the see,
Þ*at* Jordan drye thorgh was likest for to be:
And out of the grounde of the flvmme the folk toke twelue stones
To make a memorial on the bank perpetuell for the nones.
Of oþ*er* twelue stones fro the bank broght vnto the depnesse
Thai made a hepe whare the Arche stode til eu*er*lasting wittenesse.
Thus passed Gods folk the flvmme drye fote, joyous and fayne,
And Jordan, als it didde arst, held furthe the cour*e*s agayne.
The Arche of the Testament whilk stode in Jordan this wise
P*re*figu*re*d Our*e* Lord Jh*es*u Crist in Jordan to baptize.
In the Arche was Aarones ȝerde whilk floured m*er*veillously,
And be the same flour*e* was Crist fortakned figu*ra*tively.
In the Arche was manna also þ*at* in desert reynyde,
And Crist his brede of lyf þ*at* of hevenis descendid.
In the Arche was also the boke of the Lawe cald Deut*er*onomy,
And the same Godde is made man þ*at* Moyses had it by;
And in the Arche war*e* also Gods commandementes tenne,
For the same Godde þ*at* thaym gave had ordeigned baptesme to men.
The Arche of the tree of sethym eu*er* inputrible was made:
So Cristis flesshe dede & dolven never*e* to corrupcioune slade.
The Arche w*ith*inne & w*ith*out was hiled w*ith* golde polyt,
And to Crist qvhikke and dede was the Godhed eu*er* vnyt.
The twelue stones testi*mo*niales the twelue apostils signified,
Whilk thorghout alle the werld Cristis baptesme testified.
Jh*es*u, be thi baptesme gif vs so to lufe the
Þ*at* in p*er*petuele joy with the our*e* dwelling be.

1456 ij figu*re* *mar.* 1457 Jordan seven] *o.s.o.*; sithe] *(*e *o.er.)* 1465 Math. iij *mar.* 1469 had] this *add. can. and subp.* 1470 Josue iij & iiij^to *mar.* 1482 memorial] i.e. a montjoie *over.* 1483 depnesse] i.e. of Jordan *over.* 1490 fortakned] *followed by er.* 1493 Deut*er*onomy] i.e. the secund lawe bot noght of the new lawe *over.* 1494 And] in *add. subp.* 1500 vnyt] i.e. joynt *over*

The temptation of Christ
Matt. iv 1-11

Daniel destroys Bel and kills the dragon
Dan. xiv 1-27

Now last hard we how John Our*e* Lord Crist baptizid;
Here now how þ*at* the feend Crist proudely thrise temptid.
Afftere his baptisme was Crist ledde be the spirit styring
Into desert–this was of the Haly Gast moving.
Ȝe shalle noght vnderstand þ*at* Crist was caried in the ayre,
Als the aungel to Babilyone made p*ro*ph*et*e Abakuc to cayre; [f.19^{v}]
Nor no more bare the devil Our*e* Lord Crist ou*er* the Temple;
And to wit it be thus, lat vs se be ensa*u*mple,
For this worde "lede" "to bere" has noght ay signifying
Bot sometyme "inducc*io*une" ore els "a conveying":
To lede his folk out of Egipt Godde vnto Moyses spakke,
Neu*er* the rather*e* hym byd\d/yng to bere thaym on his bakke!
No more the devil be the ayre bare Crist in his leding,
Bot in shapp of a man to fylowe hym Crist tempting;
And for temptaciounes Crist wald thole of the so*u*nes of Adam,
Fylowde he the feend and w*ith* hym the Temple & the mount clame.
Crist wald be temptid to shewe til vs instruccioune
Þ*at* no man may lyve here w*ith*out temptacioune.
Sith Crist, God Son hymself, wald be tempte of the feend,
We ne may noght go without, this is the soth at eend;
And who is qwitte of one temptacioune happily,
The deville will noght dwelle lange to make ane other*e* redy.
Crist was noght temptid onely of o vice bot of thre,
Takenyng of the feendes fanding the innoumbrable diu*er*sitee:
And war ne Godde ȝaf to menne the freendful angelic keping,
Thar*e* shuld neu*er* man eschape the feendes crowell temptyng,
For als the sonne beme of motes shewes full when it is clere,
So is this werld of feendes to dere men lyving here.
Þ*er*fore whame þ*at* we see fall in temptacio*u*ne,
We shuld of thaym in hert haf grete compassio*u*ne.
We ne shuld noght thayme condempne, nor sone discou*er* be skille,
Bot excuse at our*e* myght thare trespasse, and it hille;
And if the trespas in dede excusen we ne may,
The entencione ȝit til excuse some worde shuld we forth lay;
And if we noyther*e* the entent excuse may nor the dede,
Than shuld we inwith vs self thenk thus mekely w*ith* drede:
"O wriche, how oftsithe wers shuld it haf fallen of the,
If Godde had the noght kept of his m*er*veillouse bo*u*ntee."
And *nota* the feend thoght Crist to tempt be treble vice:
Gluterie and pride war*e* two, the thred was auarice.
When Crist had fourty dayes fastid and nyghtes fourty,
The devil had than grete hope Crist to be sore hungry,
And for the feend w*ith* swilk synne to tempt men has grete wille
Als he coniettes be signes thai be most able tille,
Wharefore, for he hoped Crist was forfastid and wast,
Alder-formast thoght he be gluttery hym to tast.
Now glutterie is þ*at* vice þ*at* the feend first temptis man inne,
For rather*e* a man delicat then abstynent fallis in synne. [f.20^{r}]
Wharefore Adam and Eue of glutt*er*ye first tempt he,
The forbedde fruyte til ete, be his fals sutiletee;

1511 {Ca^{m}} xiij^{m} *mar.* 1529 No*ta mar.* 1545 Math. iiij *mar.* 1553 Gen. iij *mar.*

David kills Golias
I Kings xvii 19-51

David kills the bear and lion
I Kings xvii 34-37

For ageyns othere vices whateuer he bestrives in veyne,
Bot he the inmoderaunce of glutterye lerne to refreyne;
¶a And Crist ouercome the devil in glutterye forthy,
Als shewed Daniel in the ydole Bel and the dragon, figuratifly.
In Babiloyne wirshipt was als god the mawmet Bel,
Þat hoegely ete and dranke, als diuerse stories tell.
Brede of twelue bordes ware offred ilk day til hym redy:
Of wyne sex amphores, and flesshe shepe kaces sothen fourty.
Bel prestes to this vitaille hadde vndre the erth entree,
And ete vppe alle be nyght with þer wyves and meignee,
Whas trace be asshes strewed Daniel apparceyving
Destruyd Belle and his prestes, be leve had of the kyng.
In a caverne also lay there a grete dragon
Wham alle that landes folk held god and thare Mahon;
And certein tymes the prest gaf mete the dragon tille,
The whilk þerof was gladde and in the cave dwelt ay stille.
Daniel a masse of pikke and grees mellid with hare
Kest in the dragouns mouthe be the kinges leve, & thare
Thilk feend swalowing the lompe, anone he alle to-brast,
And thus slewe Daniel bothe th\o/s gluttons at the last.
Now Daniel, whilk this two gulows deuouratours wyried,
Crist þat the tempting ouercome of glutterie prefigured;
¶b And that Crist temptid of pride the feend ouercomen was,
Prefigured Dauid sometyme when he slew Golias.
This Golias hymself auauntid be pride vnlike in force,
Passing alle Israel childere for his gretenesse of corse:
Bot Dauid orthrewe hym sone with his stone and his slyng,
And with his awen swerd hym slewe, Godde of bataile helpinge.
This Golias so proude was like to Lucifere,
Whilk in the regne of heven of Godde wold liknesse bere;
And Dauid the hird whilk this proude geaunt thus ouerthrew,
Victoure of the fanding of pride, takenid the meke Jhesev.
Now fandinges diuerse of pride ere wyde-whare generale,
Noght onely amange seculere, bot eke in folk claustrale;
For oftsithe whaym the feend with no vice may come bye,
Be lust of mans lavde he crokes to vaynglorie.
For vndere fulle \vile/ habit lurkes oft ane hert als proude
Als othere in kinge or qwene, for alle thaire gilden shroude. [f.20^v]
And Crist ouercome the feend in his auarous temptacioune:
¶c This figured Dauid sleyng a bere and a lyoune:
For thas \two/ beestis betakened auarice–now takes kepe–
In thaire gredy ravynne reving Dauid his shepe.
Dauid, rescoving his shepe, the bere and lyoune slewe,
And this thredde fanding ouercomen, Crist than the feend ouerthrewe.
Aungels come negh to Crist, venkust and fledde Sathan,
And ministrid to that victour Jhesu both Godde and man.
Thus whoso manly feghtis, the feendes ouercomyng,
Decerves aungels comfort and thaire swete ministring.
O gude Jhesu, gif vs temptacioune to ouercome,
Þat we in joye with the dwelle euermore alle and some.

1558 Of Daniel Bel & the dragon *mar.* 1559 j figure Daniel xiiij° *mar.*; In] *1552 marked to begin the figure.* 1562 amphores] i.e. pottes of certeine mesure *over.* 1574 bothe] i.e. Bel and the dragoun *over.* 1575 ij figure *mar.* 1579 j Reg. xvij° *mar.* 1588 claustrale] i.e. of Religiouns *over.* 1590 lavde] laude *or* lande *alt.* lavde. 1593 of auarice *mar.*; And] *158 marked to begin the figure.* 1594 iij figure *mar.* 1595 j Reg. xvij° *mar.* 1598 fanding] i.e. of auarice *mar.* 1599 Math. iiij^to *mar.* 1603 corr. *mar.* 1604 Amen *mar.*

The penitent Magdalen in Simeon's house
Luke vii 37-50

The prayer of Manasses in captivity
II Par. xxxiii 1-19; IV Kings xxi 1-17
(Charles I 620-24)

Tofore herd how the feend temptede Crist threfaldelye,
Here now how þ*at* gude Lord helyd the Mawdeleyne Marye.
When Crist, his threttith ȝere bygunne*n*, was baptized of John,
The devile, als ȝe hafe herd, tempted Our*e* Lord anone.
To preche and to baptize the folk Crist than beganne
Be ensaumple & be doctryne shewyng the hele of manne.
This swete sovne alder-first shewed Crist in his p*re*ching:
"Dose pen*au*nce, for the regne of heven is negh co*m*myng."
Be penaunce taght he of heven liberale apercioune;
Tofore his co*m*myng herd never*e* man swilk a swete sermo*u*ne.
Trewe is this Lordis s*er*moune ouer*e* alle accepcio*u*ne digne;
Be penaunce co*m*mes vntil heven synner*e* vile & maligne.
In synfulle Mawdeleyne apperes the sothfastnesse of my tale,
Fulle sometyme of seven feendis, þ*at* is, seven synnes mortale,
Whilk out of hir*e* voided penaunce and contricioune,
And of hir*e* synnes gate sho fulle m*er*cy and pardoune.
Ther*e*fore shuld no synner*e* dispair*e* of Gods gudenesse,
Till alle repentantz so prest thair*e* synne fulle to relese;
And moreou*er* he revokes repentantz till heven right,
Neu*er* done, tofore his come, til any repentant wight.
¶a Godde be Kyng Manasses this thing sometyme notide,
Be penaunce fro captivitee intil his kyngdom revokide.
This king hadde wrethid his Godde: infynytly synnyng,
Be slaghter*e* of haly p*ro*phetes, Godde at right noght settyng.
P*ro*phetes þ*at* hym blamed so many did he dede,
Þ*at* stretes of Jer*usa*l*e*m with thaire blode made he rede.
Ysay whilk for his synne rep*re*hending hym grevede,
He did with a sawe of tree be the mydward be cleved. [f.21r]
For his horrible synnes his enemys at the last
Hym ledde intil exile and put in prison fast.
Att the last, when he beganne to have contricioune
Of alle his wikked dedes, thus syittyng in p*ri*soune,
W*ith* many a bitter*e* tere to Godde thus prayed he:
"My synne passes in noumbr*e* the gravell, Lord, in the see.
I am vndigne, allas, of heven the celsitude
To se, for of my synne the innoumbrable multitude.
Irrited haue I thyne ire, O swete Godde of clemence,
And in thi sight deserved alle this for myne offence."
And of hym hadde Godde reuth, and shewed hym his m*er*cy,
Accepting his penaunce of his bo*u*ntee gudely,
For he delyvred hym fro prisoune and captivitee,
And til his regne of Jer*usa*l*e*m hym als restoyred hee.
This Manasses fig*ur*es a man þ*at* synnes evre,
And wher*e* þ*at* Godde be blithe or wrothe, þ*at* rekkes he neu*er*;
To Gods p*ro*phetes dose he hym blamyng, outrage & pyne,
When he of Gods p*re*chour*s* despises the haly doctrine;
And als lange he ligges in dedely synne thus yvele,
Sothly to-whiles is he in prisoune of the dyvel.
And if he cry m*er*cy and wille trewe pen*au*nce done
Than Godde will hym socour*e* send of his grace fulle sone.

1605 Ca^m xiiij^m *mar.* 1607 Math. iiij^to *mar.* 1612 Math. iij° & iiij^to *mar.* 1613 apercioune] i.e. openyng *over.* 1614 sermoune] (r *o.er.*). 1616 maligne] i.e. wikked *over.* 1617 Luc. vij° *mar.* 1625 j fig*ur*e *mar.*; notide] i.e. shewid *over.* 1627 P*ar*alipominon xxxiij° *mar.* 1629 It. iiij° Reg. xxj° *mar.* 1630 P*ar*alipominon i.e. stories of dayes a boke i*n* whilk war*e* thinges write*n* þ*at* war*e* left out in the iiij boke of Kinges *mar.* 1639 celsitude] i.e. the heght *over.* 1641 Irrited] i.e. wrethid or styed *over*; clemence] i.e. of pitee *over.*

The prodigal son returns
Luke xv 11-32

David, admonished for adultery, repents
II Kings xii 1-23

¶b This shewed Crist be ensaumpell writen in the Gospelle-boke,
Of thilk fole-wasto*ur* son of whaym mynde makes Seint Luke,
Whilk fro his fader*e* dep*art*id to ferr*e* land vnwysely,
Consumyng his substaunce thar*e* lyving luxo*ur*iously.
At the last gane he to nede, and tholid swilk hongres pyne
Þ*at* he felle til a toune and kept a bourgeys swyne.
This p*ro*degate son may wele a synner*e* signifie,
Whilk fro his Fader*e* of heven p*ar*tis synnyng dedelye;
And swilk a shrewed son is in a ferre regioune,
For ferre er*e* synners fro hele, this is the p*ro*phetes resoune;
And swilk one leccherously lyving consumes his substaunce,
Turnyng his wittes and strengthe fro v*er*tue vnto myschaunce.
Than til a burgeys he fallis, of Lucifer*e*, his swyne to feede,
Plesyng the devils of helle ilkone w*ith* his mysdede.
Aft*er* felle \to/ swilk nede this wastour*e*, lewed daffe,
Þ*at* he langvyst to fille his wombe w*ith* sory draffe.
Than, til hymself turnyng, he thoght to do pena*u*nce,
Als nede makes naked man rynne the qwhippe, to fikke and da*u*nce;
And in this may we wele note the Salueo*ur*s miseracioune, [f.21^v]
Þ*at* wille synners compelle thus to contricioune.
For so ferforthe our*e* hele lufs he, and sekes it ay,
Þ*at* he drawes vs til hym be alle wise þ*at* he may.
For some drawes he swetly be inspiracioune,
And some dose he come inne thorgh p*re*dicacioune,
Some be weltth and softnesse benignely chyricynge,
And some compellis he oftsithe be sharpe scovrynge.
This wise the wasto*ur* son so sore for þ*at* hym smertid
Was he be penaunce ledde, and til his fader*e* conu*er*tid,
And his fader*e*, hym oferre seyng, ranne hym agayne
Hym for till hals and kisse, this gude man, for ou*er* fayne.
Thus rynnes Godde to the contrite, w*ith* his grace p*re*venant,
Thaym to receyue, and alle thair*e* trespasse relessant.
¶c This was p*re*figu*re*d sometyme be Dauid kyng full right,
Auoutrer*e* and ho*m*icide in Vrye his trewe knyght,
Whilk saying "I haf synned", when hym reproved Nathan,
The pie Godde was redy to forgyf hym right than;
For when he saide "I have synned", Natan answard swyftly:
"Godde has t*ra*nsferred thi synne and forgyven it gudely."
O Godde of hiegh pitee, inmense and ineffable,
Þ*at* no wight will refuse vnto repentaunce able,
This wille Peter*e* wittenesse, Poul, Thomas and Mathe,
Dauid, Manasses, Achab, the thefe, Achor, Zache,
Ninivee, Samaritane, Raab, Ruth and the avoutresse,
Theophil, Gilbert, Thayde and the Egipciane in sothnesse,
The enuche & Symonde, Cornely, Kyng Ezechy,
Mawdelene, Longyve the knyght and Moyses sist*er* Marye;
Whar*e*fore no vylest synne shuld make synn*er* dispair*e*,
Þ*at* wittenesse so many diu*er*s thay may to m*er*cy repair*e*.
O gude Jh*es*u, gif vs contricioune so verray
To come to thi p*re*sence and to dwelle thar*e* for ay.

1655 j fig*ure* Luc. xv *under rub. mar.* 1661 pr*o*degate] i.e. fole-large *over.* 1664 resoune] longe a pec*ca*toribuz salus *o.i.e.l.* 1669 no*ta* *mar.* 1679 Chyricynge] *(1st y o.er.)* 1683 o] of *(f erased).* 1685 provenant] i.e. co*m*myng tofore our*e* meritz *mar.* 1687 iij figur*e* *mar.* 1688 ij Regu*m* xij^o *mar.* 1689 Nathan] i.e. the p*ro*phe*te* *mar.* 1698 Thayde] i.e. strompet *over*; Egipciane] i.e. Marie *over.*

The entry into Jerusalem: Christ weeps over the city
Luke xix 28-44

Jeremias laments over Jerusalem
Lam. i

In the last chapitle ȝ*e* herd of Mawdeleynes conu*er*sio*u*ne;
Now heres on Palme Sononday what felle of Crist, Godde Son.
In that day p*ri*ncipally felle thar*e* thre thinges \not/able
The whilk be thre figu*r*es of olde tyme war*e* monstrable:
Crist wept, Je*rusale*m seen, and with grete hono*ur* was there
Resceyved, and the marchants drave out of the Temple for fere.
First is to note þ*at* Crist wepped ou*er* the citee,
Compaciant on the meschief thereaft*er* on it to be.
¶a This weping of Our*e* Lord Crist was sometyme figu*ra*tiflye
Shewed in the lamentacio*u*nes of the p*ro*phet Jeremy, [f.22^r]
Whilk wept þ*at* Je*rusale*m be Babiloignes shuld be destruyd:
So, þ*at* the Romanes shuld wast thilk citee, it Crist esnuyed.
And thus shuld we, lyke Crist, wepe for compassioune
When we our*e* neghtburs se haf any afflicciou ne.
More is \to/ rewe than to gif gude to the nedy,
For the reuthe semes to be of thiselven a p*ar*tye.
Both on our*e* freendes shuld we rewe and our*e* mavfeso*urs*:
Ensaumple of Crist p*ra*ying for his crucifixours.
Certs inpossible is hym want Gods grace and mercy
His even-Cristen at disese þ*at* kan rewe hertfully.
¶b Secundely is it to note the poeples laude in metyng
To Crist, whilk was figu*r*ed sometyme in Dauid kyng
To whaym the poeple meting when he hadde slane Golye
Hono*ur*ed with sanges made of his grete victorye,
Tofore Saul, thair*e* king, thus Dauid p*re*ferannde:
"Saul a thozand has slayne and Dauid ten thouzande."
Dauid Our*e* Lord Jh*es*u betakened figu*ra*tifly
Whilk slewe Golye, þ*at* menes the devil, hoegest enemy.
This verray Dauid, þ*at* is Crist, on Palme Sononsdaye
Be concourse of grete folke was hono*ur*ed be diu*er*s waye.
Some cryed, "To Dauid so*un* osanna," hym loving,
Some, "Blissed be he þ*at* comes in name of hevenyshe king."
Some King of Israel saide sothly þ*at* was he,
Some Salueo*ur* of this werlde þ*at* he was comen to be.
W*ith* floures some, and some other*e* w*ith* palmes ranne hym aȝayne;
Some thair*e* clathes in the strete spredde vnder*e* his fete for fayne.
Jher*usale*m "syght of peece" is to say mystikly,
Be whilk is vnderstanden a trewe saule spirituelly,
To whilk Our*e* Saueo*ur* is prest for to come eu*er*more,
And we be contricioune shuld go mete hym þ*er*fore.
Lovinges til Our*e* Lord Godde w*ith* clamouse voice we synge,
When we in shrift reherce our*e* synnes w*ith* trewe weping.
Braunches of palmes in hande than bere we sp*irit*uelly
In satisfaccioune when we disciplyen our*e* body.
Our*e* clothinges in the waye in hono*ur* of Crist we sprede
For his luf, to the poer*e* when we doŋe almuse dede.
W*ith* floures til hono*ur* Crist renne we fulle plesantlye
W*ith* vertues when we vs shroude, and w*ith* werkes of m*er*cye,
And Crist þ*at* comes in name of Godde we b*ene*dice,
Thanking done vntil vs for his grete benefice. [f.22^v]

1705 Ca^m xv^m *mar.* 1707 notable] noght able (-ght *subp.* t *ins., then* noght *can.* not *ins.*). 1709 wept] j *over*; hono*ur*] ij *over.* 1710 drave] iiij *over.* 1713 j figure Lame*n*tacio*u*nes of Jeremy j | *id* est Lame*n*tacioun trenor*um* j *mar.* 1716 Luc. xix^o *mar.* 1718 of compassio*u*ne *mar.* 1719 to¹] the *subp.* 1725 ij figu*re* *mar.* 1727 Golye] the Geant *over.* 1728 j Reg. xvij^o *mar.* 1735 osanna] i.e. I p*ra*y the sauf *over.* 1753 benedice] i.e. we blisse *over.*

David is acclaimed
I Kings xvii 57, xviii 6-7

Heliodorus is beaten
II Machabees iii

That he is Lord and Kyng *gra*unt we and beres wittnesse,
If our*e* werkes be in drede of Godde w*ith* alle mekenesse.
The thredde note is how Crist of smalle corde made a skourge
The Temple of marchandise and of marchantz to pourge.
He ou*er*threwe the bordes & shedde the monee of the numelariens
For th\a/i war*e* fals vsuriers and collibistes of the Pharisens.
¶c The shourging of thir*e* marchantz tofore thus reherced
In one Helyodre, a prince, was sometyme p*re*figured.
King Seleuchus of Asye sent this Helyodore
To robbe Jherusalemes Temple, named riche of trezore;
And he, entring the Temple w*ith* men of armes boldely,
Ageyns hym Gods vengeaunce ordeigned fand he redy.
Ar*e* he was warr*e*, on hym an hors come fulle \h/orrible,
On whilk sitting þ*er* was ane armed man fulle terrible.
This hors his forther*e* fete on Helyodre he festte,
And gnaisting and neeing hym vnder*e* his fete he keste.
Two stronge ȝonge men come als, and in a sory arraye
Dight Helyodore w*ith* thaire whippes, til he als dede thar*e* laye.
This hors and the two men than vanyst out of the stede,
And Helyodore, thus whipped, left in the Temple als dede.
Bot be the sou*er*eynes bisshops prayer*e* he lyved agayne
And til his king retou*r*nyng, saide betwix fere and fayne:
"What enemy my lord the king list haue a right shrewed jobbe,
Send hym to Jher*usale*m, Gods Temple bot for to robbe."
This Helyodre was whipped for Goddes Temple spoilling;
The Jewes scourged for thair*e* fals vs*ure* dissimuling.
For the Pharisens in the Te*m*ple sett collibists and numularies
Þ*at* who þ*at* wantid offring myght borowe of thaym some penyes;
And for th\a/i shuld w*ith* vsure nothing take be thair*e* lawe,
Smale giftes named collibies wald thai vnto thaym drawe.
Thai callid figes, razines and nuttes and apples collibies,
Almandes, chykyns and gees, pygeons and swilk als thise;
And thus vnder*e* thair*e* cloke thi cou*er*ed vsure sleghly,
And Ezechyel wordes the p*ro*ph*et*e thai toke bot short hede by:
"Ȝ*e* shalle none vsure take, nor alle sup*er*haboundaunce."
O brether*e*, haldes fast in mynde thir*e* wordes for alle chaunce;
Bot more reuth is, fulle many named Cristen men todaye
Mantilles swilk man*er*e vsure als sleghly als eu*er* thai may,
Whilk will noght lone purely for Gods dileccioune,
Bot for gift or s*er*uice, fauo*ur* or p*ro*mocioune.
Swilk folk synnes hyghly, Gods word noght pondering: [f.23^{r}]
"Gif thow thi lane, thar*e*of non encrees thens hoping."
Godde wille out of his Temple of heven elles the ferre chace,
And thi rote out of the lande of eendeles life arace.
Gods Temple and his s*er*uice lat vs thar*e*fore honoure
If we wille noght þ*at* he eurelastingly vs scoure.
Dispise we als vsure with alle the spices, dreding
Out of Gods Temple be qwhippid elles, of joye eu*er*lasting.
Jh*es*u, this forsaide thinges make vs kepe so dewlye
To disserue evre to dwelle in thi Temple of glorie.

1757 iij fig*ur*e Luc. xix° Math*e*i xxj° M*a*rc. xj° *mar.* 1759 numelariens] i.e. of the chaungo*urs* *over.* 1760 collibistes] (*1st* i *alt.* u *in black ink*; i.e. takers of smale giftes *over.* 1763 Machabeor*um* iij° *mar.* 1775 bisshops] i.e. Onyas *over.* 1781 collibists] smal gifts mang*ers* *over*; numularies] comvne chaung*ers* or vsurers *over.* 1789 Ez\e/ach xviij° & xxij° *mar.* 1792 of vsure *mar.* 1795 Luc. vj° *mar.*; pondering] i.e. noght weighing *over.* 1804 *?* r. cor. *mar.*

The Last Supper
Matt. xxvi 26-30

The manna in the desert
Ex. xvi 11-36

In the last chapitle ȝe herd of Palme Sonondayes doyng;
Heres nowe of the sacrament of eukarist insite at Cristes souping.
Aproching the haly tyme that Crist wald thole passyoune,
He made in p*er*petuel mynde the sacrament of co*m*munioune,
And wald gif vs hymself in sustenaunce benignelye,
To shewe vs his swettest luf alder-most freendfullye.
¶a **This thing was shewed tofore in the manna figu*ra*tiflye,**
Whilk Godde gaf in desert to the Jewes miraclouslye.
Hoege was his luf to thaym shewed in thilk wildernesse,
Bot infinitly more til vs his gudelynesse,
For the Jewes manna was brede temporele and mat*er*iale,
The brede gyvin vntil vs substanciel and et*er*nale.
Manna, cald 'brede of heven', come never*e* ther*e* sothfastly
Bot be Godde made in the ayer*e* als to heven bot her*e*by.
Our*e* Lord Godde of our*e* saule is brede vif and verray
The whilk descendid fro heven to make vs lyve alwaye.
The Jewes had of this brede bot fig*ur*e and likenesse,
And we no fig*ur*e, bot brede itself in sothfastnesse.
Also in manna war*e* thinges diu*er*s shewed figuratiflye,
Whilk in the seint eukarist err*e* eendid now verrayly–
The manna a nat*ur*e hadde mirable to ma*n*nes witte,
Melting ageyns the sonne and at the fire herd wax itte:
So the seint eukarist in vayne hertis wites awaye,
And in luf-brennyng sawles waxis herd, to dwelle for aye.
The wikked resceyves this brede to thair*e* dampnac*io*une,
The gude alle eu*er*lasting lif and saluacio*u*ne.
W*ith* manna the dewe of heven descendid there in the place,
Signyng þ*at* eukarist to the digne brynges Gods grace.
The manna thus oft forsaide was white like to the snawe:
So who the eukarist shalle take be clene of hert thaym awe. [f.23^{v}]
The manna hadde alle delit in it of mete erthly,
Bot eukarist alle delites whilk may be spirituelly,
Whilk swettenesse is noght felt the sacrament in etyng,
Bot Crist and hevenly thinges thenking and contemplyng.
This manna til eu*er*y man sauourde aft*er* his wilnyng,
Bot the grete swettnesse of Crist is ou*er* alle erthely sauo*ur*yng.
And wha of his swetnesse had felt ones p*er*fitely,
Alle man*er*e delites of erthe hym shuld think absinthy.
Petre, of this sauoure feling in Mount Thabor,
Tabernacles desired to make, til haf dwelt þ*er* eu*er*more.
Moyses co*m*mandid the folke go forth ar*e* sonne-risyng,
And ilkone bot o gomor of manna home w*ith* thaym bring;
And gulyards þ*at* more wald gedir*e* than thilk mesure gomore,
At home the assigned mete fande thay and lessen nor more,
And thas þ*at* moght noght gedir*e* the mesure for fieblesse
Or for swilk cause, at home thai had the even fulnesse:
So he þ*at* many hoostês receyves in co*m*munyng,
More than who takes bot oone has noght of sp*irit*uel thing,
And who a p*ar*tie of the hooeste oonely receyves also,
Has no lesse than ane oyther*e* reyceyving one hole or moo.

1805 {C}a^{m} xvj^{m} *mar.* 1806 Of Cristes soper*e* *mar.* 1808 co*m*munioune] *otiose mark over.* 1811 j fig*ur*e *mar.* 1812 Exo. xvj^{o} *mar.* 1814 of manna *mar.* 1819 vif] i.e. viu*us* *over.* 1822 itself] i.e. sp*irit*uel brede *over.* 1824 eukarist] i.e. the sacrament of Gods body *over.* 1825 Of the nat*ur*e of manna *mar.* 1835 Sapiencie xvj^{o} *mar.* 1842 absinthy] i.e. ane h*er*be alderbitt*er*est *o.i.e.l.* 1843 Marc. ix^{o} *mar.* . 1844 Math. xvij^{o} *mar.* 1846 Of the gedring of manna *mar.*; gomor] i.e. a certeine mesure *over.* 1849 Exodi xvj *mar.* 1852 Of the Eukarist *mar.*

The Paschal lamb
Ex. xii 3-11

Melchisedec brings bread and wine to Abraham
Gen. xiv (Heb. iv 14-v 9; Ps. cix 4)

¶b Cristis sup*er*e was p*re*figur*id* als in the lambe paschale,
The Thorsday tofore our*e* Paske whilk the Jewes hade festivale,
Whilk lambe Godde badde thaym ete opon c*er*teine manere,
When he wald thaym delyur*e* fro the Egipciens daungere:
So Crist of eukarist the sacrament instuyd he
When he thoght vs delyure fro the feendis captifitee.
And when the Isralitens the pasche lambe war*e* etand,
Thay stode vpright succincte, ilkone a staffe in hand:
So co*m*muning shuld we be gyrde with double chaystitee,
And stafs hald in our*e* handes of right feith firmitee.
Als shulde thai stande vpright in gude lif be thaym taken,
Noght eft fallyng in synne tofore be thaym forsaken.
The lambe with wilde letuce ete thay in bitter*e* mete,
And Cristis swete body shuld we w*ith* bitter*e* contricioune ete.
The Jewes fete shulde be shodde in the lamb paschale etyng,
For the fete of the luf in Haly Writte beres takenyng,
Wharefore of thas þ*at* commvne shodde shuld the fete bene,
Lokyng þ*at* thayr*e* desires alle man*er*e waie be clene. [f.24r]
The lambe shuld noght be sothen, bot roostid ageins the fire,
For thas þ*at* commvne shuld brynne in charitee and noght in ire.
¶c In liknes of brede and wyne gaf Crist his blode and flesshe,
Melchisedek, both king and preest, p*re*figu*r*ing this exp*re*sse:
Foure kinges waystid the lande whar*e* dwelt than Abrah*a*m
And Loth–captifs and spoilles many hadde thai w*ith* ham.
Abrah*a*m and his fylowing discomfit thaym be Gods grace,
And men and spoilles agein he broght vnto thair*e* place.
Melchisedec ran to meete hym, offring him brede and wyne,
In whilk thing he figu*r*ed the forsaid sacrament divine.
This forsaide Melchisedec was preest of Godde and kynge,
And of Our*e* Lorde Jh*es*u Crist bare he p*re*figuryng,
For Crist is King of kynges whas regne cesses nevre,
And þ*er*to verraiest preest and first þ*at* sange messe evre.
Melchisedec, king and prest, both brede and wyne offride,
And Crist in lykenes of brede and wyne this sacrament ordenid.
Thus was Crist callid preest aft*er* the ordre of Melchisedec king,
For he this sacrament figured in this forsaide offring.
Melchisedec was a preest and also a prince realle,
In whilk was fair*e* figured the dignitee sac*er*dotalle,
For preestis princes real with resoune callid may be,
For alle princes imp*er*ial passe thai in dignitee,
For patriarches and p*ro*phetes in poustee thai excede,
And vertues aungelike taking, on some wise, hede:
For preestis the sacrament makes, þ*at* aungels may noght do,
Nor patriarkes nor p*ro*phetes moght noght attigne þ*er*to.
Be Marie Jh*es*u Gods So*u*n was on tyme incarnate,
And of[t] be the preest is brede to flesshe t*ra*nssubstanciate.
Preestis for the sacrament shuld we honou*r* forthy,
Whaym Crist thus has ordeigned to sacre his p*re*ciousse body.
O gude Jh*es*u, gif vs so wirshippe this sacrament
Þ*at* we come to thi joye without dep*ar*tement.

1859 How the lambe paschale was eten *mar.* 1862 succincte] i.e. girde *over.* 1863 co*m*muning] i.e. resceyving Gods body *over*; chaystitee] i.e. both of body and of sawle *over.* 1867 letuce] i.e. letuce of the felde *over*; mete] i.e. the felde letuce *over.* 1870 luf] i.e. or of the desire *over.* 1871 commvne] i.e. þ*at* resceyves thare creature *mar.* 1875 Gen. xiiij[o] *mar.* 1893 *marked and* Of the dignite of presthode *mar.* 1900 oft] of; t*ra*nssubstanciate] i.e. turned fro o kinde of s*u*bstaunce to anothere *o.i.e.l.* 1904 Amen *mar.*

Christ fells his enemies with a word
John xviii 3-6

Samson fells a thousand with an ass's jawbone
Judges xv 15-17

How Crist the sacrament of eukarist ordeynde haf 3*e* herd alle;
Now fylows howe he metyng his enemys made thay*m* do*un* falle.
When Judas had resceyvid of the sac*ra*ment co*m*mvnyo*un*e
He went of Cristis enemys to make congregacio*un*e.
O oute, thowe fals Judas, on thy wodenesse maligne,
And m*er*cy, O pie Jh*es*u, of thi soeffrance benigne!
Crist fedde this fals trayto*ur* with his awen flesshe and blode,
And he to betraise his Lord so crwelly thoght and 3ode: [f.24^v]
Crist, this knawen, wald noght discoure, nor hym the sacrament denye,
Gifing the fo*ur*me to preestis of howseling men herebye.
The preest, k[n]awing a man ask howsill in dedely synne,
Shall noght denye it, þ*at* he diffame noght hy*m* þ*er*inne.
Than Cristis enemys to gader*e* went out trayto*ur* Judas,
And Crist to the knawen stede whar*e* he to come to was.
Than come ther*e* armyd men w*ith* swords and stafs in handes
To seke Crist in the derke w*ith* lanternes and with fire-brandes;
And Crist alle vnarmed a3eins thayme gudely 3ode,
Asking thayme whayme thai soght with fulle benigne mode,
And thai agayns hym stode, ilkone as a geaunt,
"Jh*es*u of Nazareth" crying and answeraunt.
Than alder-myldest Jh*es*u gave thaym this swete answere
In a base voice fulle meke saying, "Loo, I am here."
With þ*at*, fledde alle abakke þ*at* ost þ*at* was so felle
Tofore hym als thai war*e* deede, and to the erthe doune thai felle.
Wharto gadrid 3*e* swilke rowte, O Jewes, welle of wodenesse,
Thus fowlly thrawen to the erthe at o worde of mekenesse?
What p*ro*fits 3our*e* many heveds diu*er*s sleghtis counseillande,
Or, at a worde borne doune, 3o*ur* oost of many thowzande;
Or what may 3ow availle 3o*ur* wapeins t*er*rible of were
Laten falle out of 3oure handes of o worde for the fere?
Se 3e noght Crist, hym one more than 3owe alle myghty
To slee 3ow alle, and hym nothing disese þ*er*by,
Bot myght co*m*maunde the erthe open vnder*e* 3o*ur* fete onone,
And swalough 3ow vp alle \q/whikke like Datan and Abiron,
Or bidde brimston and fire to rayne on 3owe in haste
Lyke Sodome and Gomorre p*er*petuelly to waste,
Or be watres of the heven with bekenyng of his hande
Drown 3ow, als alle this werlde he didde at ones neghande,
Or than, als Lothis wif, haf turned 3ow alle to stones,
Or diu*er*sly haf 3ow wo*u*nded als the Egipciens ones?
Or he moght haf 3owe striken to pouder*e* w*ith* aungels hande,
Als Kinges Senacheribs oost neyne score and fyve thovsande,
Or he moght sodeynely haf made 3owe dede to be
Als he slewe sometyme Here & Onam, so*un*s of Jude,
Or els w*ith* aungels swerde he moght haf slayne 3ow alle,
Als in Kyng Dauid tyme hoege peple he made to falle,
Or els moght he haf laten the dyvel w*ith* 3owe to fare
Als he soeffrid hym to slee the seven husbandes of Sare?
Or he might have sent fire which would consume you
Like Core with his hundred men;

1905 {C}a^m xvij^m *mar.* 1911 How Judas receyved the sacramentt of co*mmun*ivnne. In the decrees Dist. ij° ca° *mar.* 1915 knawing] kawing; howsille] i.e. comyng to Gods borde als at paske amonges oþ*er* *over.* 1919 M*a*rc. xxxiiij *mar.* 1921 no*ta* ben*e* *mar. hand²*. 1922 no*ta* Cristis mekenesse *mar.* 1938 Num*eri* xvj° *mar.* 1940 Gen. xix° *mar.* 1942 Gen. vij° *mar.* 1943 Gen. xix° *mar.* 1944 Exodi xiiij° *mar.* 1946 Ysay xxxvij° *mar.*; Senacheribs] of Assyrie *over.* 1948 Gen. xxxviij° *mar.* 1950 iij Reg. xxiiij° *mar.*; hoege] i.e. seventy thovzande *over.* 1952 Thoby vj° *mar.*; Sare] i.e. the wif of 3onge Tobye *o.i.e.l.* 1953 *The MS wants a folio at this point.*

Samgar kills six hundred with a ploughshare
Judges iii 31

David kills eight hundred in one attack
II Kings xxiii 8

Or he might have sent fiery serpents against you
As he did once against your predecessors who spoke against him;
Or he might have had you rent to pieces by means of loosed lions
As he once did dwellers in Samaria, for King Salmanasar;
Or he might have rent you with the teeth of ravening bears
As he once did the forty boys mocking Eliseus;
Or he might have beaten and crushed you just like Heliodorus,
Or destroyed with putrefaction and worms, as he did Antiochus;
Or he might have struck you with sudden leprosy
As once he struck Giezy and Mary, Moses' sister;
Or he might have smitten you with blindness and confusion
Just as in the time of Eliseus the army of Syria was struck;
Or he might have made the arms of all of you dry and hard
As once he did to King Jeroboam before the altar in Bethel;
Or he might have consumed your weapons with the teeth of worms
As he consumed all the bow-strings in the army of the Syrians.
All these and more he could have done had he wished to defend himself,
But he does not so wish—only to cast you down just a little:
He did this, however, to show that he suffered death voluntarily;
And if he wished to resist, you could not seize or hold him.
When, therefore, Christ showed his victory and power,
He gave them leave to come to themselves again and get up.
¶a *This victory of Christ over [his] enemies, already described,*
Was once prefigured in Samson and Samgar and David:
With a jaw-bone of an ass Samson laid a thousand men low,
¶b *And Samgar slew six hundred with a plough-share.*
If these laid low so many enemies with the aid of God,
No wonder that in the presence of Christ all his enemies fell headlong.
¶c *Scripture calls David a most tender woodworm,*
Who killed eight hundred men in one charge;
The woodworm, when touched, seems to be very soft,
But when it touches, it is said to bore through the hardest wood;
In the same way, no one was milder than David among his household,
But in judgement and against his enemies in battle none was harder.
In the same way, Christ was most gentle and patient in this world,
But in judgement upon his enemies he will be most severe;
For he passed his life quietly, and walked unarmed,
And he endured being vilely treated like a worm;
And this seems to be plaintively lamented in the Psalm
Where he says of himself: "I am a worm and not a man."
He is called, however, not so much "a worm" as "a woodworm",
Because the wicked slew him on the wood of the Cross.
He is also appropriately called "most tender",
Because his flesh is acknowledged to have been most tender and noble,
And to the extent that his flesh was nobler and more tender,
So was his passion heavier and harsher,
And so he cries in Lamentations to all passers-by along the road
That they consider whether they have ever seen comparable sorrow.
O good Jesus, grant us so to see your bitter sorrow
That with you we may deserve to live and rejoice in the Kingdom of Heaven.

The betrayal of Christ
Matt. xxvi 46-56

Joab kills his brother Amasa
II Kings xx 8-10

In the preceding chapter we heard how Christ overthrew his enemies;
Next let us hear how Judas deceitfully greeted him.
Judas the betrayer of Our Saviour gave the Jews the sign of a kiss,
Which was a sign wicked and malignant beyond measure
For a kiss has always been regarded as a sign of love;
Wicked Judas changed this into a sign of betrayal.
¶a *This evil greeting so deceitfully delivered to Christ*
Was once prefigured in Joab and in Amasa.
Joab, greeting Amasa with deceitful intent, called him "Brother",
And Judas, greeting Christ with evil intent, called him "Master".
With his right hand Joab held Amasa's chin as if to kiss him,
And drawing his sword with his left, killed him.
In the same way Judas seemed to hold Christ's chin with his right hand,
Blandly saying (as we can read for ourselves), "Hail, Rabbi!"
With his left [hand] he drew a sword indeed, and struck him through,
Because we read for ourselves that mild words hid a trap.
O Judas, what reason do you have for betraying your Saviour?
What harm had he done you, that you should want to harm him like that,
For he gave you the apostolic honour and dignity,
And why did you vent such malice on him?
He chose you as an apostle over seventy-two disciples,
And you showed yourself falsest to him above all.
He numbered you among his twelve most special friends,
And you abandoned him and joined his enemies.
He accepted you, you received his secrets with the other apostles,
And you made secret plans with his enemies against him.
He sent you out to preach, without satchel and wallet,
And wherever you went, by the providence of Christ you lacked nothing.
You, however (forgetful, alas, of such–and so much–providence)
Came to betray him for a small sum of money. [f.25r]
That swete Lord gaf the grace to hele both halt and blynde,
And thow thoght make hym fulle seke and in hard cordis bynde.
For to cast out dyvelleres he gaf the auctoritee,
And thow traysed hym in his enemys poustee to be.
Wher*e* þ*at* gude Lord made the his bourser*e* and pairato*ur*,
His adu*er*sarie chase thow to be, and falsest stinking trayto*ur*,
Also Crist ordeynd the spendo*ur* of thas penys
Whilk be waye of almus war*e* gyven til hym and hys:
Thase myght thow vse at wille; O vnkynde and crewell
Whi wald thow than thi Lord for thus smalle moneye sell?
Thow stale of Cristes purse oftsith whateu*er* thow wolde,
So þ*at* for xxx[ti] penys neded the noght hym haf solde.
With his sacred blode he vouched sauf the to fede,
And hym to the Jewes to selle hadde thow noyther*e* shame nor drede.
He gaf the to drink his blode, pyment of hevenly swettenesse,
And thow traysed hym agein to shedde his blode saklesse.
That Lord deigned mekely thi cursyd fete for to wasshe,
And thow traysed hym aȝein falsistly þ*at* eu*er* was.
His sucrish mowth to kysse he wald the noght denye,
Bot thin hertis malice was neu*er* the lesse forthy.

Saul returns David evil for good
I Kings xix 9-10

Cain kills his brother Abel
Gen. iv 1-11

When thow in tresoune hym hailesid, he calde the freende mekely,
Bot thin hert chaunged nothing to rewe thi Lord þ*er*by.
Fro Petre and other*e* apostles layned Crist thi tresoune,
Knaweyng if thai hadde witten thai wald have striken the doune.
In the Olde Lawe 'toth for toth' is wryten, and 'ee for ee',
Bot it was neu*er* levefulle to ȝelde harme for bountee.
Bot thowe, cruwelle Judas, of alle trayto*urs* banyour*e*,
To thi bountevous Lord canseile was thow traytour*e*,
So yvel for gude ȝalde thay the wikked Jewes thi felawes,
Jh*esu* thair*e* salueour*e* crucyfying forouten cause.
¶b Saul, O crewelle Jewes, p*re*figured ȝow and Judas,
To Dauid his gude son-in-lawe þ*at* eu*er* so cruwelle was.
Dauid hadde weddid his doght*er* and luved hym hertfully,
And Saul ymagyned his deth for he didde doughtyly:
So toke Crist ȝowe to sauf of ȝour*e* lygne manes nature,
And for to slee hym didd ȝ*e* assemble force and armure.
Golyas, Sauls foo, Dauid slewe worthily,
And Saul laide for his dethe als for hys mortale enemy:
So Godde, þ*at* Pharao w*ith* ȝour*e* other*e* enemys ou*er*threwe,
Ȝour*e* wodenesse als oft tofore cont*re*pledid in Jh*esu*.
Dauid the wikked gast chacid oft fro Saul King,
And Saul wold hym a slayne with a sharpp spere kasting. [f.25v]
Also ȝour*e* salueo*ur* oftsithe cald ȝow fro ydolatrie,
And til his sakles deth armed ȝ*e* ȝow cruwelly.
Dauid at the kinges bidding allewaye ȝede in and out,
And Saul kast eu*er* agayne to bring his deth about.
So Crist went alle ȝour*e* lande the waye of sothfastnes teching,
And ȝ*e* soght hym to slee for alle his gude doing.
Dauid Sauls sekenesse harping vsed til amese,
And Saul of Dauid alwaye desired deth and disese.
So Crist raisid ȝour*e* dede men, and ȝour*e* seke folk he helid,
And ȝe hym sakkelesse to slee made gaderyng & counseillid.
¶c Also ȝe Jewes er*e* like vnto the enevyous Kaym
Whilk slewe his innocent brother*e* þ*at* neu*er* trespast til hym.
Abels offringes ware swete til Our*e* Lord Godde allemyght,
Þ*er*fore his brother*e* slewe hym Kaym þ*at* cursid wight:
So for Crist was placable to Godde and poeple of man,
Ȝ*e* saide, "If we lefe hym, the werld trowes on hym than."
Now leef thogh alle the werld suyde hym what harme moght falle
Sith his techings er*e* soth and holsome both one and alle?
With glosing wordes tillid forth his brother*e* this fals Cayme,
And having forth at the large with wikked strokes he slewe hym:
So Judas w*ith* fair*e* wordes Our*e* Lord Crist he salutyd,
And til his enemys to slee vnder*e* that hym presentid.
Abel his wombes brother*e* be Kaym to deth done was,
And Crist, thair*e* fader*e* and brother*e*, slewe the Jewes and Judas.
He is wele fader*e* þ*at* made alle man*er* creature,
\And brother*e* for þ*at* he walde become man in nature./
O Jh*esu*, þ*at* vouchid sauf our*e* meke brother*e* to be,
Be vs benigne fader*e* in keping and in pitee.

2059 Exodi xxj° *mar.* 2065 j fig*ur*e j Regu*m* xviij° *mar.* 2076 hym] i.e. Dauid *over.* 2079 kinges] i.e. of Saul *over.* 2080 his] i.e. of Dauid *over.* 2087 Gen. iiij° Fig*ur*e iij *mar.* 2102 *ins. mar.* 2104 pitee] *followed by* wheneu*er or ?* in heuen*e later hand.*

Christ is mocked and beaten
Matt. xxvi 67

Hur is smothered by spittle
Ex. xxxii; Comestor 1189-90

How Crist was traysid and kissid haf ȝ*e* herd last toforne;
Now fylows how was bespittid his hidde swete face for scorne.
When Crist was taken and bonden off his enemys cruwelle,
Petre a s*er*uantis ere stroke of, thus it befelle,
And Crist shewed thaym onone his hoege benignitee,
Heling that ere at one touching, blissed mot he be.
First ledde ther*e* cruwelle Jewes Crist to the house of Anne,
The fader*e* of Ca\y/phas wif, hiest bisshoppe for the ȝere thanne.
Thanne Anne of his doctrine askid Our*e* Lord Jh*es*u;
Crist saide, "Thas þ*at* me herd of ther*e* thinges aske shuld thov,
For my teching was noght in hirnes nor pryuitee,
Bot in the Temple whar*e* was of folk most assemble."
And o s*er*uant stode negh whilk to Crist felly speke,
And a fulle sore buffet gaf Crist opon his cheke. [f.26^{r}]
This ilke s*er*uant is trowed the same Malkus to be,
Whas ere, als was fortolde, Crist helid of his bountee.
Bot Crist wald noght hym venge, Godde and man almyghty,
Bot soeffred for ensaumple alle this fulle manswetely.
O brether*e*, if any of vs hadde taken swilk a buffette,
And myght als wele als Crist amendes þ*er*in haf sette,
W*ith* Peter*e* trow I fulle sone the swerde we hadde out hent,
Or ellis w*ith* James and John fire fro the heven haf sent;
Bot noght so, brether*e*, bot luke of Crist the doctrine meke:
"Who smytis the on þ*at* one, bide hym thyne other*e* cheke."
Aft*er* this, Crist be the Jewes fro Annes house ledde was,
And broght with many reproef til the house of Ca\y/phas.
Ther*e* war*e* thaire aldermen assemblid for counseilling,
To fynd occasioune and cause Crist to the deth to bring,
Bot alle þ*at* thas fals Jewes aȝeinst Crist feigne moght
War*e* discordant and leghe in trewth and noght ne doght.
At the last coniured he Crist be Godde this Ca\y/phas
To gr*a*unt thar*e* in ap*er*t wher*e* þ*at* he Gods Son was,
And hym to be Gods So*un* for he knewe in þ*at* stede,
The Jewes ilkone demed hym worthy to goo to dede.
And than his eghen thai hidde, in thair*e* japes & scornyng,
And alle defowlid his face with thair*e* dispitefulle spittyng,
And gyvyng til hym buffets thai badde hym p*ro*phecye
Who þ*at* was þ*at* hym stroke, and he tholid benignely.
Whateu*er* thai couth devise of shame and vilaynye,
Alle didde thir*e* cruwelle Jewes to Crist w*ith*out m*er*cye.
Alle thir*e* derisounes, the reproves and this sorowe
Durid in Cayphas hows alle nyght vnto the morowe.
O Jh*es*u Our*e* Salueo*ur*, blissed be ȝour*e* hoege mekenesse,
And thowe corsedest [Judeus], out o thi last wodenesse:
His eghen þ*at* alle thinges sees hilde thai and hym smyting
That alle thinge wote, hoped thay the doers hym vnknawing.
The \de/lytable face, to behalde whilk aungels has in desire,
Dred thai noght to bespitte in thair*e* vile wodeest ire.
The handes bonde thai fulle sore of the Lord of alle thinge
That heven and erth and helle made in the begynnyng.

2105 Ca^{m} xix^{m} *mar.* 2117 lo the wikked ȝeldes yvelle for gude *mar.* 2122 Math. xxvj^{o} *mar.* 2123 Luc. ix^{o} *mar.* 2125 Luc. vj^{o} *mar.* 2126 Math. v^{to} *mar.* 2146 No*ta* b*e*ne *rub. mar.* 2147 Of Cristis paciens *mar.* 2148 Judeus] Judas.

Noe's nakedness is mocked, then covered
Gen. ix 22-25

Samson, humiliated, destroys the house of the Philistines
Judges xvi 20-30

The Jewes who þ*at* hym stroke badde hym telle, scornfully,
Be whaym the haly p*ro*phetes to\ke/ vertue of p*ro*phecye.
His eghen hilyng, wend thai haf blyndid hym in þ*er* ire
Þ*at* lightned thair*e* auncestres sometyme with a piler*e* of fir*e*, [f.26^{v}]
His visage dredde thay nothing til hide w*ith* spitting fowlly
Thair*e* faders þ*at* with a clowde cou*er*yd fulle m*er*vellusly.
¶a The Jewes, with \þair/ spittings whilk Cristes face defovlide,
Be the ydolatiers of the golden veel ware wele p*re*figurede,
For when the Jewes in desert walde make thaym gods fals,
Aaron than thaym withstode and Hur, Maries husband, als.
Whar*e*fore thay ranne on Hur*e* for his trewe chalenginges,
And in dedeigne and dispite choked hym w*ith* thair*e* spittinges.
Thay hatid Hur*e* for þ*at* he reproved thair*e* ydolatrye,
And the Pharisens hatid Crist, blamyng thair*e* trecherye.
¶b The wikked Jewes whilk on Crist made thus scorne and laghyng
Somtyme be Kam, the son of Noe, hadde figuring.
This Kam, whilk his fader*e* shuld haf wyrshipt be res*ou*ne,
We rede made wykkedly of hym derisioune.
Right so the Jewes, þ*at* Crist shuld haf hadde in reu*er*ence,
Didde hym than fulle vile scorne, dishono*ur* and eke offence;
And thogh Noe of his son was scornyd vnhonestely
Ȝit was Crist vnlike with bejaped more vileynsly,
For in his tab*er*nacle was Noe scornyd, no man seeyng,
Bot Crist in the bisshopis hows, fulle many one on lukyng.
When he slepe and wist noght, than scornyd was Noe:
Bot Crist alle brode waking, blissid mote his pacience be.
Noe bot of o son was scorned alle onely,
Bot Crist of poeple of Jewes w*ith* alle þ*er* counseille holly.
Noe hadde two gude so*u*ns of his scorne condolent,
Bot Crist hadde none w*ith* hym of his woo compacient.
The Jewes þ*at* scorned Crist als hadde p*re*figuryng
In the Philistiens sometyme to Sampson in thayr*e* doyng:
When the Philistiens hadd taken Sampson thai made hym blynde
And scorned hym disefully in alle thair*e* myght and mynde.
¶c Nowe Sampson, it is to witt, for his grettest stroungnesse
P*re*figured Our*e* Lord Crist be some man*er*e liknesse:
Sampson soeffred hymself be bonden o tyme freely,
And Crist tholed of the Jewes bondes and scorne wilfully.
And when Sampson thoght tyme on o daye aft*er*warde,
He vengid hym on his enemys horribly and fulle harde.
Right so of Cristes enemys shalle falle o tyme to come
When he in his maiestee shalle sitte on the day of dome.
What vengeaunce Crist wille than vse ageins his enemys
May no scripture ne tonge for to declare suffise; [f.27^{r}]
For than wald thai wele levre alle man*er*e payne sustene
Than the irefulle juges face so vengeable for to sene,
Saying, "O cursyd wyghts, gos to et*er*nale fyre!"
To freendes: "Comes my blissid, joye endeles be ȝour*e* hyre."
O gude Jh*es*u, gif vs so the for to plese here
Þ*at* we the blissid callyng discerue of the to here.

2157 Exodi xiiij^{o} *mar.* 2162 Exodi xxxij^{o} *mar.* 2164 Maries] i.e. the sister*e* of Moyses *over.* 2168 trecherye] i.e. desceyving of the folk *o.i.e.l.* 2169 Gen. ix^{o} *mar.*; The] *2164 marked to begin the figure.* 2170 ij figur*e* Kam *mar.* 2185 iij figur*e* Judic. xvj *mar.* 2192 Judic. xv^{to} *mar.*

The flagellation of Christ
John xix 1-2; Comestor 1628

Achior is bound to a tree by Holfernes' servants
Judith vi 7-13, v 5-29

Howe Crist was scorned and hidde tolde the chapitle tofore;
Nowe fylowes howe he was bonden vntil a piler*e* fulle sore.
\When þai all nyght Crist scorned hadde, & þus done to*ur*ment,/
Thai ledde hym arely fro thens to Pilates dome p*re*sident.
Qvodh Pilate, "Whareof pleygne ʒ*e* on this man ʒ*e* me say."
"A mysdoer*e* and a gyloure of the folke is he," saide thai,
"And he ne has noght oonely begilt the poeple of Judee
Bot \the/ Galilens also, folk of his awne countree."
Pilat sent hym, heryng he was a Galilene,
To Herode, for vntil hym to deme Crist shuld p*er*tene.
This Herode and Pilate freendes war*e* made þ*at* day,
Þ*at* ware, the Boke says, tofore enemys: this is no naye.
Herode hadde noght sene Crist, bot herde of hym grete thinge,
Thar*e*fore was he gretely joyovs of Cristis co*m*mynge.
Some straunge thing hoped he and hoege for til admyre,
And signes or miracles to see of hym was his desire;
And when Herode hadde Crist askid of many a thing,
And Crist stode alle sylent and gaf none answeryng,
Than Herode hoped of hym a fole, his witte forlorne,
And in his japes cledde hym in white clothing for scorne,
And so sent hym ageine to the dome of Pilats lawes,
Saying in hym of deth þ*at* he hadde founden no cause.
Herode cledde Crist in whitte, what þ*at* ment vnknawing,
Þ*at* the Haly Gast Crist*es* innocence wroght þ*at* s*u*bostending–
The whilk Gast shewed be Cayphas of Cristis deth expe[d]ience,
Þ*at* shewed be Herode also the same Lordis innocence.
Pilat askid the Jewes if thai wald any cause nemne
Whar*e*thorgh thai moght be ryght Crist to the deth condempne,
And onone right, thre causes ageinst Crist thai forth laide
Tofore Pilate the juge, and thus forthmast thai saide:
"He this saide, 'I may destruye Gods Temple of hande-makeyng,
And vnhande-made an other*e* the thredde day make fyloweyng,'
And says þ*at* no tribute shuld be gyven to Cesar*e*,
And þ*at* hymselven is King of Jewes, this is his lar*e*."
The first two causes Pilat helde bot a truferye
Asking Crist of the thredde diu*er*se tymes bysylye, [f.27^{v}]
For Cesar*e* the revme of Jewes helde vnder*e* Romayns empir*e*,
And thai no king bot hym to co*m*mande at his desire.
Pilat apon the Jewes be Cesar*e* hadde powere,
Forthy of non oþ*er* king of the Jewes walde he here,
And fro Crist sayde, "Of this werlde is noght my kyngdome,"
Pilat of þ*at* accusing sette bot shorte in his dome.
Than thinking how he best myght the Jewes wodenesse ou*er*take,
It seemed hym most spedefulle Crist to be scourged make,
That thay*re* hertis, so fullfillid, shuld of Cristis deth cesse,
And of insufficiant dome he to be holden blamelesse.
Whar*e*fore Pilats knyghtis cruwelly scourgid Jhesvm,
Corrupt w*ith* the Pharisens giftes, ferre ou*er* the wont custom.
¶a Be Prince Achior hadde this scourging p*re*figuraunce,
Bounden ones til a tree be duc Olofern s*er*ua*u*nt[s]:

2205 {C}a^{m} xx^{m} *mar.* 2207 *in another script at foot of page (where* þai *is followed by* had *can. and subp.)* 2208 p*re*sident] i.e. the juge *over.* 2224 Of Cristis white cloothing *mar.* 2227 Johannis xj^{o} *mar.* 2228 s*u*bostending] i.e. shewing vnder*e* p*ri*vely *over.* 2233 No*ta* ben*e* *rub. mar.* 2234 The causes of Cristes deth *mar.* 2235 j *mar.* 2237 ij *mar.* 2238 iij *mar.* 2241 Cesar*e*] i.e. the Emp*erour* of Rome *mar.* 2253 j fig*ur*e *mar.* 2254 Judith vj^{o} *mar.*

Lamech is beaten by his wives
Gen. iv 18-19; Comestor 1079

Job is beaten by his wife and a demon
Job ii

This Achior bonden was w*ith* Olofernes cursed wightis,
And Crist bonden to the piler*e* be Pilates cruwelle knightis.
Achior, for he saide soth, als is forsaide was bonden,
And Crist for the soth p*re*ching fulle doelfully was beswngen.
Achior was bonden for he in speche Oloferne noght plesid,
And Crist for he blamyng for vices the Jewes displesid.
Achior was bonden for he Gods glorie magnified,
And Crist scourgid for he the Fader*e* name notyfied.
¶b And *nota þat* folkes two whilk scourged Crist cruwellye
Be two wyves of Lamech war*e* forshewed figuratifly.
The two wyves of Lamech war*e* callid Sella and Ada,
The two forsaide folkes payentee and Synagoga.
Sella and Ada thair*e* husband w*ith* wordes & betings turmentid,
The payentee and the Sinagoge *þer* salve*our* Crist flagellid.
Crist was w*ith* scourges and wandes bette of the payentee,
The Sinagoge scourged hym w*ith* tonges and wordes of cruwelltee.
¶c This double scourging of Crist, als Haly Writte lcryng we hope,
Was sometyme p*re*fig*ur*ed in the flagellacioune of Job,
For Job was twofalde scourged in c*er*teine tyme of his lyve:
Be beting sore of the feend and bitter*e* wordes of his wyve.
Off Satanas scourge tholed Job in his flesh outwardes smert,
And of the scourge of his wife hadde he t*ur*ment in hert.
The feend thoght noght ynogh to scourge his flesh outwards,
Bot he his wyfe entyced to troble his hert inwards:
So suffized noght the Jewes *þat* Crist with scourgis was bette, [f.28^{r}]
Bot if with bitterest wordes eu*er*ilkone on hym sette.
No hele was left in Job fro the toppe vnto the too,
And Cristes swete tenderest flesshe was alle bewondid ryght so.
And how mykel Cristes flesshe was noble \and/ tendre the more,
Was his doelfulle passioune more bitter*e*, sharper*e* and sore.
O man, think how for the Crist soeffred passioune,
And betake neu*er* thi sawle eftsones to p*er*dicioune!
If eu*er* thov see or herd any other*e* swilk payne, take hede,
And for it passis alle mesure bere hym swilk luf and drede.
Behald the brennyng to the of Cristis dileccioune,
That for thyn hele wald thole swylk payne and passioune.
Thar*e*with loke what s*er*uice, kyndenesse, labour*e* or payne
For thus innoumbrable gudenesse thow hast ȝolden hym agayne.
For alle the gude *þat* thow doos lyving thy dayes here
Til o drope of his blude may to no point answere.
Thar*e*fore to thole disese luke *þat* thov murm*ure* noght,
Bot Cristes hard passioune kepe alleway in thi thoght.
Of Cristes blude w*ith* thi woo if thow a syrope make,
Whateu*er* thow thole shalle seme to the swete for his sake.
A littel soeffre in this lif of flagellacioune
Til eschewe elleswhare eterne dampnacioune.
To chaystise the in this werlde rede I Godde *þat* thow p*ra*ye,
Þat dying thow entre heven w*ith*outen any payne for ay.
O gude Jh*es*u, strike vs here w*ith* swilk bitternesse
Þat dying w*ith*out purgatorie we come til hevenly swettenesse.

2257 Achior *mar.* 2262 Crist] i.e. was bonden *over.* 2263 ij fig*ure* *mar.* 2265 Gen. iiij^{to} *mar.* 2265,2266 *reversed, marked for reversal:* b, a. 2271 iij^{o} fig*ure* *mar.* 2273 Job ij^{o} *mar.* 2304 Amen *under rub. mar.*

Christ is crowned with thorns
Matt. xxvii 27-30

Apemen makes a fool of Darius
I Esdras (Apocrypha) iv 29 (Charles I 31); Josephus VI 339

Ho\w/ Crist was scourgid tolde ȝowe this last chapitle toforne;
Heres nowe in this howe he was crovned w*ith* sharpe thorne.
Pilat bede knyghtes sco*ur*ge Jh*es*u til c*er*tein soume,
The Jewes hired tham to bete Crist ou*er* vse and custovme.
The lawe was at the most to passe noght strokes fourty,
Bot the Jewes hired the knyghts the noumbre to multiply;
And to do hym this wronge onely suffized thaym noght,
Bot to crovne hym w*ith* thorne a newe payne vpp thay thoght.
And þ*at* thay hym als king moght hono*ur* scornfullye
Thai toke hym septre and po*ur*pre als signes of regalye.
Misdoars for to scourge in some cas was custome,
Bot to crovne thaym w*ith* thorne of lawe was noght the dome.
O Jewes of cruwelle witte in newe malice to fynde,
What paynes haf ȝ*e* to thole newe and of diu*er*se kynde: [f.28v]
For who studies to fynde in wikkednesse newe engyne
Be right newe and vnherd haf thai for to bere pyne,
For the mesure þ*at* thai mesured shalle thaym be mesured aȝeine,
And wele more eked þ*er*to, for eendeles bes þ*er* peyne.
Thay cledde noght Crist when thay hadde sco*ur*ged hym cruwelly,
Bot in a cokcyn or p*ur*pre mantelle thay wapped hym scournfully.
Pourpre to regalye p*er*tenyng was toforne,
Wharefore thay mantlid hym in swylk colour*e* for scorne.
The secunde, a crovne of golde p*er*tenes to regalye,
For whilk a croune of thorne the Jewes gaf Crist forthy.
The tredde, a septo*ur* of golde p*er*tenes vntil a king:
The Jewes in Cristis right hande a rede sette for whilk thing.
And for kinges hono*ur* askis for to be wyrshipt knelyng
Forthy Cristi*s* enemys knelid, "king" hym in scorne callyng.
Men war*e* wonte honorable giftes to p*re*sent vnto kinges,
For whilk thay p*re*sentid Crist w*ith* buffets and foule spittinges,
And with a rede stroke thay the crovned heved of Jhesev,
P*re*ssing the thornes til eke Cristes peyne newe and newe.
O cruwelle Jewes, whar*e*fore didde ȝ*e* thus to ȝour*e* king
Alle his benefetes to ȝowe done nothing remembring?
The rokkes of Arnon sharpe vnder*e* ȝour*e* fete planed hee
And his heved w*ith* sharpe thornes crovned ȝour*e* cruwelletee.
He gaf ȝow hose and shoce in desert for pitee,
And in his handes and heved wroght ȝ*e* hoge cruwelltee.
He kept ȝour*e* clothes vntorn in desert ȝeres fourty,
And ȝ*e* tirved hym stone naked aȝeinward scornfully.
King Pharao and Egipt for ȝour*e* sake turmentid he,
And hym causelesse fulle sore aȝeinward scourgid ȝe.
The kinges of Egipt corovne for ȝowe be Moises he braste,
And ȝ*e* a corovne of thorne thrange on his heved fulle faste.
Alle erthly kinges drede ȝow of hys gudenesse didde he,
And hym als kyng in scorne vnkyndely haylsid ȝe.
He hono*ured* ȝow ferre above alle oþ*er* nacioune*s*,
And ȝ*e* hym dishono*ured* w*ith* many illusioune*s*.
He ou*er*come ȝour*e* enemys one a thovzande chacinge,
And tofore two of ȝoures ten thowzande enemys fleynge,

2305 {C}a^{m} xxj^{m} *mar.* 2317 no*ta* *mar.* 2321 Luc. vj^{o} *mar.* 2325 of p*ur*pre *mar.* 2327 Crist was coroned *mar.* 2339 Num*er*i xx^{o} *mar.* 2353 Ysay xxx^{o} *mar.*; one] i.e. of ȝow *over.*

Semei curses David and stones him
II Kings xvi 5-10

Amon humiliates David's messenger
II Kings x 2-5

And a3einst Crist alle one many thowzandes gadred 3ee,
And of two poeples a3einst o man made 3e assemblee;
And how a thovzande or two chaced thovzandes ten
Bot for Godde wald shewe so his glorie ou*er* erthly men? [f.29r]
How shuld Crist have bene taken of alle 3our*e* assemble,
If he hadde noght betaken*e* hymself in 3our*e* poustee?
¶a This illusioune of Crist when he was coroned,
Appinen a kinges concubyne sometyme p*re*figured.
The kinges corovne of his heved take wolde thilk Appinen,
And on hir*e* awen heved it sette, p*re*sent hym and mo men.
So the Sinagoge Cristes corovne, þ*at* was his hono*ur* dewe,
Raft hym, and on his heved a corovne of thornes threwe.
Als wold she with hir*e* hande buffette the king sharpely,
And he nothing be wroth bot soeffre alle þ*at* gladdely,
So Crist King be the Jewes was buffett and colaphized harde,
And he, meke als a lambe, no malece shewed a3einwarde.
Thilk concubine to the king stode in so hoege grace
That whateu*er* þ*at* she didde he tholed and held solace.
3it is p*r*ouable þ*at* Crist lufed the Sinagoge wele more,
Sith he innoumbrable despits and paynes wolde suffre therfore.
¶b And swilk pacience of Crist p*re*figured Dauid the king,
Of the wikked Semey so vile reproves suffring.
Semey stones and stokkes and myre on Dauid kest;
The Sinagoge spittinges and thornes & buffets on Crist fest.
Semey callid Dauid "man of Belial" and "manquhell*ere*":
The Synagoge Crist "a wyche, gylour*e* and mysdoer*e*".
Abysey, ne hadde Dauid lettid, wold haf slayne Semey:
So hadde aungels Cristes foos, bot he thaym lettid mekely.
Crist descendid to dye for mans synne w*ith*out faille,
And with his blode vs to Godde his Fader*e* to reconsaille.
He ne come noght to this werld any man for to qwelle,
Bot peece and concorde betwixe Godde and man for to melle.
Bot he ne was noght of the Jewes aft*er* his gude wille tretidde,
Whayme w*ith* swilk vilaignyes thay hym dishono*ur*idde.
¶c This in King Dauid messages was ones p*re*figured,
Whaym King Amon of Amonytz so foully dishonested.
Dauid sent thaym for peece causeynge of thinges toforne,
And Amon thair*e* clothes to mydhips and halfe thair*e* ber*e*dis made shorne.
So Godde his oone dere Son til erth for peece he sent,
Whame the Sinagoge naknedde, his berde bespitted and shent.
Betwix Godde, aungels and man Crist come pees to restore,
Lasting ire inplacable fyve thovzande 3ere tofore.
Blode in refo*ur*myng pees to shede war*e* wont payens,
And watre in case semblable 3ettid the Judeenes. [f.29v]
Bot Crist both watre and blode shedde for vs freendfully,
For we the faster*e* shuld kepe his pees made thus swetely.
The payens shedde blode of bestis, the Jewes watre of the flode,
Bot Crist of his awen side he shedde both wat*er* and blode.
O gude Jh*es*u, gif vs to luf and kepe thy peece,
Þ*at* make vs dwelle w*ith* the in joye þ*at* neu*er* shalle ceesse.

2355 Marc. xxiiij° *mar.* 2361 j[a] figure *mar.* 2375 fug*ur*e ij *mar.* 2377 ij° Regu*m* xvj° *mar.* 2378 Semey *mar.* 2389 figure iij *mar.* 2391 ij° Reg. x° *mar.* 2392 Amen *mar.* 2396 The lange enpr*is*onement of mankynde *mar.* 2398 Judeenes] i.e. the folk of the Jewes *o.i.e.l.* 2404 amen *mar.*

Christ bears his Cross
John xix 17

Isaac carries the wood for his own sacrifice
Gen. xxii 6

ȝe haf herd last tofore of Cristis corovnement;
Now how he bare the Crosse to here is consequent.
When Crist was crovned and japed and w*ith* sco*urg*es thus beseen,
Pilat didde bringe hym forth the poeple his sorowe to seen,
Þ*at* thay, fullfillid of his thus doellfulle affliccioune,
Shuld thenk ynogh and cesse of his interfeccioune;
Bot thay gnaistid on hym ilkone als hondes wode,
Shovting, "Crucifye hym, do hym fast on the rode!"
And Pilat, desiring hym delyvre out of thair*e* handes,
Saide how þ*at* he wald thaym a p*r*isoner*e* q*whi*t out of bandes,
And thay askid to be gyven thaym a thefe heght Baraban,
And Jh*es*u the auct*our* of lif on Crosse to be done than.
O cruwelle Jewes, why wold ȝe noght þ*at* Lord assoigne
Þ*at* qwhit ȝow fro thraldome of Egipt and Babiloigne?
Pilat, þ*at* moght noght lette thair*e* noyse þ*at* on hym grewe,
His handes wesshe to seme clene of Cristis blode Jheseve.
This wroght the Haly Gast in Pilat to this intent:
That Crist shuld for vs dye rightwys and innocent.
Pylates wyf said sho hadde of Jh*es*u fulle mykelle seen
Be dreme, wharefore gude was hym to delyvred been.
Þ*at* wroght the dyvel, wilnyng to lette Crists passioune,
To lette so of mankinde the p*re*ciouse saluacioune.
And þ*at* Pilat instode for Cristis delyvring
Is hoped als of the wyves haf bene the dyvles stiring,
For be thaym thoght the feend lette our*e* redempcioune
Als he be Adam and Eue made our*e* dampnacioune:
For when the haly faders he se in the lymbe joye make,
He dredde Crist be his deth wold thaym fro thennys take,
And Cristes deth be Pilat thoght he to lette þ*er*fore,
And hym be his ledde the wyf to spede pricked he the more.
For his prikke specially is a wo*m*man gloosyng,
Be whaym he dose husbandes do many a nyce thing.
Now than the knyghtes of Pilat of p*ur*pre vncledde Jh*es*u, [f.30^{r}]
And with his spoilled awen clothes thai hym cledde eft alle newe,
Than on his shuldres thai laide a Crosse þ*at* was fulle hevy:
Þ*at* didde thai for the nones til his more contumely.
And for the crosses þ*at* tyme taknys of malyson were,
Noyther*e* wald Pilats knyghtes nor Jewes the Crosse bere;
Bot the Crosse þ*at* than was halden waried and ignomynyouse
Be Cristis passioune is made fulle blissed and gloriouse;
And þ*at* than was ordeynde for theves to*ur*mentynges
Is nowe peyntid hyegh in frontes of emp*erours*, p*ri*nces and kynges;
And be that whar*e*on misdoers, the feendes felowes, war*e* hanged,
Er*e* now the dyvels punyst, chasidde, ou*er*comen and strangled.
¶a And of this forsaide Crosse Cristes baiulacioune
In Ysaac, Abraham son, hadde p*re*figuracioune:
For Ysaac on his awen shuldr*es* wodde mekely bare & broght
Be whilk his fader*e* to Godde þ*at* tyme hym sacrifie thoght.
So Crist bare on hys shuldres a Crosse fulle hevy and lange,
On whilk the Jewes cruwelle thoght hym sakles to hange.

2405 Ca^{m} xxij^{m} *mar.* 2406 consequent] i.e. filowing *over.* 2410 interfeccioune] i.e. slaghter *over.* 2419 Math. xxvij^{o} *mar.* 2423 Of Cristis vnrightwis dampnacioune *mar.* 2426 letting of Cristes passioun be the feend *mar.* 2427 instode] i.e. bisid hym *over.* 2429 thaym] i.e. be Pilat & his wife *over.* 2440 contumely] i.e. dispising *over.* 2443 ignomynyouse] i.e. wrechid *over.* 2449 Fig*ure* j *mar.* 2451 Gen. xij^{o} *mar.*

The heir of the vineyard is killed
Matt. xxi 33

The scouts carry grapes on a stave
Num. xiii 23-28

Ysaac be ane aungels help was delyvred fro dede,
And a wethir*e* cleving in breres sacrified in his stede;
Bot noyther*e* tholed wethir*e* for Crist nor other*e* creat*our*
For swete Jh*es*u hymself wald for vs alle endure.
Ysaac, hering his fader*e* þ*at* wald hym sacrifie,
Sayde he was obedient, at his wille alle redie.
So Gods Son til his Fader*e* was meke and obedient,
In alle thinges to fullfille his wille and co*m*mandement.
For the Fader*e* and Son and Haly Gast helde a mistik counsaille,
One of thaym for to sende man-sawle to recounsaille.
The Fader*e* saide, "Whaym shalle I sende, and whilk of vs shalle go?"
The Son saide, "I am redye, I send meselven ther*e*to."
"Go to the werlde," q*uo*d the Fader*e*, "and lyve w*ith* men mekely,
And whateu*er* thai do the, soeffre it benignely."
Thus Crist Gods Son olyve sent, conu*er*sed in Judee,
And thai hym revilid and slewe w*ith* \h/orriblest cruwelltee.
¶b Als in a pytouse p*ar*able Crist shewed the Jewes this thing,
Fi*gur*ing it be a vigne a tyme i*n* his p*re*ching.
A man plantid a vigne and closid it, tellis vs the Boke,
A toure, a p*re*ss*eur* in it, and to tilmen it toke.
He sent his seruantz in tyme the frvytes hym for to fette,
And thai slewe some of thay*m* & of thaym some thay bette.
Mo s*er*uants than [t]he first the lord sent, this hering,
To whilk the tilmen didde like slaght*er* and betting. [f.30v]
At the last his \oon/ lufed so*u*n this lord sent to thaym oute,
Lyst thay hym for to slee wald oyther*e* haf shame or doute:
Whaym the tilmen taking, kest hym w*ith*out the vigne,
And cruwellerly than the s*er*uants slewgh hym w*ith* shame and pyne.
Of the Jewes or the Jewrye this vigne bare takenyng,
The clos*eur*, Je*rusal*em walles or than the aungels keping;
And takenyd is be the toure the Temple of Salomon,
Be the p*re*ss*eur* the autier*e* of holocaust and oblacioune.
The s*er*uantes sent þ*at* war*e* Gods haly p*ro*ph*e*tes and trewe,
The whilk w*ith* paynes diu*er*se the Jewes cruwelly slewe.
Thai suwe Ysay and stoned Jeremye w*ith*out faille;
Thai b*ra*yned Ezechiel, and Amos p*er*cede w*ith* a naille.
At the last Our*e* Lord Godde sent hys oone Son Crist Jhesew,
Whaym cruwellerly than thas other*e* the fals wode Jewes slewe.
On his shuldres thai laide the Crosse hym for to pyne,
And slewe hym w*ith*out the citee (so kastin out of the vigne).
And thas þ*at* Crist to his deth ledde out war*e* folkes two:
The Jewes in hert ledde hym, the hethyn in dede for so.
¶c Be two exploratours hadde this fig*ur*acioune,
Þ*at* broght the grape-clustr*e* to desert fro the lande of p*ro*missioune.
Crist was þ*at* grape-clustr*e* whilk two folkes ledde cruwellye
Out of Jherusalem to the mount of Calvarye.
The Jewes tasted be the grape of the hight lande the gudenesse,
And be Crist teching may we consider*e* of hevenly swettenesse.
O Jh*es*u, of thy lyf et*er*ne gif vs swilk gastly smelle
Þ*at* we in it with thee withouten eend eu*er* mowe dwelle.

2467 The sending of Gods son *mar.* 2471 Fig*ure* ij *mar.* 2473 Luc. xx° *mar.* 2479 oon] awne *subp.* 2492 othere] (y *after* o *erased*). 2494 citee] i.e. of Je*rusal*em *over.* 2495 Fig*ure* iij *mar.* 2497 Num*er*i xiij° *mar.* 2499 folkes] i.e. Jewes and payens *over.* 2501 hight] i.e. of p*ro*missioune *over.* 2504 amen *mar.*

Christ prays for his torturers
Luke xxiii 34

Tubalcain's forge: the discovery of music
Gen. iv 21-22

Tofore herde ȝ*e* how Crist bere on his bakke the Croice;
Nowe heres for his crucifi*ours* howe he p*ra*yd w*ith* mylde voice.
The nyght and daye forjaped was he made so wery
Hymself þ*at* hevy Crosse þ*at* he ne moght bere forthy.
Than constreyned thai a man hight Symond, mavgre his,
To help Crist for to bere the Crosse, the sothe is this–
At Mount Caluarie comen when thai see Crist fayntid
Thai gaf hym ayselle w*ith* galle mengid and wyne mirrid.
This drink the Jewes to Crist mengid maliciously
Als in the boke of the Psalmes was writen be p*ro*ph*ec*ie.
The knyghtes apon the grounde laide than the Crosse flatling,
The body of Our*e* Lord Crist alle naked on it spreding,
And w*ith* ane hoege nayle to the Crosse thai drofe one of his handis,
That other*e* hande to ane hole drawyng w*ith* cruwelle bandis, [f.31^{r}]
The whilk festnyng, his fete thai ruggid out semblably,
And thirlid thaym to the Crosse w*ith* one naille cruwelly.
Of this Our*e* Lord be the psalme pleyned openly for the nones:
“Thai delvid myne handes and my fete and thai noumbred al my bones.”
And Our*e* Lord Crist, tholing this bitt*er*est cruwelletee,
Vntil his enemys þ*at* tyme shewed his swete charitee,
Vnto his Fader*e* of heven thilk tyme for thaym praying,
Til vs our*e* enemys to luf in þ*at* exsaumple leving:
For when we our*e* enemys luf, and also for thaim we p*ra*ye,
The sonnes er*e* we of Crist and brether*e*, this is no nay,
For our*e* enemys to luf is Cristes teching fulle even,
Þ*at* we be þ*at* way mowe become Gods sonnes of heven.
Noght grete price is of freendes nor of gude-doers luving,
Bot to luf p*er*secut*ours* and enemys is grettest thing.
The knyghtes doune on the erthe nailled Crist on the Croice
And aft*er* raysid hym alle qwhikke w*ith* ane hoege shout & voice;
¶a And Cristis prayer*e* when he was this wise crucified
In Jubal, Tubalkain brother*e*, tofore was figured.
Thyr*e* two war*e* sonnes of Lamech, sometymes als clerks wote
Fynders, als bokes telle, of musik and yren note;
For when Tubalkain with hamers stroke on the yren stifly,
Juball than of thair*e* soune fande arte of melodie,
And to soune of thas hamers and fabricacioune
Cristis prayer*e* es likned and his crucifi*ours* malliacioune.
For when the crucifi*ours* ham*er*ed Crist to the Crosse wodely,
Þ*at* Lord for thaim to his Fader*e* sange fulle swete melodye:
“Fad*er*e, forgif to thaym, for thai ne wote what thai do,
Thai ne knawe me noght for thi Son þ*at* thay do thus vnto;”
For if the Jewes and the hethen hadde knawen Crist sothfastly
Thay ne hadde neu*er* crucified, doutles, the King of glorie.
And þ*at* blissed melodie was of so fyne dulcoure
That thre thovzand of men conu*er*tid thilk same houre;
And wele war*e* the Jewes figured be the fynder*e* of ham*er*yng,
For thay first of alle fande thilk man*er*e of crucifying,
For no lawe demed þ*at* man shuld to the crosse be naillid,
Bot to be bounden vppe w*ith* ropes to tyme þ*at* his lif fayllid;

2505 Ca^{m} xxiij^{m} *mar.* 2506 Luc. xxiij^{o} *mar.* 2514 Psalmes] i.e. the salter*e* *over.* 2516 Of C*ri*st was nakned *mar.* 2523 Luc. xxiij^{o} *mar.* 2526 Ensaumple to p*ra*y for o*ur* enemys *mar.* 2533 This some men holde *mar.* 2535 fig*ur*e j^{a} *mar.* 2539 The fynding of musik & yren note *mar.* 2542 malliacioune] i.e. the nailling on the Crosse with hamers *o.i.e.l.*

The martyrdom of Isaias
Comestor 1414 (Charles II 159-62)

Moab sacrifices his son
IV Kings iii 26-27; Comestor 1389

And wele was Crist prefigured be the finding of melodye
For he swilk melodie to the Fadere fande for to singe swetely;
And for his crucifiours prayed Crist noght alle onely,
Bot for the hele of alle the werlde allso fulle devoutely. [f.31^v]
And thogh many one hadde prayed for mans synne oft tofore,
For bede ne sacrifie warre thay neuer herde the more;
Bot Crist prayed with swete teres & strenghfulle voice crying,
And for his reuerence was herde his prayere he purchacing.
¶b This crucifixioune also prefigured seint Ysay,
Gods prophete wham the Jewes didde to deth \h/orribly.
For the Jewes with a sawe of tree thorgh the middis hym kitte,
Wharefore the deth of Crist right wele prefigured itte.
So the Jewes with a tree-sawe Crist be the middes departid
When thai his body and sawle with the Crosse desseueryd.
And allethogh thay Cristes sawle made fro the flesshe to parte,
To thwynne the Goddehede fro ovthere couth thas wriches none arte,
For fro the dede flesshe twynned was noght the deite,
Nor fro the sawle lyving the flesshe, this is trewe certeintee;
For allethogh Crist diedde, Godde wald hym noght forsake,
Thogh he sent hym to dye, mans reaunceoune for to make.
O Fadere of hevyn, what luf lest the shewe to mankynde,
Thyn one Son sending til erth for man thus to be pynde!
O boundless love of the divine charity,
That would give a beloved son for the sons of wickedness!
Who herde euer of swilk luf or se swilk jentellenesse,
Or sufficed to prayse it right in o poynt of fulnesse?
¶c This lufe of the Fadere Godde thus hoege and thus passing
Hadde sometyme prefigurance in Moab, a jentil king.
He was in his citee assieged with ane hoege oost and grete;
The citizeins wel negh perist, failling both drink and mete.
This king luved his citizeins so hoegely mykell at alle
That his awen son for thaym he sacrified on the walle.
Be the forsaide citee the werld is wele prefigured,
And be the citezeins mankinde is noght wronge designed.
Be the oost of the feendes of helle was sieged this citee
More than fyve thovzande ȝere are Crist come in pitee,
And the citezeins so way\k/e warre waxen thorghout and out
That thay this siege to breke moght neuer alle bring about.
At the last, Fadere of mercyes, Godde of consolacioune,
Piely beheld the disese of oure obsidioune,
Þat for hoege luf his Soun lete he for oure luf dye,
The siege of the feendes to breke, til vs delyvre frelye.
Moab for his frendes and foos his son to dye suffred,
Bot Godde for his enemys his Son vnto deth delyvred.
What may we ȝelde this Lord for swilk luf worthilye
Bot body & hert and sawle gif in his luf holely?
To the Fadere þat vs lufed first gif we dileccioune,
Whilk thus pyely beheld oure mortiel obsidioune. [f.32^r]
O gude Jhesu, lat vs here of thi luf cesse nevre,
Þat in thi joy to come with the we mowe dwelle evre.

2556 melodie] i.e. to pray for his enemys *over.* 2560 bede] i.e. prayere *over.* 2563 figura ij^a *mar.* 2565 Maister of the Stories *mar.* 2570 For the Godhede ones vnite to manhede neuer fro body ne sawle of Crist departid *mar.*; ovthere] i.e. fro the flesshe or the sawle *over.* 2574 mans] *stroke over.* 2580 sufficed] *(s alt.* c). 2582 Figure iij^a *mar.* 2583 Maister of the Stories *mar.* 2591 The lange thraldome of mankinde to the feende *mar.* 2596 The] *(e o.er.).* 2602 obsidioune] obsidioioune; i.e. our assiege be the feend *o.i.e.l.*; *catchword:* O gude Jhesus Christ *(-s* Christ *later hand) foot of page.* 2604 Amen *mar.*

Christ alive on the Cross
John xix 25-27

Nabugodonosor dreams of a tree
Dan. iv

Now last herd we howe Crist p*ra*yed in the Crosse mekely;
Her*e* fylows howe he his deth forshewed figuratifly.
¶a King Nabugodonosor a grete tree se dremyng,
The whilk tree of the same king bare verray signifying,
Bot Crist to come to this werld betaknyd it mistikly,
Þ*at* King of kinges and Lord of lords shuld be sothly,
Whas pouwer*e* ou*er* alle the hevens is raised fulle hiegh on hieght,
And spredes ou*er* alle this werld above alle erthly myght.
Alle beestis vndir*e* it and briddes in it hadde thair*e* dwelling,
And of the fruytes of þ*at* tree ete and hadde norisshing,
The whilk fulle conueniently gaf verray signifiaunce
Þ*at* eu*er*y cre\a/ture be the grace of Crist takes sustenaunce.
Bot loo, ane aungell co*m*myng co*m*manded kit doune þ*at* tree,
Whilk thing fig*ur*ed þ*at* Crist done on the Crosse shuld be.
He saide þ*at* alle the braunches of the tree shuld be kitted,
Takenyng þ*at* Cristis disciples shuld alle be fro hym seu*er*yd,
And saide more þ*at* alle the leves shuld be \s/haken of the tree,
Takenyng þ*at* alle Cristis lare of the Jewes shuld dispisid be.
He co*m*manded the fruytes of the tree to be scatred, the king thoght,
Takenyng þ*at* alle Cristis werkes the Jewes shuld sett at noght.
He saide the beestis and briddis shuld alle flee fro the tree,
For noyther*e* aungels nor men to Crist ni help shuld bee.
The aungel saide more þ*at* thogh the tree warr*e* kitted doune,
Neu*er* the laccer*e* the rote shuld leve in erth for to burgeoune–
Als so say allethogh Crist hadde of deth to thole the payne,
3it shuld noght deth hym hold, þ*at* he ne shuld rise agayne.
He saide Nabugodonosor, ment l*itte*raly be the tree,
With bandes of yren and stele bonden also shuld be,
Whilk shewed þ*at* Crist shuld be bonden til a pyler*e*,
W*ith* iren nailles on the Crosse striken w*ith* his enemys fer*e*.
He saide w*ith* dewe of heven shuld alle be wette the kinge,
For l*itte*raly fro amanges men he shuld haf his dwelling,
With hevens dewe wette (þ*at* is with his blude) ou*er*ronnen) bene,
And w*ith* the same blude we alle fro thraldome \q/whitte fulle clene.
He saide þ*at* als a beeste was to be fedde this kinge,
For Crist of ayselle and galle to drink shuld haf offring.
He addid þ*at* the kinges hert shuld haf fro ma*n*nhed chaunging,
And þ*er*fore taken hym an hert beestisshe als of feling: [f.32v]
For the Jewes Crist als a man shuld noght treet nor addmitte,
Bot als a wilde beest or a worme hym crucify and bespitte,
Or els þ*at* the Jewes to Crist shuld noght like men thaym bere,
Bot grynne on hym like beestes the cruwelest þ*at* evre were.
He saide more þ*at* seven tymes shuld be cha*u*ngid on the king,
So hadde seven houres canonyke Crists passioune p*ro*loignyng.
He saide in sentence of aungels this was c*er*tein decree,
And worde and asking of seints þ*at* this for f*er*me shuld be,
For to aungels and men Crist deth shuld be necessarie thing
Til aungels restoraunce and of seints delyvring.
He saide this king shuld be til alle the werld manifesto*ur*,
Ou*er* alle kyngdoms of men of the hiegh dominato*ur*,

2605 {Ca}^{m} xxiiij^{m} *mar.* 2607 Figure j *mar.* 2608 Daniel iiij^{to} Nabugodonosor *mar.* 2636 *A two-line space follows (see n. 2636).* 2638 qwhitte *(*q *in different ink).* 2639 He] i.e. the aungel *over.* 2649 decree] i.e. jugement *over.* 2650 ferme] fernae *(*a *subp. and minim ins.) with* fermae *ins. mar. all in hand^{2}.*

Codrus sacrifices himself for his people
Valerius V 6; *Gesta* xli

Killing the elephant, Eleazar is crushed by it
I Machabees vi 42-46

For the p*re*ching of Crist and his shuld gif the werld knawyng
Of verray Godde of alle werldis and maker*e* of alle thing.
He saide þ*at* the kyngdome of men Godde myght gif wher*e* hym list,
On whilk he p*ur*veide to sette of alle men the mekest.
This takened Crist for to be mekest of alle mankynde,
Thar*e*fore King of alle kinges, in bokes alle this we fynde.
And thus was Crist fig*ur*ed til vs be the forsaide tree:
Of his Faders ordinaunce for man crucified to bee;
And thogh his passioune war*e* ordeynde of his Fader*e* th*us* tofore
He soeffred it of free wille and invite nevre the more.
¶b And Codrus, a king of Gr*e*ce, shewed this p*re*figuratifly,
His citezeins for to delyvre the deth accepting freely.
The grete citee of Attenes stode in obsessioune
So streit þ*at* no mans witte moght fynde subvenc*io*une.
Than counseild this King Codrus w*ith* his godde Appolyn,
If any way wer*e* þ*at* he moght rescow his citee fro pyne,
And alle war*e* he payen and Godde sothfast ne knewe,
Ȝit soeffred Godde hym resceyve be Appolyn ane answer*e* trewe,
That c*er*teine thar*e* was no way to delyvre his citee
Bot if he wald soeffre hymselven of his enemys slayne be;
And the king his sugits luvid so p*er*excellently
Þ*at* he went out of the toune for to dy willfully.
His enemys, knawyng the cas, wold hym disese nothing,
The citee more than his deth vnlike w*ith* desiring;
And King Codrus, knawing of his enemys the entent,
He left his realle arraie and s*er*uants clethes on hym hent,
And co*m*myng forth eft*er*, his foos didde hym to deth als tite
For thay knewe noght the king in his s*er*vylle habite.
The enemys, knawing his deth, of thair*e* p*ur*pos dispaired,
And the siege vpbreking, to thair*e* contrees repaired. [f.33^{r}]
Thus Crist luved vs þ*at* he for vs wold dye freely
Fro the feendis assieging to qvite vs alle vtterrly,
Cledde in mans flesshe als in clothes of s*er*uyle degree,
Noght mowing dye in realle clothis of his deitee,
For if thay hym the King of glorie hadde asspied
Thay nwold neu*er* hym haf slayne nor so vily treted.
And Crist brakke noght the one siege of our*e* captivitee
Bot our*e* deth also with his for eu*er*more destruyd he.
¶c And this be Eleazar*e* was ones the Machabe p*re*figurid
Disposing hymself to deth to slee olyphaunt armyd.
The hethen oost come on the Jewes þ*at* hadde of thaym hoege fere,
And Eleazar*e* bare thorgh thair*e* olyphaunt w*ith* a spere:
The beest, wounded to the deth, felle on this Eleazare
And his sleer*e* slogh he w*ith* his grete sweght right thare.
The stronge assaylled the stronge and both felle in the stede,
And thus Eleazar*e* and the beest in this wise ware both dede.
Thus stronge Crist the stronge deth assailled chyvalerously,
And w*ith* his deth slewe oures, blissid be he eendelesly.
O Jh*es*u, þ*at* be thi deth liked to bye vs thus sore,
Make vs aft*er* this lyf w*ith* the dwelle eu*er*more.

2664 invite] i.e. maugre his *over.* 2665 Fig*ur*e ij^{a} *mar.* 2667 Historia Scolast. *mar.*; obsessioune] i.e. assiege *over.* 2668 subvenc*io*une] i.e. help of delyveraunce *o.i.e.l.* 2693 Fig*ur*e iij^{a} *mar.* 2695 Machabe*orum* vj *mar.* 2704 Amen *mar.*

The dead Christ's side is opened
John xix 34, Luke xxiii 47

Michol mocks David
II Kings vi 14-20

Herd last tofore how Crist was slayne thus cruwelly;
Here nowe howe thay hym dede scorned maliciouusly.
It suffized noght the Jewes of C*ris*t the cruwelle sleeyng,
Bot thay aft*er* þ*at* he ware dede reioyst in hym scorneyng.
¶a **Micol, Saulis dogh*ter*, this touchid p*re*figuratifly**
When scho hi*re* husbond Dauid the king scornyd proudly.
Tofore the Testaments Arche daunced Dauid harpyng,
Whaym Micol gaf scornes brode, out at a wyndow lokyng,
And ȝit suffized hi*re* noght to scorne hym doing "A" ferre,
Bot at thai*re* meting eftsones chaufed sho hy*re* husbond wele werre,
Saying he couthe a king contrefete wele hardily
Naknyng hym tofore folk als harlots vses lewedly.
Right so the Jewes scorned C*ris*t wers than ane harlot than,
Hym condempnyng w*ith* theves and lowsing thefe Baraban.
Dauid in his harping p*re*figured Crist in this thinges,
For Crist was stendid on the Crosse als in ane harpe e*re* the stringes.
O Lord, how this faire harpe gaf a swete melody
When Crist with doelfulle teres for vs cried myghtylye,
When p*ara*dise he to the thefe hight, so late repentyng,
And his mode*re* vnto John and hym to hi*re* betakeing! [f.33v]
And for ou*re* hele, "Me thristis" saying þ*at* Lord thus,
And aft*er*, "Consummatum est" þ*at* he shuld thole for vs,
And when he cryed, "Hely, Hely, lamazabatany",
And when he ȝalde vnto the Fade*re* his gast so pynefully.
The Synagoge in this harping to scorne hym gamen thoght,
And aft*er* hys gast ȝolden, to scorne thay cessid noght.
¶b **This thinge in A\b/solon, the fairest of men, rede we**
P*re*figured when þ*at* he honge be his here in a tree,
Whaym seighen, a man rynnyng to Joab this discou*er*yd,
And he co*m*myng, thre speres thorghout his hert festnyd.
Bot sqwyers of Joab thoght noght enogh thereby
Bot w*ith* thay*re* swerdes also bare hym thorgh cruwelly.
Absolon takned Crist, of mans sonnes fairest floure,
Striken w*ith* thre speres on the Crosse, þ*at* war*re* thre paynes soure.
The first of his awen paynes the innombrable hydousnesse,
Secunde of his dere mode*re* the intolerable bitt*er*nesse,
The thredde doele for the dampnable whilk C*ris*t lete on hym bite,
Knawing his bitt*er* passioune shuld noght to thaym p*ro*fite.
And thogh Crist was fest w*ith* thus many sorowes on the Croyce,
The Jewes ȝit pyned hym ovre w*ith* thai*re* wikked tonges voice.
Thus alle wilfulle synners assailles Crist on like wise
Resydyuaunt, and also in thaym Crist eftsones crucifise.
¶c **King [Ev]ilm*er*edach of swilk sometyme gaf forlyknesse**
When he in his dede fade*re* ex*er*cised his wodenesse,
Whas body dolven out of the grave in thre hondreth gobets he kitte
And to thre hondreth voltoure*s* for to devou*re* dalte itte.
So in thai*re* fade*re* Crist for thay*m* dede, haves fals C*ris*ten thaym wodely
When thay wilfully synnyng hym eftsones crucifye;
And thay synne more wrething Crist in his deitee
Then thay þ*at* crucified hym lyving here in humanitee.

2705 {Ca^m} xxv^m *mar.* 2655 Figure j *mar.* 2660 ij Regum vj^to *mar.* 2713 doing] *(*g *o.er.)* 2726 Consummatum] i.e. it is eended *over.* 2731 Fig*ure* ij *mar.* 2732 ij Reg. xviij° *mar.* 2736 thay*re*] *(*r *alt.* y*).* 2739 Of the treble sorow of C*ris*t on the Crosse *mar.* 2746 Resydyuaunt] i.e. turnyng aȝeine to olde synnes *over.* 2747 Fig*ure* iij° *mar.*; Evilm*er*edach] wilm*er*edach. 2748 Joseph*us* or the Maist*er* of Stories *mar.* 2752 Austyn *mar.* 2754 How fals C*ris*ten w*ith* diu*er*s synnes pynes Crist in diu*er*ses man*er*es *mar.*

Absolom is killed
II Kings xviii 9-15

Evilmerodach chops up his father
Comestor 1453

Crist ones crucified enforces he for to assaille
Þ*at* hym auantis of synne or vses it stably sanz faille;
Of a crosse to Cristis crucifying is þ*at* man carpenter*e*
Whilk of yvelle to be done is help or counseiller*e*:
That man lays, als men says, the Crosse on Cristis bakke
Whilk to the ordeigna*u*nce of Godde of his synne gyves the lakke.
Holy Writte beres hym on hande in Cr*is*tis face for to spitte
Whilk ony gude takes of Godde and hym thankis noght of itte;
And Crist on his bakhalve vngudely also betes hee
Who þ*at* his neghbo*u*rgh enforce diffame in priuytee; [f.34r]
And Crist in his face betes he w*ith* buffetes cruwelly
Who byses hym to confounde his neghburgh p*re*sently;
And Cristis heved w*ith* sharp thornes corones he dispitously
Who þ*at* Haly Kirk assailles w*ith* ravynes and iniurye;
And thas bisis thaym to hide Gods eghen, alle thing behalding,
Who sellys or gifes or chaunges for erthly gude haly thing;
And thas er*e* saide to depart to thaym Cristis clothinges
Who p*re*sumes for to destruye, robbe or ref neghburgh thinges,
And Jh*es*u Crist w*ith* Judas kissis he tresovnously
Who þ*at* his neghburgh gloses for to begile hym sleghly,
And with Judas trecherously hailsen thay Crist, I say,
His hest þ*at* til his neghburgh haves noght entent to pay,
And Jh*es*u Crist w*ith* the Jewes laghes he to scorne than
When he gives almovse or prayes for lavde or p*ri*se of man,
And Cristis purses beres he w*ith* Judas, þ*at* thevis lymme,
Who stelis or oght w*ith*drawes of thinges betaken hym.
Cristis fete w*ith* iren nailles is he p*ro*ved thorgh to smyte
Who tavernes and comon places wille more than kirkes visyte.
It p*ro*ves he beres the Crosse with thilk Cyrene Symon
Þ*at* noght of free wille dose gude bot be coacci*o*une,
And nailles for Crist is he p*ro*ved to forge wricchedly
Whilk amanges neghburghs discordes to sawe makes hy*m* bisy.
He is demyd Crist to scorne like to the lefthande thefe
Who þ*at* in confessioune to lyegh or feygne er*e* lefe;
Thaymself w*ith* Judas to hange p*ro*ve thas vnderstandinglye
Þ*at* mercy likes none til aske ne for thair*e* synne satisfye.
Thas thaym the handes of Crist p*ro*ves w*ith* ropes for to bynde
Þ*at* trowes noght Our*e* Lord Godde may thaym thair*e* necessaries fynde.
Gods handes vnto the Crosse wo*u*nde thay fulle grevously
Whilk of Gods gude gyven thayme deles noght almouse freely;
And thas er*e* p*ro*ved to selle Crist w*ith* Judas the trayt*our*
For money þ*at* spendes thair*e* gude to purchace thaym vayne hono*ur*;
And thas gyves myrred wyne to Jh*es*u Crist for to drinke
Þ*at* heresies vnder*e* colour*e* of trewth to teche folk swynke;
And thay menge aysell w*ith* gall to gif Crist on the Rode
Þ*at* sacrifice makes to Godde of mysbegetyn gude;
And w*ith* Judas tra\i/t*our* betrayses he Crist kissing
That resceves þ*at* Lordis body in dedely synne being.
O Jh*es*u, gif vs righ\t/ so to resceve thy body
That we neu*er* be fro the departid eu*er*lastingly.

2766 p*re*sently] i.e. openly *over*. 2780 hym] i.e. to kepe *over*. 2801 trait*our*] *(*i *in different ink)*. 2803 right] *(*-ght *in different ink o.er.)*; cor. *mar.*

The deposition: Mary's sorrow
Matt. xxvii 55-59

Jacob mourns his son Joseph
Gen. xxxvii 33-35

The last chapitle tofore tolde Cristis passioune;
Heres now his moderes doel and rewthfulle compassioune. [f.34v]
For the more hardnesse þ*at* Crist tholid in his passioune, c*er*tayne
The more doel til his moder*e* encresced be payne and payne.
Than Symeons p*ro*phecie in hir*e* fullfilled wasse:
"Thorghout thy sawle, Marye, the swerde of sorowe shalle passe."
¶a The sorowe þ*at* Our*e* Lady consuffred for hire dere son
In Jacob for Joseph deth hadde p*re*figuracioune.
Jacob ou*er* alle his sons luved Joseph tendrely,
Whar*e*for*e* alle his brethir*e* thoght hym slee for envye.
Jacob did make his so*u*n a longe cote dyu*er*sly
Colourd, w*ith* sere figu*re*s thar*e*in wroght craftyly,
Whaym til his brether*e* whare thay kept shepe his fad*er* sending,
Anone, hym seen, thay thoght of hym to make endyng.
Bot Godde wold thay hym solde til Ismalits for gude,
And his cote al to-rent thay sprenclid w*ith* gotes blude
And sent it to his fader*e* w*ith* a strainege man to see
And hym avise whether*e* it the cote of Joseph mot be.
Whilk seen, his fader*e* his clothes kitte and saide wepynly,
"The worst wilde beestis tethe has eten my sons body."
Than come his sons togider*e* til hym, this thing heryng,
Thair*e* fader*e* in thus grete doel to comford enforcyng,
And he none hede wolde take to consolacioune,
Bot in his vnmesured woo this ilk was his s*er*moune:
"Til helle vnto my son shalle I sorowing descend,"
For hym myght no comfort in this lyf here amend.
So Marie til hir*e* dere son wald have descendid to hell
Iff it hadde bene possible, foreu*er* w*ith* hym to dwelle.
O brether*e*, howe mykelle, hope ʒ*e*, sorowed this moder*e* mylde,
The cote seen of the flesshe to-torne thus of hyr*e* childe!
Joseph cote was made rede of a kidde w*ith* the blude,
Bot Cristes cote w*ith* his awen blude was alle bewette on the Rude,
And of the cruwellest wilde beest was Crist devoured sothly,
Þ*at* was of the wikked Jewes the fiercest maliciouuse enevy.
Jacob for doel of his son share his clothis vtward,
And Marie share hir*e* clothis, þ*at* was the strenghthes of hir*e* sp*ir*its inward.
Alle the sons of Jacob about hym gadred even and morowe,
Bot alle thay myght neu*er* the rather*e* soften his doel & his sorowe.
And thogh to Marie hadde gadred this brode werlde alle holly
Neu*er* thing hadde softned hir*e* doel withouten hir*e* son sothly.
Sith Jacob hadde sonnes twelf and sorowed thus oon losyng,
How mykel was Maries doel more, oon lost, no moo having!
¶b This doelfulle virgyns compleint was sometyme fortaknyd
When Abel of wikked Kayme was slayne and martirizid, [f.35r]
Whas slaghter*e* Adam and Eue thai both for causes sere
Compleynyd both nyght and day, lasting ane hondreth ʒere;
Bot thogh the sorowe of thir*e* two war*e* fulle hoege in reknyng
No dout to Maries doel it shuld seme littell or nothing,
For eu*er* the more þ*at* a thing is more luved be resoune
The more sorowe is of it tholed in the amyssioune;

2805 {Cam} xxvjm *mar.* 2806 The compassioune of Our*e* Ladye *mar.* 2809 Luc. ijo *mar.* 2811 The] *2806 marked to begin the figure.* 2812 figur*e* ja *mar.* 2814 Gen. xxxvijo *mar.* 2819 Ismalits] i.e. to men of swilk a countree *over.* 2827 *marked mar.* 2830 *marked mar.* 2839 his son] i.e. of Joseph *over.* 2847 Figure ij *mar.* 2851 The compleynt of Adam and Eue for the slaght*er* of Abel *mar.*

Adam and Eve mourn Abel
Gen. iv 1-14

Noemy mourns the death of her sons
Ruth i 20

Bot neu*er* more luf was than betwix Marie and hir*e* son
Wha*re*fore hir*e* doel alle other*e* passid in comp*ar*isoune.
The sorowe of Adam and Eue als of bokes men may here
Lastid for thair*e* gude son Abel ane hondreth ȝere;
Bot if Crist hadde bene dede of ȝeres ane hondreth thovzande
Marye alle þ*at* menetyme hadde neu*er* cessid to be wepande
When Joseph Cristis body of the Crosse toke doune, wounded so depe,
Marye stude than fulle negh in hir*e* armes hym to kepe.
The littelle birthyn of mirr*e* betwyx hyr*e* breestis dwelt than,
Als Cantica Cantico*rum* shewes til a lettred man.
A bitter*e* birthin of mirre in Maries hert þ*at* laye
The sov*m*me of Cristis paynes gadred tholed in a nyght and a day;
And als the more þ*at* a wyne swetter*e* and noble is p*ro*ved
Is it more v*er*raly sharpe and bitter*e* when it is *tur*ned,
So als Maries luf til hir*e* son alle oyther*e* passid in swetnesse,
Hadde hir*e* sorowe in hir*e* sons passioune most bitt*er*nesse.
¶c Wha*re*fore Marie sometyme was figu*re*d be Neomy,
The whilk fo\r/ hir*e* two sons waymentid doelfully:
"'Neomy', þ*at* is to say, 'fair*e*', calles me noght so, nay, nay,"
Quod sho, "bot calles me 'Mara', 'bitt*er*' þ*at* is to say,
Forwhi almyghti Godde w*ith* bitt*er*nesse hase filled me."
Beweping hir*e* childre deth swilk doelfulle wordes spake she,
And Marye be Neomy be resoune was fortaknyd,
For sho noght onely of one bot of two sons was pryvid.
O son hadde sho fairest be flesshely p*ro*geni*ture*,
Ane other*e* hadde sho adopt be law of m*er*cyfulle cure.
Crist was hir*e* oone dere son be verray bodily kinde,
The adoptif alle mankynde, in Haly Writte this we fynde.
Dede was the bodily son be verray deth corporele,
So was the son adoptif be the deth spirituele,
For in Cristis passioune mankynde hadde the trewe feyth linquist,
Wha*re*fore alle man*er*e man in sawle was dede and p*er*ist.
For both thir*e* sonnes tholed \she/ the vnhopfulle bitt*er*nesse,
Sithen she luved thaym both two w*ith* swettest luf tendernesse, [f.35v]
And thogh sho luved hir*e* dere son als hir*e*self and wele more,
Ȝit wold she soeffre hym to dye, lif til mankinde to restore,
For rather*e* to see hir*e* son for a tyme liked the moder*e* of pitee
Bere payne, than mankynde alle condampned et*er*naly to be.
In whilk thinges we may conceyve þ*at* Marye lufed vs hoegely,
When she desired þ*at* hir*e* son for our*e* redempcioune shuld dye:
For o thing gyven for ane othere or changed than may men see
The thing takne semes more chere than the thing gyven for to bee.
Than in man*er*e semes Marye haf luved vs more than hir*e* son,
That rather*e* than vs to be dampned soeffred his crucyfixion.
And how the Fader*e* of heven luved vs also may we knawe hereby
Whilk soeffred his oone Son for our*e* lufe to dye thus pynously.
And thus both the Fader*e* and moder*e* has desseruyd ineffably
Of mankynde to be luved ageyne w*ith*out mesure hertfully.
O gude Lorde Jh*es*u, gif vs our*e* luf w*ith* thyn so to melle
Þ*at* we decerve in thy heven et*er*naly w*ith* the for to dwelle.

2856 comp*ar*isoune] *o.s.o.* 2863 birthyn] bitter*e* (-tter*e* *subp.*, -rthyn *ins.*). 2864 Cantica Cantico*rum*] i.e. swilk a boke of the Bible *over*; Cantic. j° *mar.* 2867 Ensaumple *mar.* 2871 Neomy] i.e. swilk a womman *over*; Figu*re* iij^{e} Ruth j° *mar.* 2872 for] (r *in different ink*). 2880 cure] i.e. diligence *over.* 2885 linquist] i.e. lost or gone fro it *over.* 2887 she] *in different ink.* 2901 ineffably] i.e. more than may be spoken *over.* 2903 cor. *mar.* 2904 Amen *underlined rub. mar.*

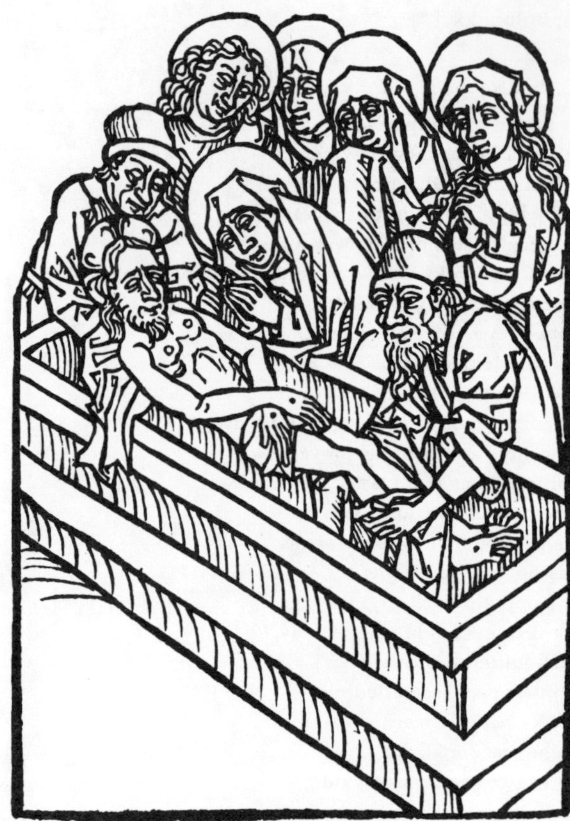

The entombment
John xix 38-42

David mourns Abner
II Kings iii 31-38

Tofore haf 3*e* herd how Crist of the Crosse was taken doune;
Nowe fylowes howe \he/ was graven to here w*ith* devocioune.
The body bewrapped in syndene be Joseph and Nicodeme
Arraied w*ith* oignementis layde thay in a newe grave fulle qweme.
The*re* was Marye fulle negh, the doelfullest creature
Þat eu*er* was mode*re* for son in erth, 3e may be seure.
The*re* moght neu*er* tonge c*er*teine declare hi*re* doelfulle wepyng,
Nor hert think hi*re* disesse and pitousest compleignyng.
She was so feynt and ou*er*comen for sorowe the day and nyght,
Þat vnnethis til hi*re*s sons grave to byry hym wyn she myght.
So many swete cosse and halsinges til hi*re* dede son gave scho
Þat alle gude wightis hi*re* rewed and saide, sore weping, "Loo,
Allas, thi*re* wikkedest men howe thay haf done cruwelly
To this fairest of wo*m*men most benigne and gudely."
This Ladye made so grete doel, compleint and inward gemyng
Þat folkes herts standing about wel negh brist for weping.
For one thus doelfulle mode*re* what hert hadde *þat* hardnesse
Whilk at the welles of weping shuld eschewe tendernesse?
For nowe the handis, nowe the feete of hi*re* son was sho kissing,
His nekke or his woundid sydes in rewthfulle army*s* bracying.
Hi*re* awen breest nowe bette sho, hi*re* handis out nowe spreding,
Nowe sho wronge thaym togydi*re* w*ith* revthfulle teres weping,
Now his smert woundis lokyng, nowe felle sho pitously
On his breest, on his eghen, on his pale mouth blody. [f.36^{r}]
Nowe c*er*tes ane ou*er*-hard hert more than a beest hadde hee
Þat rewthlesse thus gretest doele myght ony wise think or see,
For sith o swyn and of othe*re* is moved to he*re* it crye,
Who of this moderstfulle weping shuld noght than haf m*er*cye?
On Mawdelayne hadde compassioune and w*ith* hi*re* wepid Jh*es*u;
Who than on Marye virgyne shuld noght wepe and sore rewe?
O dolphin ane othe*re* dede with rewthe, says men, wille grave;
What man shuld Maries compleint heryng than no doel have?
¶a The sorowe whilk blissyd Marye in hi*re* sons graving tholid
Dauid in Abners byrying sometyme eke fortakenyd.
Abner of Joab was slayne be fraudulent dissymuiling,
And Dauid King pleyned his deth & fylowed his bere weping;
And thas doelfull birialles weppid noght Dauid oonely,
Bot othe*re* w*ith* hym for to wepe eke excitid he pitously.
He saide, "Kittis 3ou*re* clothing and wepes alle *þat* 3e may:
Whe*re* 3e ne knawe the grettest prince in Isr*ae*l haf fallen today?
Als a wriche mysdoing, witte 3e, he nys noght slayne,
Bot als wikked the rightwis makis dye be sacles payne."
Thus myght doelfulle Marye say on the Gude Fridaye
When hi*re* son of the wikked Jewes slayne in hi*re* armys laye:
"3ou*re* clothes of inward compleynt in signe of doel shere 3*e*:
Whe*re* 3e ne knawe the grettest Prince of Isr*ae*l today dede be?"
O Lord, howe grettest a p*ri*nce in Isr*ae*l tholid occisioune,
Of wham eu*ery* creat*ure* bare grete compassioune!
His hote bemes the son w*ith*drewe *þat* thay ne shuld noght Crist brynne,
The ayre wax derke also, to hille his nakednesse w*ith*inne;

2905 Ca^{m} xxvij^{m} *mar.* 2909 Of O*ur* Ladys sorowe apon hi*re* dede son *mar.* 2919 gemyng] i.e. sorowyng *mar.* 2927 No*ta* *mar.* 2938 fig*ur*e j Abne*re* *mar.* 2940 his] *(r* alt. *s).* 2942 ij Regum iij^{o} *mar.* 2941 occisioune] i.e. to be slayne *over.* 2952 Compassioune of the elementz i*n* C*ri*stis deth *mar.*

Joseph is put into the well
Gen. xxxvii

Jonas is swallowed by the fish
Jonas i-ii

The erthe whoke for to fere the crucifi*our*s, this is trewth;
The vaille of the Temple was rent to make the Pharisens haf rewth;
The roches *þat* wer*e* so hard creved both vppe and doune,
And for the disciples spak noght stones cryes w*ith* hiegh soune.
Also dede men graves opned that thay myght rise for to telle
The poair*e* of this grete prince to the werld whilk than befelle;
And mony of the dede to men aperid thilk tyme rysing,
The werkis of this grete prince fulle planely manifesting.
The dyvel apon the left brace of the Crosse alle astoned satte
To whame alle creatures obeyed m*er*veilling what was he *þat*.
The philosofres of Athenes, the so*n*ne aȝeins kinde derke seynge,
Saide godde of nature *þat* daye was some anguisse soeffringe.
Til on vnknawen godde maide thay ane autier*e* forthy
To be knawen werldis co*m*myng whoso myght come *þer*by; [f.36v]
Wharefor this princes biriales pleigne w*ith* deuocioune
Our*e* inwards hertis kerving w*ith* tendrest compassioune.
¶b Of Crist*es* scpulture the sons of Jacob gaf forliknesse,
Puttyng thair*e* brother*e* Joseph into the cisternys depnesse.
Thai hatid thair*e* brothir*e* Joseph to the deth w*ith*out skille,
And the Jewes thair*e* brother*e* Crist for his luf and gude wille.
Jacob sonnes sold thair*e* brother*e* Joseph for penys thretty,
The Jewes boght Crist of Judas for als many penys evenly.
Jacob sonnes thair*e* brother*e* cote w*ith* thair*e* handis vnsoundid,
The Jewes Crists flesshe w*ith* scourges, w*ith* thornes and nailles woundid.
Jose{p*s*} cote in no p*ar*te felt payne of dyrupcioune,
Bot Cristis flesshe in alle his membris tholid hard passioune.
Josephs cote fro his nekke rechid til his helis behynde,
Bot fro Cristis crovne to his too was none hele for to fynde.
Jacob so*u*ns thair*e* brother*e* cote sprenclid w*ith* a kyds blude,
The Jewes w*ith* Cristis awen blude dyed his cote on the Rode.
The sons of Jacob *þer* fader*e* trevblid ynogh and wele more,
And the Jewes Maryes pye hert made hoegly doelfulle & sore.
Joseph his brethers trespas to thaym relesed gudely
And Crist for his crucifiours p*ra*yed his Fader*e* pitously.
Joseph, solde of his brether*e*, lorde of Egipt befelle,
And Crist, crucifyed of the Jewes, of heven and erth and helle.
Jacob sons hono*ur*ed thair*e* brother*e*, p*ro*cesse of tyme fylowing,
And many Jewes trowed in C*ri*st fro deth aft*er* his ryseing.
Jacob heryng his son olyve hadde grete gladnesse:
Marye, hir sons rysing seen, was fillid w*ith* swetnesse.
Joseph 'a son growing' or 'increment' is for to say,
And the feith of Our*e* Lord Crist spredde wyde-wher*e* day be day.
¶c And Jh*es*u Crists sepulture be Jonas p*re*figu*r*ed myght be,
Whaym a whalle swalowed casten out of a shippe vnto the see.
Thre dayes and als the thre nyghtes w*ith*inne the whalle was Jonas
So Crist vnto the thredde day in his grave closid was:
And how this storye to Crist resonably is appropred
In the chapitle of the resurrexcioune more openly is declared.
Thi sepulture gif vs here to luf so, swete Jh*es*u,
That we dwelle eure w*ith* the in heven whar*e* joye is newe.

2958 Math. vij° *mar.* 2965 Act. xvij *mar.* 2971 Fig*ure* ij *mar.* 2972 Gen. xxxvij° *mar.* 2977 vnsoundid] i.e. made vnhole *over.* 2979 dyrupcioune] i.e. of reending *over.* 2984 Rode] *(*u *alt.* o*).* 2990 helle] i.e. is lorde *over.* 2813 increment] i.e. encrees *over.* 2997 Figure iij° *mar.* 2999 Jonas] i.e. p*ro*ph*e*te *over.*

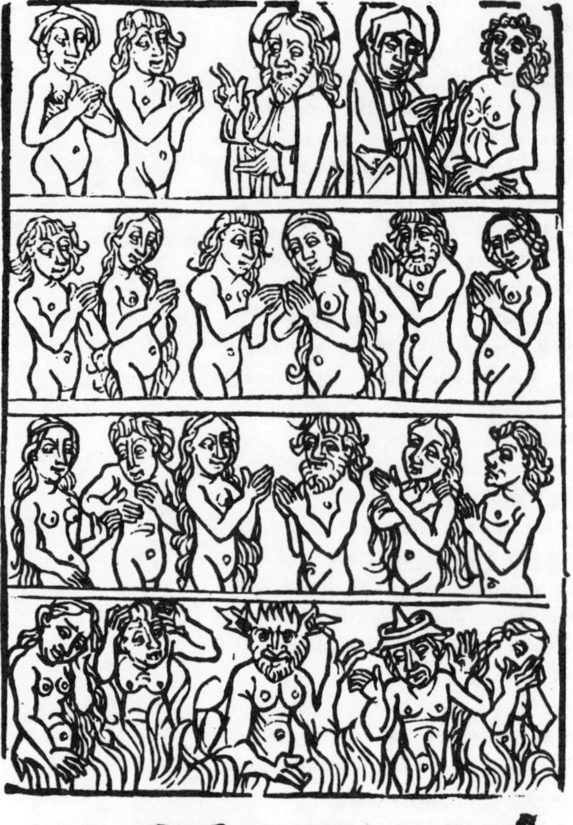

Christ's descent into hell
Eph. iv 9; I Pet. iii 18-20 (Enoch xxii)

Sidrach, Misach and Abdenago in the furnace
Dan. iii 14-100

Ʒe have herd last tofore how Joseph Crist byryid;
Now is fylowing to here how Crist in helle entrid.
The houre of Nones, Cristis soule ȝolden in the Crosse als tite,
Vnto the hellis descendid, the saule to the Godhede vnyte.
Fourefaldes or in foure stedis ere hellys, be Thomas sawe:
Of dampnyd, of childer, of purgatorie and of seints of the Olde Lawe. [f.37^r]
In the first, þat is, of dampnyd, is smeke and fire inextinguyble,
Sight of innoumbrable feendes, horrour and flaying terrible,
Wormes freetyng the con\s/cience and horrible derknesse palpable,
Inenarrable hydous coldnesse and stinking intolerable,
Eure enterchaungable envy, multiplying of malicioune,
Fleyng of desired deth, dispare of redempcioune,
The point of dying allwaye, and of deth neuer freedome–
There ere paynes euermore newe, neuer of thaym eend to come.
To this helle neuer descendid Oure Lorde Crist is no doute,
Nor fro þat horrible place boght he nevre saulys oute.
Above this helle a place for childere is thus devised
Without circumcisioune and oþer eke vnbaptized.
There nys no sensuele payne bot payne of wanting, wit ȝe:
Joie haf thay thare fulle grete of Gods vnmesured bountee.
In thilk place haf the forsaid childere so hoege gladnesse
Whilk of alle joyes erthly passes lust and swetnesse.
Thay joye þat thay thaire makere synnyng offendid nevre,
And þat fro the helle of the dampnyd seur thay knawe thaym forevre.
What Godde will do be thayme no man has the knawing,
Nor no doctour suffices to termyne it be writing.
Overe this stede is ane helle whilk named is purgatorie,
Fulle \of/ diuerse diseses, with many a payne fulle sory,
Whare Cristen saules for thaire synnes vnclensid who saved salle be
Resceves after Gods demyng certeyne penalitee.
Thire savles paynes ere lessenyd be dovoute messys singyng,
Be fastyng and be prayers, and be trewe almouse-delyng,
Be indulgence and be the haly laude of the Croyce be accepting,
And be penaunce of othere folkes for thaire freendes fullfillyng.
The paynes of purgatorie may no tonge erthly telle,
For-passing alle erthly disese, alle be thay neuer so felle.
Als is fire peyntid vnlike to self fire materiale,
So differences fire werldly fro thilk purgatoriale.
Above this stede is ane helle whare the seints of the Olde Lawe were,
Lymbus of Abrahams bosme named be clerkes sere,
Tho whilk helle alle the seintes entred, wit ȝe trewly,
Þat died or Crist vprase, ware thay neuer so haly.
This helle entred Jhesu Oure Saueour descending doune right,
And of alle savles thereinne he heryde it be his grete myght.
In this helle was Cristes sawle fro the houre of his dieying [f.37^v]
Vnto the thred day fylowing, the houre of his vprysing;
And thogh it ware that Cristis s{a}wle fro the body departid,
The Godhede fro the body nor fro the sawle no tyme was disseueryd,
For in the lymbe was the Godhede vnite to the savle partid fro the flesshe,
And in the grave to the flesshe dede, incorrupt and euer ylike fresshe;

3005 Ca^m xxviij^m *mar.* 3006 Seint Thomas in the boke of Cristis descensioune to hell after his deth *mar.* 3009 Thomas] i.e. Alqwyne *over.* 3011 Math. xiij^o *mar.* 3013 conscience] *(s in different ink)*; j helle *mar.*; 3016 dispare] *(a 2nd* s *erased)*. 3021 ij helle *mar.* 3031 iij helle *mar.* 3035 Expediencia animabus in purgatorio nota *mar.* 3043 iiij helle *mar.* 3051 sowle] *(o.er. necessitating a paper repair)*. 3052 How to Cristis flesshe dede was the Godhede vnyte *mar.* 3054 to...dede] i.e. was the Deitee vnite *over.*

Daniel in the lions' den
Dan. xiv 27-42, vi 16-27

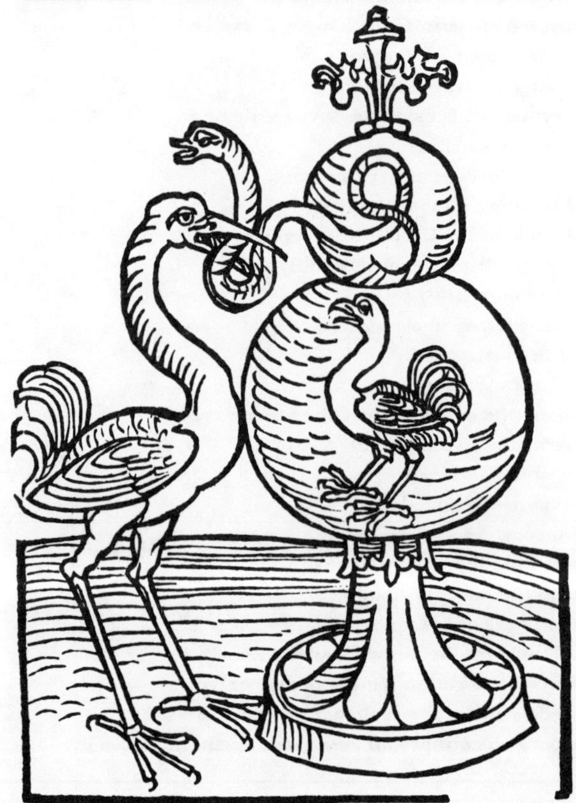

The ostrich releases her young
Comestor 1353-54

And when þ*at* Crist entred in the lymbe, the seints see the verray deitee,
And alle the joye and the blisse i*n* the heven hadde thay be free lib*er*tee.
Men sais, whar*e* the Haly Fader*e* is, thar*e* for to be the courte of Rome,
And hevenly joyes whar*e* the Godhede is shalle be hoped to the same dome.
And to the thef hanging in the crosse saide O*ur* Lord Jh*es*u on this wise:
"I saye the forsoth this ilk daye thowe shalle be w*ith* me in p*ar*adise."
And this of p*ar*adyse t*er*restre touches noght in expounding,
Bot of the contempiacioune dyvine is in trewth the vnderstanding.
The theves savle w*ith* the savle of Crist entrid in the lymbe the same day,
And the verray Godhede contemplid w*ith* othir*e* seints, th*us* the clerks say.
And when the seints see Our*e* Lord Cr*is*t thai kest a fulle joyous cry,
"Welcome, Our*e* lange desired Lord, vouching sauf vs to by."
¶a This thing p*re*figured thre childer*e* at Babiloygne in the fo*ur*nas,
When the fire at the aungels entring to swete dewe turnyd was;
For if the aungels p*re*sence to the childer*e* in the fire refrigery made,
Wele more myght Our*e* Lord Crist in helle the seints glade.
The aungelle sent into the oven to confort the childer*e* fortolde
Fig*ur*ed þ*at* to co*n*fort the faders Crist entre into helle wolde;
And als in the forsaide fo*ur*nace war*e* bot childer*e* & nan other*e*,
None was bot innocents and childer*e* i*n* the lymbe sothly, gude brother*e*;
For who tofore satisfaccioune pleyne passid, to purgatorie descendid,
And when thay wer*e* purged at the fulle vnto the lymbe aft*er* thay ascendid.
¶b Be Daniel in the lake of lyouns Our*e* Lord p*re*fig*ur*ed this thing,
W*ith* Abacuk and his sherers mete wonderfully to the lake carying.
The folk of the lande of Babiloigne into the lake hadde puttid Daniel,
In thair*e* entent for to bene devoured of seven lyons hongry & cruwelle.
Bot Godde of thas fiers beestis kept hym fro ill\e/sioune,
And sent hym fulle m*er*veillously be his aungelle refeccioune.
So Godde our*e* faders in the lymbe kept fro feendes and yvel pyne,
And co*m*myng hymself, fedde thayme w*ith* his refeccioune dyvine.
The lake of Babiloigne til helle may men likne, or it calle,
The seven lyons takenyng the noumbre of feendes alle.
The noumbre of feendes er*e* wonte be discrived be dyvels seven,
Whilk be seven dedely synnes lettis men the way til heven;
Of whilk synnes dedely the names er*e* thir*e*: pride and envye,
Ire, acide, auarice, glutterye {a}nd leicherye.
Of fendes er*e* thir*e* the wapenes, and arm*ur*es of the dyvel, [f.38r]
Warnst*ur*e of the castels of helle, of whilk man takes oft yvel.
And thogh the feendes hadde garnist the helle many ȝers so fiersly,
Ȝit Crist w*ith* his p*re*cious blode all to-brast it lyghtly.
¶c This was p*re*figured sometyme be a fowghel hight strucc*iou*ne
Whas bridde in a vesselle of glasse didde close vp Kyng Salomon.
The strucc*iou*ne, to delyvre hir*e* bridde out of the glasse desyring,
Flowgh vnto desert and broght a littel worme reto*ur*nyng,
W*ith* whas blode the vesselle touching of glasse, it al to-brast,
And so the bridde of the strucc*iou*ne freely come forth at the last.
Thus when Crist tholid in the Crosse his blode p*re*ssid out to be,
Helle als glasse brast, & man went out both qwhit and free.
O gude Jh*es*u, vouche saufe vs so to kepe fro helle
Þ*at* we in thy p*re*sence eu*er* in joye with the dwelle.

3067 Figure j *mar.* 3075 No*ta mar.* 3077 Figure ij Daniel vj[to] *mar.* 3081 illesioune] Illusioune *(1st* u *subp.*, e *ins. in different ink.)* ; i.e. fro harme *over.* 3089 The names of the vij dedely synnes *mar.* 3098 worme] it hat Thamer*e over*; The Maist*er* of Stories apon the iij boke of Kinges ca° v[to] *mar.* 3104 Amen *mar.*

Christ conquers the devil
Gospel of Nicodemus

Banaias kills the lion
II Kings xxiii 20; Comestor 1344

Now last herd ʒ*e* how Crist gladide our*e* faders in helle;
Her*e* fylowse howe he ou*er*come the p*r*ince of feendes cruwelle.
Crist wolde be man for he the feende til ou*er*come thoght,
Als he to the poeple a tyme in *par*able thus forth broght.
Whils the stronge-armed, i*d est* the dyvel, kepes his halle, lymbus,
Alle is in pees þ*at* he haves (of the Faders the glose is thus).
Co*m*myng his stronger*e*, i*d est* Jh*esu*s, swith wille he hym ou*er*come,
Bynde hym, and his arm*ur*es ref fro hym alle & some.
The dyvel, tofore þ*at* Crist come, armed was so strongly
Þ*at* neu*er* man erthly borne myght his halle breke forthy.
Than Crist–noght man oonly, bot Godde and man o p*er*son–
Entrid his halle be the Crosse, and ou*er*come hym anone.
¶a Hereof Bananias the stronge gaf p*re*figuracioune,
Þ*at* entrid a cisterne w*ith* his ʒerde and slewe ther*e*inne a lyoun.
So to the feende in the cistern of helle entrid Jh*es*u
W*ith* ʒerde and staffe of his Crosse, and thilk lyoun ou*er*threwe.
Off this the p*r*ophete Dauide thus in the Savtier*e* saide he:
"Thi ʒerde and staffe, tha thinges er*e* grete comfort to me."
The ʒerde menes here a staffe in a mans hande walking,
To holde hym vppe in the waye, and fro hondes defending.
So Cristis Croice is a staffe sustenyng þ*at* we ne falle,
And ʒerde be whilk helle-houndes we may fere fro vs alle.
Be this staffe C*ri*st the lyoun of helle nobly ou*er*come,
And for to withstande thilk feende has takne til vs the same.
Loke, brethere, what we be holden*e* til hono*ur* the Croice, alle and so*m*me,
Be whilk our*e* enemys, the dyvels, we may thus fere and ou*er*come.
Als be the tree of *par*adys the dyvel toke man prisoner*e*
So Crist be the tree of the Crosse ou*er*come the feende, dying here. [f.38v]
O brether*e*, mykelle er*e* we holde. . the seint Croice to hono*ur*e swetely,
Whilk Crist w*ith* his p*r*ecious blode vouched sauf to sacre nobly.
In the Croice the dyvels felawes, ille folk, war*e* sometyme hongid;
Nowe er*e* feendes be it chaced, ou*er*comen lightly and stranglid.
Be the Croice, tofore þ*at* C*ri*st come, eked was the noumbre of dampnable,
And nowe in it, be Cristis vertue, growes the noumbre of the sauuable.
Men were once put to death by the cross,
And now the sick are cured and the dead raised by it.
Be the Croice sometymes to the feend was eked als in man*er*e glading,
And nowe be it, to thair*e* hoege sorowe, til aungels is eked reioying.
Sometyme be the crosse wikked men toke for thair*e* synne dampnacioune,
And now be it, blissed be Jh*es*u, is to synne m*er*cy and pardoune.
The Crosse, in mount of Calverie sette for the viletee,
Is nowe sette vppe in Haly Kirke in autiers for seintitee.
The Crosse þ*at* \was/ horrour*e* to touche for the p*ro*pre shame,
Nowe hono*ur*es it king and prince, & heries the gloriouse name;
Whame alle this werld myght noght ou*er*come, the dyvel of helle,
A childe be the signe of the Crosse may hym fere and expelle.
This myght gaf he til it, our*e* awen campion stedfast
Whilk in it ou*er*come the feend and helle ʒates alle to-brast.
And Cristis victorie sometymes was fig*ur*ed be Sampson
In the vignes of Engaddi whilk to-rent a lyon.

3105 {Ca}^{m} xxix^{m} *mar.* 3109 Luc. xj^{o} *mar.* 3110 haves] (has *alt.*) 3111 hym] i.e. the feende *over.* 3116 Fig*ur*e j ij Regum xxiiij^{o} *mar.* 3120 lyoun] i.e. the feende *over.* 3129 beholden] (*o.s.o.* -den). 3133 Of the v*er*tue of the seint Croice *mar.* 3147 was] *ins. hand*[2] *should perhaps be omitted.* 3150 no*ta mar.*; expelle] i.e. chace hym away *over.* 3153 Figure ij *mar.* 3154 Judic. xiiij *mar.*

Samson kills the lion
Judges xiv 1-17

Ayod kills Eglon
Judges iii 15-24

¶b Be strongest Sampson is Crist, strongest of alle, taknyd,
Of whame the hellysh lyo*un* is of his myght depryved.
Sampso*un*, to take a wif weending out on a daye,
He slewgh a cruwelle lyo*un*, metyng hym on the way.
So Crist, Gods So*un*, fro heven to this werld descending,
Contracte a matrimoigne w*ith* mankynde desiring.
Sampson weddid a wif, a womman of Thamnataa,
And Crist in alle naciones chase hym the lande Juda.
This womman of Thamnataa deceyved Sampson sleghly;
Right so the contree of Juda tretid Crist fraudulently.
Sampson his enemys cornes and thair*e* vignes sette in fire,
And defendid hym nobly, maugre thair*e* aller*e* ire;
So Crist of the Jewes at the last vengid hym, for alle thay*re* boost,
Wher. ne the lande of Judee destruyd w*ith* the Romayns oost.
Thus Sampson alder-strongest C*ri*st takned p*re*figuratifly,
Whilk the infernale lyo*un* ou*er*come–the fende our*e* enemy.
¶c Eke Ayoth ambidexter*e* sometyme p*re*figured Jh*es*u,
Whilk Israels enemy w*ith* his swerde the fattest King Eglon ou*er*trewe.
This ilk forsaide King Eglon, the fattest man outrageously,
Verrayde of Israel the folk, oppressing thayme horribily. [f.39^{r}]
Ayothe this Eglon to slee studied fulle bysyly,
For to qwhite Israel of swilk one eneuyous enemy.
This Ayoth gat this Eglon in his awen chaumbre at the last,
And his swerde w*ith* his left hande showed i*n* the kinges body fulle fast;
For with so grete force Ayoth bare it in the body of Eglon,
That the hilts w*ith* the swerds blade was closid in his fatt wombe anone.
The whilk swerde in þ*at* plite left, Ayoth eschaped happyly,
And the folkes of his contree delyvred of so grete ane enemy.
This King alder-fattest Eglon, for his wombe brode als a targe
Bers takenyng the feende of helle, for his bely w*ith*out noumbre large
Whilk is callid fattest for he alle men devourid,
And for þ*at* alle mankynde in his hoege wombe [entrid].
At the last, come Our*e* Lord Crist and his grete wombe [decovrid]
W*ith* the swerde of his passioune when he helle ȝates p*er*cyd.
And for the feende ou*er*come man be ane apple swete taysting,
Ther*e*for Crist ou*er*come the dyvel be bitt*er*est passioune soeffring.
In whilk thing Crist for to fyght a trewe ensaumpille left vntil vs,
Þ*at* aȝeins the feende and vices vs mote feght w*ith* v*er*tuse;
For als the matiers be thair*e* contraries in sekenesse has curacio*un*e,
Be like wise, in bataille w*ith* the feende, be v*er*tuz men puttis vices doune.
Bo\t/ he þ*at* feghtis lawfully, non other*e* shalle of coro*un*e haf the p*ri*s,
For ther*e* may no man feght in this erth, bot if hym hapne to haf enemys.
Forthy Our*e* Lord has ordeyned þ*at* a man shalle haf here impugnacio*un*e,
Þ*at* þ*er*by in heven at his eende hym be eked retribucio*un*e.
Also some men in slepe Our*e* Lord soeffres temptid,
Þ*at* also thaym slepyng þ*er* mede be encressid:
For eu*er* the more þ*at* a man endures here of bataille,
So of mede more and more shalle he take w*ith*out faille.
O gude Jh*es*u, gif vs so w*ith* the feende to feght
Þ*at* we be corovned of the in hye joye vpp on heght.

3157 Sampson *mar.* 3161 Thamnataa] i.e. of þ*at* contree *over.* 3170 Whilk] i.e. C*ri*st *over.* 3171 Fig*ur*e iij Judic. iij *mar.*; i.e. for right and left hande was hym alle oon *over.* 3175 Ayoth *mar.* 3186 entrid] decovrid; deovrid] entrid. 3195 Bot] *(*t *in different ink)*; Thi. ij^{o} *mar.* 3203 corr. *mar.* 3204 corovned] *stroke over 2nd* o *erased*; Amen *under rub. mar.*

The Virgin's compassion overcomes the devil
Gen. iii 15

Judith kills Holfernes
Judith xii 15-xiii 21

Herd nowe þ*at* Crist ou*er*come the feende be his passioune;
Heres howe Our*e* Ladye ou*er*come hym be compassioune.
What Crist in his passioune suffred, þ*at* evrydele
Tholid Marye be compassioune in hir*e* sowle mat*er*nele.
The nayllis whilk handis and fete thirlid of hir*e* dere son
P*er*ced his swete modris breest be pynefulst compassioune.
The lance which penetrated the side of her dead son
Pierced the heart of the living mother with compassion.
The thornes þ*at* the heved of Crist prikkid so pynefully
His moders hert be compassioune fulle depe woundid sothly.
The swerde of sharpest tonges, herd of Crist tholemodely,
Be inwardest compassioune p*er*cyd the sawle of Marye. [f.39v]
And als Crist ou*er*come the feende be his seint passioune,
So dide eke blissid Marie be modrefulle compassioune.
W*ith* armes of hir*e* sonnes passioune armed hir*e* blissid Marie
When sho shuld aȝeinst the feende to bataille make hir*e* redy.
¶a \Be/ Judith, þ*at* Holofern withstode, p*re*figured this was fulle wele,
For Marye putte hir*e* aȝeinst the feende, prince infernele.
Judith hir*e* clothis didde on most festyvale fair*e* and swete:
With mytre hir*e* heved arraied and sandales eke on hir*e* fete.
Marie didde onne hir*e* sons cote inconsutyle, w*ith*out semyng,
On whilk sho didde the palle of hir*e* sons double scornyng:
One white, in whilk þ*at* Crist of Herode was scorned,
Þ*at* oyther*e* coccyne, redisshe, in whilk the knyghtes hym japed;
And in a palle white and rede was wele cledde Our*e* Ladye,
For Haly Kyrke singes of hir*e* son to be white and rodye.
Alle Marie compassioune of mirre til a bondel has liknyng,
Betwix the breestes of a swete savle for it shuld have dwelling.
Marye gadred bysyly alle hir*e* sons passioune and pyne,
And be compassioune made thaym of mirre a littel byrthyne;
Whilk birthyn betwix hir*e* breestes sho kept als a sevre shelde,
With whilk aȝeins our*e* enemy sho made were in the felde.
And in this fassicle of mirre ware bonden samen paynes alle
Of hir*e* der*e* wrthyest luvid son passioune, both grete and smale.
Swerdis, spere, staffes and other*e* arm*ur*e sho ne forgate noght,
Lant*er*nes, light brandes be whilk hym in the gardyn thay soght;
Drerynesse, trembling and drede, Cristis threfolde orisoune,
The comfort aungelicale, Cristis b\l/ody swete rynnyng doune;
Howe his foos freely meting he kest doune w*ith* his worde oon,
And aft*er*, restoryng thair*e* strenghe, he lete thaym take hym anone;
The signe for to knawe Crist, and Judas cusse so maligne,
The tresonouse salutacioune, and Cristis answer*e* benigne;
The cruwelle capcioune of Crist, and of his doelfullest bindyng,
The s*er*uants ere restorid, and his disciples fleyng;
And how John left the syndone and ferefully fledde fro Crist than;
The wode joye of the Jewes, of Crist the opposynge be Anne;
Be bisshops s*er*uants buffet and Cristis swete answering,
The threfald nying be Peter*e* and his conu*er*sioune weping;
The juge names tofore whayme Crist was ledde & accusat–
Anna, Caphays, Herode, the ferth was Pontius Pilate;

3205 {C}a^m xxx^m *mar.* 3217 passioune] *(*com- *subp.)* 3221 Fig*ure* j Judith xiij° *mar.*; Be] In *subp.* 3224 mytre] i.e. a man*ere* of wommans arraye *over.* 3225 semyng] i.e. þ*at* hadde no seme *over.* 3230 Cantic. j° *mar.* 3232 breestes] i.e. the pappes *over*; swete savle] i.e. a luving savle *over.* 3233 No*ta* ben*e* *mar.* 3239 shone ne] shone *with* she *over in another, faint, hand.* 3249 John] ? Joh*an* 3253 The names of Cristis juges *mar.*

Jahal pierces Sisara's temples
Judges iv 12-22

Thamar beheads Cyrus
Comestor 1474

The pilere, scourges and cordes, the thornes, the rede and wandes,
The Crosse, nailles, spere, coroune & hameres, the table writen of Pilats hande{s}; [f.40r]
The buffetts, reproves, neckings, blasphemes, derisioune,
The prophetic hiling of Crists eghen, and of his cloths departisoune;
The kavil on Cristis cote also of Herode the white clothing,
The tribunal, the cloth of purpre, of Pilat the handis wasshing;
The dremyng of Pilates wif, the lyueraunce of thefe Baraban,
The noyse, the Jewes clamoure "Crucifige" multiplying than;
Crists sorest thrist, the acetable, the aselle medled with galle,
The rede with the sponnge and ysope, the wyne myrrid withalle;
Cristis prayere, his teres, his crye, the theef to mercy takeing,
Alle Crists wordes in the Crosse, his moders and John commyndyng;
Cristis deth, of Longif the spere with his illuminacioune,
The effluxioune of blode & watere with centurys protestacioune;
The sonne derk, erth-dynne, cleving of stones and the vaille thorghby,
Of the Temple party falling, open graves, Mount Caluerye;
Thas penyes thretty be whilk Crist was both solde and boght,
Judas wannehope whaym Crist with his blode redemyd noght–
With thire and oþer of Crist paynes armed hire Oure swete Ladye,
And als oure propugnatrice ouercome the feende oure enemy.
Than ware complete in Marie sometyme forshewed figures,
And some of the prophetes sawes writen vp in Haly Scriptures:
"Apon the aspe and on the basilisk shalle thowe go, Ladye Marye,
The lyoun and dragon, the feende, shalle thowe to-trede sothly"
And "Thowe, Sathan, shal awayte hire hele, man werraying,
And sho thi hevede al to-breke be commpassioune ouercommyng."
¶b Jael, the wif of Abere, sometyme this thinge figured,
When sho Sysaram thorgh the temples with ane iren naile perced.
Sysera was a grete prince of the ost of Jabyn the king,
After the deth of Ayoth the childere of Israel wasting,
Wham thorgh the thonwonges with a naile at the last perced Jael,
And of þat grevous enemy delyvred the folk of Israel.
So Marye with the naile of the Crosse has striken thorgh oure enemy,
And of his myght on vs hadde dispoillid hym, and maistry.
¶c The qwene Thamare also Marie prefigured,
Whilk Cirus the cruwelst king and mannes qwellere hevedid
The whilk brent in swilk lust of mannes lyves vndoing
That he ne myght neuer be fillid to slee men for nothing.
Tylle alle men made he werre, alle landes assaillid he,
And slew doune tofore hym without rewth or pitee.
At the last, the qwene Thamare, hym taken, his heved of kitte,
And after in a fulle potte of mannes blode sho putte itte, [f.40v]
And saide, "Drink nowe manes blode whareof thowe hadde swilk thrist,
Þat neuer thereof lyving hadde thowe ynogh to thi list."
Right so the feende, mansleere, fro the werlde begynnyng
Might neuer ȝit be fulfillid of mans kynde perysshing;
Bot the qwene of heven hym matid with hire sons passioune,
And fillid hym with his ordeyned for vs dampnacioune.
O Jhesu, be thy gude helpe make vs ouercome the feende,
Þat oure sawles after this lif til eterne joye mowe weende.

3255 Instruments of Cristis passioune *mar.* 3260 tribunal] i.e. the see of the juge *over.* 3261 thefe] *(? 2nd* e *subp.)* 3263 acetable] i.e. the vesselle with þat drink *over.* 3266 John] ? Johan 3269 erth-dynne] *(*-dymm *alt.* -dynne *then final* e *subp., another ins.)* 3276 some] *(*-tyme *subp. and can.)* 3281 Figure ij Judic. iiij° *mar.* 3289 Figure iij *mar.* 3304 Amen *mar.*

The Holy Patriarchs are freed from limbo

Eph. iv 9; I Pet. iii 18-20; *Gospel of Nicodemus*

Moses releases the Israelites from Egypt

Ex. xiv

Howe the dyvel was ou*er*comen tolde the chapitle tofore;
Heres nowe howe man was qwhit fro priso*u*ne forthermore.
On Gude Fryday when Crist his sawle on Crosse expired,
Vnite vnto the Godhede anone it helle entrid:
Noght, als some hopes, to-whils the nyght of Sonday biding,
Bot to comfort the faders in p*ri*so*u*ne fulle fast hasting,
For if þ*at* any man myght his freende delyvre today
It war*e* yvel to the thredde morowe to putte it in delay,
Whar*e*for Crist, the trewest of alle freendes, wold noght dwelle,
Bot aft*er* his passioune anone visit the seints in helle—
Ensaumpill til vs, who wille bringe sawles out of distresse,
To p*ro*loigne thair*e* suffrages to*ur*nes thaym tylle hevynesse.
Swilk folk synnes grevously, for sawles in sore langing
Bides in paynes vntholefulle, thair*e* freendes pitee co*m*myng.
Some dose singe single messes for thair*e* freendes xxx dayes:
Wele done, bot better*e* war*e* alle the first day done always—
Longe, longe is to abide thretty days thair*e* no doute,
Eu*ery* man think the same of sawles suffrages thorghout.
Hast we þ*er*fore til help the sawles in purgatorye,
For þ*at* be Cristis hasting is proved to be spedy.
Crist noght right than the faders the same day delyvrid,
Bot with thaym dwelling w*ith* his swete p*res*ence thaym gladid.
The Sonday tofore the mornyng fro deth rysyn, the mydnyght,
The fadres out of the lymbe ledde Crist thorgh his grete myght.
¶a This captivitee be the feende tofore here reme\m/brid
In the Egipcien thraldome sometyme was p*re*figured.
Thar*e* war*e* the childer*e* of Israel be Pharao thralde hoegely
And for delyveraunce to Godde cryed thay longe doelfully.
Our*e* Lord till Moyses at the last appiered in a busshe brynnyng,
Fulle of fire and neu*er* the lesse hole in verray grennesse lasting.
Fro thens Godde sent Moyses vnto the kinge Pharaon
And of his folks captivitee be hym made lyvrisoune. [f.41^{r}]
Right so the feende mankynde thrallid ȝeres fulle many,
The whilk for delyvraunce cryed to Godde manyfaldly,
"O Lorde, in adiutorie of me like the entende;
Gude Lorde, enclyne thyne hevenes til erth for to descende;
Delyvre me, Lorde, for pore and fulle nedy am I,
Of meself noght having to delyvre me whareby.
Putte forth thyne hande, gude Lorde, for to make my ransoune,
Send thi lombe, our*e* victyme of recounsiliacioune.
Send forth thi light be whilk be fordone our*e* derknesse;
That thi p*ro*phetes be trewe send forth thi sothfastnesse."
This wise and many ane other*e* crying to Godde mankynde,
To soco*ur* it m*er*cyfully toke his gudenesse in mynde,
In a busshe descendant in flavme, it vnwasting,
Þ*at* is in virgyne Marie, hir*e* maydenhede vnlesing.
Pharao and alle his folk Godde smote, and out ledyng
The childere of Israel to the londe w*ith* mylke & hony flowyng.
So Crist woundid the feende and his foulle assembling,
And ledde seints out of helle til et*er*nale feding.

3305 Ca^{m} xxxj^{m} *mar.* 3307 how Crist descendid to helle *mar.*; expired] i.e. ȝalde *over.* 3308 Vnite] i.e. the sawle *over.* 3315 Howe p*er*illous es to tarie the almouse or p*ra*yers for sawles nota *mar.* 3327 no*ta mar.* 3329 remembrid] *(3rd minim in 2nd* m *ins. in different ink.)* 3333 Exodi iij *mar.* 3339 Psalmus lxix *mar.* 3345 Ysay xvj *mar.* 3346 Psalmus xlij *mar.*

The freeing of Abraham from Ur of the Chaldees
Gen. xv 6-7; Comestor 1091

The freeing of Lot from Sodom
Gen. xix 12-29

Thare ere thai fedde with mylke of his swete manhede to see
And hony of contempling of his dyvinitee.
Godde wilnyng delyvre the Jewes bade a lombe sacrifie,
Bot Crist to delyvre vs made hymself crucifie.
¶b And this delyvraunce of man also Godde preostendid
When he patriarche Abraham fro Hurre of Caldee delyvrid.
The poeple of Caldee worshipt als godde Hur, þat is, fyre,
And Abraham noght wilnyng do so thai wald haf brent in grete ire.
Bot trewe Godde omnipotent whaym Abraham worshept onely
Out of the fyre of the Caldiens delyvrid mercyfully;
And als Godde kept Abraham in the fire without brennyng,
So kept he the seints in helle without payne sensuel felyng;
And als Abraham rescowde he made hym fadere of folk many,
The faderes redemyd fro helle ioyned he til aungels likely.
¶c Also Godde preostendid of man the redempcioune
When he Loth delyvrid fro Sodomes subuersioune.
Out of the citee of Sodome ware onely gude men delyvrid:
The wikked with sulphur and fyre without eende perisshid.
So out of the lymbe gude sawles delyvrid Crist alle onely:
Out of the helle of the dampned toke he noght oone sothly.
Tharefore saye none þat Crist brast this ilk hellys pitte,
For who is þat moght suffize a3eyn to repare itte; [f.41v]
Wharefore it was noght brystyn bot thas whilk fro begynyng
Entred in it shalle dwelle thare euer without eendyng.
O pye Jhesu, kepe vs fro þat helle eendlesly
And vouche sauf in this lyf to purge vs mercyfully.
Here tourment and also scourge here, gif woundys here temporelle
Þat we fele neuer scourgings of cruwelle peyne perpetu\e/lle,
For thowe says that thas whame thowe lufs thowe wille in this lif chasty.
We pray the, Lorde, luf vs right so, Jhesu, for thy mercy,
For better is to suffre disese in this lif and come to the
Than for to perisshe eendelesly for temporel prosperitee;
And thogh we gruch in disese here, be noght wroth, Lorde of gudenesse,
Bot, wille we or none, scourge vs to bringe vs to eternale blistnesse.
We wricches may no sore fele without murmure for freel,
Bot forgif oure impacience, O pie Lorde Jhesu leel.
Also til ascende a mountayne how þat Oure Lorde Godde badde Loth
And forbede hym loke bakwards, is bisyly for to note.
So when Godde has delyvrid fro synne a man be penaunce
He shuld noght his left synnes eft loke be delite for no chaunce,
Bot shuld fro vertue til othere euer vp and vppere ascende,
And to satisfaccioune and gude werks als a man strongly entende.
For Loths wif, loking bakwards, was turnyd til a stone salyne
And diuerse beestis hire likkes, wittnissing Scripture Dyvyne.
So a man be resydiving hardyns in synne like a stone,
And infernale beestis hym likkes and to synne temptis hym ilkone.
The mountayne of vertuz to clymbe to be sauf rede I þerfore,
To be dampnyd be residiving, bakwardis beholding, no more.
O gude Jhesu, teche vs hevenly thinges so til ascende
Þat in thi seint mount with theself our dwelling be without eende.

3359 Figure j *mar.* 3360 Gen. xj *mar.* 3368 likely] i.e. in the like wise *o.i.e.l.* 3369 Figure ij Gen. xix° *mar.* 3383 Apocalips iij° *mar.* 3384 Ad Hebr. xiij° *mar.* 3389 murmure] i.e. gruchyng *over.* 3391 Figure iij Gen.xix° *mar.* 3399 resydiving] i.e. turnyng til forsaken synne *over.* 3400 Amen *mar.*

The Resurrection of Christ
Matt. xxviii

Samson carries away the gates of Gaza
Judges xvi 1-3

In the last chapitle herd we of manes redempcioune;
Nowe fylows of Jh*es*u Cristis gloriouse resurreccioune.
Cristis sepultur*e*, wit ȝe, is caved inwith a stone,
Like til a double chaumbre, w*ith*inne other*e* be thaym one.
A littel chaumbre men fynde first in the forthemast entring,
Caved in a stone above, and noght beneth erth ligging.
In lenght and als in brede oyther*e* halds about feet eght
And als a man may his hande reche vppe holdis the heght.
Be a dore fro this chaumbre to ane other*e*, bot littel lesse,
Þ*at* is to say als of heght, in lengthe and als of brodenesse
And fro man be the littel dore is entred the chaumbr*e* forsaide,
On the right half is the stede wher*e* Cristis swete body was laide,
The whilk is als it war*e* a fo*ur*me about the brede of thre fete,
And fro that one walle to þ*at* other*e* shalle men fynde the lengthe þ*er*of mete. [f.42^r]
The heght negh a fote and a halfe is fonden of the fo*ur*rme forsaide,
And noght holowgh, because þ*at* above & noght w*ith*inne it was the body laide.
This forme of the sepulcre onely of the pilgrimes has the name
Bot the Jewes alle the stone w*ith* the chaumbres calles the same.
The dore of the monument was stopped with a grete stone
The whilk Jewes w*ith* thair*e* seles both kept and m*er*kid anone,
And Our*e* Lorde graven, the Jewes selid the stone bisyly
Þ*at* the body ware noght stollen tofore the thredde day sothly;
And þ*er*to hyred knyghts payen to kepe surely the grave
According w*ith* thame of pris what mede ilkone shuld have;
Bot Crist, clos dore and seles and eke the stone hole about,
In his body glorified maugre his enemys went out;
And aungel in fo*ur*me of a man fro the heven after*e* descendid
And, onloking the kepers, the stone fro the dore tirvid,
Whas clothis whitte als the snawe, his face like foudr*e* shynyng,
The kepers lay als dede men ferefulle, the erthe trembling;
The whilk thair*e* strenghtis recou*er*ed and to the Jewes aft*er* weendyng
Told thaym the cas fallen to the eende fro begynnyng.
The Jewes toke thaym in counseil and gaf thaym mykel monee als
To publisse vnto the poeple a fame of Crist fulle fals,
To say þ*at* the body of Crist was stolne fro thayme sleping,
Whilk than the kepers and ȝit the Jewes er*e* aywhar*e* saying.
¶a And *nota* þ*at* Our*e* Lorde Crist his gloriouse resurexioune
P*re*figured lange tofore be alder-strongest Sampson.
Sampson in the citee of his enemys entrid
And in þ*at* ilk same nyght he dwelling thar*e*inne slepid.
Anone the ȝates of the citee closid his enemys fulle fast,
And in the morowtide arely thoght hym slee or he past.
Sampson roos vp fro sleepe at midnyght, noght biding day,
And the ȝates w*ith* the postis w*ith* hym bare he away.
So Crist his enemys citee entred strongely of helle
And to the midnyght of Sonday liked hym þ*er* for to dwelle.
The sawle to the body repayrid, helle spoillid, at the midnyght,
And so Crist, tofor dede, vpros be his almyght,
And mony bodis of the seintes w*ith* Crist vprose also,
And entering the city of Jerusalem, appeared to many.

3405 Ca^m xxxij^m *mar.* 3437 Math. xxviij^o *mar.* 3441 Fig*ure* j *mar.* 3444 he] *(2nd* e *subp. and can.)* 3447 Judic. xv *mar.* 3452 Of the resurexioune of bodys w*ith* Crist *mar.*

Jonas emerges from the fish
Jonas ii 1

The rejected stone becomes the corner-stone (key-stone)
Ps. cxvii 22 (Matt. xxi 42, I Peter ii 4-7)

It must not be thought that the bodies rose up at Easter only,
And þat day ware thaire graves oonely open and no moo.
Crist, the primogenit of the dede, rose tofore
And with hym mony a body of seint dede lesse & more,
The whilk ascendid with Crist, behynde he thaym noght left:
It nys noght to trowe thaym þat sais þat thay dyed eft.
¶b Also his resurexioune prefigured Crist be Jonas
Whilk in the whallis wombe thre dayes conserued was. [f.42v]
Jonas was in a shippe casten with tempest hoegely,
In whilk none othere hope was bot euery man for to dye.
Jonas the mariners badde cast hym into the see
And so alle the tempestis and perils cessid shuld be.
Wham when thay hadde casten out, anone a whalle hym swalowed,
And on the thredde day þerafter on the lande hym evomed.
Be the perilles of the see has this werld betaknyng,
In whilk mankynde perille tholid of deth euerlasting,
Wharefore Crist on the Crosse tholid to dye willfully
To qwite man fro thilk deth thorgh his ineffable mercy;
Bot the Fadere Godde kept hym fro alle corrupcioune
And ordeynd the thredde day after his gloriouse resurexioune.
¶c This resurexioune of Crist was be a stone fortouchid
Whilk was reprovid sometyme of thaym þat the Temple beldid.
The Jewes the Temple bigging in Kinges tyme Salomoune,
Hapned to be fonden a stone of merveillous condicioune.
The biggers myght fynde no stede covenable it in to lay,
Allethogh with grete bysynesse thay putte it oft til assay,
For oythere felle it ouer-lange or ouer-shorte hoegely,
Or ouer-thikke or ouer-brode, wondring ilk man thareby.
Thusgates the forsaide beelders, angring at it fulle sore,
Callid it be propre name "the reproved stone" tharfore.
The Temple eendid, a stone was to sett angulere
For to ioygne samne two wallis and eende the werk alle in feere;
Bot thare myght be fonden no stone þat wald be craft to þat stede falle,
Apon whilk thing the beelders merveld without mesure alle.
The stone whilk thay hadde reproved to þat place at the last thay broght,
And angulere alder-metest thai fonde it the werld to haf soght.
At whilk grete merveil ilkone ware the Temple beelders amayde,
And be it some grete thing to come betaknyng amange thaym was saide.
Crist was this reproved stone in tyme of his passioune,
Bot angulere of alle Holy Kirke in his gloriouse resurreccioune.
Than fulfillid was the prophecie of the grete prophete fulle clere:
"The stone whilk the biggers reproved in the heved is made angulere.
Of Oure Lorde is this thinge done and in oure eghen is it mirable."
And in the fest of Cristis rising is this prophecie festiuable–
In Gods Temple has this angulere two wallis ioynt sittingly,
For Crist of the payens & of the Jewes has made o Kyrke be his mercy,
And in this werke in stede of cyment our Lord Jhesu toke his haly blode
And his precyous body for stones, for oure luf hanged on the Rode.
O Jhesu, graunt vs of thi grace in thi Kyrke to lyf so swetely
Þat we discerve to dwelle without eend with the in thi Temple hevenly. [f.43r]

3461 Figure ij Jonas j° *mar.* 3475 Figure iij Lapidem quem reprobauerunt edificantes *mar.* 3478 evomed] i.e. kest out *over.* 3479 Maistere of Stories *mar.* 3498 festiuable] i.e. songen festiually *over.* 3504 Amen *mar.*

The Ascension
Mark xvi 19; Acts i 9-10

Jacob's Ladder
Gen. xxviii 10-16

Tofore herd 3*e* howe Crist fro deth ros myghtyly;
Heres nowe howe he ascendid til hevens admirably.
Crist rysing fro deth noght anone ascendid,
Bot dwellyng fourty dayes aft*er*, oftsith he hym ostendit.
The fourtith daye to his disciples Crist shewed hym openly,
And in thair*e* sight be a white cloude he p*er*ced heven maiestyfly,
And his deciples aft*er* hym stode towardis heven behalding;
So war*e* two aungels white cledde right than be thaym standing,
Whilk saide, "Ȝit to the dome thus shalle come Crist Jh*es*u
Als 3e see hym stegh vp til heven in grete vertue."
¶a This ascensioune of Crist was in a ledder*e* figured
Sometym to patriark Jacob in his slepe ostendid,
Of whilk one eende the erth, þ*at* other*e* the heven touching,
Hadde on it aungelik turmes nowe vppe, nowe doune clymbing.
So Crist descendid fro heven and ascendid a3ein thider*e*,
When hevenly thinges and erthly hym liked eft festyn togider*e*,
Whar*e*fore both Godde and man neded be the mediat*our*
Or of peece betwene thaym myght be no refo*ur*mo*ur*:
For Godde was hiest of alle and man lawest fulle even,
Whar*e*fore Crist ordeynd a leddir*e* betwyx erth and the heven
Be whilk aungels descendis nowe, grace til vs bringing,
Nowe reascende thai til heven*e*, our*e* sawles thider*e* restoryng.
Swilk a ledder*e* in this werld was neu*er* other*e* ther*e* tofore
Nor neu*er* sawle intil heven*e* myght ascend arst þ*er*fore.
Blissid be and alder-blissed this notablest ledder*e* of alle,
Be whilk is thus refo*ur*med our*e* hyest lange wikkedest falle.
¶b And this ascensioune til heven Crist in a p*ar*able techid
When he the folk of a shepe lost and a3ein fonden p*re*chid.
A man ane hundreth shepe hadde and for one of thaym lesyng
Soght it, the iiij^{xx} and xix in desert meentyme leving.
Whilk fonden, this gude man in alle his hert joyous
Laide it in his shuldres and broght it home til his hous,
And his freendis callid togider*e*, told thaym of his gladnesse,
And to reioie w*ith* hym als prayed thaym w*ith* bisynesse.
Be this man toforsaide is Our*e* Lorde Godde takenyd,
The whilk for mankynde hele to become man deynyd.
Ane hundreth shepe makes one and nyentene and four*e* score,
Be whilk vnderstand nyen ordres of aungels and men þ*er*fore.
O shepe p*er*ist no dout of this fair*e* company
When man, Gods maundement broken, disse*r*uyd deth eendlesly,
And Godde left ordres nyen of his aungels in heven,
And soght man lost in erth, this is trewe sothe fulle even.
He soght and labourde so sore 3eres here thre and thretty,
Whils swete blody ranne doune on alle his p*re*cious body. [f.43^{v}]
Loo nowe, O man, howe mykel Gods awen Son of the roght,
When he w*ith* swilk labo*ur* and so lange tyme the soght!
The fonden shepe on his shuldres laide he & broght to flokke
When on his bakke for our*e* synne of the Crosse he bare the stokke.
Loke, man, þ*at* noght onely Crist weryed hym the sekeing
Bot laboured als to the deth til heven the for to bring.

3505 Ca^{m} xxxiij^{m} *mar.* 3508 ostendit] i.e. shewed *o.i.e.l.* 3515 Figure j Gen. xxviij^{o} *mar.* 3518 turmes] i.e. companyes *over.* 3531 Figure ij Luc. xv *mar.* 3541 one] j *over*; nyentene] xix *over*; four*e*score] iiij^{xx} *over.* 3542 ordres] ix *over*; Inquirat*ur* *mar.*

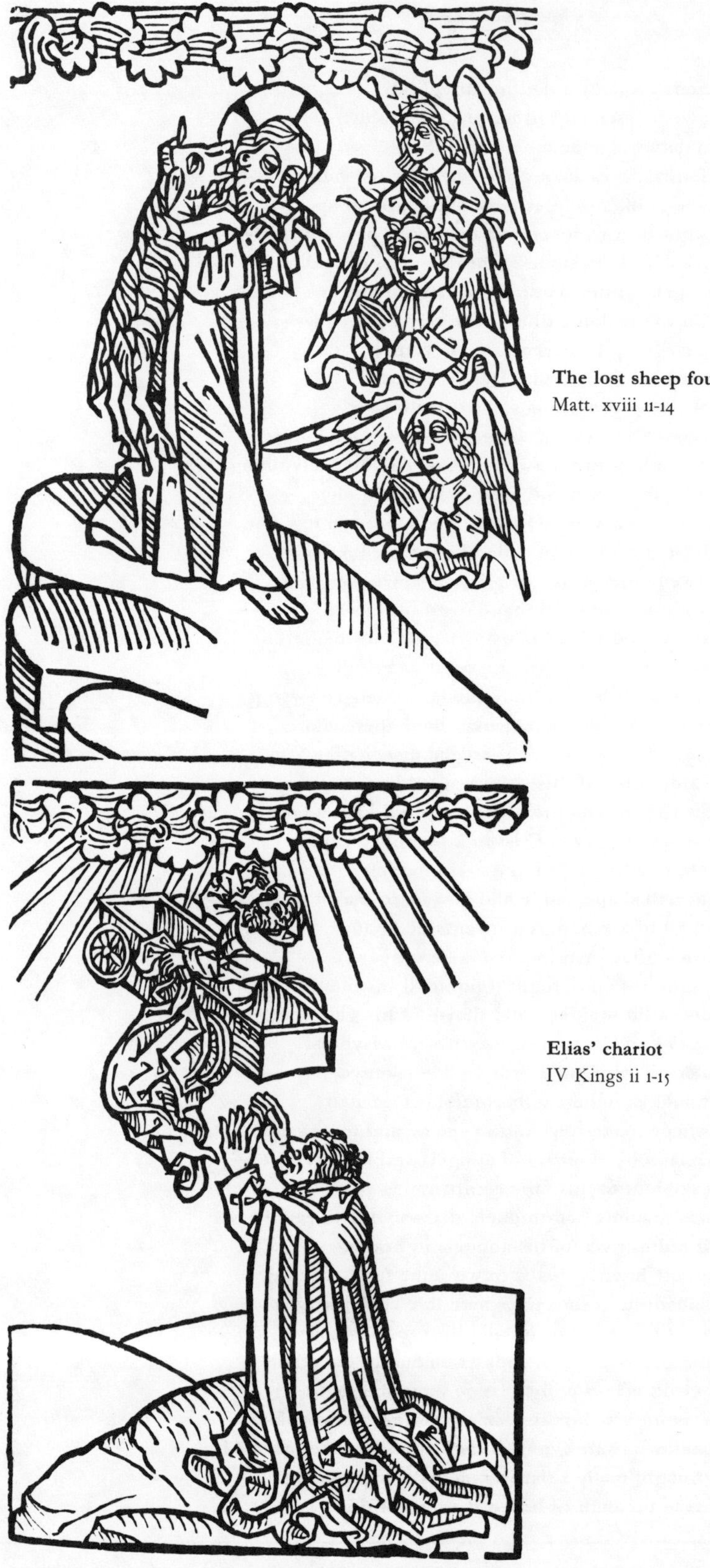

The lost sheep found
Matt. xviii 11-14

Elias' chariot
IV Kings ii 1-15

And for to be glade w*ith* hym his freendes excited he than,
Glading the court of heven when he stegh vp w*ith* man.
Whar*e*fore who wille plesaunce to the court of heven sende,
His awen and other*e* men*ne*s lyves studie he for til amende;
For teres of synners c*er*tein whilk er*e* contrite trewely
Er*e* wyne and ciser*e* to seintis and to Godde almyghty.
Pure shrift eke of synners and thair*e* devout praying
Er*e* harping to Godde and seintis and symbales fulle wele sownyng.
Brede delitable to Godde and til his seintis eke gif we
When*ne* we Gods maundements fille and his wille w*ith* hert free.
And als many mes to Godde and til haly seintis we p*ro*fer*e*
Als in diu*er*se gude werkis to thaym our*e* strenghthis we offer*e*.
The mes of Godde & his seints of spices has swete savo*ur*
When we be discrecioune vses our*e* gude labour*e*.
¶c Also the sacred forsaide of Crist ascensioune
Was sometyme prefig*ur*id in Helyes translac*iou*ne.
The p*ro*ph*e*te Helye p*re*chid the lawe of Godde in Judee,
And lawbrekers and ydolatrers w*ith* bolde visage blamed hee,
Whar*e*fore of the Jewes he tholid hoege p*er*secucioune,
Bot of Godde he desservid in p*ar*adys translacioune.
So Jh*es*u Crist in Judee the waye of sothfastnesse taght,
Þ*er*fore of the Jewes cruwelle mykel p*er*secucioune he raght;
Bot Godde has hym dignely rased vp above alle hevens,
And gyven hym a p*re*cious name ou*er* alle names þ*at* men nevens,
Þ*at* in the name of Jh*es*u alle man*er*e knee it bowe
And hym in the Faders joye be ilk tongue confesse nowe.
Lo, man, what mysese Crist for the tholid, and passioune,
Ar*e* he come til his sou*er*ayn hevenly exaltacio*u*ne.
Nowe brether*e*, if Crist most thole thus til entre vnto his blisse,
Mikelle more aght vs to thole gladly for heven ywisse.
Jh*esus* þ*at* neu*er* trespast, sustened grete passioune,
And we gruche for his regne a littel tribulacioune.
Littel thing, or als right noght, soeffre we here sothfastly
In regarde of the joye tyme to come eendlesly.
For als the leest watres drope is vnlike als to the see
So is alle erthly disese to ioye þ*at* eu*er* shalle be: [f.44^r]
Forto with poudre or w*ith* st*er*nes alle erthly joie multiply
War*e* absinthe als in regarde of alder-leest joye hevenly;
And if the welkyn and the werld war*e* turnyd to p*ar*chemyn white,
Men myght noght the leest joye of heven on it fulle write;
And thogh alle watres war*e* enke it shuld be thorgh wastid
Ar*e* be it the leest joye of heven war*e* descryvid;
And thogh trees, herbes and corns war*e* alle pennes swith writyng
Thai suffized noght of the leest blisse et*er*ne in descriving.
Thogh men and alle creat*ur*es war*e* p*re*chours w*ith* facounde
The beautee of Godde and hevenes thai myght neu*er* telle to the rounde;
And thogh \ilk/ poudre myght shyne thovzandefald ou*er* the sonne
Alle ware bot derknesse to lyght of Gods comparisoune.
O gude Jh*es*u, lede vs to thir*e* joyes wayes even,
Passing what hert may thenke or what al tonges may neven.

3557 No*ta* *mar.* 3569 Fig*ur*e iij iiij Reg. ij° *mar.* 3579 Philip. ij° *mar.* 3580 *a radiating heart inscribed* IHC M *under rub. mar.* 3601 ilk] it *subp.* 3604 Amen *mar.*

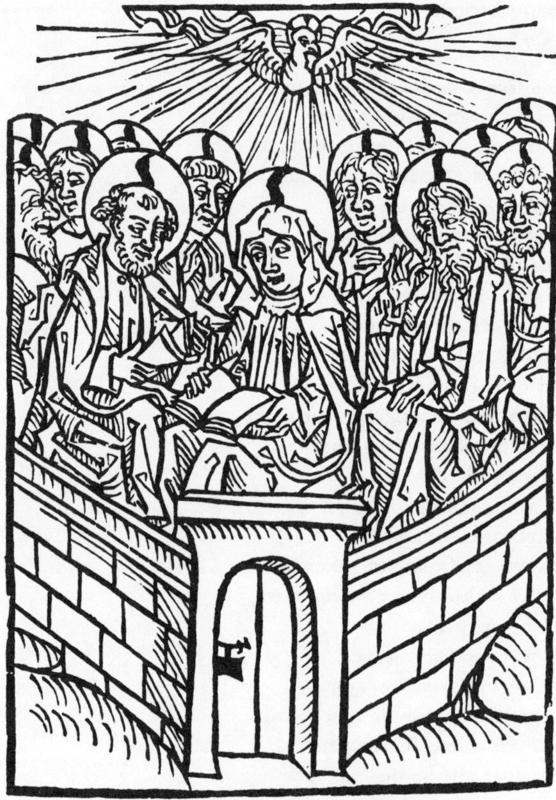

Pentecost
Acts ii 1-4

The tower of Babel
Gen. xi 1-9

O brether*e*, the chapitle tofore told of Crists ascending;
Nowe fylowys to the disciples the Haly Gastis sending.
When*ne* þ*at* the tyme come negh of Cristis harde passioune
He co*n*fortid his disciples w*ith* mony a swete s*er*moune.
His deth and his rysing told he thaym or he went,
His ascensioune and howe the Haly Gast shuld be sent.
"A littel am I w*ith* ȝowe and to the Fader*e* go I.
I shalle come aȝein to ȝowe, treuble noght ȝour*e* herts forthy.
I go to heven," q*uo*d he, "a stede for ȝowe to ordeyne,
And to take ȝowe to meself I shalle come eft aȝeyne.
Ȝe er*e* thay þ*at* have dwelt in my temptacio*u*nes w*ith* me,
Whar*e*fore w*ith* me in my regne both ete and drinke shalle ȝ*e*.
Dwellis in my luf, and I w*ith* ȝowe shalle than dwelle evre,
And thogh my manhode depart, my Godhede shalle ȝowe leve nevre.
Als a braunche beres no fruyt bot dwelling in the vigne-tree,
No more may ȝ*e* right so, bot ȝ*e* be dwellyng in me.
Ȝe er*e* the braunches c*er*tayne and I the vigne am verray;
If ȝe be dwelling in me fulle mykel fruyt bere ȝe may.
This wise er*e* ȝe braunches and I the verray vigne than,
And my Fader*e* of heven is vigno*ur* and eke tilman.
Ilk braunche þ*at* beres no fruyt he shalle kit of at the last
And in helle-fire to brenne et*er*nally it kast;
And þ*at* braunce þ*at* beres fruyte shalle he make clen\e/ þ*er*fore,
For to make it abounde in fruyt ay more & more.
The werld shalle make grete joye & ȝ*e* shalle hevynesse
Have, bot þ*at* shalle ȝowe turne til imprivable gladnesse.
A womman has hevynesse til hir*e* childyng be done
Bot, hir*e* childe borne, hir*e* sorowe has sho forgetyn sone. [f.44v]
So shalle ȝ*e* thole disese in this werld her*e* lyvyng
Whilk in joye for to come shalle renne to forgetyng.
Bot for I telle thir*e* thinges of my dep*ar*ting nowe
Has ȝour*e* hert hevynesse and gretely troebles ȝowe,
Bot my departing with ȝ*e* shalle be to ȝowe spedefulle
For an othere, P*ara*clit, I shalle send ȝowe nedefulle;
And the P*ara*clyt comes noght bot so be þ*at* I weende,
And if I goo, than shalle I doutles hym to ȝow sende,
And when he comes than shalle he teche ȝow alle sothfastnesse,
Of whas comfort shalle than ȝour*e* hert haf grete gladnesse.
For he shalle informe ȝowe c*er*teinly of alle thinge
And also to ȝowe a*n*no*u*nce the thinges þ*at* er*e* co*m*myng."
Be this and many other*e* wordis his disciples gladid he
And heght be hym the Haly Gast to thaym sent for to be;
And in Jer*usa*lem to dwelle bade he thaym, ascending,
Vnto tyme þ*at* Haly Gast come thaym of his sending.
So fro the mount of Olyvet alle thay the citee entrid
And in a littel hovs togider*e* in orisoune p*er*seu*er*id.
Aft*er*, on the Witsondaye thredde hovre, above thair*e* hovse
Was herde a voice of a wynde whilk was fulle hoegely sonovse,
So þ*at* thorgh alle the citee it was herde without faille,
And the poeple gadrid thider*e* to knawe of this m*er*vaille.

3605 {C}a^m {x}xxiiij^m *mar.*; O] *a face upside-down inside in different ink.* 3611 Joh. xiiij *mar.* 3622 Joh. xv *mar.* 3627 clene] clens (s *subp.*). 3629 Joh. xvj *mar.* 3637 Joh. xiiij *mar.* 3654 m*er*vaille] (? e *alt.* a).

Moses receives the Law
Ex. xx 1-17

The widow's cruse of oil
IV Kings iv 2-7

Thay se als a tonge of fyre ou*er* thair*e* hevedes ilkone sere,
Þ*at* was a flavme of fyre whilk lengthe of a tonge bere.
The Jewes þ*at* tyme hadde bene thorgh the werlde in disp*er*sioune
And war*e* thar*e* than, Godde wolde, some of ilk regioune:
Alle thas herde the disciples diu*er*se langeges speking
Als the Haly Gast to speke gaf thaym be his styring.
Ilk one of thaym herde tonges of landis whar*e* thai war*e* borne,
And m*er*veillid in hoege stupo*ur* in thir*e* thinges alle þ*er*forne.
Some of this evident miracle war*e* wroth and alle sory,
And saide þ*at* thai war*e* dronken and fulle of must hardily.
Bot Peter*e* answerde and saide þ*at* thay war*e* ȝit alle fasting,
For it was bot Tierce of the daye, ou*er*-ayrly than for drynking,
And saide more þ*at* that tyme thilk p*ro*phecie was complete
Whilk the Haly Gast sometyme spak be Joel p*ro*phete:
Þ*at* s*er*uants and ancilles of Godde shuld resceve the Spirit Haly,
And diu*er*se tonges als p*ro*ph*et*es speke even forth openly.
And this p*ro*ph*ec*ie þ*at* day was fulfillid, for wymmen
Spak ther*e* diu*er*se langegages in same wise als did men.
Loo, Godde of m*er*veilles his myght shewed þ*at* tyme m*er*veilly,
Als eu*er*y man may considre loking his werkis bisyly.
¶a At the tour*e* of Babel in mony sometymes was changed a tonge [f.45r]
And ȝonder*e* til eu*er*y man of alle was knawyng gyven, olde and ȝonge.
And howe myght Our*e* Lorde Godde þ*at* tyme this myracle haf forth laide
Bot he tofore hadde devidid o tonge in diu*er*se forsaide?
Whar*e*of diu*er*se tonges thus formade gyves resoune
Þ*at* of this miracle to do þ*at* was p*re*figuracioune;
And als he the biggers confusid than of the to*ur* of Babel
So confusid he be tonges nowe his enemys of Israel.
The Jewes, ȝ*e* may wele witt, war*e* confused hoegely
When thay thus strange a miracle herde and see openly.
¶b The fest whilk our*e* Kyrke nowe worships on Witsononday
Hono*ur*ed in figure sometyme the Synagoge be grete noblay.
The fiftithe day aft*er* the Jewes out of Egipt war*e* passid,
Ten co*m*mandementz thay of Godde in Mount Synay rescevid.
Right so the fiftith day aft*er* man was delyvrid fro helle
The disciples receyved grace of the Gast þ*at* on thaym felle.
Thus alle thing about the Jewes war*e* forwith done in liknesse,
The whilk we Cristen men nowe has receyved in sothfastnesse.
¶c Als was this thing figured be the oyle habounding
Gyven to the pore wydowe, be p*ro*ph*et*e Helise p*ra*ying.
Helisei apon this wydowe (moved be fulle grete m*er*cy)
Praying, gat hir*e* of Godde oyle habound*au*nt hoegely.
This wydowe hadde noght bot a littel of oyle whilk m*er*veillously grewe
To-whils sho hadde ony vesselle to resceyve it, olde or newe.
This wydowe of Haly Kyrke bare figure in sothfastnesse,
Whilk, hir*e* spouse Crist berefte, was wydowe in liklynesse,
To whayme haboundance of oyle Crist gaf of his clemence
Grace of the Haly Gast and eke of tonges intelligence.
O gude Jh*es*u, gif vs this oyle haboundantly
Þ*at* in our*e* passing we mowe haf thy grace and m*er*cy.

3655 thaire] i.e. of disciples *over*. 3658 regioune] religioune (-li- *erased*). 3659 Act. ij *mar*. 3667 Joel iij° *mar*. 3671 No*ta* *mar*. 3675 Figure j *mar*. 3676 Gen. xj° *mar*. 3678 Ba\b/el *mar*. 3679 resoune] i.e. significacioune *over*. 3685 Fig*ure* ij *mar*. 3688 Exodi xxvj *mar*. 3690 Gast] i.e. the Haly Gast *over*. 3693 Fig*ure* iij *mar*. 3698 Regum xvij *mar*. 3701 clemence] i.e. benignitee *over*.

The Virgin visits the places Jesus knew
Voragine IV 234

Tobias' mother laments her son's absence
Tob. v 23, x 4-7

The chapitle tofore tolde vs of the Haly Gastis sending;
Nowe forwarde like ȝow to here of Maryes blissid conu*er*syng.
After Cristis ascending was sho in Jer*usal*em dwelling
Swetly stedes of hir*e* son whar*e* sho myght wynne visityng.
Ilkon sho kissid mekely for of luf grettest swetnesse,
W*ith* many a devout knelyng and p*ra*yer*e* of hir*e* sawles excesse.
Oftsith thas places wette sho w*ith* many teres doune rynnyng,
Hir*e* dere son melliflwe p*re*sence piely tille hir*e* mynde bryngyng.
In Nazareth wold sho visit the stede of his concepcioune,
Also the place in Bethlem of his byrth and adoracioune,
In the mount of Thabor the stede of his t*ra*nsfiguraci*ou*ne,
In Jer*usal*em of his contumelies and the place of his passioune,
And in the Mount Syon eke whare he wesshe his disciples feet,
And whare he alder-first ordeynd the sacrament of his body swete,
The toune of Gethsemany, the gardyn whar*e* he blode swette,
Whar*e* Judas and his companye toke Jh*es*u when he thaym mette, [f.45v]
The hovse of Anna to whilk he was first p*re*sentid
Whar*e* of the s*er*uant a buffett and many accusings he suffrid,
Cayphas hovse whare thay hym bespittid & his eghen hidde,
Beiapid, buffetid and bett and in the nekke collaph[i]zidde,
Herodes hovse whare he was cledde for verray scorn alle in white,
And of þ*at* king and hys ost beiaped alle for dispite,
Pilats mot-halle whare he was accusid falsestly,
Sc*our*gid, bette and corowned w*ith* thornes sharpe pynously,
The stede of Gabatha whilk als Litostratos be name hatte
Whar*e* Pilat dampned Our*e* Lorde Crist when for tribunal þ*er* satte.
Oft went this swettest virgyne weping sore in the way
Be whilk Crist bering the Crosse was ledde to deth o day:
The mount of Caluarie whilk men named Golgatha withalle,
Whare crucified thay Crist, bedde to drink ayselle and galle,
The ȝarde whar*e* he was graven of Joseph of Aramathie,
The mount of Olyvet whare he stegh to heven openly,
The Temple and other*e* places whar*e* he lerned folk p*re*ching
And stedes whar*e* he appered oft aft*er* his gloriouse rysing.
Thir*e* and many other*e* places soght sho w*ith* many a tere,
For hir*e* sons absence sho ne myght w*ith*out grete compleint bere.
To condole and for to geme, more than to make ioye, levre
Hadde sho, hir*e* son absent, hadde it bene so lange nevre.
¶a This trewest sorowe and this doel of this swete virgyne Marie
Was sometyme p*re*figured be Anne, wif of Thoby,
Whilk wept and made evre doel for hir*e* sons dep*ar*tyng,
Þ*at* neu*er* thing myght hir*e* glade tofore his ret*our*nyng.
Alle wayes loked sho oftsithe als he shuld come, tovne & feelde,
And diu*er*s mountaynes clymbing, oft thiderwards sho behelde.
Hir*e* sons p*re*sence, sayde sho, til hir*e* passid hoege rychesse
And hym p*re*sent at the fulle suffized it hir*e* porenesse.
Thus Marie virgyne alwaie dwelt in doele and gemyng,
Alle the wayes of hir*e* son, als sho myght, visitting.
Hir*e* sons p*re*sence ou*er* alle richesse hadde sho reknyd:
Hir*e* povert, and hym p*re*sent, a revme of revmes co*u*ntyd.

3705 Ca^{m} {x}xxv^{m} *mar.* 3707 The pillerimage of Our*e* Ladye *over.* 3713 *an omitted link-line upsets the rest on f.45r.* 3714 adoracioune] i.e. be the kinges & shephirds *over.* 3716 contumelies] i.e. whare vylenyes ware done hym *over.* 3728 corownid] (? v *alt.* w). 3743 Fig*ur*e j Anne wif of Thoby *mar.* 3747 sithe] *followed by erasure.*

The tenth drachma is lost
Luke xv 8-9

Michol is married against her will
Comestor 1327; I Kings xxv 44, II Kings iii 15-16 (cf. vi 23)

¶b And in the gospelle is noted also this doele of Marie
Of a dra*m*me be a womman soght, tellyng Crist openly,
Whilk womman hadde ten dra*m*mes of whilk for sho lost oone
Bysily sho soght hir*e* hovse, a lant*er*ne lighte vp anone.
This dra*m*me fonden vp, was sho noght littelle gladde & myrye,
And hir*e* neghburghes p*ra*yed sho to bere hir*e* companye.
Be this womman Marie noght causeles liknes men,
Þ*at* in this werld lyving sho hadde drammes also ten, [f.46r]
Off whilk one semed hir*e* be some resoune lesing,
And alle thas ix re*m*naunt alwaye til hir*e* dwelling.
The ix dra*m*mes war*e* p*re*sence of diu*er*s spirits hevenly,
Of ordres ix aungelik whilk visit alwaye Marie.
The p*re*sence of Crist manhode the tenth was be resoune,
Whilk sho lost in manere at his ascensioune.
This diu*er*s ȝeres c*er*tayne soght sho fulle bysily
When sho the places of hir*e* son forsaide soght so drery.
Bot at the last sho fonde it in hir*e* assumpcioune
When sho was dowyd w*ith* eterne Cristis fruyc*i*oune.
A lant*er*ne lightid sho also at hir*e* dere son sekeing,
Shewing the seint ensaumple of hir*e* swete conu*er*syng,
Whilk als a clere lant*er*ne brent in alle v*er*tues playnly,
Ensaumpling til alle gude folk for to lyf vertuously.
The forsaide stedes eght vs to visit in luf fulle depe,
And Cristis passioune, like hire, hertly compleyn and wepe,
And who þ*at* may noght wele come to visit thaym corporaly
Lik thaym the wantyng fulfille w*ith* gude hert spirituelly.
¶c Also the doel and mo*ur*nyng of Marie nowe fortouchid
Was in Michol the spouse of Dauid King figurid,
Whaym fro hir*e* husband bereft Saul, hir*e* fader*e* cruwelle,
And til an other*e* man hir*e* weddid, þ*at* heght be name Falthiel.
Þ*at* rightwise man Falthiel walde noght this Michol knawe,
Witting wele þ*at* sho was the wif of Dauid be lawe.
This Michol was eu*er* trewly in grete doel and wepande
To-whils sho was broght aȝeine til Dauid, hir*e* awen husbande.
This may be wele expovned of the blissed virgyne Marie,
To whaym Crist Godde Son was spouse and alle hir*e* joye sou*er*eynly,
In whas absence alwaye sho brent in swilk langour*e*
Þ*at* eu*er* sho contynuyd in weping and in meroure.
So feruent ard*our* and luf hadde Marie hir*e* spouse vnto
Þ*at* neu*er* other*e* wymmen alle langvist so sore als sho.
Forthi the boke of Sanges makes of Marie menyng,
The feruo*ur*, ard*our* and luf of hir*e* desir*e* thus shewing:
"Doghters of Je*rusal*em, telles to my luf bisily
I langvisse for luf of hym, body and hert alle holely."
Mikelle doel es to the moder*e* of hir*e* dere sons absence,
Bot mykel more of the spouse wantyng hir*e* spousis p*re*sence.
Than Maries doele alther-most p*ro*ues to be open resoune,
Absent God Son of heven, both til hir*e* spouse & dere so*un*.
O gude Jh*es*u, make vs so thenk on alle this thing
Þ*at* w*ith* ȝowe both eendlesly in joye be our*e* dwelling. [f.46v]

3755 Fig*ure* ij Luc. xv *mar.* 3763 Of the dra*m*me lorne *mar.* 3767 manhode] (d *alt.* h). 3779 no*ta mar.* 3781 Fig*ure* iij *mar.* 3783 j Regum vj^{o} *mar.* 3795 Cantic. v^{o} *mar.* 3804 Amen *under rub. mar.*

The Virgin enthroned after her assumption
Voragine iv 234-47

The Ark before which David harped
II Kings vi 1-15

Off Marie herde ȝe tofore the conu*er*sacioune;
Nowe fyllowes it for to here hir*e* gloriouse assumpcioune.
Howe lange Marie ou*er*lyved hir*e* sons ascensioune
Hase no clerke left c*er*teine det*er*minacioune.
Some says twelfe ȝere, some more, als bokes enfo*ur*mes vs,
Bot twenty and four*e* ȝeres telles Seint Epiphani*us*.
And thogh the c*er*tayne hereof als ȝit det*er*mynde be noght,
We may say for c*er*teyne, and holde sothly in thoght,
Þ*at* if sho hadde bot one houre lyved aft*er* hir*e* dere son here,
Til hir*e* sou*er*ayne desire hadde it semed fulle fyve ȝere.
Jacob ȝeres fourteen of seruytute and distresse
Acco*m*pted bot dayes fe\e/we, of his luf for gretenesse.
So Marie of hir*e* dere son one houre hym absentyng
For hoege lango*ur* in luf hadde holden a lange dwelling.
For til a sawle disirrouse lange is a short tyme thoght,
And for thing ȝerned labours, whateu*er* thay be, dredes noght.
Aft*er* hir*e* swete sons p*re*sence was Maries hert so brennyng
Þ*at* alle labo*urs* of this lif sett sho att right nothing.
That in this werlde Godde suffred dwelle so lange Our*e* Ladye
Was for luf and comfort of his disciples sothlye,
And þ*at* ilk man þ*er*by may p*er*ceve p*er* resoune
The way til heven stends it be many tribulacioune.
Loke Our*e* Ladye, loke eke hir*e* son: no littel while
His labo*urs*, his passioune and of his moder*e* the exile;
Loke his apostles and loke his other*e* freendes alle so dere,
Loke thair*e* treuble and disese for Crists luf suffred here,
The Baptist, amange wyves sons ou*er* whaym had risen none more.
Thir*e* thinges remembred, aght the bere disese light*er* þ*er*fore,
And hope noght w*ith*\oute/ disese for to come to corovne,
Gods moder*e* suffring so lange exile and tribulacioune.
Wharefor, aft*er* lange exile and mysese tholid, Marie
Was assumpt \til/ hir*e* dere so*un* w*ith* hym to dwelle eendlesly,
¶a And this assumpcioune of Marie was sometyme figurid
When in the Kyng Dauid house Gods Arc was translatid.
Dauid harped and daunced tofore thilk Archa Domini,
And til his hovse he broght it w*ith* alle his myght festivaly.
In this Arche wyrshipfully was hevenly manna closyd,
And be it accordantly is virgyne Marie taknyd,
For sho broght to this werlde hevenysh brede verrayly:
Crist w*ith* his seint sacrament þ*at* fedes vs m*er*cyfully.
Of sethym wodde imputrible was Archa Dom*ini* made,
Takenyng þ*at* Marie virgyne neu*er* into rotyng ne slade,
For thogh Haly Writte telle noght we may trowe sekerly
Our*e* Ladye assumpte til heven body and sawle entierly. [f.47^r]
We ne shalle trowe in no wyse þ*at* Marie ne soeffred dying,
Bot hir*e* flesshe dede tholid neu*er* ony man*ere* corrupting.
The sawle to the body was joynt eftsones, this is soth even,
And w*ith* the body glorified assumpt right so til heven.
King Dauid tofore Gods Arche þ*at* daunced and harped
Crist, King of heven and of erth, sothly p*re*figured.

3805 Ca^m xxxvj^m *mar.* 3806 Of O*ur* Ladyes being in erth aft*er* hire sons ascensio*u*ne *mar.* 3815 Figure j Gen. xxix *mar.* 3822 Be t*ri*bulaciones comen men to ioye *mar.* 3825 Apocal. iij^o I thas þ*at* I luf I chasty *mar.* 3827 Deut*er*ono*mii* xxxiij the t*ri*bulaciones of Marie *mar.* 3831 Math. v^o blissed thas þ*at* soeffre p*er*secuc*io*une *mar.* 3833 withoute] *(*-oute *in different ink.)* 3836 til] of *subp.* 3837 Archa d*o*mini *mar.* 3840 ij Reg. vj *mar.* 3850 Our*e* Ladye was assumpt body and sawle *mar.*

The woman clothed in the sun
Apoc. xii 1, 14

Solomon places his mother by him
III Kings ii 19-20

It is to trowe þ*at* gude Crist his mode*re* mette p*er*sonely
And til his hovse w*ith* grete joye broght hi*re* festivaly,
And his dyvine kyssinges felt his mode*re* and his spouse,
His hevenly zucrys halsinges ineffable and gloriouse.
The aung*e*les w*ith*outen mese*ur* thi*re* thinges musyd seyng
And askid many one of othe*re*, "Who is this, the farest thyng
Ascending out of desert in delyce affluaunt,
Lenyng on hi*re* awen luf als a swete spouse glozaunt?"
And than answard Marie the spouse of God Son verraye,
"I haf fonde whame I soght; hym þ*at* my sawle luved aye,
Hym shalle I halde plesing, for hym shalle I leve nevre
Als fade*re*, als son, als spouse, alle my joy nowe and evre.
W*ith* o cusse of his mowthe like my Lorde to kisse me,
Of whilk the dyvine dulco*ure* in me eu*er*lasting be.
Vnde*re* myne heved softly mot he lay his left hande,
Þ*at* I be eu*er*more w*ith* hym in joye and gladnesse lyvande.
His right hande shalle me embrace so fast, fast and trewly,
Þ*at* he ne shalle neu*er* me putte fro hym fulle seure am I."
¶b Also this assumpcioune of Ou*re* Ladye Marie
Was shewed vnto Seint John in the ile of Pathmos say I,
In heven pierd, als he says, a signe grete and notable,
A womman fairest of alle til alle werlds admirable.
This wo*m*man was alle about closid in a sonnysshe clothing,
For Marie w*ith* the deitee was alle bewrapt ascending.
Vnde*re* hi*re* feete was the mone \sene/ whilk betaknyd wele
The stedfastist stablenesse of Marie p*er*petuele.
The mone lastis neu*er* in oone, in fulnesse nor wastyng,
Taknyng this werlde chaungeable and alle othe*re* erthly thing
Whilk Marie vnde*re* hi*re* feete trade doune ilkone alway,
Vnchaungeable hevenly thinges \thrustyng/ evre nyght and day.
Als hadde this womman on heved a fulle bright p*re*ciouse corovne
Whilk twyse sex sterris lusa*u*nt contyned about in virone.
A corovne custumably of hono*ur* halden is a signe,
Taknyng this gloriouse virgyne til hono*ur* of qwenehode condigne.
Twelve sterres apostles twelve taknyd, and resonably,
Whilk at hi*re* joyfulle decesse wa*re* p*re*sent, men trewe, mekely. [f.47^v]
To this womman wa*re* gyven two wenges als for fleghyng,
Whilk notes both body and sawle of Marie the vptaking.
¶c Also this virgynes feest of hi*re* assumpcioune
Was figurid in the mode*re* of riche King Salomo*u*ne.
He made hym a throne of glorie for to be in sittande,
Ane othe*re* throne for his mode*re* to sit on his right hande,
In whilk he hi*re* made sitte besyde hymselfe hono*ur*ablye,
And sayde it was noght levefulle anything til hi*re* denye.
So Crist on his right hande has sette his mode*re* hyeghly,
And whateu*er* sho wille aske grauntis he hi*re* favo*ur*ably.
Pray thi dere son take vs, O mode*re* Marie virgyne,
Til hymselfe aft*er* exile of this werlde fulle of pyne.
O gude Jh*es*u, here thowe thi mode*re* for vs praying
And graunt vs eendlesly w*ith* ȝowe both ou*re* dwelling.

3865 Cantic. j *mar.* 3873 Fig*ure* ij *mar.* 3874 John] *?* Joh*an)* ewang. *over.* 3875 Apocal. xij° *mar.* 3879 sene] (videbatur L) *in different ink*; whilk] *followed by* whilk *subp. and can.* 3884 thrustyng] *hand², in a gap with* dub*iu*m *mar.* 3891 ware] was *alt., or vice versa.* 3893 Fig*ure* iij *mar.* 3903 corr. *mar.*

SS Dominic and Francis see the Virgin appease God
Voragine IV 179

Abigael appeases David
I Kings xxv 2-35

Nowe last of th\e/ assumpcioune herde we of Our*e* Ladye;
Howe sho our*e* mediatrice is heres nowe ententifly:
Howe sho the ire of hir*e* son ageynst this werlde makes softe,
And synners be hir*e* praying recounseilles vnto Godde ofte.
This werlde thorghout is sette to wikkednesse and errour*e*
And nothing condignely to worship the Creatour*e*.
Charitee and sothfastnesse stands aywher*e* nowe wakely,
Pride, auarice and lux*ur*e beres vp thair*e* heve[d]s boldly.
W*ith* thir*e* thre vices the werlde is filled thorghout w*ith*inne;
Fulle fewe may thaym excuse in none of thir*e* to synne.
Some, keping chastitee, flees to be leccherous,
And lettis noght to fyle thayme w*ith* covitise auerous.
Some flees this auarice, chesing wilfulle povert,
And neu*er* the lesse wille fyle thaym in vayne p*ri*de of thair*e* hert.
Some flees for to be proude, mekenesse of hert keping,
Bot thay synne be luxuree or elles myscoveyting.
And leccherie thogh þ*at* some als in dede vses noght,
ȝit err*e* thay luxuryouse in fowle words or in thoght.
Thay wille be chaste and neu*er* the lesse of filthes flesshely confable,
And in hering and sight flesshely be delicable.
Also some shewes no pride als outwards in thair*e* arraye,
And neu*er* the lesse of vayne p*ri*s inwards grete lust haf thaye;
And some blames auarice and takes thaym to pooretee
Whilk ȝernes many thinges & haves ou*er* thair*e* necessitee.
Some wille be so pure men þ*at* thai ne haf no failling,
Some wille also be meke bot w*ith*out despisyng.
Than pride, luxurie, thir*e* two, and thair*e* thredde auarice,
May be p*ro*ved verrayly rote til alle man*er*e vice: [f.48r]
The aungelle felle out of heven, man put fro p*ar*adys,
Nabugodonosor fro his rewme of pryde for wrongwis empris.
For auarice [Achan] and Naboth war*e* stonyd and lost thair*e* lif,
And Ananye died sodaigne deth and Saphira eke his wif.
For luxuree negh alle this werld drovned wat*er* in Gods ire,
Sodome and Gomore to helle sanke thorgh bronstone and fyre.
Be thir*e* thre thinges is Godde wroth to this werlde ilk day,
Bot Marie softnys his ire, als our*e* best mediatrice ay.
Ane avisioune p*ro*ves this of olde tyme autentyke,
Shewed be Gods ordenance to the holy man Seint Domynyke.
He se Crist fro the heven, his right hande vp liftyng
Thre speres ageynst this werld and w*ith* wroth chere shakyng,
Bot Our*e* Lady Marie als mediatrice come nere
And softned hir*e* dere sons ire w*ith* hir*e* succ*ur*able prayere,
Offring til his p*re*sence two champyons fulle doghty
For to convert synners whilk to the werld shuld thaym hy.
Seint Domynyk was þ*at* oone, fader*e* of alle Freres P*re*chour*s*,
Þ*at* other*e* was Seint Fraunceys, pat*ri*ne of Fre*res* Menour*s*.
Be thys shewed Godde this werld to be til it p*ro*pice,
Be the vnwithsayable p*ra*yer*e* of Marie our*e* mediatrice.
¶a And þ*at* this gloriouse virgyne shuld our*e* mediatrice be
Was shewed lange tyme tofore be fulle fair*e* fig*ur*es thre.

3906 Ca^m xxxvij^m *mar.* 3912 heveds] heves. 3921 No*ta* *mar.* 3931 Howe noyous err*e* thre synnes w*ith* thair*e* volence *mar.* 3933 Ysay xiiij° Luc.x° Genes. iij° *mar.* 3934 Daniel iiij° *mar.* 3935 Josue vij° | iij Reg. xxj° *mar.*; Achan] Achior. 3936 Actum ap*osto*lor*um* v^to *mar.* 3937 Gen. vij° *mar.* 3938 Gen. xix° *mar.* 3941 A tale *mar.* 3948 synners] (-rs *o.er.*) 3951 thys] (a *alt.* y), i.e. avisioune *over*; p*ro*pice] i.e. merciable *over*. 3953 Figure j *mar.*

The woman of Thecua reconciles David to Absolom
II Kings xiii-xiv 21

The woman of Abela throws Seba's head to Joab
II Kings xx

First be fonde Nabals wif, the jentyle Abigael,
Whilk pesid the king Dauid, co*m*myng w*ith* hir*e* camel.
This angry nyce foole Nabal be sturdynesse and folye
Made to hym Kyng Dauid his vnmesurable enemy.
Als "Of alle folys the so*u*me be noumbre no man it kan,"
Menyng of werdly synners, thus says vs the wisman.
For what thing, reso*u*ne the juge, is fonden gretter*e* folye
Than for a vile passing synne selle ioye eu*er*lastyngly?
Neu*er* the lesse thus in this werld dos many foole synnfulle shrewe,
And thir*e* dayes er*e* fonden of thas, more harme is, noght a few;
Err*e* thay noght folis and more and alther-most wriches at alle
Whilk to thayr*e* almyghti Godde p*re*sumes for to gaynecalle?
The p*ro*ph*et*e says, "Waa til alle thas whilk wille þ*er* maker*e* gaynsay:
A pot-sharde of the slyme of the erth, þ*at* is to say vnthrefty clay."
Foly ware to swilk sharde to countresay the potter*e*,
Bot alther*e*-grettest folys er*e* thay whilk wrethis Godde thair*e* maker*e*.
And swilk folys our*e* verray Dauid in his ire wald slee verrayly,
Ne war*e* his wreth oftsith amesid be our*e* Abigail, virgyne Marie.
¶b And the wyse womman Thecuytes sometyme p*re*figu*re*d this thing,
Absolon whilk slewe his brother*e* til his fader*e* recounseilling. [f.48^v]
Be this ilk Absolon, his awen brother*e* sleer*e*,
Shalle we vnderstand als here ilk voluntary synner*e*.
For he a fratricide is calde þ*at* synnes in Godde baldelye,
For he enforces Crist his brother*e* èftsones to crucifye.
Fro Absolon toke on boldnesse to slee his brother*e* c*ru*welly,
W*ith*in the lande of beheste dwelt he neu*er* aft*er* forthy.
In Gessur*e*, a payens lande, aft*er* þ*at* he dwellyd,
Til the womman Tecuytes hym w*ith* his fader*e* accordid.
So of a synne dedely a man aft*er* p*er*petracioune:
Fro than has he no dwellyng in lande of p*ro*missioune
Tofore be the womman Thevcuytes he be to Godde recounseild,
Þ*at* is our*e* mediatrice Marie, Gods moder*e* and mayden myld.
¶c Also was fortakned Marie our*e* mediatrice
Sometymes in Abela be a womman fulle wise.
Aȝeins King Dauid ros on the son of Botrus, Syba,
And to make his lord werre entred in Abela,
Wharefore the p*ri*nce Joab asseiged þ*at* citee sone,
And because of Syba he wold haf it vndone.
So felle a wise womman dwelt than in þ*at* citee
Whilk turned the prince ire to pece thorgh hir*e* tretee,
Be whas counsaile the tovne the heved of Syba of kitte
And it kest to Joab, the tovne rescowed and qwitte.
Syba betaknes pride rysing ageins Godde King,
In the citee of Abela–the sawle of a synner*e*–entryng.
The Prince of the chyvalrye of heven has dedeigne to this citee
To-whils the wise womman Marie of the citee mediatrice wold be,
Be whas rede we shalle the heved of kitte of Syba, þ*at* is, of pride,
And of the Prince of heven, Crist, in grace alway abide.
O gude Jh*es*u, teche vs vices so to werraye
Þ*at* aft*er* this lif w*ith* the we come to joye for aye.

3955 iij Regu*m* xxv° *mar.* 3956 Abigael *mar.* 3967 Ys. xlv° *mar.* 3971 Dauid] i.e. Crist *over.* 3973 Thecuytes] i.e. of swilk a citee *over*; Figure ij *mar.* 3974 ij Reg. xiiij° Absolon *mar.* 3977 fratricide] i.e. a brother*e* sleere*e over.* 3980 beheste] i.e. of p*ro*missioune *over.* 3981 Gessur*e mar.* 3983 p*er*petracioune] i.e. fro a man haf synnyd dedely *over.* 3985 recounseild] *(-d o.er.)* 3987 Fig*u*re iij *mar.* 3988 Abela] i.e.a citee *over.* 4000 citee] i.e. of the sawle *over.* 4003 corr. *mar.* 4004 Amen *under rub. mar.*

The Virgin as protectress
Caesarius of Heisterbach II 79-80

Tharbis defends Saba against Moses
Josephus ii 10, Comestor 1144

Herde howe virgine Marie is our*e* swete mediatrice;
Nowe fylowes it how sho is our*e* blissed deffensatrice,
Sauvyng fro Gods vengeaunce and indignacioune,
Fro assauts of the feend and werldis temptacioune.
¶a Marie hils vs when we er*e* in tribulacioune,
Als in Moises and Tharbis this hadd p*re*figuracioune.
Moises w*ith* Egipciens sieges Saba the grete tovne
So sore þ*at* no man myght louse his obsidioune.
Tharbis, the kynges doght*er*, dwelt than in þ*at* citee
And made the siege forsaide thus broken vp for to be.
Moises fair*e* and gudely was, and ȝonge man and bolde,
Whaym the kynges doght*er* forsaide wold of the walles oft beholde, [f.49^{r}]
And in so mykel payed hyr*e* of Moises the fairnesse
Þ*at* hym til haf husband sho didde alle hir*e* bisynesse.
At the last told sho hir*e* fader*e* hir*e* desire openly,
Howe sho luved of þ*at* ost Moises the prince worthy.
It plesid right wele the king þ*at* this mariage shuld be
And gaf his doght*er* to Moises w*ith* Saba the citee.
Thus was Saba delyvred be help of the ilk womman,
And the citezeins rescowed out of thair*e* disese than.
Our*e* Lord Godde is betaknyd be Moises fair*e* and formouse,
Als tofore alle man sons of fo*ur*me most spec*i*ous.
Ageins this werld was this p*ri*nce to grete ire excitid
Be our*e* forme-fader*e* and moder*e* whilk to hym hoegely mysdid.
Whar*e*fore w*ith* the ost of Egipt, þ*at* is of feends, he sieged vs
Passing fyve thovzande ȝere, the bokes enfo*ur*rmes vs thus.
In alle the werld was noght fonden any man þ*at* myght be reso*u*ne
Pees this grete ire of Godde and louse this obsidioune,
To-whils the doghter*e* of a kinge luved hym, virgine Marie
Whilk be hir*e* graciouse p*ra*yer*e* peesid þ*at* Lords ire swetely.
Marie eke deffendid vs fro the feends temptacio*u*nes,
Fro alle sleghtis infernale and thair*e* inpugnacio*u*nes.
Gretely nedefulle til vs is this deffensatrice
For thassautis of the feende er*e* many, dyvers and nyce.
For some man wille he inpugne be p*ri*defulle bolnyng right ȝerne,
Als shewed in qwene Jezabelle, Balthazar*e* and Holoferne.
Some be hatred, and other*e* of envie, chokes he fulle,
Als Kaym, als Jacob sons pat*ri*arche and King Saull.
Some eke \of/ vengeaunce temptis he als shewed in Semey
In Absolon, John and Jacob the sons of Zebedei.
Be vntrest and incredulitee he dos so*m*me grete disese,
Als shewed in Achab, Achaz, Jeroboam and Moises.
Be irreverence and rebelling and be inobedience vses he
To tempt so*m*me, als Dathan, Abyron, Cham and Chore.
So*m*me temptis he for to gif counsailes werst þ*at* may be,
Als shewed in Achitofel, Balaam & Jonadab alle thre.
So*m*me temptis he be vnrewth and other*e* so*m*me be tresoune,
Als shewed was in Chayn, Joab, Judas, Tripho*u*n.
So*m*me for to shedde mans blode temptis he to con neu*er* hoo,
Als Cyre, als Manasses, Antyochus, Herode also.

4005 Capitulum xxxviij^{m} *mar.* 4009 Historia Scolastic*a* super Exod. The stori callis hir*e* Tharmis *mar.* 4011 Saba] i.e. a citee in Ethyore. 4012 obsidioune] i.e. the siege *over.* 4017 payed] *(*-d *overwritten).* 4026 Psalme xliiij Speciosus forma p*re* filius hominu*m* *mar.* 4039 Howe the feende temptis diuers dyuersly *mar.* 4044 John] *?* Joh*a*n.

A Theban woman kills Abimelech
Judges ix 50-54, Comestor 1282

Michol helps David to escape
I Kings xix 11-18

Some folk thaymself to slee makes he bolde & cruwelle,
Als Judas, Abymalech, Saul, Achitofel.
W*ith* thir*e* and many other*e* vice the feend mankinde inpugnys,
Bot our*e* deffensatrice Marie for vs alway p*ro*pugnys. [f.49v]
¶b Whare\fore/ a p*ri*sefulle womman Our*e* Lady p*re*figurid,
Whilk the tour*e* of Thebes fro Abymalech deffendid.
The folk, Abymalech dredeing, went on the tour*e* w*ith*inne,
And he both thaym and the tour*e* wald in fyre sette and brynne.
A pece of a mylnestone threwe doune ther*e* a womman,
And the heved of Abymalech touchyng, brayned hym right than.
Abymalech, of a womman to be confusid sorowyng,
Saide thus til his sqwyer*e*, of his lif disparing:
"Out w*ith* thi swerde," quod he, "and slee me hastily,
Þ*at* I neu*er* be demed of a womman to dye."
This provde Abymalech, whilk betaknys the feende,
Thas þ*at* er*e* in the toure of Haly Kyrke wolde he sheende,
Bot our*e* deffensatrice Marie, moder*e* of Jh*es*u God Son,
Hils vs fro his assautz vnder*e* hir*e* p*ro*teccioune,
And fro the malice of the feend sho kepes vs noght oonly,
Bot fro the temptacio*u*nes of the werld deffendis vs this Ladye,
And this p*ro*teccioune is vs fulle necessarie
For the temptyngs of the werld er*e* many one & fulle varie.
Bot most tempts vs this werld of lordship covatyng,
Be pride and brynnyng lustes of fals richesse gadering,
Als shewes in Alexandr*e*, Nembreth and Nabugodonosor,
Athalia, in Absolon, Adonybeseth and Codorlamor.
Some temptis it w*ith* vaynglorie and other*e* swilk vanitee
Als Aman, King Ezechye, Herode Ag*ri*ppa, thir*e* three.
So*m*me temptis it w*ith* avarice, be stu\l/th or be robberye,
Als Cusy, [Achan], Elyodre and many one other*e* by.
So*m*me er*e* temptid be luxuree or be fornicacioune
Als war*e* Zambry, Amon, King Dauid and Salomo*u*n.
So*m*me er*e* stirde be fole speche and so*m*me to blaspheme gretely,
Als Nabal, Senacherib and Roboam the sturdy,
So*m*me to detraccio*u*nes, contencio*u*nes and contumelye,
Als Marie sister*e* of Moises, the wyves of Job and Thobye.
Alle werldly temptings may we wele eschape & ou*er*come
Luving our*e* mediatrice w*ith* our*e* hert alle and so*m*me.
¶c This was p*re*figurid also be Dauid the noble king
Michol, Saulis doght*er*, w*ith* alle his hert wele luving,
Wharefore sho qwitte hym of awayt of hir*e* faders s*er*geantz
And lete hym out at a wyndowe, so making his delyvrance.
So dos til alle hir*e* lovers Our*e* Ladye, seint vi[r]gyne Marye,
In alle nede and temptinges thaym helping fulle bisyly.
Luf we than this virgine w*ith* alle our*e* hert als the wise, [f.50r]
Our*e* mediatrice in alle nede and fervenst propugnatrice,
Þ*at* fro alle werldly p*er*ils hir*e* like vs kepe and defende
And aft*er* this lif passing vntil hir*e* son sho vs sende.
O gude Jh*es*u, here thowe thi moder*e* for vs praying
And help hir*e* against our*e* foos for our*e* hele eu*er* feghting.

4058 p*ro*pugnys] i.e. feghts for vs *mar*. 4059 Fig*ure* ij° Judic. j *mar*. 4073 Diu*er*s temptings of the werlde *mar*. 4081 Machab. iij *mar*. 4083 stulth] *(l in different ink)*. 4093 Figure iij ij Reg. xix *mar*. 4097 virgyne] Vigyne. 4103 corr. *mar*. 4104 Amen *under rub. mar*.

Christ shows his wounds to The Father
Aquinas *ST* III q.54, a.4; *PL* CLXXXIX 1726; John of Ford, Sermon CXX

Antipater shows his wounds to Caesar
Comestor 1531

In two last chapitles herde ȝe howe Marie is mediatrice
To Godde, and in disese our*e* sevre deffensatrice.
Howe Crist his woundes to his Fader*e* shewes is to here fylowingly,
And hir*e* blissid brestes to hir*e* son for vs shewes virgine Marie.
Als Crist descendid to helle fro the heven for mankynde sake,
So to heven is he reascendit, our*e* pees *with* his Fader*e* to make.
We shuld noght falle in wanhope thogh we haf synned forthy,
Having to the hevenyssh Fader*e* so trewe auokette and myghty.
¶a Þ*at* Crist his cicatrices wold shewe his Fader*e* for vs,
Tofore lange in figure was it p*re*ostendid thus:
Antipat*er*, a noble knyght, was wryed to the emp*erour* Julian
Þ*at* he was wikked and vntrewe vnto the Empir*e* Roman,
And he tyrved hym stone nakid, p*re*sent this emp*er*our*e*,
Shewyng the erres of his woundes for thaym in many a stour*e*,
And saide, "What shuld my wordes p*ro*ve me wreche or worthy?
Bot heres thir*e* cicatrices alle cry out þ*at* trewe am I."
And thus the emp*erour* approved his excusacioune,
And a trewe knyght held hym, his accusing put doune.
Right fair*e* was Crist figured be this Antipater*e*,
Alway just and for vs tofor the hevenyssh Fader*e*,
Be his woundis hy*m* shewyng a noble knyght & doghty,
And his Fader*e* comaundementz to haf fulfillid trewly,
Whar*e*\fore/ Godde til hono*ur* cessis neu*er* this worthy knyght
And his askings freely grantes hym eu*er* day & nyght.
That Our*e* Lord Jh*es*u Crist was knyght noble and worthy
Shewed in his cicatrices and in his clothing blody:
Fore rede sangvinolent was alle ou*er* Cristis clothing,
Like to clothes of the men of rede wyne grapes treding;
Whar*e*fore of Cristis clothis thus askid aungels dyv.ine
Whi thai war*e* rede als of men out of *gra*pes stampyng the wyne.
"The presso*ure* of my passioune tholid I alle one," quod he,
"And of alle folk in erth was noght o man *with* me."
And þ*at* no man *with* hym was, Crist saide notably
For bot a virgyne *with* hym left than–his moder*e*–onely.
Crist toke the ordre of knyght with the colee *cer*tayne
Als vse is to make knyghtes in the lande of Almayne. [f.50^{v}]
Bot this knyght Crist myght noght *with* o colee be qwitte,
Bot he ne hadde strokes dovblid to noumbre als infynyte.
Ane asse on Palme Sondaye was his stede *cer*teynly,
The felde of his bataille was the mount of Caluarie,
The la*un*ce of blynde Longyve the knyght was Cristis spere,
The sharp corovne of thornes was his helme for the were.
The criste of Cristis helme the table was of his title,
\And the girdel of his swerde al his bandis grete & litel./
The patible of the Crosse for sheeld and targe hadde hee,
For spors ane yren naile thorgh his fete to the tree.
The haub*er*geo*u*ne whilk his body shuld kepe both vp and doune
His tendrest skynne al to-rent with flagellacioune.
His swerd was Haly Doctrine taght in Judees landes,
And two herde nailles of iren war*e* als gloves to his handes.

4105 Capit^{m} {x}xxix^{m} *mar.* 4112 B*ernard* in Cant. last chap*itle mar.* 4113 cicatrices] i.e. merkes of his woundes *over*; Figure j *mar.* 4118 thaym] i.e. for the Romayns *over.* 4125 Hym] *letter(s) alt.* -ym. 4127 Wharefore] *(-fore in different ink).* 4134 Ysay lxiij *mar.* 4139 The makyng of a knygh and his array *mar.* 4148 *ins. mar.*

The Virgin shows her breasts to her son
Ernaldus *PL* CLXXXIX 1726

Esther pleads with her husband Assuerus
Esther v 3, vii 2-10

The sqwyer*e* for his body was his swete moder*e* Marie,
The whilk alle his arme*ur*s bare in passioune trewly:
For als the sqwyer*e* at nede held hym negh Jonathas,
So in Cristis passioune his moder*e* a negh sqwyer*e* was.
The baner*e* of this noble knyght Crist was of two colour*e*s:
Þ*at* o part was alle white, þ*at* other*e* rede als rose flour*e*s.
That one was of the white clothe at Herodes illusioune:
The coccyne, þ*at* was taken hym in his coronacioune.
With thir*e* a\r/me*ur*s this knyght faght so wele at devis
Þ*at* be his deth he ou*er*come alle our*e* cruwelle enemys.
After þ*at* w*ith* gloriouse trihumphe vntil heven he ascendid,
And to his Fader*e* praying for vs his cicatrices he ostendid.
Thar*e*fore no wight disespair*e* for his synnes innoumbrable
Bot trist in this aduokat allemyghty and m*er*cyable,
For in the Fader*e* or the Haly Gast thogh we nevre so synne,
Crist may vs recounseil and p*ar*dou*n* haboundant wynne.
And if we synne in the Son, þ*at* is in Crist Jh*es*u,
We have, to pray til hym, on aduocat fulle trewe.
¶b Crist to his Fader*e* shewes his cicatrices for m*er*cy,
And til hyr*e* son hir*e* bristes shewes for vs swete Marie.
And Crist "Antipater*e*" may be callid resonably,
So "Antefilia" men may calle Marie semblably.
O trewest Antipat*er*, and Antefilia swettist,
Howe seurly may synners in succ*our* of ȝow two trist–
For how myght thar*e* be hopid of anything denying
In heven, erth or in helle to thus swettist praying?
Howe shuld the Fader*e* of pitee noght fille the Sons entent
Wham hee sees swilk woundes haf suffred at his ma*un*dement?
How shuld a son his moder*e* oght mow warne in praying,
Whare oyther*e* oþ*er* als thaymself lufs eu*er* without feynyng? [f.51r]
Than wher*e* Crist here his moder*e* nedes noght to doute, I wene,
Wham ou*er* alle mortal folk he hase made hevens qwene.
¶c This was p*re*figurid sometyme be the grete Kyng Assuer*e*,
Whilk, wele chaufid w*ith* the wyne, saide thus to Qwene Hester*e*:
"Aske me whatevre thow wilt, thi prayer*e* I graunt the,
Thogh it war*e* half my roialme, fulfillid thi wil shalle be."
And sho hir*e* folk fro Naaman asked to be deffendid,
Wham Kyng Assuwer*e* anone on gibet maide be suspendid.
Hester*e* a pore mayden was borne of the Jewrye
And the king chase hir*e* to qwene ou*er* alle other*e* sou*er*eynly.
So chase Godde mayden Marie above alle virgynes erthly
To be qwene of alle heven now and eu*er*lastyngly,
And has dampnyd our*e* enemy be hir*e* intervencio*u*ne
And taken hir*e* half his kyngdome be twyp*art* dep*ar*tisoune.
Godde has his regne dep*ar*tid in p*ar*tis two jentillye,
Þ*at* one kept for hymself, þ*at* oyther*e* gyven til Our*e* Ladye.
He kepes til hymselven justice, delyvred til his moder*e* m*er*cye,
W*ith* the first he vs manaces, w*ith* þ*at* oþ*er* helps vs Marye.
O gude Jh*es*u pray thow for vs thi Fader*e* of m*er*cy,
And thi dere moder*e* for vs p*ra*ying here benignely.

4155 Fig*ure* ij j Reg. xiiij° *mar.* 4163 armo*ur*s] *(1st* r *in different ink)*; knyght] i.e. Crist *over.* 4166 ostendid] i.e. shewed *over.* 4172 on] *followed by* the *subp.* 4174 Bernard apon Cantic. vlt. *mar.* 4175 Antipater*e*] i.e. tofore his Fader*e* *over.* 4176 Antefilia] i.e. tofore hir*e* son *over.* 4183 oght...praying] *o.er.* 4184 Whare...thaymself] *o.er.* 4187 Fig*ure* iij Hest*er* xlv° *mar.* 4197 intervencio*u*ne] i.e. p*ra*yer*e* *over.* 4203 corr. *mar.* 4204 Amen. *under rub. mar.*

The Last Judgement
Matt. xxiv 30; Apoc. iv 2-3, xx 11-13

The parable of the talents
Matt. xxv 14-30

Last herde 3*e* how þ*at* Crist for vs cessis noght to praye;
Nowe fylowes howe streit a juge he bees on Domesday.
¶a This notid Crist on a day a p*ar*able p*ro*ponyng,
When he in this werld here went in Jewerye p*re*ching.
He saide a man weending intil a regioune lontaigne
For to take hym a rewme and eftsones turne a3eine,
Whilk til his men bezauntes toke ten for emprowyng,
And at his gayncome to gif hym trewly the wynnyng.
The rewme taken, and reto*ur*nyd fro thens whar*e* he was went,
He askid of ilkone reknyng aft*er* his rather*e* entent.
Who mykel hadde wonne was mykel his remuneraci*ou*ne;
Who littel wanne was lesse mede taken hym for his gerd*ou*ne.
Hym þ*at* 3alde the bezaunt with none vsur*e* a3aine,
The lord helde hym noght payed, and putt þ*at* s*er*ua*un*t to payne.
This wise shalle Crist haf hym the day of his demyng,
Whare shall take eu*ery* man aft*er* his labourde wynnyng:
And who noght wele hase done shalle fele the juges ire,
And for his negcligence to bote brenne eu*er* in hellis fyre,
For it nys nothing ynoghe onely to forebere synne,
Bot also mot men do gude whar*ewith* heven for to wynne,
For the auster*e* juge wille repe in place whar*e* he noght sewe,
Asking of the payens gude werkis, and thaym no movth-sede sewe. [f.51^v]
How negh wil he gude werkis of Cristen than seke streitly,
To whame so saluter*e* techinges he mynystres so freely!
He shalle shewe synners his woundes w*ith* the armes of hy\s/ payne
For thaym soeffred, to see what thay 3alde hym a3aine.
Alle Cristes armes shalle stande ageynst the synners stifly
And alle his woundes apon hym sharply shalle vengeance cry.
Alle creat*ur*es shalle thaym arme til inpugne the synner*e*
And alle the elementes on hym shal pleyne and m\a/ke hym were:
The erth þ*at* hym bare and hym for to fede fructified,
And he it als a tree vnfruy\t/fulle occupied;
The fyre shalle pleygne þ*at* hete it mynistred hym and light,
And he his light, the Maker*e*, wald noght knawe day nor nyght;
The ayer*e* whilk hym brething was ay to gif redy
Whar*e*of his Creato*ur* he thankid noght bisyly,
The water*e* þ*at* hym gaf drinke & w*ith* fysshes hym fedde,
And he the Maker*e* of this ne serued nor g*ra*ces bedde.
His gude aungel on hym shalle stir*e* Gods rightwisnesse
Þ*at* he cessid noght to synne for Gods, nor his, clennesse.
The moder*e* of m*er*cy þ*at* nowe to synners is so p*ro*pice
Þ*at* doelfulle day to none shalle sho bene adiutrice.
The piest Jh*es*u þ*at* wald for synners thole passioune
Shal at thaire deth lagh than in thair*e* dampnacioune.
The feends \of/ alle p*ri*uest synnes shalle than shewe forth thair*e* taillies
And of alle gude werkes left aungels make rehersaillies.
Crist alder-piest shalle than to m*er*cy be seen so stra*un*ge
Þ*at* noyther*e* prayer*e* ne teres his sentence shall than mowe chaunge.
If Marie and seints alle wepped blode for m*er*cy
Thai shuld noght rescowe o sawle fro dampnacioune sothly.

4205 Cap^m xl^m *mar.* 4207 p*ro*ponyng] i.e. puttynge forth *over.* 4209 Fig*ur*e j *mar.* 4211 men] i.e. seruaunts *over*; Luc. xix^o x bezauntz *mar.* 4222 No*ta* *mar.* 4226 and ... sewe] i.e. he prechid noght p*er*sonely to thaym *over.* 4228 The crying of Cristis woundes for vengea*un*ce apon synners *mar.* 4232 make] *(a in different ink).* 4244 clennesse] i.e. of the aungel *over.* 4246 none] er synners *over.* 4247 P*ro*u*er*b. I shalle lagh in 3*our* p*er*isshing *mar.* 4249 Psalms And thov Lord shalle scorn thay*m* *mar.*

The parable of the wise and foolish virgins
Matt. xxv 1-13

The warning to Baltasar
Dan. v

¶b The fierstee of this streit dome is noted be virgines ten,
Of whame Crist in p*ar*ables p*re*ched in erth to men.
The virgynes wise of thair*e* oyle gaf noght virgines fole,
To shewe þ*at* seintis nothing shal of the dampnyd condole:
And als oyle of m*er*cy the foles of the wise none hadde,
So in the vengeaunce of thaym seints shall be joyouse & gladde.
And the wise virgynes scorned the virgynes fole myrily
When thay to the oyle-sellers sent thaym oyle for to by;
Ryght so the seints shall seme the dampnid scorne on Domesday,
And send thaym til oyle-sellers for thair*e* laumpes, als so say:
"Ȝe solde joye et*er*nale for vayne voluptuostee,
Goos bye more, ȝe have nede of ȝ*our* marcha*un*ts lat see:
Alle almouse-dede and gude werks be ȝow done vnwisely
Solde ȝ*e* for ma*n*nes praysing and this werlde passing glorie.
What profits nowe ȝ*our* grete pride of erthi wricchid p*ra*ysyng?
Whar*e* is alle ȝ*our* plesa*un*ce of ȝowre apocrisyng? [f.52[r]]
Off the fruyte of ȝour*e* gude dedes nowe may ȝ*e* se what failles,
And ȝ*our* lust transitorie what nowe it ȝowe availles."
And when the foles of the wise no parte of oyle myght wynne,
Thay went than to the spouse and cried to lat tha[m] inne,
Bot no m*er*cy of hym gate thay in alle the werde
And þ*at* he ne knewe thaym noght sothly of hym thay herde.
Thus wille falle be synners on Domesday *cer*teinly,
For of Godde nor his seints get thay than no m*er*cy.
¶c In þ*at* scriptu*re* of this was shewed figure and note,
Ageynst King Balthazar*e* when a hande on the walle wrote.
'Mane, thechel, phares' was writen apon the walle,
Þ*at* noumbr*e*, weght and twynnyng gifs to mene til vs all:
For Gods dome shall be tretid be noumbre and be weghyng,
And eendid be the gude fro yvel p*er*petuel dep*ar*tyng.
For be noumbre of decerts shall Godde gif jugement,
Þ*at* our*e* thoght, worde or dede knawes alle in o mo[m]ent.
Our*e* wille and our*e* movinges knawes he wele evry whitte,
And alle the tyme til vs taken howe we dispendid itte.
The giftes be vs resceved has he wele noumbred alle,
What tyme & howe besette–alle thir*e* shalle he forth calle.
Alle thir*e* thinges noumbred nowe wille he weghe streytly thare,
And to the prikke thair*e* value tofore alle men declare.
Than shalle so*m*me pore mans myte weighe als mykel in valo*ur*
Als some thovzande besauntes of pope or emp*er*our*e*.
Than shalle one eye weigh, gyven out of synne dedely \q/white,
More than in dedely synne golde gyven noumbre infynite.
And o Pat*er* Nost*er* more weygh in swete devocyo*un*e
Than a savter*e* w*ith* sleuth, w*ith*out attencio*un*e.
At the last comes forth *phares*, þ*at* is to say, devisyng,
When the noumbre dampnable fro Godde & fro his seints takes twynnyng:
Than shalle the dampned to helle w*ith* dyvles eu*er*lastingly,
And the gude entre in the joye of thair*e* Lord sempit*er*nely.
To the whilk bring vs, Jh*es*u, als thowe art King of the hegh heven,
W*ith* the Fader*e* and the Haly Gast of substa*un*ce & of joye even.

4255 Fig*ure* ij *mar.* 4274 tham] than. 4276 Math. xxv[to] *mar.* 4279 Fig*ure* iij Balthazar*e* Danyel *mar.* 4286 moment] C, monent; i.e. in so short space þ*at* may noght be dep*ar*tid *o.i.e.l.* 4293 myte] or peny or half peny *over*; P*rou*erb xvj *mar.* 4295 qwhite] (q *in different ink*); Off offring in gude lyfe and prayers *mar.* 4303 corr. *mar.* 4304 Amen. *mar.*

The damned
Matt. xxv 46; Apoc. xxi 8

David punishes the city of Rabbath
II Kings xii 31; Comestor 1334

The passid chapitle shewed vs the last examynacioune;
Heres nowe howe gude and yvel shalle both take thaire gverdoune.
Oure Lorde Godde in this we\r/lde list evre do benignely,
Bot in the werlde for to come rewardis he rightwisly.
And for a man body and sawle dos joyntly gude or harme here,
Therefore in oþer werlde bere thay payne or joy both yfere.
At Domesday, bodyes and sawles shal be revnit certayne,
And euermore both togidere haf joye or suffre payne.
The wikked mens bodies shall rise vnshaply and passible,
Bot the gude mens fulle faire without eend impassible.
A dampnid bodie shalle rise in swilk deformitee [f.52^{v}]
Þat infinite horrour bes it the awen fote or hande to see;
And the more þat thaire synne here haf bene abhomynable,
So mykel thaire bodyes than shalle be more defourmable,
And of the grettere desertes þat rightwise men haf bene here,
So mykel shalle thaire bodyes be fairere and more clere.
The body of the leest childe þat shalle entre into hevene
Clerere than is the sonne shalle be be faldes sevene,
And if an oythere passes hym ten tymes in halynesse,
His body shalle passe þat othere eke tenfolde in clerenesse.
If one more than an othere be haly ane hundrethfolde,
He shalle passe in clerenesse an hondrethfald wele tolde;
And if another is a thousand times more holy,
His body will be a thousand times more bright.
So als Crist ouer alle seints is haly innoumbrably,
His body more than alle seints bes clerere infinitly.
The bodies of seints shalle be glorified in lyf to come
Fovrefolds, and ere thire the parcelles of þat soume:
Claritee take for the first, the secounde impassibilitee,
Sutyltee for the thredde, the feerthe agilitee–
Thire foure dowairs whilk I ȝowe have tofore noumbrid
Ware in Cristis body sometyme in manere prefigurid.
Crist shewed the claritee in his transfiguryng,
His face in Mount Thabor bright als the sonne shynyng.
The sutiltee was shewed in his natyvitee,
When he was borne savyng his moders integritee.
The agilitee may be taken, and noght vnresonably,
When Crist went in the see, his fete both lasting drye.
The inpassibilitee shewed hee betaking in manere
His bodie til his disciples til ete at his sopere.
And haly sawles shal be dowed be treble dotacioune,
The whilk ere "knawing" and "luf" and "comprehensioune".
The dampned sawles & the bodies shal haf no swilk dowyng,
Bot eternal helle payne without eend vncessyng.
Als thay to thaire Godde etern here synnyd willfully,
So shal he thaym in helle put to payne eendlesly.
The dampned neuer of thaire synne shal haf verray penitence,
Wharefore Godde of thaire payne shalle nevre turne his sentence.
So grete is the payne of helle and so inenarrable
Þat no payne in this werld is to it comparable.

4305 Capi^{m} xlj^{m} *mar.* 4307 werlde] (r *in different ink*). 4307 revnit] i.e. fast togidere *over*; Of resurexione of men *mar.* 4313 He is passible þat may fele payne *mar.* 4319 no*ta* *mar.* 4323 ten] x *over.* 4331 Of the dowaires of the sawle *mar.* 4334 agilitee] i.e. delyvrenesse *over.* 4337 Marc. ix^{o} Math. xvij *mar.* 4340 borne] *o.s.o.*; integritee] i.e. her maydenhod *over.* 4347 Of the payne of thas þat shall be dampned *mar.* 4352 sentence] i.e. jugement *over.*

Gideon's revenge on Socoth
Judges viii 11-17; Comestor 1280

The Red Sea overwhelms Pharao
Ex. xiv 21-25

Who couthe of martres alle the paynes in o so*u*me telle,
C*er*teyne thaym shuld seme noght to paynes þ*at* er*e* in helle.
Ysay p*ro*phete was sawen, and stonyd was Jeremye,
Amos p*er*ced thorgh the temples, Ezechiel brayned foullye,
Poul w*ith* ȝerdis bette thris and aft*er* þ*at* o tyme stonyd,
Sithen aft*er* v. [quadragenaries], one less, ar*e* thay hym hevedid.
This wise Seint Jame martir toke his deth, aft*er* tale:
Al to-kytt w*ith* sharpe knyves & raso*ur*s kene gobettmale— [f.53^{r}]
Barthelmewe slayne alle qwhikke and Peter*e* postle croisid,
Piers martir*e* stikt w*ith* a swerde, Seint Laurance deken roistid;
And the payne of alle martirs who myght in a sovme telle
Alle thas shuld noght be comparable vnto the lest payne of helle:
For alle the to*ur*ment of m*ar*tirs war*e* shorrt and transitorie,
Bot the paynes of the dampnid lastis in helle eendlesly,
For thay brynne in the fyre of helle þ*at* lastis in evre
And er*e* gnawen w*ith* the worme of conscience þ*at* dies nevre.
Bot a worme mat*er*ial this nes noght to devise
For no swilk beest lyving may ther*e* be in no wise:
Then is this forsaide worme remorse of conscience
Gnawing the sawles dampnyd be Gods eu*er*lastyng sentence.
Ther*e* shalle be continuel lokyng on dyvles terrible,
Cold, gnaysting of teth, hungre & thrust importible,
Crying, horro*ur* and drede, tremblyng, doel p*er*durable,
Byndyngs, priso*u*ns, bronstone and stynking intolerable,
Envie, cursyng and smeke and ferefulst derknesse palpable,
Sorowing, confusioune & shame, wepyng, teres inenarrable,
Dispair*e* of delyvrance or of the leest confortyng,
Neu*er* ony ent*er*cesing of contynuel punysshing.
¶a The vengeance her*e* toforsaide of Godde on the dampned
Was be the citee of Rabath and Dauid p*re*figured.
The pople of þ*at* citee the king punyst strangely:
So*m*me w*ith* sawes did he kitte, so*m*me w*ith* knyves membratly,
So*m*me made he yren-boune cartes in his ire ou*er* thaym rynne,
And so*m*me made he to-drawe w*ith* many a dyu*er*se gynne.
¶b This shewed also be men of Socoth and Gedeon
On wham he venged hym hoegely for thair*e* derisioune.
The poeple of Socoth scornyd Gedeon the duce worthy
And he, his tyme abiden, venged hym fulle horribly,
For aft*er* that, his scorners he punyst fulle sore scornyng
W*ith* breres and w*ith* sharpe thornes thair*e* bodyes al to-racyng.
Thus Crist shalle his scorners, synners þ*at* is to say,
Thogh her*e* he thayme forbere, elleswhare fulle sore pay,
For Wisdom says that torments have been prepared for scorners,
And shattering hammers for the bodies of fools.
¶c In Pharao and the Egipciens was this be figure enclosid,
Whame Godde in the rede see ilkone at ones conclosid.
Right so the dampnid w*ith* feendes and Lucifer*e* at the last
In helle foreu*er* togider*e* shalle be shette alle fulle fast.
Jh*es*u, for thyn helefulle and bitt*er*est passioune,
Make ferre fro vs foreevre this horrible conclusioune. [f.53^{v}]

4355 Maist*er* of Stories and Josephus *mar.* 4357 Jeremye] *(-ere- blotted).* 4359 Corinth. xj^{o} *mar.* 4360 quadragenaries] quinquagenaries. 4368 Math. xxix *mar.* 4369 Ysay xxx^{o} *mar.* 4370 Judith ix^{o} *mar.* 4382 ent*er*cesing] *(a 2nd* s *erased).* 4385 Fig*ur*e j *mar.* 4387 king] i.e. Da*ui*d *over.* 4391 Socoth] a citee *over*; Figure ij Judic. viij *mar.* 4395 scorners] *o.s.o.* 4397 *2-line space follows where 2 lines are omitted (see n. 4397).* 4399 Fig*ur*e iij Exodi xiiij *mar.* 4403 corr. *mar.* 4404 Amen *mar.*; *at the foot of the page, in another hand:* Dicit e*n*im Sapiens quod parata sunt tormenta derisorib*us* Et malleis percutientes stult*orum* ordib*us*.

The blessed in heaven
Matt. xxv 46; Apoc. xxi 1-5

Solomon in his glory
III Kings x

Tofore the paynes herd to dampnid eendlesly;
Nowe er*e* the joyes of seints to here of fylowingly,
Whas blisses er*e* so many þ*at* thay may neu*er* be noumbrid,
So hoege þ*at* thay shalle neu*er* be any wise mensurid;
Thay shal neu*er* mowe be tolde, thay er*e* so ineffable,
Nor thay ne shalle neu*er* take eende, so er*e* thay p*er*durable.
The joye to Gods luvers p*re*paryd egh se thayme noght,
Nor neu*er* war*e* be er*e* herde nor in hert of man thoght.
Ther*e* is alle man*ere* beutee lustfulle to beholdyng,
Alle armonye melodyouse þ*at* p*er*tenes til hering.
Ther*e* is alle delicacye vnto smelle suppetyng.
Ther*e* is alle suavitee delitable to touching;
Ther*e* is alle man*ere* swetnesse vnto tast influyng.
Ther*e* is p*er*fitest boond of inwardst hertly luvyng.
Ther*e* shalle we of Godde the Fader*e* conceyve the omnipotence,
The wisdome of his dere So*un*, the Haly Gastis clemence.
Ther*e* shalle be of alle gudes contynuel affluence,
Ther*e* shalle be of alle yvels without eende alle absence.
Ther*e* shalle be rest eterne w*ith*out alle man*ere* laboure,
Ther*e* shalle be pees and suretee w*ith*out alle man*ere* terrour*e*.
Ther*e* shalle no feendes awayte nor laye temptacioune,
Ther*e* bes of werlde nor flesshe none inpugnacioune.
Ther*e* bes connyng and witte w*ith*out any ignoraunce.
Ther*e* bes freendship and luf without contrariaunce.
Ther*e* bes p*er*petuel hele w*ith*out alle man*ere* sekenesse,
Ther*e* shal be strengh stably w*ith*out alle werynesse.
Ther*e* bes eu*er* clerest light w*ith*out ony clowde sothly.
Ther*e* shal be gladnesse et*er*ne and jubilyng bisyly.
Ther*e* bes beutee and shappe w*ith*out deformytee,
Wightlayke delyvrenesse without ony torditee;
Ther*e* shalle be richesse and myght w*ith*out any man*ere* failling,
Ther*e* bes joye and honou*r* w*ith*out any dispising.
Ther*e* is the flo*ur* of ȝouthede þ*at* neu*er* shal knawe welknyng,
Ther*e* shalle be lyf eu*er* grene, neu*er* more til haf eendyng;
Ther*e* shulde seme bot a point the age of Matussale,
And the strenthe of Sampson bot pallesye for to be.
Ther*e* the whightlake of Azael war*e* irksome tarying,
And the helth of Caleph war*e* dedely sekenyng;
Ther*e* war*e* difformitee the beutee of Absolon,
And folie als to acconpt the witte of Salomon;
Ther*e* the counsaile of Jhetro & of Achitofel folenesse,
Aristotil and alle philosofres thair*e* scionce bot lewednesse; [f.54r]
Ther*e* Tubalchaym and Neoma, Irams suttlist werkemen,
Besleel and [O]oliab to deme vnkonnyng couth thay swilk ten;
Ther*e* Dauid harpe and the musik of Jubal war*e* absurditee,
Manna bitt*er* and the wyne made in Cana Galilee.
Ther*e* Adams p*ar*adys and the lande of p*ro*missio*un*e seme exile,
And alle Ecclesiastes delices seme absinthe or aysile.
Ther*e* alle Octavianes regne shulde seme prison or desert.
Ther*e* tresore of Cresus and Antecrist shuld be demed ther*e* povert.

4405 Capitulum xlij^{m} *mar.* Tofore] *(rub.* T *has* IHC *rub. inside).* 4407 Of the joye of the seints *mar.* 4412 Ysay lxiiij *mar.* 4428 luf] i.e. charitee *over*; contrariaunce] i.e. envie *over.* 4433 bes beutee] *o.er.*; deformytee] i.e. vnsitingnesse *over.* 4434 torditee] i.e. slawnesse *over.* 4448 Ooliab] Coliab. 4449 absurditee] *?* i.e. envysom *(*u *alt.* v*) over.*

Assuerus' feast
Esther i 1-8

Job's feast
Job i 4

Ther*e* shalle thowe, man, haf more myght than Cresus & August*us* Cesar*e*,
Cyrus, Nabugodonosor, King Alexandr*e* and Balthasar*e*.
Ther*e* shalle thowe be stronger*e* than Sampson, Sangar*e*, Abisay,
Or Dauid or Semma, Bononay or Sobokay.
Fairer*e* than Absolon & Joseph or Moyses, witt thowe this wele,
Judith and Susanne, the fair*e* Rebecca, Sara & Rachele.
Ther*e* shalle thowe langer*e* lyve than Enoc, Matussale & Elye,
Be swifter*e* than is the sonne, Asael, H*er*cules and Cusy.
Ther*e* shall thowe eke wiser*e* be than King Salomon or Austyn,
Pope Gregoir*e* or Jerom, Ambros and Thomas Alqwyn.
Ther*e* shalle thowe more clerely se Godde þ[*an*] Pet*er* did, John or Jame,
Ezechiel, Ysay, Moyses and deken Steven be his name.
¶a Figure of this et*er*ne joye moght Salomons gl*or*ie be,
For we rede of none other*e* so delicat als was he,
And noght onely passid he other in delices hyghly,
Bot in richesse also passid he \all/ other*e* strangely.
To Je*rusal*em, his fame herd, come than of Saba the qwene,
And saide, for m*er*veils ravist, his incredible glorie sene,
"More is thi glorie than fame of thi p*ro*sp*er*itee,
I have p*ro*ved *þat* the half was noght talde vnto mee."
So shal a sawle say for joye, comen intil heven blisse,
"I ne herde neu*er* half sothly nor thovzande parte of alle this."
The face of Salomon to se alle the werld desiryd,
Whilk thing the face Jh*es*u right wele prefiguryd,
For alle the joye of the heven and sp*irit*uel reioying
Is of the graciouse visage of Jh*es*u the contempling.
For better*e* war*e* a sawle in helle Crists visage seyng to be,
Than in heven for to dwelle and his face noght to se:
For if a sawle ware in helle it war*e* noght paynes suffrable,
Seyng *þat* joyfulle visage ou*er* alle thing delectable.
¶b Ane other*e* figure of this joye may the feest of Asswer*e* be,
For neu*er* other*e* *þat* we rede heeld swilk feest als did he,
To whilk feest noght grete lordis gert he pray alle onely,
Bot alle the poeple, alle so men and wymmen holely.
And Gods feest was gretter*e* of alle folk grete and smalle,
Saying, "Passis to me, ȝe *þat* coveites me alle." [f.54v]
The feest of Kyng Aswer*e* was ix^{xx} dayes duryng,
Bot the feest of Jh*es*u Crist shalle be eu*er*more lasting.
¶c The thredde figure may be taken in the feestes of the sons of Jope,
For of so contynuel feestyng of other*e* we ne rede, I hope.
Of Job the sons seven ilkone about his day
Calling thair*e* thre systres contynuyd feestis alway,
Be whilk feestes vnderstande hevenly felicitee,
Be the cyrcuyt of seven dayes p*er*petuel et*er*nitee.
Seven sons men may the seints of the seven eage devise,
Thre doghtres, the vertues of thre angelik ierarchies.
Alle thay haf sempiterne festes w*ith*out cessyng,
Alle shalle thay be in joye *þat* neu*er* shalle have styntyng.
O gude Jh*es*u, gif vs for thy benigne bountee
In thy feestes toforesaide eu*er*more to dwelle w*ith* the.

4465 þan] quam L, þ*at*. 4467 Figure j *mar.* 4470 all] *in different ink.* 4472 iij Reg. x P*ar*alipo. ix *mar.* 4476 No*ta* *mar.* 4481 Of the sight of Godde *mar.* 4485 Figure ij *mar.* 4487 Hest. j *mar.* 4489 Eccl*es*iastic. xxiiij *mar.* 4493 Figure iij Job j *mar.* 4501 thay] i.e. aungels & seints *over.* 4504 Amen. *mar.*

Tofore herde we the paynes to dampned intolerable
And of the joyfulle gerdon to seintis ineffable;
Now fylows howe þ*at* we may the paynes forsaid eschewe
And eu*er*lasting joye wynne w*ith* Crist eu*er* newe & newe.
Who to the blissednesse forsaide of seints wilnes to come,
Hym awe s*er*ue and luf Godde w*ith* his hert alle & so*m*me,
And what so be most greable to Godde in gude entent,
To þ*at* aspire alwaye with bisy hert and fervent.
§ Sometyme a man dwellyng devoutly in his celle
Was bysy in alle his hert to s*er*ue Godde; bokes telle
This man his Godde besoght, p*ra*ying contynuelly,
To shewe hym in what s*er*uice he myght plese hym most by.
Felle on a tyme he se towards hym Crist co*m*myng
W*ith* a Crosse lange and grete on his bak vpbering,
And saide, "Me may thowe neu*er* s*er*ue here more plesantly
Than me help for to bere this hevy Crosse tenderly."
"O my swete Jh*esu* Godde, like ȝowe to declare me
What wise, and I shalle help w*ith* body and sawle", quod he.
"In hert", answered Jh*esus*, "my bitt*er*est passioune pleygnyng,
And in mouthe be devout oftsith & tendr*e* thankyng,
In erys be my doelfulle paynes feruent heryng,
On thy bakke thyne awen flesshe contynuelly chastying."
O war*e*fore the paynes of helle for til eschape saufly
And to the joye w*ith* the seints for to come graciously
In hert, worde and in dede thanke we Our*e* Saveour*e*,
Saying this oris*ou*nes in his passiounes honour*e*.
† I thanke the, Lorde Jh*esu* Crist Gods Son verrayly
One Godde and neu*er* moo, my salveo*ur* sothfastly,
Þ*at* in hour*e* of Evensonge thyne hoege luf shewed to me
When thowe gaf me ensaumple of deppest humilitee. [f.55^{r}]
Jh*esu*, of thi s*er*uants wesshe thowe the fete mekely,
And of thyn awen trayto*ur* wald thowe the fete wesshe and drye.
Jh*esu*, of this mekenesse be the sup*er*haboundaunce
Dystruy in me, synfulle, alle pride and arrogaunce,
And fille myne hert w*ith* p*er*fit and verray humilitee
For til ascende in vertue til hevenly sublimitee.
And Jh*esu* Lorde, fayne wald I thank the some man*ere* wise,
If I couth or war*e* digne or myght any way suffize
For thus ineffable grace and vnherd dileccioune
Shewed vnto wrichidist me in thi seints co*m*mvnyo*u*ne,
For thi sacroseint body has thowe taken me etyng
And thyn awen ryale blode in salut*er*e swettest drinkyng.
Who shal suffice to telle this hoegest luf of luvyng,
Or of thir*e* grettest benefaites ȝelde to point anything?
Thogh I my body to the deth toke thovzande tymes infinite,
Thus eendles mirable gudenesse myght I neu*er* come to qwyte.
I pray the, piest Jh*esu*, for alle this luf and honour*e*,
Thi benefaites above m*er*velle, O sawles lif and dulcour*e*,
Thi sac*ra*ment at my deth to thi plesance gra*u*nt me,
And in thi melliflewe p*re*sence w*ith*out eend be w*ith* the,
Whilk thing grant vs, Jh*esu*, for thyne ineffable m*er*cy,
Þ*at* w*ith* the Fad*er*e and the Haly Gast lyves and regnes eendlesly.

4505 Capitulum xliij^{m} *mar.* 4513 A tale *mar.* 4529 No*ta* bene *mar.* 4531 Graces to Godde at hour*e* of Evensonge *mar.* 4549 nota *mar.* 4553 plesance] *otiose mark over.* 4556 Amen *mar.*

† Graces to the, Jh*es*u, benigne Crist Goddis Son,
Thowe ert my Godde sothly and my saluacioune.
Thi luf shewed thowe to me in the hour*e* of Completorie
When thowe tremblyng for me swette blode ou*er* alle thi body.
To þ*at* stede, vndestressid, of free wille thowe the drewe
Whar*e* thyne enemys wald the take and bynde, swete Jh*es*u.
Thi benignest mansuetude shewed thov þ*at* tyme ywys
When to the trayto*ur* thi mowthe thov warnyd noght for to kysse.
The Jewes, whaym thow hadd shewed grete luf oft and relefe,
Toke and bande the fulle sore, and ledde forth als a thefe.
Thi disciples saide thay wolde dye w*ith* the, bot no dout
Thay fledde ilkone, seing of thyne enemys the rout.
Bot thow alle onely, Jh*es*u, bode in þ*at* hardest stour*e*
Amanges thyne enemys w*ith*out any help or defensour*e*.
W*ith* swerdes and staves and lant*er*nes was thow taken & w*ith* brandes,
W*ith* many iniurie and reprove p*re*sentid til Anna handes.
Of thy lore and disciples askid he the to this eende:
For he of thaym both two thoght the to reprehende;
Bot w*ith* alle mansuetude answerde thov, Lorde, wisly,
A buffet of his s*er*vant thar*e*on tholing mekely.
O swte Jh*es*u I pray, be thy blody swet, the,
Be thi sharppest byndyngs and wrongwys captivitee, [f.55^{v}]
Wasshe me out of the bandes of my stynking synne vile,
And to thyn awen joye lede me aft*er* this werldis exile,
Whilk thing graunt vs, Jh*es*u, for thi swettest m*er*cy,
Þ*at* w*ith* the Fader*e* and the Haly Gast lyves & regnes eendlesly.
† Graces to the, Jh*es*u, sou*er*eyn welle of mercy,
My Godde and my maker*e* and my salueo*ur* sothly.
In the hour*e* of Matynes thi luf to me freely shewed was
So to be japid soeffring in the house of Caphays.
Ther*e* war*e* the prince*s* of the poeple gadrid be conspiracye,
Witnesse and causes sekeing ageinst the for enevye,
And sekeing oft vp and doune of deth fande thay cause none
Rightwise, for thair*e* witnesse war*e* insuffissant ilkone.
At the last Cayphas askid the wher*e* thowe was Goddis Son,
And thow grauntid þ*at* ȝa be sothfast confessio*u*ne.
Þ*at* iuste cause of thi deth demed thay ther*e* alle about,
"He is of the deth coupable!" crying alle at a shovt.
Thi visage, Lorde, amiable hild thay, thyne eghen hyding,
Buffets & many a choppe who myght gif the stryving,
And saide in thair*e* wodenesse, "Have done, thow Crist, lat se
Telle nowe of alle this rovte be p*ro*ph*e*cie who stroke the."
Thi face so delitable til aungels for to beholde
W*ith* thair*e* \h/orrible spyttyng for to fyle war*e* thay bolde.
Thi brighter*e* eghen than the sonne, whilk sees clerely alle thing,
To hil, obumbr*e* and to blynde was thair*e* wode enforcyng.
Jh*es*u, for thi paynes of thyne eyghen thus hydeyng,
Thy contumelye and neckyng, buffets and bespitting,
My wikkidnesse forgif me, w*ith* alle the payne & the plight,
The whilk innoumbrable sithes I haf trespast in thy clere sight:
Whilk thing graunt vs, Jh*es*u, for thi swettest m*er*cy,
Þ*at* w*ith* the Fader*e* & the Haly Gast lyves and regnes eendlesly.

4559 In the houre of Completorie *mar.* 4561 Luc. xxij *mar.* 4575 Luc̣. vj^{o} *mar.* 4580 thyn] the *alt.* 4582 Amen *mar.* 4585 The hour of Matynes *mar.* 4596 Luc. xxij *mar.* 4608 Amen *under rub. mar.*

† Graces to the, Jh*es*u, sou*er*eyn welle of m*er*cy,
My Godde and my maker*e* and my salveo*ur* sothly.
In the houre of Pryme dayes thyne hoege luf shewed thow me
When thow of Herode and his ost for my sake scorned wald be,
When thow was alle nyght beiaped in bisshops house Cayphas,
Than to the p*re*sident Pilat be the morowe ledde forth thow was,
Whilk hering the a man of the lande of Galilee beyng
Til Herode sent the anone, als til his dome p*er*tenyng.
Herode was fulle gladde, hoping of the some m*er*velle to se,
Holdyng a fals wikked nygromancer*e* the to be.
The Jewes w*ith* cruwelle insta*u*nce tofore Herode the accusid,
And Herode of thinges dyu*ers* w*ith* many wordes the apposid.
Bot thow, Lorde, in no worde wald make hym responsioune,
Knawing alle the malice of his wikked entencioune.
Than cledde he the in qwite for scorne & contumelye,
Als a fole scornyng the Herode w*ith* alle his famylye, [f.56r]
Remyttyng the to Pilat aft*er* this illusioune,
And thus thas enemys gadrid ent*er*reconsiliacioune.
Alle this tholid thow, Jh*es*u, in paciens sup*er*suffrable,
Noght in thi gilt, bot for our*e* wricchednesse innoumbrable.
Lorde, be thir*e* contumelyes and thi benigne clemence,
In alle my tribulacio*u*nes graunt me swete pacience,
In alle adu*er*sitees þ*at* I so tholemode ay be
Whar*e*thorgh i*n* thy kyngdome my dwelling be eu*er* w*ith* the,
Whilk thing graunt vs, Jh*es*u, for thy swettest m*er*cy,
Þ*at* w*ith* the Fader*e* and the Haly Gast lyves and regnes eendlesly.
† Graces to the, Jh*es*u, hono*ur* and benediccioune,
My gude Godde and maker*e* and alle my saluacioune.
Thi luf in the houre of Tierce shewed thow me tenderly,
For me sco*ur*gid and w*ith* thornes corovned most pynefully.
Als a misdoer*e* thy foos til a cold piler*e* bande the,
W*ith* ȝerdes and scovrges beting, alle gode wightes doel to se,
To-whils ther*e* hele no left in alle thy tendrest body,
Of whilk like welle-strondys thi blode brast out freely.
A corovne of sharpest thornes mayde thyne enemys plettyng,
In stede of a diademe it on thyne heved settyng;
And for a mantel real in coccyn cledde thay the,
Putte in thyn hande a rede for regale septre to be,
And on thair*e* knees tofore the sat thay, the saluting,
W*ith* many mowe & w*ith* scorne the kyng of Jewes callyng.
Thy ven*er*able heved w*ith* the rede stroke thai fulle angrily,
And w*ith* thair*e* handes on thi cheke and in thi nekke pynously.
Thi blode w*ith* thair*e* spittynges so thi faire face ouer*r*anne
Þ*at* thow was like to behalde ane \h/orrible seke mesel man.
I the beseke, swettest Jh*es*u, for thi sharpe rewfulle sco*ur*ging,
And pray the, Prince of pitee, for thyn hard corovnyng,
Þ*at*, wher*e* I wil or wil noght, thow me here so chastie
Þ*at* w*ith* scourges of thyn ire in other*e* werlde I ne bye,
Nor þ*at* I neu*er* fele sco*ur*ging of purgatories sharpnesse,
Bot w*ith*outen any to*ur*ment come to joye eu*er* eendlesse:
Whilk thing graunt vs, Jh*es*u, for thi swettest m*er*cy,
Þ*at* w*ith* the Fader*e* and the Haly Gast lyves & regnes eendlesly.

4609 Hour*e* of Pryme *mar.* 4625 Luc. xxj *mar.* 4626 thas] i.e. Herode & Pilat *over.* 4632 i*n*] *o.er.* 4635 Hour*e* of Tierce *mar.* 4641 left] *(*-ft *o.er.)* 4646 scorne] *o.s.o.* 4652 horrible] *(*h *in different ink).* 4653 Nota a gude p*ra*yer*e* *mar.* 4660 Amen *under rub. mar.*

† Graces to the, Jh*es*u, sou*er*eyn welle of m*er*cy,
My Godde and my maker*e* and my salveour*e* sothly.
The Sext hour*e* to me thow shewed both hoegely luf & pitee,
Tholing dome for my sake and to be nayllid on a tree.
Pilat his handes wesshe aft*er* thow was oft accusid,
Bot forthwith to be honged apon the Crosse he the demyd.
On thyne awen shuldres thay laide the Crosse to bere fulle hevie,
For thi shame and reprove to encrees more notablie, [f.56v]
And with ropes on the Crosse thyn enemys extendid the
And drofe thyn handes and thi fete w*ith* yren nailles til a tree,
And aft*er* the w*ith* the Crosse thai raised with a fulle grete crye,
And w*ith* mowes & w*ith* japes scorned the contynuellye.
And ther*e*, Lorde Jh*es*u, shewed thowe thyn hoegest dileccioune
For thi foos to thi Fader*e* praying a swete orisoune,
And ou*er* this, swettest Jh*es*u, war*e* thi paynes hoegely cressid
Thi moder*e* seen be thi Crosse w*ith* sorowe on ilk syde pressid,
And two thefes broght to place to encrees thy contumelye
Betwyx thaym two the hanged thyn enemys wode & vnselye.
Þ*at* one thi hoegest m*er*cy, Jh*es*u curtays & heende,
Shewed thowe, p*ar*adys grauntyng be contricio*un*e at his eende.
O Jh*es*u, I the beseke be the dome gyven on the,
And prays the be alle thy paynes innocent soeffred for me,
Þ*at* I bere neu*er* the sentence \h/orrible of the left p*ar*tye,
Bot ledde me to thi fair*e* regne of the right half compaignye,
Whilk thing graunte vs Jh*es*u for thyn ineffable m*er*cy,
Þ*at* w*ith* the Fader*e* and the Haly Gast lyves and regnes eendleslye.
† Graces to the, Jh*es*u Crist benigne Goddis Son,
Thow ert my Godde sothly, my lif and salvacio*un*e.
In the houre of None thi luf shewed thow to me holely,
On the gibet of the Crosse deignyng for me to dye.
A doelfulle lamentacioune made thow, Lorde, c*er*teynly,
When thow saide, "Hely, Hely, lamazabatany,"
Þ*at* is, "My Godde, my Godde, why has thowe forsaken me?"
When neu*er* the lesse in no tyme was thy Godde twynnyd fro the.
Aft*er* saying "I thrist" thay profred the mirred wyne
And ayselle medlid w*ith* galle, þ*at* thow shuld dye w*ith* more pyne,
And with dyuers scornyngs thyn enemys the blasphemyd,
And alle the shame þ*at* thay myght to the, Jh*es*u, thay did.
Aft*er* this, swete Jh*es*u, "Consummatum est", thow sayde,
And ȝalde thi spirit to the Fader*e*, and than died at a brayde.
Than thi side w*ith* a spere thay p*er*ced thorght at the last,
Of whilk riche blode and water*e* in my sawles hele out brast.
Alle creatures condoelid on thy payne than at ones,
The sonne blakke als an hayre & clevyng hard roche & stones,
Terremote and of graves notable apercioune,
And many body of the seintes roos w*ith* thi resurexioune.
O Jh*es*u, als thowe for me dyed in Mount Caluarie,
In me shewe thowe thi grace, þ*at* be thi swettest m*er*cy
I mot here in this lif so the both luf and s*er*ue
At my decesse thi joye eendlesly may deserue, [f.57r]
Whilk thing graunt vs, Jh*es*u, for thi grace and m*er*cy,
Þ*at* w*ith* the Fader*e* and the Haly Gast lyves and regnes eendlesly.

4662 The sext houre *mar.* 4664 Math. xxvij *mar.* 4687 The houre of None *mar.* 4704 The co*m*passioune of the element in Cristis deth *mar.* 4711 vs] J *alt.* 4712 Amen *under rub. mar.*

Now last herde we tofore the sevenfald graces accioune
Aght til Oure Lorde Jhesu for his dere passioune;
Nowe fylowes seven orisounes to say with tendernesse
Til Oure Ladye for hire grete sevenfold hevynesse.
For als it pleses Jhesu Crist his paynes in mynde be soght,
So likes Oure Ladye þat we hire sorowes kepe in oure thoght.
§ Als sometymes was a man religious Frere Prechoure
Þat hadde Oure Lady and hire son in dere luf and honoure.
His thoght was alway bisy in Cristis harde passioune,
And on the doel of Oure Ladye in erth hadde on hire soun.
This man prayed day & nyght, with alle the luf of his hert,
Þat Crist walde graunt hym to fele somme of his paynes smert;
And at the last, his pie askings lyked Oure Lorde Crist so wele
Þat of his passioune partie a littel he lete hym fele.
Hym thoght his handes & fete ware drawen out streitestly,
And with harde iren nayles perced most pynously.
After prayed he mekely Oure Ladye Marie virgyne
For alle hire swettest bountee, to lat hym fele of hire pyne.
Hym thoght thorgh the werlde to seke a swerde alder-sharpist
Was thrusten thorghout his hert, with sorow alder-grettist.
Thilk frere be swilk thinkyngs in graces acciounes
Hadde revelings dyvine and consolaciounes;
Wharefore rede we gladly to Crist the forsaide thankynges,
And to his gloriouse modere Marye the fylowyng hailsynges,
That we be qwitte in this lif fro alle manere hevynesse,
And atteyne in werlde to come euerlastyng joye and gladnesse.
† Hayle Marie, modere of Crist, of heven meke emperice,
Thow ert named virgyne dyvine, of sorowfulle consolatrice.
I praye the, modere of pitee, for alle the sorowe and distresse
Þat euer thow tholid in this lyf, without gilt more & the lesse,
To me, wriche, be socoure in alle tribulacioune,
Swettist and after thi soun next consolacioune.
Many ware thi sorowes in erthe and dyuers, this nys no tale,
Bot namely amanges alle othere, seven ware the princypale.
The first doel þat thyn hert thrast, be myne entencioune,
Was in the Temple when thow herde the prophecie of Symeoun.
With great joy and delight you came to the Temple;
With great grief and sadness you departed from the Temple.
In offering your son to such a Father you felt great joy,
But it was suddenly turned into a great sadness:
That old man Simeon announced sad news to you
When he prophesied to you about the sword of your beloved son
Which he declared would pass through your most holy soul.
Your heart felt no small sadness as a result of these words.
You understood the meaning of this prophecy completely,
And as a result you carried sorrow in your heart thereafter.
For the sake of this your sadness, most merciful mother, I beg you
Pray for me to your beloved son, the Lord Jesus Christ,
That on account of his most bitter Passion
He lead me, after this exile, to eternal consolation,
Which the Lord Jesus Christ deign to grant to us all,
Who with the Father and the Holy Spirit is for ever blessed.

4713 Capi[m] xliiij[m] *mar.* 4719 A tale *mar.* 4735 thankynges] i.e. of the seven Houres *mar.* 4738 Amen *mar.* 4739 Of seven sorowes of Oure Ladye – The first sorowe *mar.* 4745 tale] i.e. for þat was certeyne *over.* 4748 Recte viij° fol. sequente *mar.*; *folios 57v, 58r, and the beginning of 58v are left blank; the missing 100 lines are in Latin on ff. 64r, 65v, hand².*

† *Hail Mary, devoted mother of Christ, heavenly empress!*
You are, virgin goddess, the merciful comforter of sorrow in this life.
You then felt a second sadness, most sweet mother,
When you fled into Egypt with your beloved son.
King Herod was thinking of ways of killing your son,
And the angel of the Lord announced this to Joseph in a dream:
"Get up," he said, "take the boy and his mother and flee into Egypt,
For it will come to pass that King Herod will seek the boy to destroy him."
These things, virgin most gentle, truly wounded your soul,
And brought great sorrow to your virgin heart.
Then you had to leave relatives and acquaintances and homeland,
And flee by night through the desert to a land of pagans;
But King Herod was searching for your son with such hatred
That on his account he slew a hundred and forty-four thousand boys.
Most merciful Lady, you came to an alien land
Where you had neither relatives nor friends nor acquaintances.
There you endured great hunger and penury:
By distaff and needle you gained food and clothing for your son and yourself.
You endured this exile and sorrow for seven years,
And then, Herod being dead, you returned to your homeland with your son and Joseph.
For the sake of this sadness, most merciful mother, I beg you
Pray for me to your beloved son, the Lord Jesus Christ,
That in this pilgrimage he may preserve me from all evil,
And after this exile he may lead me to the heavenly homeland,
Which the Lord Jesus Christ deign to grant to us all,
Who with the Father and the Holy Spirit is for ever blessed.
† *Hail Mary, devoted mother of Christ, heavenly empress!*
You are, virgin goddess, the merciful comforter of sorrow in this life.
You felt the third sorrow then, most sweet mother,
When you lost your beloved twelve-year-old son;
For when your most beloved son was twelve
He went with you from Nazareth to Jerusalem on the day of the Paschal Feast;
But when that Feast had been observed and come to an end
You returned, and he, without your knowledge, remained in Jerusalem.
This did not happen, devoted mother, because of your negligence,
But as a result of the plan and design of the divine wisdom.
You thought the boy was with Joseph in the crowd of men;
Joseph thought he was with you in the crowd of women,
For the men used to go to the Feast alone, and the women by themselves,
But boys could go with either, as they wished.
When, therefore, you were a day's journey from Jerusalem
And you did not find the boy with Joseph, his putative father,
What grief and immense sadness overcame you then:
It is difficult for the heart to conceive, and difficult to describe.
With great sorrow you looked for him for three days,
Until you found him sitting among the learned men in the Temple.
For the sake of this sorrow, most merciful mother, I beg you
Pray for me to your beloved son, the Lord Jesus Christ,
That he may teach me to search for him as diligently in this life
So that I may deserve to find him happily in the heavenly Temple,
Which the Lord Jesus Christ deign to grant to us all,
Who with the Father and the Holy Spirit is for ever blessed.

† *Hail Mary, devoted mother of Christ, heavenly empress!*
You are, virgin goddess, the merciful comforter of sorrow in this life.
Then sweetest mother, you had a fourth sorrow,
When you heard that your most sweet son had been betrayed and taken prisoner.
The Jews, to whom he had very often given many benefits,
And the gentiles, to whom he had never been troublesome in anything,
Having got together, set out against him with swords and cudgels,
And took him and bound him as though he were a thief and brigand.
That disciple whom he had made administrator of his group
Betrayed him most faithlessly and deceitfully with a kiss.
All the disciples, who had said they were willing to die with him,
Leaving him alone, all fled from him.
Your son was led alone to the judges,
And suffered many insults, words and blows.
From place to place, from house to house they dragged him:
They did not hold back strokes and blows and spittle.
Oh what sorrow, and how much sorrow, you had then, devoted maiden,
When you heard such things, and so many, reported to you about your son!
I think that no mind could understand her,
Nor could any tongue fully describe her.
For the sake of this sorrow, most merciful mother, I beg you
Pray for me to your beloved son, Lord Jesus Christ
That for the sake of his captivity and the bonds of his chains
He may absolve me from the chains of all my sins,
Which [grace] the Lord Jesus Christ deign to grant to us all,
Who with the Father and the Holy Spirit is for ever blessed.
† *Hail Mary, devoted mother of Christ, heavenly empress!*
You are, virgin goddess, the merciful comforter of sorrow in this life.
You had a fifth sorrow then, most sweet mother,
When you beheld your most beloved son hanging on the Cross:
When thow se hym pyned sakles so many a folde, [f.58v]
And thow myght noght help hym, thyne hert was than fulle colde.
Hym see thow hange naked w*ith*outen reso*u*ne or skille,
And thai ne walde noght lat the w*ith* thyn awen mantel hym hille.
His thrist herde thow hym pleyne with grettist doel and disese,
And w*ith* a leest watres drope wold thay noght lat the hym ese.
Thow see his heved on the Crosse hynge doune most mis*er*ablye,
Bot w*ith* thi handes it support tholid noght thair*e* harde envye.
Thow herde scorne hym and jape his foos innoumbrable wise,
And thow myght noght redresse his wronges and iniuries.
Thow herde hym his goost commende til his Fader*e* on the Crosse,
And was noght suffred gif hym of luf a fynal kosse.
For thai ne wald noght thole the come negh, when he shuld dye,
For to close his swete eghen als vse is moderfulli.
Thow ne myght hym ese, nor help in nothing vtt*er*ly;
Þ*at* eked alway thi doel, swete virgyne moder*e* Marie.
Be this doel I p*ra*y the, O welle of verray swettnesse,
P*ra*y for me to thi son Jh*es*u, Lord of gudenesse,
Þ*at* in the houre of my deth his swete help I ne mysse,
And aft*er* this wricchid lif he bringe me to his blisse;
Whilk thing graunt vs Jh*es*u for his grace & m*er*cy,
With the Fader and the Haly Gast o substaunce p*er*fitly.

4857 scorne] *o.s.o.* 4857 commende] *o.s.o.* 4863 verray] *o.s.o.* 4868 Amen *under rub. mar.*

† Hayle, Cristis moder Marie, pie hevenyssh emperice;
Thow ert named virgyne dyvyne, of sorowfull consolatrice.
The sext doel al to-thrast thi tendre hert, mekest Ladye,
When thow thi son of the Crosse resceyvid so miserably.
When hym layde in thyn armys, moder*e* of luf and m*er*cye,
Colde, dede, bla and blody, Joseph of Aramathye.
Hym þ*at* thow bare in thi wombe virginel joyfully,
Wounded, dede, in thi kne halsid thow doelfully.
A newe sorowe and gemyng wellid in thyn hert þ*er*fore,
More than mans tonge can telle, & eu*er* wex more & more.
How mykel, moder*e* of pitee, was than thi doelfulle pleynyng,
What flodes thurgh thyn hert ran of trewest sorow and wepyng!
What hert brists noght to think thi bas waikest shrikyng?
Other*e* rist was to the none tofore thi son seen rysing.
So mykel sorowe and swilk doel hadde thow than c*er*tes, Ladye,
Þ*at* for thi son, or w*ith* hym, wolde thowe haf dyed gladlye.
Thow langvised day and nyght, and to-wepe neu*er* cessing
To-whils the melliflowe p*re*sence of thy son was wanting. [f.59^{r}]
O Godde, harde and stonysshe war*e* þ*at* hert be resoune
Þ*at* of thi doel thus immense shuld noght haf compassioune.
Be this doel I pray the, Marie, welle of swettnesse,
Pr*a*y for me to thi son Jh*es*u, Lorde of gudenesse,
Þ*at* in alle my disese he be my help and socour*e*,
And my sawle take to hym gladly in my last houre:
Whilk thing graunt vs Jh*es*u for his grace and m*er*cy,
Þ*at* w*ith* the Fader*e* and Haly Gast lyves & regnes eendlesly.
† Hayle, Cristis moder*e* Marie, pie hevenyssh emp*er*ice:
Thow ert named virgyne dyvyne, of sorowfulle consolatrice.
The sevent doel, suavest Ladie, was thi lange exilyng
Aft*er* thi son in erth*e* til his Fader*e* ascendyng.
In lango*ur*, doel and disese here was thi conu*er*syng
Whils thow the desiderable p*re*sence of thi son was wantyng.
O thyn hoege ardent desire of his reto*ur*nyng to the,
W*ith*out whame neu*er* other*e* joye nor comfort myght to the be;
Or who shuld thy langyng aft*er* hym telle to fulnesse,
Whame thow conceyved virgyne, and childed w*ith*out destresse?
O desire of desires, aft*er* his p*re*sence thinkyng,
To whame inviolat childid thi maydenes mylke was fedyng.
How oftsith, moder*e* tendrest, soght thow the stedes of thi son,
Kyssyng, halsyng ilkone in wepfulle devocioune.
Alle places devoutly thow visited of Jh*es*u:
Whar*e* thow hym virgyne conceyved, childid & hym dede knewe;
Whar*e* he was taken and betrasid, scornyd, bonden, offendid,
Bespittid, sco*ur*gid and corovned, dede, dolven and ascendid.
Thir*e* stedes & many ane other*e* ȝede thow oft dreryly,
Als sais Ephyphanius, twys twelve ȝere lastyngly.
Be this doel I pray the, Marye, welle of swettenesse,
Pray for me to thi son Jh*es*u, Lorde of gudenesse,
Þ*at* I thi sorowes forsaide be here so remenbring
Þ*at* w*ith* thi son and w*ith* the my joye be eu*er*lastyng–
Grauntyng the same Jh*es*u for his grace & m*er*cy,
Whilk w*ith* the Fader*e* and the Haly Gast lyves & regnes eendlesly.

4869 The vj doel *mar.* 4895 hevenyssh] hevenynssh; The vij doel *mar.* 4914 Of Our*e* Ladyes dwellyng in erth aft*er* hir*e* son *mar.* 4920 Amen *under rub. mar.*

Herde of the sorowes seven of Our*e* swete Lady Marie;
Now fylowes of hir*e* seven joyes to here consequently.
Hir*e* joyes ilk Cristen man eght wele luf and hono*ur*,
Þ*at* when our*e* nede is grettest, sho be our*e* help & soco*ur*;
§ And how this s*er*vice hertly is to Gods moder*e* greable,
In a preest ones devout til hir*e* is right notable,
Whilk hir*e* joyes to remenbre oft vsed comfortably,
W*ith* orisounes and w*ith* songes, at his myght devoutly. [f.59v]
This preest felle at the last in a fulle grevouse sekenesse,
And, his synnys remembring, he hadde grete hevinesse.
"Allas I wricche!" quod he, "What shalle I answer*e* or say
Tofore the juge all rightwyse, when he my lif wille assay?
Whar*e* he shalle aske me reknyng of alle my lyves dispence,
Of thoght, worde and of tyme, and my vile negliegence."
And anone, inprovise, he se the moder*e* of m*er*cy,
Whilk w*ith* gladde cherre and blith til hym saide comfortably,
"Joye to the, son wele luved, be glade, the thar*e* neu*er* drede,
For here come I myself til help in thi last nede.
Ofttyme greable seruice has thow done me sothly,
So mykel hono*ur* beryng to my joyes bysyly;
For grete joye is to me wher*e* my joyes er*e* in mynde,
Als in speche or heryng or thoght w*ith* freendes kynde;
And for thow has thaym hadde in thi mynde so trewly,
Now shalle I the rewarde innoumbrable thovzandly."
Wharefore gude is hir*e* joyes we hono*ur* w*ith* gude chere,
And w*ith* fervour*e* rede oft thir*e* orisoune fylowyng here.
† Joye to the, moder*e* of Crist, pie, riche and delicable;
To thi joyes ware neu*er* other*e* in alle werlds comp*ar*able;
And thogh neu*er* man suffize thi joyes to shewe be tale,
Als nowe ȝit I honour*e* thir*e* seven in speciale.
The first inopynably war*e* ouer*e* mesur*e* to telle,
How the archaungel fro Godde grette the, Seint Gabriel,
Þ*at* God Son hadde the chosyn and liked onely to calle,
To take flesshe of thi wombe forbe other*e* wymmen alle.
Anone als thi swete sawle to the message gaf assent,
Thi chastest bosme God Son conceyved the same moment.
Thus was thyn wombe sacrid be the Arche of sethym notid,
And thi sawle alder*e*-blissidst be the golden potte figurid.
In thilk Arche and the potte was manna kept p*re*ciously,
And in the brede of lyf Crist was closid sothfastly.
The p*re*ostendid the ȝerde whilk florisshed for Aaron,
And the figurid the flees fillid w*ith* dewe for Gedeon.
Aarons ȝerde agein kynde floured, of Gods special gyvyng,
And thow above kynde conceyvid be the Haly Gast inspiring.
Fillid was the flees w*ith* dewe, and the erth about al drye:
So was thi wombe fulle w*ith* God Son, neu*er* other*e* ther*e*to worthye.
Be this firist joye pray I the, Marie, moder*e* of pitee,
To Jh*es*u Crist thi dere son for to beseke for me, [f.60r]
At my deth to be me gladnesse and comfortyng,
And kepe my sawle fro the deth secunde and eu*er*lasting:
Whilk thing graunt vs Jh*es*us for his grace and m*er*cy,
Þ*at* w*ith* the Fader*e* and the Haly Gast lyves and regnes eendelesly.

4921 Capi^m xlv^m *mar.* 4925 A tale *mar.* 4934 negliegence] negcliegence *(c subp.).* 4947 The first joie *mar.* 4951 The j joie *mar. hand*². 4972 Amen *under rub. mar.*

† Joye to the, mod*er*e of Crist, be the sonne taknyd art thow
In diu*ers* joyes and delices for thyn incomp*ar*abletee now.
The seconde joye hadde thow than, message of gudliest gretyng,
When Elizabeth thy co*u*syne thi graciousest enbracyng
Felt and the son in hir wombe made a strange reioying,
And thi sawle alder-swettest a magnyfy jubylyng,
Thi sawle alder*e*-graciouseste in Godde thi salut*er*e gladyng,
Thi swete movthe a newe songe to Godde of gods endityng.
And til a vesselle of bavme was likned thi chastest wombe,
Redemptif bavme contenant Jh*es*u, Gods awen lombe.
Thow art the busshe fulle of fyre, the grenesse noght wastyng,
For thow was grete w*ith* Gods So*un* and neu*er* thy maydenhode lesyng.
Thow art the gardyn conclose of swettest aromatyze alle,
Of the whilk Godde bare the kaye, fulle of delices ou*er* alle.
Abigael the Sunamyte, Ladye, p*re*tendid the,
Confoving Dauid in hir*e* barme, and sauf hir virgynitee.
So norist thow in thi bosme ix moneths the hevens Kynge,
And thi maydenhode intacte inmaculat eu*er*lastinge.
For thus grete benefices thanked thow Godde plesa*u*ntly,
"*Magnificat*", a newe songe, makyng p*ro*pheticaly.
Be this joie seco*u*nde p*ra*y I the, Marie, mod*er*e of pitee,
To Jh*es*u Crist thi dere son for to beseke for me
(Whilk ix moneths restid in thi chast wombe) forevre
To bringe me to þ*at* rist whar*e* vnrest shalle be nevre;
Whilk thing graunt vs Jh*esu*s for his grace and m*er*cy,
Þ*at* w*ith* the Fader and the Haly Gast lyves and regnes eendl[esl]y.
† Joye to the, mod*er*e of Crist, swete flouryng ȝerde of Jesse,
P*ar*adys of alle delice art thow p*ro*ved for to be.
This was thi joye the thredde, als thorghe this werld is loos,
Thi pu[e]rpure wombe childyng God Son intacte and cloos.
In the shette ȝate figured shewed til Ezechiel,
And in the mountayn mirable revelid to Danyel.
So thi wombe kept the cloistre of maydenhod, Crist childyng;
Godde oonely be þ*at* shette ȝate and vnbrosten passyng.
W*ith*out mans handes a stone of the saide mountayn was shorne;
So Crist of the, vacant touchyngs maritales, was borne:
For als the sonnebeeme passis the glasse it noght hurting,
So was Crist borne of the, thy maydenhode vnsheendyng.
O Godde, what joye hadde thow O mod*er*e swettest for fayne
The fairest face oft lokyng of thi son, Godde sou*er*ayne. [f.60v]
O what gladnesse inmense hadde thow oft, mayden mylde,
Thi fairest bristes bedyng to þ*at* melliflewe childe.
O swettest of embracyngs streynyng a son so dere,
Conceyvid of the Haly Gast and neu*er* of erthly man here.
O suave and swettest kyssyngs of swilk a son singuler*e*,
So lordfulle and so benigne, so myghty, so familer*e*.
Be this thridde joye p*ra*y I the, Marie, mod*er*e of pitee,
To Jh*es*u Crist thy der*e* son for to beseke for me
Þ*at* aft*er* this lyf hym lyke to his realme me to bringe,
Whare I his delicable face be eu*er*more behaldyng;
Whilk thing graunt vs Jh*esu*s for his grace and m*er*cy,
Þ*at* w*ith* the Fader*e* and the Haly Gast lyves and regnes eendlesly.

4973 The ij joye *mar.* 4998 eendlesly] in perpetuum L, eendly (e *alt.* y); Amen *mar.* 4999 The iij joye *mar.* 5002 puerpure] puarpure (ua *subp.*, a *and letter over it erased*, a *ins. different ink*), parpure *mar. different ink has* d *over it.* 5003 Ezechiel xliiij *mar.* 5004 Danyel ij *mar.* 5018 familere] (u *alt.* i *by erasure*). 5024 Amen *under rub. mar.*

† Joye to the, moder*e* of Crist, sterne of the see lumynouse:
Fulle of gladnesse art thow, bright and thorghout radiouse.
The ferth joye hadde thow than, moder*e* of sou*er*eyne swetnesse,
Of thi son be the thre kynges hering so notable witnesse,
Whilk, tofore hym knelyng, knewe hym both Godde and kynge,
Encense and golde and mirre to hym mystykly offrynge.
Whar*e* thay felle doun*e* ano*ur*nyng thy son, thir*e* kynges thre,
Godde of lyve and verraye shewed thay him for to be.
Oblacio*u*ne of encense to preestis is wont p*er*tene,
Wharefore þ*at* offring thi son a preest p*re*tendid to bene.
Dede mens bodyes to byrye w*ith* mirre was the olde wonne,
Whilk shewed for vs to dye þ*at* borne was thi dere Sonne.
Offring of golde sometyme p*er*tened to gift reale,
Whilk offrande shewed thi dere son to be Kinge potenciale,
And this King, Crist, vsed for throne of regalie
Thi swete bosme sacrid, virgynel eendlesly.
The, mekest mayden, thilk throne figurede yvoriene
On whilk the kyng wysest Salomon to sitte was sene.
Thow art thilk turtyle trewest, swete doufe w*ith*out galle:
Thow art glorie til aungels and corovnne to seints alle.
Be this ferth joye pray I the, Marie, moder*e* of pitee,
To Jh*es*u Crist thi dere son for to beseke for me
To g*ra*ce haf here to lyve vnder*e* his luf and deffence,
And in the lif for to come haf eu*er* his swete p*re*sence;
Whilk thing graunt vs Jh*esu*s for his grace and m*er*cy,
Þ*at* w*ith* the Fader*e* and the Haly Gast lyves & regnes eendlesly.
† Joye to the, moder*e* of Crist, swete rose w*ith*outen thorne,
Thow ert of ligne reale gentilst to this werld borne.
Thi fift joy, moder*e* vntacte, of inmense reioying,
Hadde thowe of thi dere son in Goddes Temple offring.
W*ith* joye isshed thow the citee of his swete birth, Bethelem;
W*ith* joye, hym for til offre, entred thow Je*rusal*em. [f.61r]
With joye in the Temple of Godde was thyn entring:
W*ith* joye of thi dere son to Godde made thow offring.
To Godde qwhikke and verray offred thow thi dere son than,
Whame thow his Fader to be knewe, and neu*er* other*e* man.
O Godde, how thi swete hert was gladde inenarrably,
Thi Son so noble a Fader*e* to haf, and so myghty.
Symeon w*ith* swilk desire so lange hym abidyng,
Hym seen, lyst here no more in this lif make dwelling.
To this joye come also Anna the p*ro*phetesse,
And blissid hym & colloved w*ith* alle hir*e* hertis gladnesse.
Alle þ*at* war*e* negh laved hym, and magnifiant blissid,
And hym seen, w*ith* grete joye and jubilyng reioyid.
Lady, what joye was than in thyn hert abo*u*ndyng,
The \s/wilk a son of alle sons to swilk a Fadir*e* offring.
Be this fift joye pray I the, Marie, moder*e* of pitee,
To Jh*es*u Crist thi dere son for to beseke for me
Þ*at* in alle my disese he be my comfortyng,
And til his joye bringe me, þ*at* neu*er* shalle haf eendyng;
Whilk thing graunt vs Jh*esu*s for his grace and m*er*cy,
Þ*at* w*ith* the Fader*e* and the Haly Gast lyves and regnes eendlesly.

5025 The iiij joye *mar.* 5033 Encense *(followed by rubricator's paragraph mark obscuring scribe's) mar.* 5035 Mirre *(followed by rubricator's paragraph mark obscuring scribe's) mar.* 5036 borne] *o.s.o.* 5037 Golde *(followed by rubricator's paragraph mark obscuring scribe's) mar.* 5050 Amen *mar.* 5051 The v joye *mar.*; thorne] *o.s.o.* 5052 borne] *o.s.o.* 5070 swilke] *(*s *and* h *subp. different ink).* 5076 Amen *mar.*

† Hayle Marie, moder*e* of Crist, pie dawenyng delicable,
Fairest and fulle of luf and alle desiderable.
Thi sext joye, swettest Ladie, was this, I vnderstonde:
Thy dere son þ*at* was lost when thow in the Temple hym fonde,
Whilk, when thow hadde hym fonden, was to the subgit mekely,
Sou*er*eyn Godde and thi son and thow moder*e* most sely.
O purest virgyne, thow toke be thi bright chastitee
The stereneste vnicorne þ*at* of no man myght taken be;
A lombe made thow mansuet of the stronge lyon ferefulle,
And the egle indomable thow reclamed at the fulle.
Thow bande and thow ou*er*come the wisest King Salomon;
Thow defovlid w*ith* thi feete the olde cruwellest dragon;
Thow toke, mayden soliter*e*, the pellican of desert,
The salamandra soght to the fyre of thi charitable decert;
Thow meked the felle panter*e*, mayden, floure of myldnesse,
And the hoege olyphaunt obeyide to thy mekenesse;
Thow made a ȝonge fenix of the oldest, and bot one.
The Ydicus made a skippe fro heven to the anone,
When þ*at* hyeghest Godde \Son/ wolde of the be incarnat,
And, als a childe to the moder, to the be subiugat.
Be this sext joye pray I the, Marye, moder*e* of pitee, [f.61v]
To Jh*es*u Crist, thi dere son, for to beseke for me
And in this werlde graunte me to be so his subgit
Þ*at* he bringe me to the joye eu*er*lastingly p*er*fit;
Whilk thing graunt vs Jh*esu*s for his grace and m*er*cy,
Þ*at* w*ith* the Fader*e* & the Haly Gast lyves and regnes eendlesly.
† Joye to the, moder*e* of Crist, piest qwene of alle heven,
The sevent joye passis what hert may think or tonge may neven:
Whilk, sou*er*eyne emp*er*ice, thow hadde in the last eende
When thow, both body and sawle, foreu*er* til heven shuld weende,
And thi son in his throne corovnd the eendlesly
With the corovne of his regne, aft*er* hymself most sely.
Thow was figurid sometyme be þ*at* welle alder-leest,
Whilk aft*er* growed, rynnyng forth in a flude grettest;
And als the grete King Assuer*e* meke Hest*er* enha*un*cid,
So Crist King the mekeest in heven has the corovnid.
The wise Abigael also sometyme p*re*figured the,
Whame Dauid for hire prudence made his wif for to be;
So the King of heven chase the his spouse and luf to bene,
His moder*e* and his felawe, his sister*e* and hevens qwene;
And Salomons moder*e* also figured the resonably
Whame he on his right half sette in a throne hym by.
The king of hevens so the als moder*e* to this joye mette,
And on his honorable right hande in his throne he the sette.
What joye ineffable hadde thow, O Ladye fairest and heende,
Entring both body and sawle in joye þ*at* neu*er* has eende.
Be this joye ineffable, qwene of heven, I pray the
To thi dere son Jh*es*u like the beseke for me
Þ*at* aft*er* this exile he me lede thorgh his g*ra*ce benigne
To dwelle withouten eende in the throne of his regne;
Whilk thing graunt vs Jh*esu*s for his sou*er*eyne m*er*cy,
That with the Fader*e* and the Haly Gast lyves & regnes eendlesly.

5077 The vj joye *mar.*; Hayle] *rubricator's* H *partly obscures the scribe's.* 5095 son] *different ink* (Filius L). 5102 Amen *under rub. mar.* 5103 The vij joye *mar.* 5128 Amen *mar.*

And thus eendes right here this ruyde translacioune
Off the boke named 'Mirour*e* of Mans Saluacioune'.
Jh*es*u alle thas encreece, in his grace and m*er*cy,
Whilk to lerne to do wele heres or redes it hertly. [f.62^{r}]

THE MIDDLE ENGLISH INDEX

Chapter references wholly in {} are conjecturally derived from the information given in the index itself, since they are wholly obliterated on the page. Those in [] are, of course, emendations: in order to avoid visual confusion, the square brackets always contain the whole reference, not just the portion emended.

Absolon is hanged	**xxv^{o}**
Abner is pleigned	**xxvij**
Abraham is delivred	**[xxx]**
Abigael plesid Dauid	**xxxvij^{o}**
Abymalech slayne	**xxxviij**
Absolon slewgh his brother	**xxxvij**
Achior is bonden	**xx**
Adam & Eue sorowed	**xxvj**
Ayoth slewgh Eglon	**[xxix]**
Amon defouled þe messages of Dauid	**xxj**
Antipater is accusid	**xxxix**
Anna wif of Thobie wept	**xxxv**
Appinen concubine	**xxj**
Archa of þe Testament is O*ur* Ladie	**x**
Archa *tra*nslat to Dauid house	**xxxvj**
Archa Noe	**ij**
Astiagis doghter	**iij**
Ascensio*un* of Crist	**xxxiij**
Assu*m*ptione of Our*e* Ladie	**xxxvj**
Assuers feste	**[xlij]**
Affix\i/one of C*ri*st to the Crosse	**xxiij**
A noble man	**xl**
A mans state tofor he sy*n*ned	**j**
Babel tour*e*	**xxxiiij**
Baris tour*e*	**vj**
Balaam proph*et*e	**iij**
Bananyas slewgh the lyon	**xxix**
Balthazar Kynge	**xl**
Baptesme of Crist	**xij**
Baptesme threfold	**xij**
Bel and þe Dragon	**xiij**
Brynnyng busshe	**vij**
Cham scorned his fader	**xix**
Candelabr*e* of gulde	**x**
Corovned is Crist	**xxj**
Conceptio*un* of Crist	**vij**
Co*n*solac*iou*ne of o*ur* Faders be Crist	**xxviij**
Clamo*ur* of	**.......**
Crucified is Crist eft.......	**{xxiiij}**
Creat*ur*es had co*m*pass{ioun}	**{xxvij}**

5133 *See Explanatory Note.* 5135 xxxj] xxxiiij. 5141 xxix] xxxix. 5152 xlij] xlj.

Crist ou*er*come the f{eend} {xxix}
Cristis soper {xvj}
Clustre of grapes brogh{t} {xxij}

Daniel in the lake {xxviij}
Dauid slew viij[C] {xxvij}
Dauid slewgh a lyon & a bere {xiij}
Dauid slewgh Golias [xiij]
Dauid repentyng [xiiij]
Dauid resceived w*ith* lovyng [xv]
Domynyks Avisio*u*n [xxxvij]
Dowaires of þe soule & þe body [xlj]

Eleazar is dede xxiiij
Ewilmeradac xxv
Eissue of Israel out of Egipt xxxj
Epiphanye of Crist ix
Excellent p*er*sones xlij

Fasci[c]le of mirr*e* xxx
Flagellacio*u*n of Crist [xx]
Flagellac*iou*ne of m*a*rchandz be Crist xv
Floure is Crist iiij
Fo*ur*naise of Babiloigne xxviij

Gedeons flees vij
Gravyng of Crist xxvij
Gret joies of heven xlij
Grete joies of O*ur* Ladie xlv
Grete tree of Nabugodonosor [xxiiij]
Giftes of þe Holy Gost seven xxxiiij [f.62v]
.... iij
.... v

J{acob} .... xxxiij
J....... xxxij
J....... xlj
J....... xxviij
J{onas] .... xxvij
J....... xxxj
J{ephte} .... {d}ought{er} v
J{eremies lamentaci}one xv
I{dols of Egi}pt felle xj
J{ordan} ....d bakward xij
J{ob was t}ormentid xx
J{oab} slew Amasa xviij
Joseph putte in þe cist*er*ne xxvij
Jonas casten out of þe shippe xxvij
Jonas casten out of þe whalle xxxij
Japid is Crist tofor Cayphas xix
Japid is Crist tofor Herod xx
Image of a mayden in Egipt xj
Isaac beres wode xxij
Joseph cote xxvj

5179 xiii] xiiij. 5180 xiiij] xv. 5181 xv] xxx. 5182 xxxvij] xlj. 5183 xlj] xxxviij. 5189 Fascicle] Fascile. 5190 xx] xl. 5198 xxiiij] xxj.

Ysay was sawen [xxiij]
Jubal fande music xxiij
Judith slewgh Oloferne xxx

Kaym slewgh Abel xviij
Kitte was a stone out of a hille xj
Kynges thre ix

Lameth was bette xx
Lagh gyven in Syna xxxiiij
Loth was delyvred xxxj

Maryes concept*io*une iij
Maries birth iiij
Maries offryng to the Temple v
Maries lif descrivyng v
Maries sponsyng vj
Maries conceyvyng of C*ri*st vij
Maries fleyng til Egipt xj
Maries compleynt xxvj
Marie lufs vs xxvj
Marie ou*er*com þe feend xxx
Marie p*ra*ys for þe werld xxxix
Marie bare Crist viij
Maries co*nuer*sac*iou*ne in þe Te*m*ple v
Maries co*nuer*sac*iou*ne aft*er* Crist ascension xxxv
Marie is o*ur* mediat*ri*ce [xxxvij]
Marie is o*ur* defensat*ri*ce xxxviij
Mare enen*e* xij
Manna gyven xvj
Maudeleines conu*er*sion xiiij
Manasses dide penance xiiij
Michol sorowed xxxv
Miracle of Cristis Passio*u*n xliij
Moab Kyng sacrified his so*u*n xxiij
Michol lete out Dauid xxxviij

Nabal offe[illegible]did Dauid xxxvij
Naaman Syr*us* xij
Neomy doelid xxvj

Orisones of þe Passio*u*n xliij
Occ\o/ours of C*ri*st til his e*n*myes [xvij]
Octovian Emp*er*our*e* viij
Oyle gyven to þe wydowe [xxxiiij]
Orison of C*ri*st for his c*ru*cifio*urs* xxiij
Ostensio*u*n of Cristes wo*u*ndes to the Fader [xxxix]

The porte close iiij
Preceps x x
Purificac*io*une of Our*e* Ladie x [f.63r]
Prodegat so*u*n xiiij
Palmesonday xv
Pharao is drovned xlj

5222 xxiij] xxxiij. 5245 xxxvij] xxxviij. 5247 Mare enen*e*] i*d est* þe lauatorie att \þe/ entree of þe Temple *over*. 5259 xvij] xvj. 5261 xxxiiij] xiiij. 5263 xxxix] xxxij.

Rabaath is taken	xlj
Rebecca Batuel	vij
Repentanz er receyved of God	[xiiij]
Riches er not ay to da*mp*natione	ij
Sara Ragnel	vj
Samuel is offred	x
Sac*er*dotale dignitee	xvj
Sa*m*pson slevgh a thovzand	-
Sa*m*pson slevgh a lyon	xxix
Sa*m*pson bar*e* þe ȝates	xxxij
Sa*m*pson blyndid	xix
Sangar slevgh vj^{C}	[xvij]
Saul p*er*suyed Dauid	xviij
Salomons moder is worshipt	xxxvj
Salomons glorie	xlij
Semey myssaide Dauid	xxj
Sepulcr*e* of Crist	xxvij
Sibille see a sercle	viij
Syba so*un* of Botrus	xxxvij
Signe grete seen in heven	xxxvj
Sodome ou*er*tirved	xxxj
Socoth citee	xlj
Scala Jacob	[xxxiij]
Statue of Nabugodonosor	xj
Spirit septiforme was sent	xxxiiij
St*ruciou*ne of Salomon	[xxviij]
Stone kytt of þe mounte	xj
Stone rep*ro*ued	xxxij
Seven doels of Marie	xliiij
Thama{r}	{xxx}
Te*m*ptac*iou*ne of þ.......	....
Te*m*ptac*iou*ne of the.......	....
Te*m*ptac*iou*ne of Cris{t}	x{iij}
Temple Salomon	{iiij}
Tour*e* Dauid	{vj}
Tubalchaym	{xxiij}
Traysyng of Crist	{xviij}
Throne of Salomon	{ix}
Virgynes x	{xl}
Vengeances many of God	x{vij}
Vigne planted a man	xxij
Wo*m*man in Abela	[xxxvij]
Wo*m*man in Thebes	xxxviij
Wo*m*man Thecuytes	xxxvij
Xprist is a vigne	viij
Ȝerde of Aaron	[viij] [f.63v]
Ȝerde of Jesse	iiijd

5272 xiiij] ix. 5281 xvij] xv. 5292 xxxiij] xxxiiij. 5295 xxviij] xx. 5311 xxxvij] xxxviij. 5315 viij] vij.

........................eend fro the begynnyng
.....................en / and thus pore rymayng
.... latyn / has it þorghout right so
..............at \e/end / metyng lynes mekely two
...........rwith answers to þe latyn
..........her / in nou*m*bre & lyne
........esses streynyng co*n*tinuelly
.......to filow / my wyser thus symply

5317-24 *The status of the lines at the top of f.63v, on a new page after the Index, is uncertain: perhaps they should not be treated as a postscript, but in the Description of Manuscripts as if they were annotations. The left half of the paragraph, almost obliterated by damp, does not respond to u.v. To the right, in another contemporary hand, are the marginal comments. Neither postscript nor commentary is in the hand of the scribe or the writer of the Latin on ff.64r,v, but the commentary may be in the hand which wrote the Index on the two previous pages, which may belong to one of the correctors of the main text.* 5317 in regarde of sutile & crafty metryng als in many places accordyng or filowyng l*itter*ae *(?* l*itter*at*e)* or swylk other *mar.* 5320 mekelye . homely for the Aucto*ur* toke more hede to fede þe sowles hert þan to soften þe bodely ere *mar.* 5322 For craft may be calde riches *mar.* 5323-24 *In a different 15th-century hand, using bright brown ink partly erased and faded:*.....may.....be / my depatry in moste...

APPENDIX

The Original Author's comments on his Prohemium, and his Prologus (passages found in the Latin manuscripts but not translated in the ME).

The Latin text opens with this brief introduction to the Prohemium.

Here begins the Prohemium of a certain new compilation. It seems helpful and useful to set down chapter by chapter, in a Prohemium, the elements and stories used in this book. Anyone who reads this Prohemium carefully will easily be able to understand the whole book.

After the Prohemium (which begins the ME manuscript) are several more lines in which the author further describes his purpose.

This is the end of the chapter-headings of this little book. I have compiled the said list of contents, providing a summary, for the sake of poor preachers, so that if by any chance they cannot afford to buy the whole book they can, if they know the stories, preach from the Prohemium itself.

Next follows this Prologus.

Those who instruct many men in righteousness will shine like stars forever. For this reason I decided to compile a book to teach many people, from which they can both receive and give instruction. I think nothing is more useful in this present life than for a man to learn to know God his creator, and understand his own condition. Men of letters can gain this knowledge from Scripture, but the uninstructed must be taught in the books of the laity–that is, in pictures.[1] So for the glory of God and the instruction of the unlearned I have decided to compile, with God's help, a laymen's book. But so that it may instruct both laymen and clerics I try to clarify matters for the reader by the use of simple precept.

But first I intend to describe the overthrow of Lucifer and the angels, and then the fall of our first parents and their descendants. After that I shall show how God freed us by his Incarnation, and with what prefigurations he earlier foreshadowed that Incarnation. However, it must be noted that in this little work various stories are mentioned that are not presented word for word in every detail, because a preacher is not obliged to expound anything of a story that is not relevant to his argument. An example or parable will make the truth of this clearer. A certain monastery had a huge oak standing in its grounds, which had to be felled and grubbed out on account of the smallness of the site. When it had been felled, servants of the monastery gathered there and each chose the pieces appropriate to his office. The master smith cut off the lower trunk which he realised was suitable [for an anvil-base] in his smithy.[2] The master of the leather-workers chose the bark for himself, which he crushed into powder for tanning his hides. The master of hogs took the acorns, with which he intended to fatten his piglets. The master builder chose the tall trunk, from which to cut beams and roofs. The master fisherman chose the curved parts, to make the ribs of ships from them. The master of the mills grubbed out the roots, which he realised would be suitable for the mill on account of their strength.[3] The master baker gathered together the branches with which he afterwards heated his oven. The sacristan carried away green leafy boughs and with them decorated his church for a feast. The scribe picked about a hundred galls or oak-apples with which he made up ink. The master cellarer took various pieces from which he wanted to make amphoras and other vessels. Last of all, the master cook collected the fragments and took them away for the kitchen fire. Each one selected things useful in his duties. That which was suitable for the task of one was not appropriate to another. The same applies to the telling of a story: any preacher takes from it what seems to meet his needs. In this little work I shall use the same method, including only such details of the story as suit my purpose: I do not want to retell the whole story in full, in case I bore readers and listeners.

---

1 The image is found in a letter from Gregory the Great to the Bishop of Marseilles (*PL* LXXVII 1128).: *Nam quod legentibus scriptura, hoc idiotis praestat pictura cernentibus, quia in ipsa etiam ignorantes vident quid sequi debeant, in ipsa legunt qui literas nesciunt.* Patristic references to this idea are listed by Gougaud (q.v.): several later citations mention *litteratura* or *libri laicorum*.

2 The use of the bottom part of tree-trunks as bases for anvils was commonplace: see Tubalcain's forge in ch.23 of the *Mirour*.

3 The roots were presumably used as drive shafts and spindles, requiring strength in torsion.

It should also be understood how conveniently Scripture is like soft wax which on the impression of a seal adopts its shape, so that if the seal contains a lion, the soft wax when impressed at once takes its form; and supposing that another seal contains an eagle, the same wax will, when impressed by it, have the shape of an eagle. In this way the same thing may sometimes signify the devil, sometimes Christ. We should not be surprised by this quality in Scripture: it can give an object (or person) different meanings according to their behaviour. When King David committed adultery and murder he prefigured not Christ but the Devil; when he loved his enemies and behaved well to them he prefigured not the Devil but Christ.[4] Nor must one object to Christ's sometimes being represented by an evil-doer. On these occasions an appropriate interpretation of name or act must be made. For example, although Absolom wickedly took revenge on his father, nevertheless Christ is prefigured by him on account of some similarities–not because Absolom treated his father badly, but because he was the most beautiful of men and was hanged on a tree: for Christ was 'beautiful above the sons of men'[5] and hanged from the tree of the Cross, yielding up his spirit.[6] On one occasion Samson entered the town of Gaza and slept that night with a prostitute. His enemies closed the gates of the town and meant to kill him in the morning. In the middle of the night Samson rose from sleep and lifting the gate of the town carried it away with him. Although Samson may have sinned with that whore, he prefigured Our Lord Jesus Christ–not because he lay with a prostitute but because in the middle of the night he rose up and broke the gates of the town. In the same way Christ rose in the middle of the night from the sleep of death, and destroying the gates of Hell carried off its prisoners with him.[7] I have introduced and explained these interesting examples, which I thought might be useful to students of Holy Scripture, so that if by any chance they come across similar things in studying this little book (for such is its method of exposition) they will not misunderstand me.[8]

O good Jesus, grant that this little work may please thee, instruct my fellows and make me pleasing to thee!

---

4 See ch.38 and 17 of the *Mirour*.

5 Ps. xliv 3, one of the Messianic psalms.

6 See ch.25 of the *Mirour*.

7 See ch.31 of the *Mirour*.

8 *mihi non invertant* (? 'they will not be put off').

EXPLANATORY NOTES

The notes which follow are not exhaustive. In the interests of brevity no attempt has been made to give patristic sources for all the types, or to discuss the art history of all the images. Basic references for the iconography of the scenes which appear in the woodcuts are given, as a rule, only for the antitypes, since types are often discussed in articles on the antitypes. After l.406, iconographical references occur at roughly regular intervals, e.g. 406, 506, 606, etc. Since the first two chapters do not follow the typological pattern of chs.3-42, each of the eight woodcuts comprising them is treated separately. Literary references for the scenes illustrated appear only once: if they are in the captions they do not appear in the notes. Attributions in Migne's *Patrologia Latina* (hereafter referred to as *PL*) are given in the light of Glorieux's tables of re-attribution.

11ff The Latin manuscripts' text begins here. Notes on the subject-matter summarised in the *prohemium* or Table of Chapters are in the notes to the chapters. Lutz and Perdrizet (1907–hereafter referred to as L-P, their text being cited as L or without attribution) do not print the Latin Table: it may be found in Neumüller's facsimile manuscript (1972:ff.4^{v}-5^{v}), or in Berenson and James (1926:Pl.6).

12 estories] There may be a small, faint *h* inserted at the front of this word: the insertion, if present, is not scribal.

30 riȝt] Emendation of the scribe's *rist* (subpuncted, with *right* in the margin in a corrector's hand) is made on the assumption that he momentarily read the yogh in *riȝt* as a *ʒ*, and transposed it to *s*. The assumption presupposes a ME exemplar.

46 Temple of the so*nn*e] *templo sol* in the Latin manuscript; in ME the pun on sun/son is implicit, but since the Latin speaks of the 'sun' not the 'son' I have not capitalised *sonne*.

108 in] Did the translator misread an abbreviated form of *cum* as *in*?

157 Two ModE lines here are the equivalent of two Latin lines not accounted for in the manuscript: *Hoc est praefiguratus fuit per regem Ioab cum filium suum domino immolaret / Vt deus ab obsidione civitatem suam liberaret*; Joab] L has *Joab*, but 2582 below correctly refers to Moab.

191 *Et Noemi qui orbata filiis pulchra noluit vocari* 'And Naomi who, deprived of her sons, did not wish to be called Beautiful'.

203-4 'And the ostrich freed her young (which had been shut in a glass bottle by Solomon) by means of the blood of a snake found in the desert.' The desert, not mentioned in L, is in Comestor: the bird *de deserto tulit vermiculum*. (Petrus Comestor *Historia Scholastica PL* CXCVIII 1353; this major source for *SHS* is hereafter cited simply as 'Comestor' followed by a column number).

250 To Seinte Benet] *beato patri Dominico* (see 3942); the substitution suggests a Benedictine translator.

264 so*u*n] There is no precedent in the MS for this spelling, which occurs unabbreviated only as *son* or *sonne*; however, the distinctive separate stroke over or preceding *n* in the word occurs in 20 cases, one of which (4722) rhymes with *passioune*.

306 Here most Latin MSS have, before another section on the use of the book, the well-known but nonetheless surprising observation that the contents of the *prohemium* will provide for poor preachers unable to afford the whole book a summary from which to preach (Neumüller 1972:f.5^{v}); a translation into ModE of these Latin passages, neither of which is translated in the ME manuscript, appears in the Appendix at the end of this book.

313 For the iconography of *The Fall of Lucifer* see Réau (1955-58:IIi 56-64) and Kirschbaum (1968-76:I 642-43).

316 Woodcut: the empty throne at the top left awaits Christ or the Virgin to represent mankind in taking Lucifer's former position in heaven (see n.1058). The falling angels grow deformed as they descend.

320 vpright] Until cursed, the serpent was 'erect, like a man' (Comestor 1072); a womans face] ibid.: the image in Bede to which Comestor refers is untraced (Bonnell 1917:257).

323 bokes] For example Comestor 1072 and Aquinas *ST* IIii q.165 a.2.

328 The doctrine of The Fall is explained in *NCE* V 814-16.

329 Damacens feelde] The Hebrew word corresponding to the Vulgate *de limo terrae* (Gen. ii 7), referring to the material from which Adam was created, is *adamah*, mistakenly thought to have some connection with Damascus (Dama-scus). The popular legend (found in Comestor) is also in Voragine I 77, Vincent of Beauvais *Speculum Historiale* I xli and is referred to in Chaucer *Monk's Tale* B3197.

331 For the iconography of the *Creation of Eve* see Schiller (1971-80:IVi 90-92 and Abb.217-227).

337ff This theory of Eve's creation is in Aquinas *ST* I q.92 a.3. God made woman from clay: as the equal of Adam, she would not obey him, so God made another woman from Adam's side, to ensure her obedience to her husband (Ginzberg 1909-38:I 65-68).

390 For the iconography of the *Marriage of Adam and Eve* see Schiller (1971-80:IVi 90-92 and Abb.217, 221).

341 ȝit] L has *si in honore pertitisset* 'if she had remained in this [position of honour]'; the scribe's *þat* is probably due to misreading of a ME source.

343 For the iconography of the *Temptation of Eve* see Réau (1955-58:IIi 83-86) and Kirschbaum (1968-76:I 41-61).

348 Adam was guilty of uxoriousness in being more reluctant to offend Eve than to offend God.

350 *Non tamen ea Deum vel deos esse putavit* 'Yet he did not think it was either God or gods'; the translator seems to have momentarily read *deosesse* as a feminine noun, giving his *goddesses*.

353-54 Two ModE lines here are the equivalent of two Latin lines not accounted for in the MS: *Mulier ergo plus quam vir peccavit / Quia se similem posse fieri Deo aestimavit*; see Aquinas *ST* IIii q.163 a.4.

364 'If you are not of that kind [strong and wise], make it your responsibility to be on your guard while there is still time'; L has *Quomodo tu, qui non es talis et tantus a muliere securus eris?* 'How will you, who are not like them, or so many as they are, be safe from woman?'.

365-66 *Virum Adam, diabolus tentare none audebat, / Hunc mulier, audacior diabolo, defraudare praesumebat* 'The woman, bolder than the devil, dared to trick the man Adam, whom the devil did not dare to tempt'.

377-78 These two lines represent four in L: *Aures ejus nunquam obsurdescerent, Et dentes eius nunquam obstupescerent, / Oculi ejus nunquam caligarent, Et pedes ejus nunquam claudicarent.* This compression accounts for the chapter's being only ninety-eight lines long.

389 for ... witte] L *nullus autem homo praesumat investigare* does not account for the ME, but Miélot's version of 1448 has *tant soit il sage et prudent* (L-P 1907:122).

390 Comestor 1075 observes that it is futile to question the divine will in this matter.

391-92 Two ModE lines here are the equivalent of two Latin lines not accounted for in the MS: *Cur etiam ipsos angelos creare volebat, / Quorum casum certissime praecognoscebat.*

404 Rom. ix 18; cf. Ex. xxxiii 19.

406 For the iconography of the *Fall* see n.343.

415 Cf. the behaviour of The World in *The Castle of Perseverance* (Eccles 1969:8-9, 16-27, 74-82).

416 Heghting ... gude] L *Multa bona promittentem* 'promising many good things'; perhaps *one*, which may be in hand², should not be accepted.

427-28 'Look, your wealth, which gives you great power now, barely ensures you a shroud at your death to cover your revolting body.' L has *In extrema necessitate nullum praestant homini juvamen / Sed vix tribuunt corpori vilissimum linteamen* 'In extreme necessity they [possessions] give man no help: they can provide only the paltriest shroud to the body.'

437-38 Matt. xxvi 48.

438 *Ipse est: tenete eum, aeternaliter cruciando* 'That is he, take him to torment forever'; the ME line is punctuated on the assumption that a scribe read *tenete* as *tene te*, and that he meant 'Take him–that one–to you, to everlasting torment'.

442 Dan. iv 24.

445-46 Tob. iv 9.

496 The Fathers give many explanations of the olive (usually, as might be expected, in terms of peace, as in Augustine *PL* XXXIV 47), but I have not located one precisely equating it with redemption. In Bede (*PL* XCI 102) the olive is equated with grace and eternal life, in Hildefonsus (*PL* XLVI 180) it is pity or mercy, the oil being the 'fruit of mercy acceptable to God'; in Alcuin (*PL* C 531) the olive represents renewal and light, announcing peace to the world.

499 to then closed ... arca] *hiis qui erant in arca* 'to those who were in the ark': a stroke separates *then* from *closed*; presumably *then* is dem.pron.dat.pl. (*OED tho*) but this form is not used elsewhere by the scribe, and it is possible that the reading should be *the[m]* or even, if one assumes that the dividing stroke is not scribal, *thenclosed* ('th'enclosed').

506 For the iconography of the *Annunciation to Joachim* see Mâle (1961:238-41), Schiller (1971-80:IVii 57-59).

510 The parable is similarly interpreted in Langland B Text Passus XVII ll.47-123, cf. nn.1285, 4266.

511 Luke x 30-36.

531 kepere] III Kings xvi 24. Samaria in Hebrew is *Shomeron*, one meaning of which is 'belonging to Shemer'. Shemer is probably from *shamar* 'to keep, watch, observe', originally meaning '(May God) watch over (him)'. In Ḥebrew, *Shomeron* is similar to *shamar*.

539 The marginal note erroneously refers to the Virgin's conception of her son, rather than her own conception by her mother, announced by an angel to Joachim (Voragine V 100, and see n. 506).

545 Comestor 1470 is more direct than the designer of the woodcut: he describes how Astiages saw rise from his daughter's genitals a vine that filled all Asia.

551 Cyre] I Esdras i.

571-72 For the iconography of the *Enclosed Garden* (Cant. iv 12) see Kirschbaum (1968-76:II 77-82). The Canticle of Canticles was interpreted in terms of both the Virgin's life and the love of Christ for his Church (see *Song of Songs*). The popularity of the theme is attested by the illustrated blockbook version of the *Cantica Canticorum* (q.v.).

572 seled] The exact meaning of the 'sealed fountain' (*fons signatus*) is clarified in the facsimile by Neumüller (1972:cap.6/d) where the fountain is called *fons signatus id est sigillatus*, and is shown not only lidded but padlocked: the idea is that it is closed with a personal seal, not merely with a cover.

574 yette] Consonantal *y*- occurs only twice in the MS: here and at 921 *yhit* (a unique departure from the scribe's normal *ȝit*).

578 of ... witt] *sitientium amarum* 'for thirsty souls'; *sitientium* was misread as *scientium* by the translator or his source.

586 The curse on Eve (Gen. iii 16) is turned to blessing in the Virgin (*Eva* becomes *Ave [Maria]*).

589 *Stella Maris* 'Star of the Sea' is one of Mary's ancient titles (see Jerome's *Liber de Nominibus Hebrais PL* XXIII 833). The *Golden Legend* gives three reasons for Balaam's comparison of Mary to a star: her beauty, opening heaven to us; her illumination of the Church; her virtue, constant as the fixed stars (Voragine II 124-25).

590 tempestuouses] The adj. may carry a French pl. ending: see n.1501.

601 The oriental legend of Theophilus became very popular in medieval literature: see Fryer (1945) and Mäle (1961:260-61). He modestly refused the bishopric of Adana in Cilicia, but beginning to desire power, signed a document promising his soul to the devil in return for worldly honour. He became more valued than the bishop, but remorse tormented him. The Virgin appeared in a dream, returning the document she had taken from the devil. After confessing publicly, he died.

606 For the iconography of the *Nativity of the Virgin* see Schiller (1971-80:IVii 63ff). The genealogy of Christ (Matt. i) ends with Joseph: for an explanation of its relation to Mary see ll.817-20, and Voragine II V 96-99.

607 For the popular image of the Tree of Jesse see Watson (1934) also Mâle (1961:165-70), Schiller (1971-80:I 15-22) and Kirschbaum (1968-76:IV 549-58). For the iconography of the Gifts of the Holy Spirit see Schiller (1971-80:IVi 36-38).

608 Of ... ȝe] The Latin equivalent is in two lines: *De quo Isaias per Spiritum Sanctum pulchre vaticinavit; / Prophetia Isaiae legitur haec esse*; the translator omitted the second, redundant, line meaning 'The prophecy of Isaias is as follows'; however, the ModE equivalent is not inserted in the text at this point as other omissions are, because the translator added a similar line of his own (612) to make up the rhyme deficiency he had created.

613 by hevenysh dewe] See n.971.

649 I Mach. vi 34.

650 To vices ... be more cruwelle] *ad laborem fortificatur* 'is strengthened for labour'.

654 covetye] The rhyme shows that this unrecorded form of *covetise* is intended.

663 Two ModE lines here are the equivalent of two Latin lines not accounted for in the MS: *Succus enim habet colorem viridem, qui visum* clarificat, / Et dono intellectus Christus ad cognitionem coelestium *invitat*. The omission was clearly due to eyeskip from two lines beginning *Succu* and *Et dono* to two beginning *Succus* and *Et dono*. For green as a rest for the eyes see Isidore *PL* LXXXII 240, cited by Bartholomaeus Anglicus (Trevisa II 1290).

666 The sense is 'intelligence gives knowledge of heavenly things by means of earthly ones'.

679 For the iconography of Ezechiel's vision of the Closed Gate as a symbol of Mary's perpetual virginity see Schiller (1971-80:I Abb.22), Kirschbaum (1968-76:III 424). The easternmost gate of the Temple was used only by God, and kept closed as a sign that he remained within. (Cf. Ezech. xi 23.) The symbolism is explained by Jerome (*PL* XXV 427) and developed by Rupert (*PL* CLXVII 1493-94).

687 The image carries more connotations than are apparent. Every part of the Temple of Solomon had long been allegorised (see, e.g., Bede *De Templo Salomonis Liber PL* XCI 758-808). For the iconography of the Temple symbolising the Church (and so Mary) see Kirschbaum (1968-76:IV 255-60).

701 III Kings vi 8.

706 For the iconography of the *Presentation of Mary* see Schiller (1971-80:IVii 67-75).

707 Woodcut: the Virgin ascends a flight of steps, saying a psalm on each; cf. *Ludus Coventriae* (1922:74-77).

709 The legend of the table of the sun is found not only in Valerius Maximus but also in Plutarch's *Life of Solon* V (*Plutarch's Lives* I 132-33), Diogenes Laertius' *Thales* (Diogenes I 29-35), and in *Gesta Romanorum*, ch.28.

721-22 And for ... þerby] L *Sabulum enim arenosa terra appellatur / Et ibi templum solis in arenoso loco habebatur* 'Since sandy ground is called *sabulum*, the temple of the sun was set in a sandy place'. This seems to imply some pun on *sabulum*: perhaps an oblique reference to Zabulon (Ex. i 3) who like this temple (l.715) 'shall dwell on the sea shore' (Gen. xlix 13), and whose name means, among other things, 'their dwelling place'; alternatively it might be 'dwelling place of strength' (Jerome *PL* XXIII 830, 834), or a reference to the Land of Zabulon, associated with prophecies of Salvation (Is. ix 1-2 echoed in Matt. iv 15-16).

724 sonne] *soli*: see n.46.

726 sonne] *solis*: see n.46.

736 *Per quam collata est nobis esca tam salubris et tam immensa* suggests that the ME *salutere* is an awkwardly placed adjective, giving the ME sense 'By which this beneficial food of God's is given to us'; however, if *salutere* is a noun, the sense is 'By which this food, God's agent of salvation, is given to us.'

758 The legend of Mary's early life is in the *Gospel of Pseudo-Matthew* and the *Evangelium de Nativitate Mariae* (used in the *Golden Legend* [Voragine V 96-104]), also in the *Protoevangelium* of James. See Tischendorff (1876:51-112, 113-21) for the first and second, and Hennecke (1965:I 370-88) for the third.

760 The Queen of Babylon looked longingly out to the land of her birth, Media (in Persia, to which Babylon may be said to belong only in the general sense); Comestor perhaps took the story from Josephus Bk.X secs225-27 (Josephus VI 283). The garden was one of the seven wonders of the ancient world.

769 *Psalmodiam aut versus hymnidicos jubilando psallebat*: *songe jubilynge* may be n. and ppl.a. 'rejoicing song, song of rejoicing', or ppl.a. and vbl.n. 'sung rejoicing' (*MED jubiling* cites only 4978, 5068).

781 She doune] *Nunquam dormitare, nunquam dormire consuevit* 'she used never to drowse or sleep'.

786 Cant. v 2.

793 Sho ... telle] *Ultra, quod dici potest* 'Moreover, it can be said, she was...'; *craft to telle* may be an (unrecorded) idiomatic equivalent of 'it can be said' or it might mean 'to describe (her) behaviour'.

808 Comestor 1538-39 gives only three reasons for Mary's marriage; Aquinas *ST* III q.29 a.1 gives twelve.

829 Cf. Langland B Text Passus XVI ll.67-78.

835-36 Aquinas *ST* Supplement III q.96 a.4 based on Matt. xiii 8, 23. Daniels (1949:xxxiv, 33) cites this as an example of direct borrowing from *ST*; threttism] this (unrecorded) word would normally, like *centisme* in the next line, be a numeral, giving 'a thirtieth' and 'a hundredth' respectively. But L's *trigesimus* can also mean 'thirtyfold' and 'a hundredfold' (Niermeyer 1976:*s.v. trigesim*), the sense required by the Gospel reference.

846 Aquinas *ST* Supplement III q.96 a.5 discusses the aureole of virginity.

869 Tob. vi 16-22.

886 *Quod nunquam aliqua hostilis impugnatio eam impedivit* 'Because no enemy's assault ever caused her trouble' shows that the sense of the ME is 'no enemy's trick could cause her any trouble' (*OED turn v.* 43b).

899 This legend, which L-P found so elusive, is in Rabanus Maurus *PL* CXI 517, and Voragine ch.37 *De Purificacione* (Graesse 1846:164– the image is not in Caxton's version) where the cypress is replaced by cedar with which it was often treated, for example by Richard de Saint Laurent *De Laudibus Beatae Mariae* (Albertus Magnus, *Opera* XX 412), who interprets the cypress as the Virgin. The two trees occur together in Cant. i 16, Ecclus. xxiv 16.

901 The serpent's fear of the vine-flower is interpreted in terms of the Virgin in Richard de Saint Laurent *De Laudibus Beatae Mariae* (Albertus Magnus *Opera* XX 396).

902 For the iconography of the *Annunciation* see Schiller (1971-80:I 33-52).

903 The marginal note *corr.*, presumably for *correctus* or *corriguntur* indicating the end of a section checked by the corrector, occurs also at 1104, 1603, 3203, 3903, 4003, 4103, 4203, 4303, 4403.

912 To ... creature] 'to whom no-one, apart from God, was of interest'.

913 Gen. xxxiv 1-2. Bernard *PL* CLXXXII 958 associates Dina with curiosity, perhaps suggesting sexual curiosity by making her a goatherd.

914 Gen. xxxviii 13-18.

915 Tob. iii 16.

916 Judith viii 4-6.

919-48 The monologue was perhaps inspired by Matt. i 19-20 as expanded in the Gospel of Pseudo-Matthew, used by Voragine (V 102).

921 yhit] See n.574.

926 Brynnyng ... grace] *Tantummodo in rebus divinis et coelestibus delectabatur* 'she delighted only in heavenly things'.

934 Is. vii 14.

936 See 579.

940 See 607.

941 Two ModE lines here are the equivalent of two Latin lines not accounted for in the MS: *Forsan haec est illa Virgo, de qua Christus nascetur, / Qui de semine David, filii Jesse, nasciturus perhibetur.*

950 Matt. iii 14.

951 Matt. viii 8.

952 Luke v 8.

953 IV Kings iv 8-10.

960 The Burning Bush is an ancient type of the virginity of Mary in conceiving and giving birth: Gregory of Nyssa *PL* XLIV 332, and see Schiller (1971-80:I 71). Woodcut: Moses is traditionally shown horned (Mellinkoff 1970).

971 Gideon's Fleece is another ancient type, this time of the Annunciation (see n.960). The story was interpreted in the light of Ps. lxxi 6: 'He shall come down like rain upon the fleece'. Woodcut: the angel's words 'The Lord is with you, bravest of men' (which come in fact from Judges vi 12, not 36-40, the occasion illustrated) echo those to Mary at the Annunciation.

977 Prov. xxxi 29.

1006 For the iconography of the *Nativity* see Schiller (1971-80:I 58-84).

1006 Woodcut: all the printed versions of *SHS* show the Brigittine form of the Nativity, influenced by St Brigit's vision of the Virgin adoring the Child born to her painlessly while she knelt (Cornell 1924).

1008 Lord ... be] L offers no precedent.

1009 Is. xvi 1.

1010 Ps. xlii 3.

1011 Ps. xxx 17, lxvi 2, lxxix 2-3; (Apoc. xxii 3-5; Num. vi 25-26?).

1012 als ... day] L offers no precedent; this is a rare additional image.

1013 Is. lxiv 1.

1015 Ps. cxliii 5.

1017 Ps. xxiv 6.

1018 Col. i 13.

1021-22 Come ... trespasse] The response to the 7th reading in the Office for the 3rd Sunday of Advent.

1027 Gen. vi 7.

1050 See 4133.

1052 See 3043-66.

1063 vines of Engaddy] The vines of Cant. i 13-15 were, according to legend (Comestor 1370), grown from a stock given to Solomon by the Queen of Sheba: this stock flowered and fruited at the Nativity (Voragine I 27); see also Bernard *On the Song of Songs II* Sermon 44 (1976:225-31) and John xv i.

1068 aungelkinde ... restorid] The nine orders of created beings depleted by the Fall of Lucifer and his associates were made up again by the creation of man (Alan of Lille, *PL* CCX 318).

1074 of] L *super*: perhaps *of* should be emended to *[o*fer*]* ('against').

1079 The image of Christ as a nut is common in medieval literature. It derives from Cant. vi 10 'I went down into the garden of nuts', and Num. xvii 8, the fruiting of Aaron's rod, prefiguring Christ's birth (Kaske 1960:33-34, Raby 1953:356). (Raby's ch.xi, para.3ff is a good, brief introduction to medieval symbolism).

1084 s\a/intite] The insertion may not be by the original scribe, whose form of the first element of the word is (72 times) *seint-*, and whose original *-e-* has been obscured, with *-a-* inserted over it.

1091 The immediate source is probably Voragine I 27; L-P (1907:192-94) give a long account of other versions of the Sibyl Tiburtina's prophecy to Octavian; for an account of the legend in English drama and literature see Vriend (1928:26). For the subject in northern European art see Mâle (*la fin*:255) where the influence of the *SHS* image is noted.

1101 Two ModE lines here are the equivalent of two Latin lines not accounted for in the MS: *Potentiam hujus regis Augustus Caesar formidavit / Et ab hominibus deus vocare et computare recusavit*; Augustus Caesar]. See n.2237.

1106 For the iconography of the *Magi* see Schiller (1971-80:I 94-114).

1109-10 The appearance of the star is described in Voragine I 26.

1123 The kings' names are in Voragine I 43; for their treatment in art and literature see Kehrer (1908-9).

1124 Sobokay] Cf. 4458. II Kings xxiii names only Abisae and Banaias; Sabochi is in Comestor 1344, and cf. Sobochai II Kings xxi 18, Sabachai I Par. xx 4, Sobbochai xi 29.

1128 bottellere celestre] L has only *patria* 'fatherland'; perhaps the scribe saw an abbreviated form of *patria*, and erroneously translated it in the light of 1118's *coelestis pincerna* 'heavenly drink-giver'.

1132 water ... offrid] *aquam oblatam* ... *offerebat* 'he gave water as an offering'; lovyng] *pro gratiarum actione* 'as an act of thanks'.

1135 toke ... conu*er*sioune] 'took delight in the conversion of pagans signified by the coming of the three kings.'

1139 Voragine I 45.

1143 Dan. xiv 32-38.

1149 a child ... he] 'though still a child, was the wisest [of men]' (III Kings ii 1, 9).

1150 'And God as a child was as wise as he was before, as one of the Trinity.'

1155 Saba] In the Vulgate, two places bear the same name, though they are distinct in the Hebrew. This was probably the 'Sheba' of S. W. Arabia (*JB*:433/10a). The Queen's gifts, prefiguring those of the Magi, were interpreted in the light of Ps. lxxi 10, 15 where the Hebrew mentions both Sheba, and Saba in Ethiopia. The Vulgate, unable to use the same name twice at this point, says that to Solomon 'the kings of the Arabians and of Saba shall bring gifts' and he 'shall be given the gold of Arabia' (referred to at 1191), 'Arabia' referring to Sheba to distinguish it from Saba.

1157 For the iconography of *Solomon's Throne* see Schiller (1971-80:I 23-25).

1181 whare] This form of *were*, not used elsewhere by the scribe, is suspect, the *-ha-* being over erasure; perhaps the reading should be *[warre]*.

1185 Two ModE lines here are the equivalent of two Latin lines not accounted for in the MS: *Summitas ipsius throni erat rotunda, | Quia Maria erat sine angulo sordium et tota mundi.*

1193-1202 One of the Responses to the 1st reading in the Office for Epiphany mentions these meanings of the gifts.

1195 *Thus autem oblatio erat sacerdotalis* ('The offering of incense was a priestly function') shows that *is*[1] is a form of *his*, giving the sense 'the burning of incense ...'.

1206 For the iconography of the *Presentation* see Schiller (1971-80:I 90-94). *SHS* echoes the traditional conflation of three separate events: the legal purification of the mother forty days after a birth, the presentation of the child by his father, and the witness of Simeon.

1209 Voragine III 24.

1211 Lev. xii.

1218 III Kings viii 9. This variation on the ten commandments (Ex. xx 3-17) is found in Comestor 1165.

1247 Num. xvii 10; als ... mynde] L offers no precedent; Miélot's version of 1448 has *contra la cours de nature* (L-P:1907:121-63).

1252 The Virgin's repose on her deathbed is thus the 'Dormition'–a sleep, as it were, since she did not suffer dissolution before her Assumption.

1256 Cf. Langland B Text Prologue ll.100-6 and Passus XIX ll.253-313.

1261 Als] The word is not marked in the MS as beginning a figure.

1264 The Seven Corporal Works of Mercy are derived from Matt. xxv 34-46, with the addition of the burial of the dead.

1271 *Mater misericordia* is one of the Virgin's titles in the 12th-century hymn *Salve regina* (on which see *NCE* XII 1002).

1280 Candlemas, 2 February, commemorates both the Presentation and the Purification.

1285 Voragine III 23: cf. Langland B Text ll.203-30.

1301 Luke ii 34-35.

1306 For the iconography of the *Flight into Egypt* see Schiller (1971-80: I 117-23).

1310 Comestor 1543. The *Fall of the Idols* is treated in Schiller (1971-80:I 127-23), Mâle (1961:217). The earliest printed *SHS* and Zainer's edition show it, but Drach's edition appears to show to show only the *Return from Egypt*, or, as is suggested by Joseph's gesture and glance, the *Flight into Egypt* (reversed, for it normally moves left to right). For the usual image of the *Flight*, from which Drach's woodcut may derive, see the *Biblia Pauperum*, sig.e.

1333 Ex. i 22.

1335 Ex. ii 2-10; Comestor 1143 names Aram or Amram and Jocabeth.

1343 Termuth] (Terimith in Comestor 1143) is not named in L or Ex. ii 5.

1368 Woodcut: having broken the crown, the boy Moses tastes the live coals offered to him, demonstrating his immaturity, and so his innocence of any offence to the king.

1378 slathe] Apart from one thirteenth-century example in *Ancrene Riwle*, the earliest example in *OED slat* is of 1611.

1400-1 Ps. xxiii 3-4.

1402 *Et misericordiam a Deo salutari suo* suggests that *salutere* is *n.* 'saviour' or 'salvation' (Ducange *s.v. saluta*, Niermeyer *s.v. salutaris*).

1406 For the iconography of the *Baptism of Christ* see Schiller (1971-80: I 127-43).

1409 Aquinas *ST* III q.39 a.1.

1413 Bradley 1954:111 (cited by Silber 1982:12) points out that this interpretation of the 'Sea of Brass' was influenced by St Bernard's commentary on Ex. xxxviii 8 (*PL* CLXXXIV 788).

1419 For the three forms of baptism see Aquinas *ST* III q.66 a.3-4.

1432 Aquinas *ST* III q.56 a.3-4; q.57 a.3-5; Durandus Bk.VI ch.82, para.2.

1435 *ibid.* para.30.

1437 Aquinas *ST* III q.67 aa.3-5.

1443 folk in towards] *ingressuri* 'those being about to enter'.

1449-50 Matt. iii 7.

1463 *Et si statim, antequam iterum peccarent, morerentur* 'And if they died at once, before they had sinned again'.

1469 had] In view of L *istud*, perhaps the cancelled and subpuncted *this* after *had* should be retained.

1481 Josue iv 1-19.

1489 Hebrews ix 4.

1497 Ex. xxv 10-11.

1501 testimoniales] This may be an adj. with a French pl. ending (see n.590) or simply L's *testimoniales* transplanted.

1506 For the iconography of the *Temptation of Christ* see Schiller (1971-80:I 143-45).

1509 The point is stressed to show that Christ went to his temptation 'not, as it were, by force, but because as Origen says ... he followed ... like a wrestler advancing of his own accord' (Aquinas *ST* III q.41 a.1); the Origen is in *PG* XIII 1879.

1510 Dan. xiv 32-33.

1519 Aquinas *ST* III q.41 a.1 explains that signs of Christ's human weakness caused the Devil to doubt the Lord's divinity, and so seek to tempt him.

1531-32 Voragine V 189.

1551 Gen. iii 1.

1561 brede of twelue bordes] *panes duodecim mensurarum* 'Twelve measures of bread'; *mensurarum* was read as *mensarum*.

1562 flesshe ... fourty] *carnes quadraginta oveum coctarum* 'the carcases of forty roasted sheep'; *kaces* is difficult–perhaps an earlier example of *case* 'body' than is recorded in *MED*. Alternatively, a puzzled scribe may have retained an abbreviated form of *kar*kaces, in which case the reading should be *[kar*kaces*]*.

1574 th\o/s] The scribe does not use this form for 'those' elsewhere; if the inserted letter is *e*, not *o*, this is only one of three uses of *thes* ('these'), the others being at 119, 170.

1579-80 *Golias superbissime de fortitudine sua se jacabat | Et nullum sibi similem inter omnes filios Israel existimabat* 'Goliath most arrogantly boasted of his strength, and he thought there was no-one like him among all the sons of Israel'; *vnlike in force* thus means 'unequalled in strength'.

1606 The 'sinful woman' of Luke vii 37-50 is traditionally identified with Mary Magdalene (see n.1619); for the iconography of the *Repentance of Magdalen* see Schiller (1971-80:I 157-58, II 16-18).

1607 Matt. iii 13-17.

1612 Matt. iv 17.

1619 Luke viii 2.

1631 The killing of Isaias is illustrated in ch.xxiij (l.2565).

1638 The image is found in the fourth-century pseudo-Clement (*PG* I 647).

1695 Peter] Matt. xxvi 69-75; Poul] Acts ix 1-18; Thomas] John xx 24-29; Mathe] Matt. ix 9 as expanded in Voragine V 154, 165, where Matthew is described as having abandoned an avaricious occupation to follow Jesus, and is cited as an example of the fact that no sinner need despair of pardon.

1696 Achab] III Kings xxi 25-29; the thefe] Luke xxiii 39-43; Achor] Judith v-vi; Zache] Luke xix 8-9.

1697 Ninivee] Jonas iii 4-10; Samaritane] John iv 6-42; Raab] Joshua vi 17, 25; Ruth] i-iv; avoutresse] John viii 1-11.

1698 Theophil] See n.601; Gilbert] According to L-P (1907:202), Gilbert de la Porrée, A.D. 1076-1154, who was involved in a major theological dispute which ended amicably (*NCE* VI 478). However, context suggests a saint and a notable example of divine pardon. Gilbert of Sempringham fulfils the first but not the second requirement (ibid., 479); could L's *Gilbertum* be a corruption of (St) *Guibertum*, who gave up riches to found the Benedictine monastery of Gemblours, and embrace a life of poverty (*Acta Sanctorum* 23 May 260)? Thayde] Voragine V 240-44; the Egypciane] Mary of Egypt: Voragine III 106-9.

1699 The enuche] Acts viii 26-38; Symonde] Acts viii 18-24; Cornely] the centurion, Acts x; Kyng Ezechy] IV Kings xix 1-7.

1700 Mawdelene] see n.1606; Longyve] see n.3267; Marye] Num. xii.

1706 For the iconography of the *Entry into Jerusalem* see Schiller (1971-80:II 18-23).

1709-1710 Woodcut: the antitype illustrated is the *Entry into Jerusalem*, but the types relate successively to all three events mentioned in these lines–lamentation, victorious entry and punishment for sacrilege. Such a close relation between text and picture is unusual in *SHS*.

1714 The relation between the images of Jeremias and Christ is briefly discussed by Von der Osten (1953:154).

1715 In Lamentations (and L) Jeremias laments the past, not future, fall of Jerusalem.

1757 John ii 13-16.

1759 numelariens] *MED* cites only the *Mirour*'s use of this word and of *numelaries* at 1781, both derived from L *nummularius*: on this slight evidence it assumes that they are two distinct words. However, it is at least possible that a suspension mark over *-iens* was lost in transmission.

1760 th\a/i] The scribe uses *thi* twice for 'they' (at 1114, 1787) but he uses *thai* 94 times; the *a* is inserted again at 1783.

1775 sou*er*eynes bisshops] *summo pontifice*: if not an error, the double genitive is due to the two words being felt as a compound title (as in the plural *lords-justices*): see Jespersen (1909-49:PtII, sec.2.37).

1777-78 II Mach. iii 38: 'If thou hast any enemy or traitor to thy kingdom, send him thither, and thou shalt receive him again scourged'; the sense of the ME is 'Send any enemy whom my lord the king wants to have a really rough time, to Jerusalem, to rob the Temple': *jobbe* is probably an earlier example with the sense 'stab' than is recorded.

1783 th\a/i] See n.1760.

1789 Ezech. xviii 8.

1796 Luke vi 35.

1801 alle the spices] The scribe or his source may have read *omnem spe*m *usurae* ('all hope of usury') as *omnem spe*cies *usurae* ('all kinds of usury').

1802 temple ... of joye eu*er*lasting] *de templo gloriae futurae*: 'temple of future glory'.

1806 For the iconography of the *Last Supper* see Schiller (1971-80:II 24-40).

1808 Woodcut: Christ offers the wine-sop to Judas, who is not haloed.

1818 als ... her*e*by] *sive in coelo aereo* 'or in the high heavens'. The ME means 'relating to the heavens which are only those near [the earth]': the manna's name 'bread of heaven' means only that it was made in the heavens, not that it was in Heaven itself.

1835 Wis. xvi 20.

1843 Matt. xvii 1-4.

1886 The Mass is described in Voragine VII 225-62. For a full modern account see Jungmann (1949).

1896 'And in some ways having more power than angels' (literally: 'taking precedence over the power of angels'); see *OED head sb.* 26, but neither *OED* nor *MED* records this precise usage.

1906 For the iconography of the *Falling Back* see Schiller (1971-80:II 56).

1907 Aquinas *ST* III q.81 a.2 says that this is an example to priests, who should refuse communion to no-one.

1911 The marginal note *Dist* refers to Gratian, *Decreti*, *Distinctio* II, *De Consecratione* (*PL* CLXXXVII 1731; ibid. 1763, ch.lxvii, is about Judas).

1938 Num. xvi 1-33, Ps. cv 17.

1940 Gen. xix 24.

1942 Gen. vii.

1943 Gen. xix 26.

1944 Ex. vii-xiv.

1946 IV Kings xix 35-36, Is. xxxvii 21-36.

1948 Gen. xxxviii 7-10.

1950 II Kings xxiv 15.

1952 Tob. vi 14.

1953 Here eighty-two lines of ModE are the equivalent of eighty-two in the Latin (L-P 1907:36/49-37/100) unaccounted for in the ME, where a folio is missing.

1954 hundred] two hundred and fifty, according to Num. xvi 35, xxvi 10.

1955 Num. xxi 6-7.

1958 King Salmanasar] IV Kings xvii 24-26, and Comestor 1407. *For King Salmanasar* is an attempt to render the puzzling *regi Salmanasar* which, if not an error for *regis* ..., may suggest that the lions were sent to prompt the Assyrian king to correct the erring Israelites over whom he ruled.

1960 forty] forty-two, according to IV Kings ii 24.

1961 II Mach. iii 24-27.

1962 II Mach. ix 5-10.

1964 Giezy] IV Kings v 20-27; Mary] Num. xii 1-10.

1965 IV Kings vi 8-18: the 'confusion' (L *acrisia*) is from Comestor 1393.

1968 III Kings xiii 4 (Comestor 1373).

1970 IV Kings xix 35, describing the destruction of the Assyrians, is traditionally associated with Herodotus Bk.II sec.141, where mice eat 'their quivers and their bows, and the handles of their shields likewise, insomuch so that they fled the next day'.

1978 Samson] Judges xv 15; Samgar] Judges iii 31; David] II Kings xxiii 8.

1984 Comestor 1345 (interpreting II Kings xxiii 8: *quasi tenerrimus ligni vermiculus*, which refers to Jesbaham), echoed in Voragine I 68.

1994 Ps. xxi 7.

2001 Lam. i 12.

2006 For the iconography of the *Betrayal* see Schiller (1971-80:II 51-56). Woodcut: at the moment of his betrayal Christ reaches out to replace the severed ear of Malchus (in the foreground).

2015-16 Woodcut: the traditional image, rather than the text, is followed.

2031 Matt. x 7-10.

2039 pariato*ur*] The sense of L *procurator* 'financial adviser' is needed; perhaps the reading should be *[pro*cu*ra*tou*r]*, assuming that an abbreviated form was misread.

2059 Ex. xxi 24, Lev. xxiv 20.

2061-62 In L, p.39 l.57 is the only equivalent: *Sed tu, iniquissime Juda, malem pro bono reddidisti*: a line, the source for 2062, has dropped out of L after this one (and subsequent lines in this chapter in L are consequently misnumbered: it has only 99 lines). In Neumüller (1972) the missing line reads: *Quia talem & t*antu*m* bene*fact*orem tu*um tradidisti*: 'For you betrayed such–and so great–a benefactor of yours'; canseil] If not an error for *conseil* or *cunseil* this is an unrecorded form.

2071 Golyas] is not marked as the start of a figure in the MS.

2075 Woodcut: David soothed Saul with his harp. In both Richel's and Drach's editions the instrument is replaced by a bowl, perhaps as a result of some misunderstanding in pictorial transmission. For example, Neumüller (1972) shows, in the equivalent MS picture, David playing a psaltery–like that illustrated in Munrow (1976:23)–in which the circular sound-hole in the frame of the instrument might well be mistaken for a bowl.

2084 'And Saul always desired David's suffering and death.'

2092 John xi 48.

2106 For the iconography of the *Buffeting* see Schiller (1971-80:II 58). Woodcut: in *SHS* (unlike *BP*) the *Buffeting* shown here is not conflated with the *Crowning with Thorns* (ch.xxi).

2108 John xviii 10.

2111 John xviii 13.

2114-2116 John xviii 20.

2121 Luke ix 54-55.

2126 Luke ix 54: cf. their name Boanerges 'Sons of Thunder' (Mark iii 17).

2128 Luke vi 29.

2130 John xviii 24.

2148 *O, quanta erat Judaeorum saevitia et incipentia* 'O, how great was the savagery and senselessness of the Jews'. In view of *thai/thay* in the next two lines I have assumed that the scribe meant or misread a form such as *Judeus* meaning 'Jews'–but he does not use the word elsewhere.

2149 Voragine I 71 carries a somewhat similar passage which he attributes to St Bernard. I am indebted to Dom Edmund Mikkers of the Cistercian Abbey, Achel, for his use of the unpublished Bernard concordance to locate the nearest sources, in *Sermones Super Cantica Canticorum* Sermon 10 para.8 (Leclercq 1957:52, ll.25-29) and *In Epiphania Domini* Sermon I, para.6 (Leclercq 1966:298 l.4).

2158 Ex. xiii 21.

2161 þair] The insertion may not be scribal: the scribe's normal form of this word is *thaire* (132 times).

2176 *Tamen multo inhonestior videtur fuisse Christi derisio* 'The mocking of Christ was clearly much more degrading'; the odd *vnlike with* appears to mean 'incomparably' or perhaps 'in contrast' (cf. 1678).

2201 Matt. xxv 41.

2202 Matt. xxv 34.

2206 For the iconography of the *Flagellation* see Schiller (1971-80:II 66-69). In his 'Meditations on the Passion' (Tierce) in the *Vitae Christi* (II lxii), Ludolph of Saxony mentions a small part of the column in Rome, a larger part in Jerusalem, and cites Bede's reference to Christ's blood still being visible on it.

2209 John xviii 29-31 and Luke xxiii 2.

2224 Luke xxiii 11.

2226 Pilate, not Herod, said this: Luke xxiii 14, John xviii 38, xix 4.

2228 *Spiritus Sanctus, occulte hoc agens, innocentiam Christi ostendebat*: 'The Holy Spirit, secretly bringing this about, made the innocence of Christ plain'.

2235 Mark xiv 58.

2237 Cesare] The word denotes the Imperial throne rather than the person occupying it. The emperors contemporary with the NT were: Augustus 27 B.C.- A.D. 14 (see ll.1101, 4455); Tiberius A.D. 14-37; Gaius (Caligula) A.D. 37-41; Claudius A.D. 41-54; Nero A.D. 54-68; Galba A.D. 68-9; Otho A.D. 69; Vitellius A.D. 69; Vespasian A.D. 69-79; Titus A.D. 79-81; Domitian A.D. 81-96.

2245 John xviii 36.

2264 For the iconography of Lamech see Kirschbaum (1968-76:III 5-7), where *SHS* is cited as the only example of this scene's being a type of the *Flagellation.*

2272 For the iconography of Job in the context of *Christ in Distress* see Von der Osten (1953).

2273 Job ii describes metaphorical beatings: Job struck by disease, and given a tongue-lashing by his wife.

2306 For the iconography of the *Crowning with Thorns* see Schiller (1971-80:II 67-73). Woodcut: two of Christ's tormentors use staves to press and lever the sharp thorns into position, a third gives mock homage.

2309 Deut. xxv 3.

2320 *Recipient nova et inaudita tormenta* shows that the sense of the ME is 'they shall deservedly suffer new and unheard-of pain.'

2321 Luke vi 38.

2324 John xix 2.

2337-2258 The pattern of this passage recalls the 11th-century portion of the 'Reproaches' recited during the Veneration of the Cross on Good Friday (*NCE* VII 407).

2339 Num. xxi 13-15 as interpreted in Comestor 1235.

2341 Deut. xxix 5.

2345 Ex. vii-xii 33, xiv.

2347 Comestor 1144.

2353 Is. xxx 17.

2356 two peoples] Jews and heathen (cf. 2499).

2357 I Kings xviii 7.

2369 colaphized] The traditional development of the scene in which Christ was beaten with rods or reeds is discussed by Marrow (1974:82, 142-3).

2376 stokkes] are not mentioned in the Biblical account of Semei's attack, but the woodcut shows them curiously placed as if in echo of the staves used, in the first scene of the chapter, by the torturers to lever the Crown of Thorns into place.

2386 melle] It is not wholly clear (*pace MED medlen 2c(c)*) whether this is *OED melle v*[1] 'to speak of, preach' or *v*[2] 'cause'; neither translates *reficeret* 'restore', but the second verb is used elsewhere by the translator (1571, 2903).

2391 'David sent them to offer friendship (? comfort) in view of what had happened.' David's messengers took condolences to Amon on the death of his father: they went *ad pacem instaurandam* 'to offer condolences (and maintain peace)'.

2398 Heb. ix 19.

2406 For the iconography of the *Carrying of the Cross* see Schiller (1971-80:II 78-82).

2408 John xix 2-6.

2419 Matt. xxvii 24.

2423 Matt. xxvii 19.

2434 *Et ipsum per stimulum suum, id est feminam, magis instigabat* 'And [the devil] by means of his goad, the woman, strongly urged him on'; the confused sense of the ME seems to be 'And [the devil] by means of his control (the woman) urged him further (to conclude the matter).' But this sense of *ledde* (*MED lede n. 1b*) is awkward.

2437 Matt. xxvii 31.

2445 Voragine I 66 citing Augustine, for whom he gives no reference: the image is an Augustinian commonplace, for example *PL* XXXVI 292, 366 (*A locis suppliciorum [crux] fecit transitum ad frontes imperatorum*), 637, 663, 934; *PL* XXXVII 1228.

2451 Woodcut: oddly, the scene is dominated by the sacrifice of Isaac, rather than by the more usual type, Isaac bearing his own pyre (which is omitted altogether in Zainer's edition, though in the background here).

2463 The council of the Trinity is dramatised in the *Ludus Coventriae*, 'Parliament of Heaven' (1922:130); the image appears in art (Schiller 1971-80:I 10-12).

2473 Isidore (*PL* LXXXIII 122) interprets the parable.

2489 Ysay ... Jeremy] See n.4357.

2490 Ezechiel ... Amos] See nn.4357-58.

2497 The grapes carried on a stave commonly represent Christ suspended on the Cross, e.g. in Augustine *PL* XXXIX 1800, Rabanus Maurus *PL* CVIII 845. In the latter their interpretation as Christ carrying the Cross is implicit, as Rabanus repeats Augustine's explanation of how the hindmost bearer represents the believer who responds to Christ's 'If any man will come after me, let him ... take up his Cross, and follow me' (Matt. xxvi 24); see Kirschbaum (1968-76:II 700-1).

2506 For the iconography of the *Nailing to the Cross* see Schiller (1971-80:II 82-86).

2509 Matt. xxvii 32: Simon of Cyrene in N. Africa.

2512 Matt. xxvii 34 + Ps. lxviii 22.

2518 Woodcut: for this 'racking' of Christ cf. *Meditations on the Life of Christ* (1966:334), *Ludus Coventriae* (1922:296-97) and especially *The York Plays* (1982:315-22).

2522 Ps. xxi 17-18.

2546 I Cor. ii 8.

2550 Acts ii 41.

2565 The marginal note points to Comestor's account of the prophet's legendary martyrdom.

2570 Aquinas *ST* III q.50 a.2-3.

2577 Two ModE lines here are the equivalent of two Latin lines not accounted for in the ME: *O inaestimabilis dilectio divinae caritatis, / Ut dilectum filium daret pro filiis iniquitatis!*

2582 jentil] This might mean *noble* or *gentile*, but the former is more likely in view of the use of the adjective to describe Abigael at 3955.

2601 I John iv 19.

2606 For the iconography of the *Crucifixion* see Schiller (1971-80:II 88-158). Drach erroneously depicts the opening of the dead Christ's side both here and (repeating a woodcut) in ch.xxv. The woodcut used here in the present edition, correctly showing Christ alive on the Cross, is taken from his illustrations to The Seven Sorrows of the Virgin (ch.xliv below, which like each of the last three chapters is unillustrated in the present edition).

2613 Woodcut: the 'Pelican in her Piety', whose reviving of her young with blood from her own breast traditionally signifies the Crucifixion, appears at the top of the tree (see White 1954:132-33).

2621 \s/haken] L's *excutienda* shows that *haken* ('hacked') is technically correct, but I retain the inserted *s-* since it may be a scribal correction made when the Latin was no longer to hand (in any case it would be retained, as other doubtfully scribal insertions are).

2636 The ME omits any equivalent for L's *nudum* ('naked'), so destroying the point of the image of Christ exposed to the elements–there follows a two-line gap in the MS where the equivalent of one Latin line is omitted: *Per hoc praefigurabatur quod Christus extra vrbem deberit crucifigi* 'By this it was prefigured that Christ would have to be crucified outside the city'. However, no equivalent ModE translation is given in the text (as it is at other points where lines are omitted) because finding his couplet pattern upset by the omission, the scribe or his source added at 2637 a line without precedent in L.

2647 'He said also that seven ages should pass in the king's lifetime'.

2648 See ch.xliii (l.4505) below: the Hours of the Passion.

2665 This version of the story, mentioning Apollo, is not, as the MS marginal note suggests, in Comestor, but in Valerius, Bk.V, ch.6 ext. 1. It is also in *Gesta Romanorum*, ch.41.

2678 *Cupientes potius civitatem quam ipsius mortem habere* 'Desiring the city more than his death'; *vnlike with* appears to mean 'incomparably' or perhaps 'on the contrary' (see n.2176).

2699 Jer. xlvi 12.

2706 Woodcut: Mary and John flank the Cross; to the right the centurion points to Christ, saying: 'Indeed this was a just man'; to the left is Longinus, who in the Bible is simply the nameless man sent to break Christ's legs. For the iconography of this form of *Crucifixion* see Schiller (1971-80:II 151-58). The relevance of the illustration is not at first apparent, since Longinus' opening of the dead Christ's side is normally associated not with abuse but with the miracle of his blindness healed (Comestor 1633-34). However, the Jews' intended abuse of Christ's body in sending their servant to hasten his death may be as significant as the piercing of his side (note that the last two types present the killing of a victim and the abuse of a victim already dead). Longinus' expression in the woodcut may suggest that here he is simply the Jews' tool, not the Longinus of legend.

2713 doing "A" ferre] The phrase seems to mean 'making mocking noises from a distance' (*OED ah* 4). However, in view of L's *Nec suffecit ei quod intra citharizationem derisat* ('Nor was it enough for her to mock him when he was involved in the music of the lyre'), the ME might be punctuated thus: *to scorne hym, doing "A", ferre* ('to scorn him, [while he was] making song, from afar'). The reading could also be *to scorne hym doing [aferre]*: 'insulting him from a distance', if one assumes that the scribe, who wrote a capital *A* in *A ferre*, misunderstood a ME source.

2716 harlots] L has *scurra* 'scoundrel', but the sexual (though not feminine) connotations of the modern word are contextually implied.

2722 Luke xxiii 34.

2723 Luke xxiii 43.

2724 John xix 26-27.

2725-26 John xix 28-30.

2727 Matt. xxvi 46 and the 'Passion Psalm' Ps. xxi 1, of which these are the opening words; Hely] This Greek form of the Hebrew means 'My God': the *-y* ending is equivalent to the personal pronoun; lamazabatany] For *lamma sabacthani* 'why hast thou forsaken me?' Aquinas *ST* III q.50 aa.2-3 explains that this cry does not imply dissolution of the union between the first and second divine Persons, but the Father's permitting of the Passion.

2728 Luke xxiii 46 and Ps. xxx 6.

2747 The marginal note cites Josephus instead of Comestor, but Josephus (*Jewish Antiquities* Bk.X, ch.xii) merely mentions Evilmeredach, omitting any reference to his murder of his father.

2752-80 Heb. vi 6. For the notion of sins causing suffering to Christ cf. the image of his bearing the tools of work forbidden on Sunday (Schiller 1971-80:II 204-5, Kirschbaum 1968-76:II 20-21).

2794 John xiii 29.

2806 For the iconography of the *Deposition* see Schiller (1971-80:II 164-68) and Parker (1975). The hymn *Stabat Mater Dolorosa*, known by the 14th century (*Analecta Hymnica Medii Aevi* LIV:312-18), celebrates the Virgin's sorrows at the Crucifixion–her 'co-passion'. The Feast of the Seven Sorrows of the Virgin (1st Friday after Palm Sunday) was established in the 15th century.

2810 Luke ii 35.

2845 sonnes] ? sounes.

2857-58 Comestor 1076.

2863 Cant. i 13.

2906 For the iconography of the *Entombment* (and *Lamentation*) see Schiller (1971-80:II 168-79). Daniels (1949:157) suggests that the Virgin's anguish resembles a passage in Anselm (*PL* CLIX 286-

88, which according to Glorieux is Anselm though Daniels refers to the pseudo-Anselm); but the resemblance is very general.

2914 hires] This may be an error for *hire*, since *MED hires pron. (b)* records only one early, doubtful example meaning 'her'.

2931 and of othere] *Bestialis porcus porco clamanti commovetur*–'The pig, a [mere] beast, is moved by the squealing of [another] pig'–is little help in determining the function of *and*, which is possibly adv. ('also', *MED and 7*); if, however, the ME shows erroneous prepositional use of *and* for *on* (*MED on prep. 7a*, 'in the presence of'), emendation should perhaps be made to *[on] of othere*.

2939 dissymuiling] The spelling at 1780 is *dissimuling*, for which this may be an error.

2941 thas ... Dauid] 'Not only David lamented over those sad obsequies'. L has *non solum ipse super exsequias ejus plorabat* 'Not only David himself lamented at that funeral'. Since the ME *thas* is pl., the strictly sg. *birialles* (*OED buriels*) has clearly been felt as a pl., perhaps under the influence of L, where the pl. form *exsequias* has sg. meaning.

2953-65 Matt. xxvii 45, 51-53, which Comestor 1631 conflates with Acts xvii 18-23.

2958 Luke xix 40.

2963 Comestor 1630, cited in Ludolphus of Saxony II lxiv. The sense in L is 'The devil, sitting on the left arm of the Cross, wondered who this could be, whom all creation held in awe.'

2965 Comestor 1631.

2987 Gen. xli 41-xlv.

2995 Jerome *PL* XXIII 420 interprets the name as *augmentum* ('increase'); Isidore *PL* LXXXII 282 repeats him.

3000 Sheol or Hades is divided into four levels, two for the righteous and two for the wicked, in the pre-Christian Book of Enoch (Charles 1893:93-96); Aquinas *ST* III q.69 a.7 describes a similar structure. Christ enters only what came to be called Limbo, the top level (cf. the Creed: 'He descended into hell'). For Limbo see *NCE* VIII 762, and for the theology of the Descent into Hell see *NCE* IV 789-93. It is curious that the woodcut (like that in Richel's but not Zainer's edition) shows the Virgin present.

3006 For the iconography of the *Descent into Hell* see Schiller (1971-80: III 41-47).

3008 The saule ... vnyte] Aquinas *ST* III q.50 a.3; see also q.52, a.3.

3009 be Thomas sawe] 'according to the account by Thomas [Aquinas]'; see n.3000.

3009-54 Daniels (1949:165) uses this passage to show that the *SHS* author's source was sometimes not *ST* but the abridgement, *Compendium Theologicae Vertitatis*.

3012 horrour ... terrible] *et horror terribilis*: in the absence of any L equivalent it is not clear whether *flaying* is from *fleien* 'frighten' or *flen* 'flay'; the former, less specific sense is more likely in context: on the other hand, the scribe elsewhere uses the *flee-* form of this verb.

3023 *Ibi non est poena sensus, sed tantum poena damni* 'Where there is no pain to the senses, but only the pain of loss'; this condition of those in Limbo, where the only limitation on happiness is the absence of the vision of God, is of course quite different from that experienced by the damned (Aquinas *ST* III Supplement Appendix 1 q.1 aa.1, 2).

3037 be the haly ... accepting] L *acceptionem crucis* is little help with the reading *haly laude*; context suggests an unrecorded *laude* = *lod* ('burden' or 'way'), but *laude* 'praise' is not impossible. Just conceivably the reading should be *Haly Lande*, assuming a reference to pilgrimage as an extension of the idea of indulgence gained. Miélot's French version has *prendre la signe de la croix* 'become a crusader'.

3045 Tho] The scribe uses this form of *the* only here.

3060 Luke xxiii 43.

3066 Voragine I 97.

3081 *Dominus autem illum illaesum a leonibus custodivit* 'The Lord, however, preserved him (uninjured) from the lions'. The translator's original *fro Illusioune* ('from scorn, derision, sport') ostensibly rendered *illaesum* ('uninjured'). As *MED illusioune* implies, he seems to have misunderstood *illaesum* as part of *illudo* 'I sport with, destroy in sport' (note that *MED*'s reading *illeusionne* is an error, as the critical apparatus shows: the corrector turned *illusioune* into *illesioune*). *OED* records correct derivatives from *illaesum*, such as *illesed* 'uninjured, unhurt' and *illaesive* 'harmless', but only from 1551, 1597, 1627-47 respectively.

3086 Woodcut: only six of the seven allegorical lions are shown.

3098 See n.203-4; the legend is in Comestor 1353 and also in Vincent of Beauvais *Speculum Naturale* Bk.XX ch.170. Solomon's experiment was to find out how to cut marble for the building of the Temple without breaking the law which forbad its cutting by iron. The legend's interpretation in terms of the Harrowing of Hell is one of several varied ones mentioned by Kirschbaum (1968-76:IV 218). For the equating of Christ with a serpent, cf. 'As Moses lifted up the serpent in the desert, so must the Son of man be lifted up' (John iii 14).

3106 For the iconography of *Christ the Victor* see Schiller (1971-80:III 32-41). Christ's conquest of the Devil is described in *The Middle English Harrowing of Hell and the Gospel of Nicodemus*, pp.112-13. The Latin is in Tischendorff (1876:429), and a ModE version is in Hennecke (1965:I 474).

3109 Luke xi 21-23.

3110 Alle ... haves] Those in Limbo did not suffer (Aquinas *ST* III q.52, a.5). For a summary of the patristic arguments about their state see *NCE* VIII 762; faders] e.g. Bede *PL* XCII 477.

3115 For the relation between Christ's body (in the tomb) and soul (in Limbo), his manhood and his divinity, see Aquinas *ST* III q.52 a.3.

3117 Comestor mentions Banaias' staff and the roaring of the trapped lion.

3122 Ps. xxii 4.

3139 Two ModE lines here are the equivalent of two Latin lines not accounted for in the MS: *Per crucem olim homines* mortificabantur, / Et per eum nunc aegri curantur, et mortui *suscitantur*.

3153-54 Samson went in fact to the vines of Thamnatha (see 3161); the vineyards of Engaddi are mentioned in Cant. i 13.

3165 Judges xv 1-8.

3183-88 Job xl and xli refer to the huge mouth and size of Leviathan, who for most commentators on Job was a figure of Satan (Mâle 1961:379-80, and Kirschbaum 1968-76:III 93-95).

3185-89 *Quis totum genus humanum in ventrem ejus introivit. / Tandem Dominus noster Jesus Christus ventrem ejus perforavit.* The words *decovrid* and *entrid* at the ends of the ME lines are transposed in the MS: except for the addition of the *hoege* and *grete* the ME as emended represents the sense in L '... Because all mankind entered his belly / Eventually Our Lord Jesus Christ opened up his belly.'

3195 II Tim. ii 5.

3206 The idea of the Virgin using the Instruments of the Passion against the Devil is a fulfilment of Gen. iii 15. For the iconography of the *Arms of Christ* (which are both weapons and charges on a coat of arms) see Schiller (1971-80:II 184-97, 207-11); Kirschbaum (1968-76:I 183-87); Berliner (1955).

3211 Two ModE lines here are the equivalent of two Latin lines not accounted for in the MS: *Lancea, quae latus filii fui mortui perforavit, / Per compassionem cor Matris viventis penetravit.*

3215 Woodcut: the text's 'sword' is omitted, but in addition the lantern of the Arrest, pillar and scourge of the Flagellation, reeds of the Mocking, vinegar and sponge of the Crucifixion are shown.

3220 Gen. iii 15.

3219 armes] (L *armis*) see n. 3206.

3225 John xix 23.

3230 Cant. v 10.

3231 Cant. i 12.

3249 Mark xiv 50-52 as interpreted in Comestor 1623.

3252 John xviii 15-17.

3256 The events in this 'bundle' of remembered sufferings (3233-74) are in historical order until this point, where the Crucifixion is suddenly recalled in the midst of the Trial sequence.

3258-59 With an emotional effect similar to that at 3256, the memory of the distribution of Christ's clothes and the lots cast for his seamless garment at the Crucifixion interrupts the recall of his humiliation by being clothed in white and purple during the Passion (Luke xxiii 11); cf. Comestor 1627-28 and John xix 2.

3263 John xix 29.

3267 Longif] This has not been emended to *Longis*, since at 4123 *Longyve* occurs, and these forms derive from a common misreading of Latin *Longinus* as *Longiuus*. His legend, developed from John xix 34, is in Voragine III 70-73, ch.xlvii. By the 15th century Longinus was distinguished from the centurion who gave witness (Mark xv 39): both appear in the Crucifixion scene introducing ch.xxv of *SHS*.

3269 cleving ... thorghby] *scissio veli et petrarum*; *thorghby* is unexplained: perhaps it is an odd form of *thereby*, meaning either 'in addition' or 'as a result (of the earthquake)'.

3270 Of ... falling] *Ruina partis templi*; this event, not mentioned in the New Testament, is in Comestor 1633, where he derives his material from the lost Gospel of the Nazareans–on which see Hennecke (1965:I 139-53).

3277 Ps. xc 13.

3279 Gen. iii 15.

3289 Thomira in Comestor 1474 (perhaps from Herodotus Bk.I secs212-14, where she is Tomyris): see ll.219-20 in the text.

3290 Cirus] Cyrus as an example of bloodthirstiness (here and at 219-20, 4054) is in marked contrast to his more usual Bible-based citation as a type of Christ, his people's deliverer (552, 558).

3306 For the iconography of the *Freeing of the Patriarchs from Limbo* (*Harrowing of Hell*) see Schiller (1971-80:III 47-68), and for the theology see n.3000 above. The scene is described in the *Middle English Harrowing of Hell and the Gospel of Nicodemus* (1907:97-112); the Latin is in Tischendorff (1876:422-30) and a modern version is in Hennecke (1965:I 470-75). Woodcut: Adam and Eve, first to fall, are released first from Limbo.

3319 St Gregory said thirty masses for the soul of a sinful monk Justus, who finally appeared to say that he had been freed from Purgatory. This gave rise to the custom of thirty Gregorian Masses said for the dead (*NCE* XII 384d).

3322 'All those [in Purgatory] think in the same way, all the time, about prayers for souls.'

3325 Aquinas *ST* III q.52 a.4.

3327 'The midnight before the morning of the Sunday when he rose from death'.

3333 Ex. iii 1-14.

3339 Ps. lxix 1.

3340 Ps. cxliii 5.

3341 Ps. cviii 21-22.

3343 Ps. cxliii 7.

3344 Is. xvi 1.

3345 Ps. xlii 3, and Is. ix 2, traditionally applied to the Harrowing of Hell (Voragine I 98, derived from the Gospel of Nicodemus, and cf. Matt. iv 16).

3346 Ecclus. xxxvi 18.

3347-48 crying ... mynde] *homo ad Dominum clamabat, / Et Dominus misertus ejus, ipsum hoc modo liberabat*; the ME construction requires ... *he toke his gudenesse* ....

3357 Ex. xii 3-11.

3373 Aquinas *ST* III q.52 a.6.

3383 Apoc. iii 19.

3397 Gen. xix 26.

3406 For the iconography of the *Resurrection of Christ* see Schiller (1971-80:III 68-87).

3408 'Like a double room, one being within the other'. Woodcut: Christ rises from the sarcophagus which though unhistorical is the iconographic convention of the time. His being shown emerging through the closed lid is uncommon, but not unknown: cf. Kirschbaum (1968-76:I 216-17) and in addition Musper (1976:Abb.49) and the late 15th-century Italian panel-painting now in Romsey Abbey.

3423 Matt. xxvii 60.

3454 Two ModE lines here are the equivalent of two Latin lines not accounted for in the MS: *Et intrantes civitatem Jerusalem, multis apparuerunt. / Non est putandum quod in Parasceve corpora surrexerunt*; did the translator omit the lines owing to their momentary difficulty?

3456 And ... moo] 'And that the graves were open only on that day.'

3457 Aquinas *ST* III q.53 a.3 cites Jerome's opinion that the rising of the dead (Matt. xxvii 52-53) occurred after the resurrection of Christ, who is thus truly 'first-born' or 'first fruits' of the dead (Col. i 18, I Cor. xv 20), and Augustine's opinion (rejected here) that Christ remains primogenitor of the dead because those who rose with him at this time later died again.

3475 The 'corner-stone' (either a major foundation stone, or the topping-stone of a defensive tower) becomes, in the illustration, a medieval key-stone which is to hold up the whole vault of the building. The unexpected female figure in the woodcut perhaps represents Ecclesia.

3496 The verse from Ps. cxvii is used in the Gradual of the Mass for Easter Thursday.

3506 For the iconography of the *Ascension* see Schiller (1971-80:III 141-64).

3509 openly] *bis* L: the ME omits any suggestion of Christ's appearing twice on the fortieth day, a popular tradition (echoed in Voragine I 108).

3530 *Per quam parata est ascensio tam long et tam mala* 'by which preparation was made for such a long and difficult ascent'. The translator's source probably carried variant readings, such as ... *reparata est descensio* (L-P record *ablata est destructio* in their MS C, which is one of the two dated 1324).

3534 $4 \times 20 + 19 = 99$.

3542 Isidore *PL* LXXXIII 121. At the ascension, mankind in Christ made up the ninth order left vacant with the fall of the angels (see n.1068).

3577-80 Phil. ii 9-11.

3591 *Si totum gaudium mundi tanquam stellae et pulvis terrae multiplicaretum* 'if all the joys of the world were as numerous as stars or dust particles of the earth.'

3593 Cf. John xxi 25: the idea is ancient (Opie 1952:436).

3598 the ... eterne] *numerum gaudiorum eternorum* 'numbers of everlasting joys'; *numerum* was misread as *minimum* by the translator or his source.

3601 ilk poudre] *quilibet pulvis terrae* '... dust of the earth'.

3603-4 A very free rendering of *O bone Jesu, doce nos illuc taliter adspirare, / Ut tecum mereamur ibi in perpetuum habitare!* 'O good Jesus, teach us to so aspire to that place, that we may deserve to live there with you forever.' It is not easy to determine the sense of *wayes even*. It might mean 'by the direct route' or 'by similar means' (referring back to the accepted suffering of 3587).

3606 For the iconography of *Pentecost* see Schiller (1971-80:IVi 11-33).

3609 Matt. xx 18-19.

3611 John xvi 16.

3613 John xiv 2-3.

3615 Luke xxii 28-30.

3617 John xv 9.

3619-28 John xv 1-8.

3629-32 John xvi 20-22.

3635-40 John xvi 6-7.

3641 John xvi 13.

3647 Acts i 4.

3649 Acts i 12-14.

3651-66 Acts ii 1-16.

3664 For the accusation of drunkenness cf. *Ludus Coventriae* (1922:353).

3667 Joel ii 28.

3679-80 'In this connection, the creation of various languages like this demonstrates that [Babel] was a prefiguration of the miracle to come.'

3684 strange] L's *grande* is no help in clarifying whether this is adj. *OED strong 15* or *strange 9*. The latter is most likely, though the scribe uses this form only twice, using *stronge* on 22 occasions (55, 69, 206 etc.) The sense is similar in either case.

3693 Woodcut: this extraordinary design (very different from that in Zainer's edition) shows the widow and one of her sons as if heraldic 'supporters' to the inexhaustible cruse. There may be a deliberate echo (cf. 3699) of the Virgin/Church and John by the Cross (see ch.xxiv above). The design is found also in one of the early MS reproduced by L-P: Munich, Bayerische Staatsbibliothek clm. 146. Eliseus' miracle echoes Elias' in III Kings xvii 8-16.

3706 Conu*er*syng] *MED* gives 'conduct', as it does for *conuersacioune* (3805), but L. *conversatione* in both places suggests, as does the context, 'haunting of (certain) places (once visited by Jesus)'.

3708 Woodcut: the four sections on either side recall more than eight events. Beginning in the bottom right-hand corner and moving anti-clockwise they cover the Annunciation, Nativity,

Cleansing of the Temple and Washing of the disciples' feet, Arrest, Buffeting and Flagellation, Crucifixion, Appearances to Magdalen and the disciples, Resurrection, Ascension. Daniels (1949:202-3) sees in the first fourteen places mentioned by name in the text a reference to the Stations of the Cross, but the correspondence is not exact.

3729 John xix 13. *Lithostratos* ('pavement') may have been so called because of a Roman pavement which excavation revealed in Pilate's palace-citadel, in the N-W corner of the Temple enclosure, but opinion on the site of Pilate's Judgement is divided (*ODCC* 1974:543).

3756 tellyng Crist openly] L's *recitatur* is little guide to the sense, which is probably 'Christ telling [this parable] plainly'.

3774 conu*er*syng] L. *conversatio*: see n.3706.

3797-8 Cant. v 8.

3805 Schiller (1971-80:IVii 83-147); conu*er*sacioune] See n.3706.

3806 Woodcut: the scene shown is the Enthronement of the Virgin. For Mary's death and assumption in art see Mâle, (1961:246-58); Schiller (1971-80:IVii 83-147).

3810 St Epiphanius] The 8th-century Epiphanius wrote on the Life of the Virgin (*PL* CXX 216ff); reading his name in Voragine (IV 234), the author of *SHS* mistook him for St Epiphanius, the 4th-century polemist.

3815 Gen. xxix 1-10.

3831 Matt. xi 11.

3838 Woodcut: the designer (or copyist) omitted the figure of David dancing, and so reduced the celebratory element in the type (see 3853-54).

3860-61 Cant. viii 5.

3864 Cant. iii 4.

3867 Cant. i 1.

3869 Cant. ii 6, viii 3.

3877 For the iconography of the *Woman Clothed in the Sun* see Schiller (1971-80:IVi 77-84). Woodcut: the usual rays of light round the figure (present in Richel's equivalent woodcut in his *Spiegel*) are absent.

3906 For the rare iconography of this vision of Mary appeasing God see Réau (1955-58:IIIi 395-96) and Kirschbaum (1968-76:VI 77), where the earliest example is 16th-century. St Dominic stands in front of Francis (see n.3942).

3909 I John v 19.

3911 I John ii 16.

3929 'Some are willing to be poor men as long as they lack nothing.'

3933 the aungelle] Is. xiv 12 and Luke x 18. man ... paradys] Gen. iii 23-24.

3934 Dan. iv 26-30.

3935 Achan] Joshua vii 24; Naboth] III Kings xxi 1-15. Even the Latin MSS have *Achior* for *Achan* (to which L-P also emend). KC suggests confusion between Achan and the valley of Achor in the same verse; an alternative explanation is confusion with 'Achior and Nabath' in Tob. xi 20.

3936 Acts v 1-6.

3937 Gen. vi-vii.

3938 Gen. xix 1-28.

3942 The vision of the Virgin Mediatrix is also in The Life of St Dominic *Acta Sanctorum* 4 August 442D, E, and in Gerardus de Fracheto (1896:9-11); it may be read in French in Sausseret (1854:278-79). It is attributed to Dominic and Francis in L, and to Dominic's vision as described by a Franciscan companion in Voragine IV 179. Woodcut: Dominic is identified by his staff and book; the fact that Francis is unnimbed may suggest Dominican influence on the designer–cf. Réau (1955-58:III 395, 524)–or simply that Voragine's Franciscan, rather than Francis himself, is depicted. In Drach's edition (ch.38, ll.24-32) the text refers only to Dominic. See 'Le Thème des trois flèches', ch.VIII in Perdrizet (1908).

3959 Eccles. i 15.

3967-70 Is. xlv 9.

3989 Seba was the son of Bochri. In L, *filius Bocri* occurs in the variant form *filius Botri*. The translator took *Botri* for a genitive, and so invented a nominative, *Botrus* (though perhaps a dot over *u*, as if the reinstatement of *Botri* had been considered, has been erased).

4006 For the iconography of the *Virgin of Mercy* see Mâle (*fin* 198-201), Perdrizet (1908), A. Thomas 'Schutzmantelmaria' (1974), Schiller (1971-80:IVii 195-205 especially Abb.822-828). The image derives from the legal concept of a defenceless person coming under the 'protective cloak' of a person of rank.

4011 The marginal note refers to *Ethyore* for *Ethyope*: Tharbis is 'the Ethiopian' of Num. xii 1.

4026 Ps. xliv 3.

4040 Jezabelle] III Kings xxi 1-23 and IV Kings ix; Balthazar*e*] Dan. v; Holoferne] Judith ii-xiii.

4042 Kaym] Gen. iv; Jacob sons pat*ri*arche] the patriarch Jacob's sons hated his favourite, Joseph (Gen. xxxvii); Saull] I Kings xviii.

4043 Semey] II Kings xvi 5-13.

4044 Absolon] II Kings xiii; John and Jacob] Luke ix 52-56.

4046 Achab] III Kings xvi 29-33; Achaz] II Par. xxviii 21, IV Kings xvi; Jeroboam] III Kings xii 26-xiii 34; Moises] Ex. v 22-23, Num. xx 12.

4048 Dathan and Abyron] Num. xvi 1-33; Cham] Gen. ix 18-25; Chore] Num. xvi 1-33.

4050 Achitofel] II Kings xvi 20-xvii 23; Balaam] Num. xxxi 16; Jonadab] II Kings xiii.

4052 Chayn] Gen. iv; Joab] II Kings iii 27, xx 8-10; Judas] Matt. xxvi 14-16, 47-49; Triphon] I Mach. xii 42-xiii 24.

4053 to con ... hoo] Presumably 'without caring whom': L offers no precedent.

4054 Cyre] See n.3290; Manasses] IV Kings xxi 16; Antyochus] I Mach. i 17-67, II Mach. v 1-3; Herode] Matt. ii 16.

4056 Judas] Matt. xxvii 5; Abymalech] Judges ix 53-54, but see 4059; Saul] I Kings xxxi 3-4; Achitofel] II Kings xvii 23.

4079 Alexandre] I Mach. i 1-8; here (in contrast to 4456) he is recalled for his excessive ambition; Nembreth] (*Nemrod* L) Gen. x 9-12, Comestor 1088; Nabugodonosor] IV Kings xxiv-xxv 22.

4080 Athalia] IV Kings xi 1-3; Absolon] II Kings xv; Adonybeseth] *Adonibezech* L, *Adonisedec* in Josue x 1-8; Codorlamor] *Chodorlahomor* L and Gen. xiv 1-17.

4082 Aman] Esther iii 1-vii 10 or, if *King* (which has no precedent in L) belongs to *Aman* and not *Ezechye*, IV Kings xxi 18-23: the latter interpretation would give a logical group of three kings. Ezechye] Is. xxxix, IV Kings xx 12-18; Herode Agrippa] Acts xii.

4083 stu\l/th] The corrector's insertion was strictly unnecessary: for *stulth* see *OED stouth* 'theft'.

4084 Cusy] *Giezy* in IV Kings v 20; Achan] Joshua vii 19-26: the MS's *Achor* is found in some Latin MSS (see n.3935); Elyodore] II Mach. iii 1-29.

4086 Zambry] Num. xxv 6-14; Amon] (*Amnon* L) II Kings xiii; Dauid] II Kings xi: the reading might be *Amon King, David*; Salomo*un*] III Kings xi 1-11.

4088 Nabal] I Kings xxv 2-22; Senacherib] Is. xxxvi; Roboam] III Kings xii.

4090 Marie] Num. xii 1-10; Job] Job ii 9; Thobye] Tob. ii 19-23, (x 4-5?).

4107 For Christ displaying his wounds to the Father (the earliest images of which are found in 14th-century MSS of *SHS*) see Schiller (1971-80:II 224-26 and Pls.798-99 where the Virgin reveals her breasts to the Father also) and see II 197-205 for the related image of Christ as *Man of Sorrows*, which is probably a development of Rom. viii 34, Heb. vii 25, I John ii 1 (see n.4112).

4108 Ernaldusc Abbot of Bonneval (d.1156), cited in the caption to the woodcut in this chapter, mentions the Virgin showing her breasts to Christ, and Christ showing his wounds to the Father in appealing for mankind. The Virgin baring her breasts in appeal is rare in art until the influence of *SHS* is felt–L-P (1907:294-98) list later examples–but it occurs at the top of the 13th-century English *mappa mundi* in Hereford cathedral.

4112 The marginal reference–Bernard *in Cant. last chap*itle–is to John of Ford's last sermon in his continuation of St Bernard's sermons on the Canticle of Canticles: Sermon CXX para.6 comments on the last verse of the Canticle: *Fuge ergo et excurre in coelestia, recurre in locum tuum, qui est omnipotentis Patris tui sinus. Exhibe Patri aeterno manipulos oboedientiae tuae, et repraesenta ei passionis tuae signa uictricia, infer coelo gloriam crucis tuae; et sanguis tuus ille uiuificus pro ecclesia tua clamans uiscera paterna concutiat* (John of Ford 1970:809): 'Hurry then, and hurry to heaven; run back to your rightful place, the bosom of your almighty Father. Show to the eternal Father the maniples of your obedience, offer him the conquering signs of your Passion, bear to heaven the glory of your Cross, and may your life-giving blood crying out for your Church move the Father's heart.' The maniples may be meant to suggest the sacramental clothing of Christ's body in wounds, from 'maniple' as vestment, a form of stylised hand-towel. In this case there may be an intended relationship between *sinus* (the fold in a garment which is the origin of the image of Abraham's Bosom or the haven of the blessed) and *manipulos* as ceremonial garment. Just conceivably the reference may be to a rare meaning of *manipulus* 'bleeding-bowl': see Mâle (*la fin*:108-15) for the image of the *Fountain of Life* in which Christ crucified bleeds into a fountain, and 1053 in our text for the image of the Father offered the wine of Christ's blood. I am indebted to Professor Christopher Holdsworth for tracing this reference and observing that the marginal note may offer rare evidence for John of Ford (though identified as Bernard) being read in the late Middle Ages. See also Aquinas *ST* III q.54 a.4.

4115 The story appears also in *Gesta Romanorum* ch.87 (1905:160).

4133 The mystic wine-press derives from Is. lxiii 1-3; Num. xii 1-26 (the grapes brought from the Promised Land by the two spies) also contributed to the iconography: see Mâle (*la fin*:115-22ff), Schiller (1971-80:II 228-29). Early 15th-century woodcuts of the image are reproduced in Körner (1979:Abb.43, 65); see also A. Thomas (1936) and Weckwerth (1960).

4139 See Gaffney (1931) and Le May (1932).

4140 Almayne] This has been seen as evidence of the original author's familiarity with Almannia, thought to have been the Alsace-Swabia area of S. W. Germany divided by the Rhine (L-P 1907:248); but the area implied by 'Almannia' at this date is uncertain, and it is an odd way to refer to a familiar rite (Silber 1982:56-57).

4145 Longyve] See n.3267.

4157 I Kings xiv 1-15.

4168 I John ii 1-2.

4174 See n.4107.

4185 where] 'Then I think there is no question of whether or not Christ would listen to his mother.'

4191 Naaman] *Aman* L, as in Esther vii.

4206 For the iconography of the *Last Judgement* see Mâle (1961:ch.6, and *la fin*:457-61); also Réau (1955-58:IIi 731-37).

4207 Daniels (1949:230-31) points out that though the original author used the version of the parable found in Luke xix 12-17 (as shown by *mna* and *austerus* for the money and its owner, where Matthew has *talentum* and *durus*), he followed Matthew's use of the parable as an illustration of the Last Judgement.

4225 Matt. xxv 26.

4226 Daniels (1949:232) finds this attitude to pagans odd, but it is perhaps implicit in Aquinas *ST* IIii q.10 a.4 and *De Veritate* q.14 a.11 (see Aquinas *The Disputed Questions on Truth*) where even a man 'brought up in the forest or among wild beasts' is required to follow the 'direction of natural reason in seeking good and avoiding evil'; cf. Langland B Text Passus XI ll.135-47, XII ll.275-93; and ... sewe] The gloss explains, but this metaphor for preaching was common cf. Langland Passus XV ll.464-70 (1886:468) and Guillaume de Deguileville (Henry 1985:ll.50-56).

4229 See n.3206.

4233 Voragine I 23.

4238 he] KC's emendation to *be* (following H) is unnecessary: as L's *ipse* makes clear, the sense is 'And man would not acknowledge his light, the Creator, by day or night'.

4247 Ps. ii 2-4.

4248 Prov. i 26.

4270 apocrisyng] KC suggested derivation from OF *hypocriser*; *OED hypocrise* offers no example earlier than 1680 and *MED* does not record the verb, though *hypocrisy* is common from the 13th century. The L equivalent of ll.4269-70 is *Quid prodest vobis nunc superbia et gloria vana? / Ubi est nunc omnis placentia et laus humana?*; it looks therefore as if the ME *apocrisyng* ('practising of hypocrisy') is a loose translation of *gloria vana* in the previous line, while *wricchid praysyng* in 4269 represents *laus humana*.

4278 Aquinas *ST* III Supplement q.94 aa.2-3 explains that the blessed will be incapable of compassion for the damned: as Daniels points out (1949:234), the wise virgins' advice to the foolish–to buy more oil–is a bitter irony.

4281 Mane, techel, phares] The Vulgate *mane, thecel, phares* in Dan. v 25 represents three Aramaic nouns: *m^{e}nē, t^{e}gēl, p^{e}rēs*. These are measures of weight or money: mina, the shekel (one-fiftieth of a mina) and the half-mina. The Vulgate goes on to explain the enigmatic inscription by a play on words in which the three nouns are interpreted in terms of three somewhat similar verbs: *m^{e}nē* means 'God has numbered thy kingdom' from the verb *m^{e}nāh* 'to count or number'; *t^{e}gēl* is 'thou art weighed' from *t^{e}gal* 'to be weighed'; *parsîn* is 'thy kingdom is divided' from *p^{e}ras* 'to divide'. Thus though the three words of the inscription are entered in the Glossary as nouns, their 'meaning' is the warning to Baltasar that his sins will result in the breakup of his kingdom (i.e. his death).

4282 Dan. v 26-28 as interpreted in Comestor 1457.

4313 Aquinas *ST* III Supplement q.86 aa.1-3.

4320 Aquinas *ST* III Supplement q.76 aa.1-3.

4331ff For the gifts of the soul (*claritee, impassibilitee, sutyltee agilitee*) see Aquinas *ST* III Supplement qq.82-85. Daniels (1949:238) points out that the immediate source here was the *Compendium* Bk. VII ch.27.

4337 Matt. xvii 1-13.

4339-42 Luke ii; for the doctrine of the Virgin Birth see *NCE* XIV 692 and Aquinas *ST* III q.28 aa.1-3 (a.2 mentioning Christ's *sutiltee* at his birth, and *agilitee* in walking on water).

4342 Matt. xiv 22-27.

4344 Matt. xxvi 26-28.

4345-46 Aquinas *ST* III Supplement q.95 a.5 the direct source being *Compendium* Bk.VII ch.25.

4357 Ysay] See the illustration in ch.xxiij and n.2565; Jeremye] his legendary stoning is mentioned by Tertullian *PL* II 160, Isidore *PL* LXXXIII 142 and Comestor 1440. The marginal note may refer to Comestor's account of the deaths of Isaias and Jeremias, and perhaps to Josephus' account (*Jewish Antiquities* Bk.X secs114-40) of Jeremias' sufferings (though not his death). However, the author could have found the martyrdoms of Isaias, Jeremias and Ezechiel (see 4358) together in the apocryphal *Apocalypse of Paul* (James 1975:551).

4358 Amos] St Epiphanius *PG* XLIII 406, Isidore *PL* LXXXIII 144; Ezechiel] Comestor 1446, and see n.4357 above.

4360 *Quinquies quadragenas una minus accipiens, decollabatur* derives from *A Judaeis quinquies, quadragenas, una minus, accepi* (II Deut. xxv 3 as practised in Cor. xi 24-25–Paul's suffering, five times, the official flogging which consisted of forty strokes less one to ensure that the legal limit of forty was not exceeded). In view of the probable familiarity of the Biblical quotation (and Paul's sufferings are also described in Voragine IV 28-29, 41) I have assumed that *quinquagenaries* is a scribal error for *quadragenaries*, made under the influence of the preceding *v* ('five') or L. *quinquies*. *MED* does not record *quadragenary*, but cf. *quinquagenary*, which though not recorded in this sense clearly does refer to various 'sets of fifty'. An alternative emendation might be to *quadragenes* (*OED quinquagene* 'set of fifty'.)

4361 Jame] St James the Martyr, d.421 (Voragine VII 34-39), famous for the horror of his martyrdom.

4363 Barthelmewe] Legend says that the apostle was flayed alive (Voragine V 37); Peter] Tertullian (*PL* II 59, 174) refers to Peter's crucifixion; Origen (*PG* XII 91) adds that it was upside-down (so too Voragine IV 27).

4364 Piers martire] The mention of Peter of Verona, a Dominican Inquisitor-General martyred near Milan by Cathars in 1252, has suggested to some (e.g. L-P 1907:234, Daniels 1949:240) that the origin of *SHS* is Dominican; Laurance] a 3rd-century Papal archdeacon roasted in Rome (Voragine IV 208-16).

4369 Daniels (1949:240) shows that this derives from the *Compendium* Bk.VII ch.21.

4370 Judith xvi 21; the Worm of Conscience is a common *topos*, found for example in the 14th-century Guillaume de Deguileville's *Pèlerinage de la vie humaine*: see Guillaume de Deguileville *Þe Pilgrimage of þe Lyfe of þe Manhode* (1985:ll.1170-87), and *Pèlerinage de l'âme*: see Guillaume de Deguileville *The Pilgrimage of the Sowle* (1975:ch.xix).

4397 Two ModE lines here are the equivalent of two Latin lines not accounted for in the MS: *Dicit enim Sapiens quod parata sunt tormenta derisoribus / Et mallei percutientes stultorum corporibus*. The reference is to Prov. xix 29.

4405 In this chapter the antitype is treated at unusual length, the types being treated with corresponding brevity.

4411-2 Is. lxiv 4, I Cor. ii 9.

4415 suppetyng] In view of L *sufficiens* this may be a nonce formation on Lat. *suppeto*, and mean 'satisfying': but perhaps it is due to a misreading of ME *suffecyng*, in which case the reading should be *su[ffec]yng*.

4439 Matussale] Mathusala lived 969 years (Gen. v 25-27). Daniels (1949:243) points out that the people mentioned in ll.4439-41 and 4443-44 occur together in the *Compendium* Bk.VIII ch.30.

4440 Sampson] Judges xiv 5-6, xv 6-16, xvi 1-30.

4441 Azael] II Kings ii 18.

4442 Caleph] Num. xiv 3-38.

4443 Absolon] II Kings xiv 25.

4444 *Ibi stultitia reputaretur sapientia Salomonis* 'There the wisdom of Salomon would be considered foolishness.' Though its general sense is the same, the ME is difficult, both *als* and *acconpt* being ambiguous. Assuming *accompt* to be a noun, and *als to* to be the phrase described in *OED as 33*, it means 'And as far as its value is concerned (*als to accompt*) the wisdom of Solomon [would be] foolishness'; but if *accompt* is a passive infinitive, the sense is 'And the wisdom of Solomon [would be] regarded (*to accompt*) as foolishness, too', see n.1149.

4445 Jhetro] Ex. xviii 13-24; Achitofel] I Par. xxvii 33, II Kings xvi 20-xvii 14.

4447 Tubalchaym and Neoma] Gen. iv 22; Irams] III Kings v.

4448 Besleel and Ooliab] Besleel and Coliab (Ex. xxxi 1-11).

4449 Dauid harpe] I Kings xvi 13-23; Jubal] Gen. iv 21; the interlinear gloss to *absurditee* ('cacophony') may be *envysom* (H, *enuy soin* C).

4450 Manna] Ex. xvi; Cana] John ii 1-10.

4452 Eccles. ii 3-10: Ecclesiastes as a whole presents the vanity of worldly joys.

4454 Cresus] King of Lydia 560-c.540 B.C., famous for his wealth (Whiting 1968:C556); Antecrist] the prince of Christ's enemies, who is to appear at the end of time (I John ii 18, 22; iv 3), the reference to wealth perhaps deriving from II Thess. ii 3-11 or Dan. viii 23-25, and xi 21-45, where antiochus is an ancient type of antichrist. For varying identifications of antichrist see *NCE* I 616. See Musper (1970) for a facsimile (with summary) of the medieval blockbook illustrating antichrist's coming.

4456 Cyrus] Esdras i 2-11; Nabugodonosor] Jer. xxvii 6-7, Ezech. xxix 19-20, Dan. ii 37-38; Alexandre] the Great: the 5th-century king of Macedonia laid the foundations of a Hellenistic world stretching from Gibraltar to the Punjab. Balthasare] Dan. v; the line might read: ...*Nabugodonosor King*....

4457 Sampson] Judges xiv 5-6; xv 14-16; xvi 3-30; Sangar*e*] Judges iii 31; Abisay] II Kings xxi 16-17, xxiii 18.

4458 Dauid] I Kings xvii 34-35, II Kings viii, etc.; Semma] II Kings xxiii 11; Bononay or Sobokay] see n.1124.

4459 Absolon] II Kings xiv 25; Joseph] Gen. xxxix 6-7; Moyses] (? Ex. ii 2) Comestor 1144.

4460 Judith] Judith viii 7; Susanne] Dan. xiii 31; Rebecca] Gen. xxiv 15-16; Sara] Gen. xii 10-15; Rachele] Gen. xxix 17.

4461 Enoc, Matussale] Gen. v 21-27; Elye] Heli, I Kings iv 15-1, but Daniels (1949) has Elias, IV Kings ii 11.

4462 Asael] II Kings ii 18; H*er*cules] The mythical hero's third labour was the capture of the swift stag of Oenoe; Cusy] II Kings xviii 21.

4463 Salomon] III Kings iii 5-28.

4463-64 Augustine, Gregory, Jerome and Ambrose are the four Doctors of the Church renowned for their commentaries on the Gospels (cf. Langland, *Piers Plowman* B Text Passus XIX ll.257-68); in art too they are commonly associated with the Four Evangelists for this reason–as on the buttresses which form part of the figure screen on the west front of Exeter Cathedral, for example. Kirschbaum (1968-76:II 530) gives a general account of their appearances in art. Thomas Alqwyn] this spelling of Aquinas occurs also in the gloss to *Thomas* at 3009. According to L-P (1907:244-45) and Daniels (1949:249) the placing of the Dominican Aquinas in the company of the Doctors implies a Dominican origin for *SHS*.

4465 The three apostles were present at the Transfiguration (Matt. xvii 1-7).

4466 Ezechiel] Ezech. i; Ysay] Is. vi; Moyses] Ex. iii, xix 17-25; Steven] Acts vii 55-59.

4490 Ecclus. xxiv 26.

4491 ix^xx] 9 × 20 (*centum octoginta*).

4499 seven eage] The seventh of the Ages of the World is the age of the dead, begun on Doomsday: it is the sabbath or rest of the blessed souls. The seventh age is contemporaneous with the previous six (of Adam, Noah, Abraham, David, Moses, Christ), and inaugurates eternity, the eighth age. See Kolve (1966:89-99) for these and other details of the Ages, and their use in medieval literature and drama. The Ages were described by Augustine (*PL* XXXIV 190-94) and later in his *City of God* XXII 30 (Augustine 1972:383); they appear in Voragine I 37.

4505 The first of the three non-typological chapters presents the Hours of the Passion. For an account of the Canonical Hours see *CE* II 771 and *Dictionnaire de Spiritualité* 'Heures'. For a full account of the Hours as they appear in the Breviary, and of their meaning for religious, see Baudot (1929:112-40). Liturgically, the day is divided into Canonical Hours based on the ancient Roman divisions into roughly three-hour periods, varying with the seasons: Prime, Tierce, Sext, None, Vespers (Evensong); the night vigils are Matins and Lauds, Matins being itself divided into three nocturns. Lauds was theoretically said at dawn; Compline (*Completorie*) is a later addition to this scheme, and was theoretically said at nightfall. Each Hour is described in its appropriate place, below. Their seven-fold structure derives from Ps. cxviii 164.

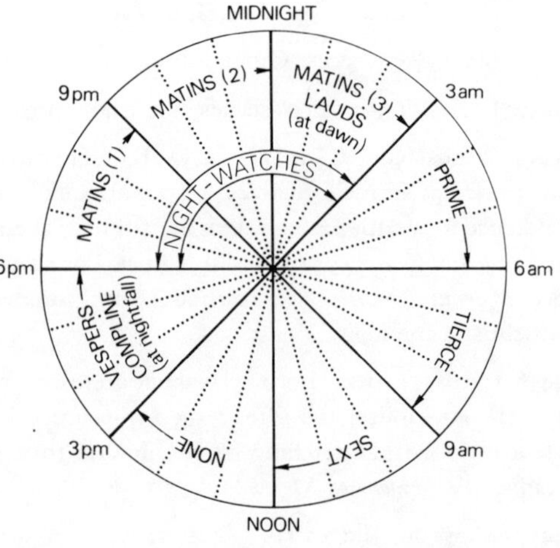

4513 The tale is in Ludolph of Saxony 'The Hours of the Passion' in his *Vitae Christi* II lviii.

4524 'And in [your] mouth by frequent, devout and loving thanks': the sense is clarified by L: *Et in ore per crebram et devotam gratiarum actionem.*

4532 One ... moo] *Quia tu es deus meus* 'For thou art my God'; *meus* was misread *unus* by the translator or his source.

4533 Evensonge] Vespers, originally the last of the daytime Hours, covering the three-hour period to 6p.m.

4559 Completorie] Compline, a later addition to the original series of Hours, set for nightfall.

4560 The Passion is described in Matt. xxvi-xxvii, Mark xiv-xv, Luke xxii-xxiii and John xiii-xix, but this account is also influenced by popular tradition deriving from Comestor 1628 (see n.2369).

4577 swte] KC's emendation to *swete* of this recorded form is unnecessary.

4585 Matynes] The first of the two Night Vigils among the Canonical Hours. It is divided into three periods corresponding with the watches of the night: to 9p.m., to midnight, to 3a.m. It was often said at midnight and immediately followed by Lauds, the second of the Night Vigils, theoretically set for dawn.

4592 And ... confessio*une*] *Et tu, Filium Dei vivi te esse, confessus fuisses* ('And you acknowledged being the Son of the living God') does not clarify the grammatical ambiguity of *ȝa*: it might be an adverb, giving the sense 'you acknowledged that to be the case' (*OED yea adv.* 1e) or 'you acknowledged that indeed' (ibid. 2); it might be the adverb used substantivally: 'you gave that assurance ...' (ibid. *sb.* 1b). The general sense is clear, however.

4611 Pryme] The Canonical Hour set for the three-hour period to 6a.m. or sunrise, and so called because occupying the ancient first hour of the day.

4637 Tierce] The Canonical hour set for the three-hour period of the day to 9a.m., and so called because occupying the ancient third hour.

4640 alle ... se] L's *immaniter* ('savagely') is no guide to the exact sense: *wightes* might be nom. pl., and *doel* pre. pl. ('all good people sorrow to see it') or *wightes* might be gen.pl. and *doel* a noun ('a torture for all good people to see').

4649 rede] see n.2369.

4663 Sext] The Canonical Hour set for the three-hour period of the day to noon, and so called because occupying the ancient sixth hour.

4689 None] The Canonical Hour set for the three-hour period of the day to 3p.m., and so called because occupying the ancient ninth hour.

4692 See n.2727.

4704 blakke ... hayre] The image (absent in L) is not of fog (*haar* KC) but of haircloth. It is a common echo of Apoc. vi 12: 'there was a great earthquake, and the sun became black as sackcloth of hair' (*tanquam cilicinus* in the Vulgate), as in both *Cursor Mundi* l.22510: *þe sun ... sal becum ... dune and blak sum ani hair* and *the sun shall be black as a sack* (Voragine I 12); *MED her 3d* cites *Yn reward ȝoven for hayres, to stoppe owte þe sunne yn the grete wendowe* (cf. Laȝamon I 130 *blac ... as a blac cloth*).

4713 Here the Seven Sorrows of the Virgin begin. Only in 1482 was the devotion formally expressed in the liturgy, the feast being on the Friday after Passion Sunday. The sequence *Stabat mater* contained in the Mass for this day is probably fourteenth-century (see n.2806).

4719 Slightly similar to the tale is a prayer found at the end of the Hour of None in Ludolph of Saxony (*Vitae Christi* II lxiv) where the author begs to be permitted to share in Christ's Passion, and feels his body wounded and his heart pierced. The fact that the tale is about a Dominican might again suggest a Dominican origin for *SHS*.

4748 Luke ii 34-35. The marginal comment at the foot of f.57^{r} explains that the Latin equivalent of the missing text for which space is left in the MS is supplied eight folios later (f.64). Assuming that the scribe meant the two incomplete and the two empty pages eventually to carry their normal 42 lines, he miscounted the spaces left, which are ten short: 2 full pages of 42 lines would leave 16 line spaces in all required at the bottom of f.57^{r} and the top of 58^{r}. There is only room for 4 and 2 respectively.

4766 virgin goddess] (L *virgo dea*) Ducange, under *dia*, suggests that this may be used for *dea*, and cites the 13th-century *Statutam Canonicorum Regularium*: *Dic et ave Dia prae cunctis Virgo Maria*; the title does not imply the literal divinity of the Virgin. Daniels (1949:261) points out that Luther also referred to the Virgin as *divam Virginem Mariam*!

4847 *Tu videbas eum pendere nudum omnino sine velamine* 'You saw him hanging totally naked, without covering.'

4897 According to Daniels (1949:260) it is unusual to find the Ascension, rather than the Entombment, as the seventh Sorrow.

4899 conu*er*syng] L. offers no equivalent: see n.3706.

4914 Ephiphanius] See n.3810.

4921 The feast of the Seven Joys of the Virgin is held on 22 August in the Franciscan rite.

4947 riche and delicable] *dives in deliciis* ('rich in delightful qualities') does not suggest wealth or nobility.

4952 Luke i 26-38.

4957 Ex. xxv 8-10.

4958 Ex. xvi 32-34 and Heb. ix 4.

4961 Num. xvii.

4962 Judges vi 36-40.

4976-78 Luke i 39-55.

4977 strange] The word may be the adjective *OED strong* 13, or *strange* 9: L offers no guide.

4978 *Et anima tua sanctissimum Dominum in jubilo magnificabat*: L suggests that *magnificabat* is translated by *made* (in the previous line) ... *a magnify*: in this case *magnify* is an unrecorded noun formed on *magnificat* (see 4992), and *jubylyng* is a present participle, the sense being 'rejoicing, made a song of praise'. An alternative, requiring the editorial removal of *a* from *a magnify*, is that the latter is an infinitive, the intended construction being *made* ... *magnify* meaning 'magnified'.

4983 Ex. iii 2.

4985 Cant. iv 12.

4992 Magnificat] Luke i 46-55: the text is traditionally the canticle of Vespers.

5002 Thi ... cloos] *Quando dilectum Filium tuum clausa et intacta peperisti* 'When, a virgin and intact, you gave birth to your beloved son'; L gives no precedent for *pu[e]rpure*.

5003 Ezech. xliv 1-2.

5004 Dan. ii 35.

5028 Matt. ii 1-12.

5084 The *Bestiary* describes how the ferocious unicorn may be caught only as it lays its head in the lap of a virgin (White 1954:20-21). For the iconography and background of the scene see Einhorn (1976:136-218). The image controls the subsequent list of strong animals and men representing Christ 'subdued' by Mary at the Incarnation.

5085 For the lion which represents Christ because like God becoming man it covers its tracks, sweeping the sand behind with his tail; see White (1954:7-8).

5086 Like an eagle, the resurrected Christ rose to his Father bearing his 'prey', mankind; in addition, Prov. xxx 19, the unfathomable 'way of an eagle in the air' was interpreted as a reference to Christ's coming down to earth at the Incarnation, and to the Ascension (pseudo-Ambrose [Grégoire d'Elvire] *PL* XVII 718, 719). The *SHS* elaborates the image, the eagle being *reclamed* like a trained falcon.

5087 L has *Tu vinxisti et ligasti fortissimum Samsonem, / Tu vicisti et superasti sapientissimum Salomonem* 'You overcame and bound Samson the most strong, / You conquered and subdued Solomon the most wise.' The reference to Solomon may derive from Cant. iii 9: 'King Solomon made him a litter of the wood of Libanus', interpreted as signifying the Incarnation (Honorius of Autun *PL* CLXXII 505). Samson is more difficult to explain. The Fathers invariably interpret Dalila, who bound Samson three times (Judges xvi 6-15), as the corrupt flesh trying to enslave the human spirit. That image has here been transmuted to one in which the Virgin's purity 'subdues' God. However, both Samson and Solomon are ancient types of Christ, so the transmutation is not as surprising as it might seem. Whether the translator conflated two lines here because he objected to the equation of Dalila and Mary or as a result of eyeskip, he or his copier added l.5088 in order to complete the couplet. Unfortunately, substitution of the dragon/devil for Samson breaks the pattern of ferocious but noble animal symbols of Christ in which it occurs. The Virgin's trampling of a dragon is based on Gen. iii 15.

5089 For Christ signified by the 'Pelican in her Piety' see n.2613; for Christ as conceived by a virgin being compared to a pelican which is by nature solitary see Hugh of Fouilly *PL* CLXXVII 29, and cf. Ps. ci 7.

5090 The fire-loving salamander (White 1954:183-84) does not itself commonly signify Christ (McCulloch 1962:161-62); however, it is described in a chapter on snakes in Rabanus Maurus (*PL* CXI 233) at the end of which the snake is said to represent Christ on account of its wisdom. Perhaps *SHS* fuses two traditions: those of the salamander and of the Virgin as the Burning Bush (see n.960).

5091 The panther which terrifies the dragon–the devil (White 1954:167)–by its cry and by the sweet breath which attracts all other animals, signifies Christ also because it is many-coloured (as God has many attributes) and is beautiful and kindly (McCulloch 1962:148-49; White 1954:14-18).

5092 The elephant which in the form of the 'most insignificant of elephants' is small enough to be able to help up a fallen comrade signifies Christ (White 1954:26-28).

5093 The phoenix, the 'rebirth' of which normally represents Christ's Resurrection (McCulloch 1962:158; White 1954:48, 49), here signifies the eternal God become a child, the godhead yet remaining undivided. The taming of allegorical beasts by Mary, of which the image forms a part, may be a deliberate echo of the prelapsarian naming of the beasts by Adam: in the Incarnation represented by their subjection, Christ is the New Adam.

5094 Ydicus] ydicus (*iditum* L). I capitalise *Ydicus* on the assumption that *The Ydicus* ('The Leaper') designates Christ. The translator (like KC) seems to have taken it merely as the name of an animal like those in the preceding lines. Idithun was a cantor and choirmaster of the Temple (Par. I xxv 3, II v 12), to whom Psalms xxxviii, lxi, lxxvi are inscribed. His name on the first of these is explained by Jerome (*PL* XXVI 997): 'leaping them'. In his *Etymologia* (*PL* LXXXII 285-86) Isidore of Seville explains the name further: 'He who is called "leaper" sprang over those clinging to the ground, bent to the earth, and those thinking about worldly and unworthy matters and placing their hope in transient things.' It is clear from the first citation in Ducange that (no doubt under Isidore's influence) *idithum* came to signify a 'leaper' in general, secular terms: it is applied to a man who though initially boastful, was the first to flee in battle: *ut vulgo dicitur vento citatior, montes et colles modernus idithum transmittebat* ('so that swifter than the wind he crossed the mountains and hills, like a modern idithum, as the saying has it.') The mountains and hills recall Cant. ii 8: *Ecce iste venit saliens in montibus, transiliens colles*, commonly interpreted as a reference to Christ: in his commentary on the Canticle, the pseudo-Ambrose (*PL* XV 1975, in a passage quoted in Voragine I 113-14, 118-19, 158) says: 'We see the leaper. He leaps from heaven to the Virgin, from the womb into the crib, from the Jordan on to the Cross, from the Cross to the grave, from the tomb to heaven.' (The so-called

Honorius of Autun *PL* CLXXII 502 gives a variation on Ambrose.) The translator's *ydicus* is probably due to an illogical alteration of a normal nominative proper noun in *-um* into a second declension noun in *-us* and to the common misreading of *t* as *c*.

5133 The ME index is in a hand not the scribe's, though contemporary with it. The errors in copying chapter references (listed in the critical apparatus) often show displacement by one line, suggesting copying from an extant list.

5256 Syr*us*] The expansion of a large 9-shaped abbreviation mark is doubtful (this scribe does not use it elsewhere): the sense of the word, 'Syrian' is clear.

5281 Occ\o/ours ... e*n*myes] The chapter reference is presumably a slip for *xvij*, since *xvj* is an account of the eucharist, not of enemies. Chapter *xvij* (l.1906) describes how Christ, *metyng his enemys made thaym doun falle*. This suggests that the doubtful first word is a form of *occurse*, though this is recorded in *MED* not at all, and in *OED* only A.D.1621ff (*occursion* A.D.1533ff). This interpretation is supported by the L. equivalent of l.1906: *hostibus suis occurens, ipsos prostravit*.

BIBLIOGRAPHY

Acta Sanctorum. Ed. J. Bollandus and G. Henschenius. 58 vols. Antwerp etc., 1643-1867.

Albertus Magnus. *Opera Alberti Magni*. Ed. P. Jammy. Lyons, 1651.

Alessandrini, A. 'Un prezioso codice Corsiniano di origine francescana (Speculum Humanae Salvationis, c. 1324-30)'. *Miscellanea Francescana*, 58 (1958), 420-83. [Bib. Corsiniana MS 55.K.2 (2617) formerly Rossi XVII.]

Analecta Hymnica Medii Aevi. Ed. G. M. Dreves, C. Blume, H. M. Bannister. Vol. LIV. Leipsig, 1911.

Ancrene Riwle. See Dobson.

Appuhn, H., ed. *Heilsspiegel: die Bilder des mittelalterlichen Erbauungsbuches 'Speculum Humanae Salvationis'*. Die Bibliophilen Taschenbücher, 267. Dortmund, 1981. [Darmstadt: Hessischen Landes- und Hochschulbibliothek MS 2505 (c.1360)].

Aquinas, St Thomas. *The Summa Theologica of St. Thomas Aquinas*. Trans. the Fathers of the English Dominican Province. 22 vols. London, 1920-1924.

———. *The Disputed Questions on Truth*. Trans. R. W. Mulligan. 3 vols. Chicago, 1952-1954.

Auerbach, E. 'Figura'. In his *Scenes from the Drama of European Literature: Six Essays*. Gloucester, Mass., 1973, pp. 11-76.

Augustine, St. *The City of God Against the Pagans*. Vol. III. Trans. W. M. Green. Loeb Classical Library. London, 1972.

Baer, L. 'Weitere Beiträge zur Chronologie und Lokalisierung der Werke des Hausbuchmeisters'. *Monatschefte für Kunstgewissenschaft*, N.F. 3 (1910), 408-24.

Baier, W. *Untersuchungen zu den Passionsbetrachtungenn in der 'Vita Christi' des Ludolf von Sachsen: ein quellenkritischer Beitrag zu Leben und Werk Ludolfs und zur Geschichte der Passionstheologie*. 3 vols. Analecta Cartusiana, 44. Salzburg, 1977.

Bartsch, J. A. von. *Le Peintre-Graveur*. 21 vols. Vienna, 1803-21.

Baring-Gould, G. *The Lives of the Saints*. 16 vols. 3rd edn. Edinburgh, 1914.

Baudot, J. *The Breviary: its History and Contents*. Trans. the Benedictines of Stanbrook. Catholic Library of Religious Knowledge, 4. London, 1929.

Becano, M. *Analogia Veteris ac Novi Testamenti in qua Primum Statvs Veteris deinde Consensus, Proportio, & Conspiratio illius cum Nouo Explicatur*. Louvain, 1620.

Beckman, J. H., and I. Schroth, eds. *Picture Bible of the Late Middle Ages: M.334 from the University Library Freiburg im Breisgau and M.719-720 from the Pierpont Morgan Library New York*. Bodensee, 1960.

Berenson, B. 'Due Illustratori Italiani dello *Speculum Humanae Salvationis*'. *Bollettino d'Arte del Ministero della Pubblica Istruzione*, 2nd Ser., 5i (1925-1926), 289-320, 353-84. [BN MSS Lat. 9584; Bib. de l'Arsenal MS N.593].

Berenson, J., and M. R. James. *Speculum Humanae Salvationis, Being a Reproduction of an Italian Manuscript of the Fourteenth Century*. Oxford, 1926.

Berjeau, J. P. *Speculum Humanae Salvationis: le plus ancien monument de la xylographie et de la typographie réunies*. London, 1861.

Berliner, R. 'Arma Christi'. *Münchner Jahrbuch der bildenden Kunst*, III, Bd. VI (1955), 35-152.

Bernard, St. *Song of Songs I*. Vol. II of *The Works of Bernard of Clairvaux*. Cistercian Fathers Series, 4. Kalamazoo, 1977.

——. *On the Song of Songs II.* Vol. III of *The Works of Bernard of Clairvaux.* Cistercian Fathers Series, 7. Kalamazoo, 1976 (sic).

——. *On the Song of Songs III.* Vol. IV of *The Works of Bernard of Clairvaux.* Cistercian Fathers Series, 31. Kalamazoo, 1979.

——. *On the Song of Songs IV.* Vol. V of *The Works of Bernard of Clairvaux.* Cistercian Fathers Series, 40. Kalamazoo, 1980.

——. See also Leclercq.

Bernheimer, R. 'The Martyrdom of Isaiah'. *Art Bulletin*, 34 (1952), 19-34.

Beuken, W. H., and J. H. Marrow. *Spiegel van den leven ons Heren (Mirror of the Life of Our Lord): Diplomatic Edition of the Text and Facsimile of the 42 Miniatures of a 15th-Century Typological Life of Christ in the Pierpont Morgan Library.* Dornspijk, 1979.

Biblia Pauperum. See Henry.

Biblia Sacra iuxta Vulgatam Versionem. Ed. R. Weber. 2 vols. Stuttgart, 1969.

Bierens de Haan, J. C. J. *De meester van het Amsterdamsche kabinet met reproducties in lichtdruk van het geheel gegraveerde werk.* Amsterdam, 1947.

Bishop, H. 'The Vocabulary of the English Translation of *Speculum Humanae Salvationis*'. *English Studies*, 53 (1972), 105-9.

Bodenstedt, M. *The Vita Christi of Ludolphus the Carthusian.* The Catholic University of America Studies in Medieval and Renaissance Latin Language and Literature, 16. Washington DC, 1944.

Bonnell, J. K. 'The Serpent with a Human Head in Art and Mystery Play'. *American Journal of Archaeology*, 21 (1917), 255-91.

Bossert, H. Th., and W. F. Storck. *Das mittelalterliche Hausbuch nach dem Originale im Besitze des fürsten von Waldburg-Wolfegg-Waldsee im Auftrage des deutschen Vereins für Kunstwissenschaft.* Leipzig, 1912.

Bradley, R. 'Backgrounds of the Title *Speculum* in Mediaeval Literature'. *Speculum*, 29 (1954), 100-15.

Brandis, T. 'Eine illuminierte Handschrift des Speculum Humanae Salvationis'. *Jahrbuch Preussischer Kulturbesitz*, 16 (1979), 177-85. [Staatsbibliothek Preussischer Kulturbesitz W. Berlin MS.175].

Breitenbach, E. *Speculum Humanae Salvationis: eine typengeschichtliche Untersuchung.* Studien zur deutschen Kunstgeschichte, 272. Strassburg, 1930.

Briquet, C. M. *Les Filigranes: dictionnaire historique des marques du papier dès leur apparition vers 1282 jusqu'en 1600 avec 39 figures dans le texte et 16,112 fac-similés de filigranes.* 4 vols. 2nd edn. Leipzig, 1928.

——. *Les Filigranes: dictionnaire historique des marques du papier dès leur apparition vers 1282 jusqu'en 1600 avec 39 figures dans le texte et 16,112 fac-similés de filigranes.* Ed. A. H. Stevenson. 4 vols. Amsterdam, 1968.

Brix, O. *Über die mittellenglische Übersetzung des Speculum Humanae Salvationis.* Palaestra: Untersuchungen und Texte aus der deutschen und englischen Philologie, 7. Berlin, 1900.

Broszinski, H., and J. Heinzle. 'Kasseler Bruchstück der anonymen deutschen Versbearbeitung des *Speculum Humanae Salvationis.*' *Zeitschrift für deutsche Altertum und deutsche Literatur*, 112 (1983), 54-64.

Buchner, E. 'Der Meister der Drachschen Offizin.' Section II of 'Studien zur Mittelrheinischen Malerei und Graphik der Spätgotik und Renaissance'. *Münchner Jahrbuch der bildenden Kunst*, N.F. 4iii (1927), 276-83.

Burger, K. *The Printers and Publishers of the XVth Century with Lists of their Works: Index to the Supplement to Hain's Repertorium Bibliographicum, etc.* Milan, 1902.

Burke's Genealogical and Heraldic History of the Peerage Baronetage and Knightage. Ed. P. Townend. 105th edn. London, 1952.

Caesarius of Heisterbach. *Dialogus Miraculorum.* Ed. J. Strange. 2 vols. Cologne, 1851.

Cantica Canticorum: Societatis in Honorem Marées Pictoris Conditae Opus Tricensimum Quartum. Editio Archetypum Anni circiter Millesimi Quadringentesimi Sexagesimi Quinti Imitans. Marées Geselleschaft, 14. Berlin, 1922. [Facsimile of Dutch coloured blockbook edition].

Catalogue of Manuscripts and Early Printed Books from the Libraries of William Morris, Richard Bennett, Bertram, Fourth Earl of Ashburnham, and Other Sources, Now Forming Portion of the Library of J. Pierpont Morgan. Vol. I. London, 1907.

The Catholic Encyclopedia: an International Work of Reference on the Constitution, Doctrine, Discipline, and History of the Catholic Church. 16 vols. New York, 1907-1914.

Caviness, M. H. *The Early Stained Glass of Canterbury Cathedral, circa 1175-1220.* Princeton, 1977.

———. *The Windows of Christ Church Cathedral, Canterbury.* Corpus Vitrearum Medii Aevi, 2. London, 1981.

Caxton's Mirrour of the World. Ed. O. H. Prior. EETS ES 110. London,1913; repr. 1966.

Charles, R. H., ed. and trans. *The Book of Enoch.* Oxford, 1893.

———. *The Apocrypha and Pseudepigraphia of the Old Testament in English with Introductions and Critical and Explanatory Notes to the Several Books.* 2 vols. Oxford, 1913; repr. 1963.

Chaucer. *The Works of Geoffrey Chaucer.* Ed. F. N. Robinson. 2nd edn. London, 1957.

Chydenius, J. *The Typological Problem in Dante: a Study in the History of Medieval Ideas.* Societas Scientiarum Fennica: Commentationes Humanarum Litterarum, 25. Helsingfors, 1958.

Clair, C. *A History of European Printing.* London, 1976.

Cockerell, S. C. *Some German Woodcuts of the Fifteenth Century.* London, 1897.

Compendium Theologicae Veritatis. Nuremberg, ? 1470.

Colquhoun, K. H. 'A Critical Edition of the Middle English Translation of *Speculum Humanae Salvationis*'. M.A. thesis. London, 1964.

———. See Bishop.

Comestor, Petrus. See Petrus.

Conrad of Saxony. *Speculum Beate Marie Virginis Compilatum ab Humili Fratre Bonauentura.* Augsburg, 1476.

Copinger, W. A. *Supplement to Hain's Repertorium Bibliographicum Part I.* Milan, 1895.

———. *Supplement to Hain's Repertorium Bibliographicum Part II.* 2 vols and addenda. London, 1898 and 1902.

Cornell, J. H. *The Iconography of the Nativity of Christ.* Uppsala Universitets årsskrift 1924. Filosofi, språkvetenskap och historiska vetenskaper, 3. Uppsala, 1924.

———. *Biblia Pauperum.* Stockholm, 1925.

Cursor Mundi: a Northumbrian Poem of the XIVth Century Edited from British Museum MS. Cotton Vespasian A.III, Bodleian MS. Fairfax 14, Göttingen University Library MS. Theol. 107, Trinity College Cambridge MS. R. 3. 8. Ed. R. Morris. 7 Parts. EETS OS, 57, 59, 62, 66, 68, 99, 101. London, 1874-1893; repr. 1961.

Daly, S. R. 'Peter Comestor: Master of Histories'. *Speculum*, 32 (1957), 62-69.

Daniels, L. M. 'Ludolphus van Saksen en Henricus Suso'. *Ons Geestelijk erf*, 20i,ii (1946), 142-50.

———, ed. *De spieghel der menscheliker behoudenesse: de middelnederlandse vertaling van het 'Speculum Humanae Salvationis'*. Studiën en tekstuitgaven van Ons Geestelijk erf, 9. Tielt, 1949.

Dan Michel's Ayenbite of Inwyt, or Remorse of Conscience. Ed. R. Morris. Rev. P. Gradon. EETS OS 23. Oxford, 1965.

Dan Michel's Ayenbite of Inwyt. Vol. II. Ed. P. Gradon. EETS OS 278. Oxford, 1979.

Deguileville. See Guillaume de Deguileville.

Dictionnaire de spiritualité: ascétique et mystique doctrine et histoire. Ed. M. Viller. Vols. I-VIII. Paris, 1937-1974.

Diogenes Laertius. *Lives of the Eminent Philosophers*. Trans. R. D. Hicks. Loeb Classical Library. 2 vols. London, 1925.

Dives and Pauper. Ed. P. H. Barnum. Vols. Ii, ii. EETS OS 275, 280. London, 1976, 1980.

Dobson, E. J., ed. *The English Text of the Ancrene Riwle Edited from B.M. Cotton MS.Cleopatra C.vi*. EETS OS 267. London, 1972.

Dodgson, Campbell. *Catalogue of Early German and Flemish Woodcuts Preserved in the Department of Prints and Drawings in the British Museum*. 2 vols. London, 1903-1911; repr. Vaduz, Liechtenstein, 1980.

Du Cange, C. du F. *Glossarium Mediae et Infimae Latinitatis*. Paris, 1937-1938.

Duff, E. G. *Fifteenth-Century English Books*. Illustrated Monographs Issued by the Bibliographical Society, 18. Oxford, 1917.

Dugdale, W. *Monásticon Anglicanum: a History of the Abbies and Other Monasteries, Hospitals, Frieri and Cathedral and Collegiate Churches, with their Dependencies in England and Wales*. New edn. Ed. J. Caley, H. Ellis and B. Bandinel. Vol. II. London, 1819, pp. 246-47. [Tituli of lost St Alban's glass; see also Schlosser]

Durandus of Mende. *Rationale Divinorum Officiorum*. Lyons, 1584.

Eccles, M., ed. *The Macro Plays: The Castle of Perseverance, Wisdom, Mankind*. EETS OS 262. London, 1969.

Einhorn, J. W. *Spiritualis Unicornis: das Einhorn als Bedeutungsträger in Literatur und Kunst des Mittelalters*. Munich, 1976.

Fairbairn, P. *The Typology of Scripture*. 2 vols. Edinburgh, 1845-1847.

Falk, F. 'Zur Entwicklung und zum Verständnis des Speculum Humanae Salvationis (Heilsspiegel).' *Zentralblatt für Bibliothekswesen*, 15 (1898), 420-23.

Fischel, L. *Bilderfolgen im frühen Buchdruck. Studien zur Inkunabel-illustration in Ulm und Strassburg*. Konstanz and Stuttgart, 1963.

Flechsig, E. 'Der Meister des Hausbuchs als Zeichner für den Holzschnitt.' *Monatshefte für Kunstwissenschaft*, 4 (1911), 95-115, Pls 26-33.

Flores, N. C. 'The Influence of the *Speculum Humanae Salvationis* on the Cathedral Cloisters Wall-Paintings at Bressanone'. *Manuscripta*, 27iii (1983), 172-73. [Abstract of paper 10th St Louis Conference on Manuscript Studies, 14-15 Oct. 1983.]

Friedländer, M. J. *Der Holzschnitt*. Berlin, 1970.

Fryer, A. C. 'Theophilus, the Penitent, as Represented in Art'. *Archaeological Journal*, 92 (1935), 287-333.

Gaffney, W. 'The Allegory of the Christ-Knight in *Piers Plowman*'. *PMLA*, 46 (1931), 155-68.

Geisberg, M. *Geschichte der deutschen Graphik vor Dürer*. Forschungen zur deutschen Kunstgeschichte, 32. Berlin, 1939.

Geldner, F. 'Probleme um den Speyrer Druckherrn und Buchhändler Peter Drach'. *Gutenberg-Jahrbuch* (1962), 150-57.

Gerardus de Fracheto. *Vitae Fratrum Ordinis Praedicatorum*. Ed. B. M. Reichert. Monumenta Ordinis Fratrum Praedicatorum Historica, 1. Leuven, 1896.

Gesamtkatalog der Wiegendrucke. Ed. Kommission für den Gesamtkatalog der Wiegendrucke. 7 vols. (A-Fed). Leipzig, 1925-1940.

Gesta Romanorum. Trans. C. Swan. Rev. W. Hooper. London, 1905.

Ginzberg, L. *The Legends of the Jews*. Trans. H. Szold. 7 vols. Philadelphia, 1909-1938; repr. 1967-1969.

Glaser, C. *Gotische Holzschnitte*. Berlin, 1924.

Glorieux, P. *Pour revaloriser Migne: tables rectificatives*. Mélanges de science religieuse, 9. Lille, 1952.

Göbel, H. 'Die gestickten Wandteppiche des Klosters Wienhausen.' *Cicerone* (1928), 9-23.

Goff, F. R., ed. *Checklist of Incunabula in American Libraries: a Third Census of Fifteenth-Century Books Recorded in North American Collections*. New York, 1964; rev. F. R. Goff, Millwood, 1973.

Gospel of Nicodemus. See Tischendorff, James, Hennecke.

Gougaud, L. 'Muta Praedicatio.' *Revue Bénédictine*, 42 (1930), 168-71.

Grabes, H. *The Mutable Glass: Mirror Imagery in Titles and Texts of the Middle Ages and the English Renaissance*. Trans. G. Collier. Cambridge, 1982.

Graesse, Th., ed. See Voragine.

Graul, R., ed. *Das Hausbuch. Bilder aus dem deutschen Mittelalter von einem unbekannten Meister*. Insel-Bücherei, 452. Leipzig, [1934].

Grimm, H. 'Die Buchführer des deutschen Kulturbereichs und ihre Niederlassungsorte in der Zeitspanne 1490 bis um 1550'. *Archiv für Geschichte des Buchwesens*, 7 (1967), cols. 1153-772.

Guichard, J. M. *Notice sur le 'Speculum Humanae Salvationis'*. Paris, 1840.

Guillaume de Deguileville. *Þe Pilgrimage of þe Lyfe of þe Manhode: Translated Anonymously into Prose from the First Recension of Guillaume de Deguileville's Poem* Le Pèlerinage de la vie humaine. Vol. I (Introduction, Text). Ed. Avril Henry. EETS OS 288. Oxford, 1985.

———. *Þe Pilgrimage of þe Lyfe of þe Manhode: Translated Anonymously into Prose from the First Recension of Guillaume de Deguileville's Poem* Le Pèlerinage de la vie humaine. Vol. II (Notes, Bibliography). Ed. Avril Henry. EETS, Oxford, forthcoming 1987 or 1988.

———. *The Pylgrymage of the Sowle*. Trans. William Caxton. London, 1483; repr. The English Experience, 726. Amsterdam, 1975.

———. *Le Pèlerinage Jhesucrist*. Ed. J. J. Stürzinger. Roxburghe Club. London, 1897.

Hain, L. *Repertorium Bibliographicum in quo Libri Omnes ab Arte Typographica Inventa usque ad Annum MD. Typis Expressi Ordine Alphabetico vel Simpliciter Enumerantur vel Adcuratius Recensentur*. 2 vols. Stuttgart and Paris, 1826-1838.

Haussherr, R. *Bible Moralisée: Faksimile-Ausgabe im Originalformat des Codex Vindobonensis 2554 der Österreichischen Nationalbibliothek*. Reihe Codices Selecti, 40. 2 vols (facsimile and commentary). Graz, 1973.

Heinecken, C. H. von. *Idée générale d'une collection complette d'estampes avec une dissertation sur l'origine de la gravure et sur les premiers livres d'images*. Leipzig and Vienna, 1771.

Hennecke, H. *The New Testament Apocrypha.* Ed. W. Schneemelcher. Trans. R. McL. Wilson. 2 vols. London, 1965.

Henry, A. K. '*Biblia Pauperum*: Schreiber Editions I and VIII Reconsidered'. *Oud Holland,* 95iii (1983), 127-50.

———. '"Eliseus Raises the Sunamite" in Context: Observations on Some Late Medieval Glass Now in Exeter Cathedral Lady Chapel, Part I'. *Friends of Exeter Cathedral Fifty-third Annual Report* (1983), 10-17.

———. '"Eliseus Raises the Sunamite" in Context: Observations on Some Late Medieval Glass Now in Exeter Cathedral Lady Chapel, Part II'. *Friends of Exeter Cathedral Fifty-fourth Annual Report* (1984), 12-18.

———. 'The Woodcuts of *Der Spiegel menschlicher Behältnis (Speculum Humanae Salvationis)* in the Editions Printed by Drach (Speier n.d.) and Richel (Basel 1476)'. *Oud Holland,* 99i (1985), 1-15.

———, ed. *Biblia Pauperum: a Facsimile Edition of the Forty-page Blockbook, with Translation, Commentary and Notes.* London, 1985 or 1986, forthcoming.

Herodotus. *Herodotus* Ed. and trans. A. D. Godley. Vol. I. Loeb Classical Library. London, 1920; rev. 1966.

Hind, A. M. *An Introduction to a History of Woodcut with a Detailed Survey of Work Done in the Fifteenth Century.* 2 vols. London, 1935; repr. New York, 1953.

Hodnett, E. *English Woodcuts 1480-1535.* Oxford, 1973.

Hollstein, F. W. H. *German Engravings, Etchings and Woodcuts ca. 1400-1700.* Ed. K. G. Boon and R. W. Scheller. Vols. I-VIII-. Amsterdam, 1954-1968-.

The Holy Bible Translated from the Latin Vulgate Diligently Compared with the Hebrew, Greek, and Other Editions in Divers Languages: The Old Testament First Published by the English College at Douay, A.D. 1609 and The New Testament First Published by the English College at Rheims, A.D. 1582, with Annotations, References, and an Historical and Chronological Index to the Whole Revised and Diligently Compared with the Latin Vulgate. Baltimore, 1899; repr. Rockford, Ill., 1971.

Honorius of Autun. *Speculum Ecclesiae. PL* CLXXII 813-1108.

Hoyt, A. C. 'The Mirror of Man's Salvation'. *Bulletin of the Museum of Fine Arts Boston,* 54, no. 298 (1956), 88-92.

Hughes, A. *Medieval Manuscripts for Mass and Office: a Guide to Their Organisation and Terminology.* London, 1982.

Huth, A. H., ed. *The Miroure of Mans Saluacionne: a Fifteenth-Century Translation into English of the Speculum Humanae Salvationis and Now for the First Time Printed from a Manuscript in the Possession of Alfred Henry Huth.* Roxburghe Club. London, 1888.

James, M. R. *Proceedings of the Cambridge Antiquarian Society with Communications Made to the Society,* N.S. 7 (1888-1891), 64-69. [On the lost glass of St Alban's cloisters.]

———. *The Apocryphal New Testament Being the Apocryphal Gospels, Acts, Epistles, and Apocalypses.* Oxford, 1924; repr. 1975.

———. 'Pictor in Carmine'. *Archaeologia,* 94 (1951), 141-66.

James, M. R., and B. Berenson. See Berenson.

Jareš, Stanislav. 'Traktát *Zrcadlo člověčieho spasenie* jako hudebně ikonografický pramen'. *Hudební věda,* IIIi (1976), 81-85, Pls 1-8. [Prague, National Museum Library, MS 1 Ac 75/I-IV and MS III B 10].

The Jerusalem Bible. London, 1966.

Jespersen, Otto. *A Modern English Grammar on Historical Principles*. 7 Parts. London, 1909-1949; repr. 1970.

John of Ford. *Super Extremam Partem Cantici Canticorum Sermones CXX Sermones LXX - CXX*. Ed. E. Mikkers and H. Costello. Corpus Christianorvm Continuatio Mediauelis 18. Turnhout, 1970.

Jolliffe, P. S. *A Check-list of Middle English Prose Writings of Spiritual Guidance*. Subsidia Mediaevalia, 2. Toronto, 1974.

Josephus. *Josephus*. Trans. H. St. J. Thackeray. 8 vols. Loeb Classical Library. London, 1956-1963.

Jungmann, J. A. *[Missarum Solemnia]: the Mass of the Roman Rite: its Origins and Development*. Trans. F. A. Brunner. Rev. C. K. Rieps. London, 1959.

Kaske, R. G. 'Patristic Exegesis: the Defense'. In *Critical Approaches to Medieval Literature*. Ed. D. Bethurum. New York, 1960, pp. 27-60.

Kehrer, H. *Die heiligen drei Könige in Literatur und Kunst*. 2 vols. Leipzig, 1908-1909.

Kessler, H. L. 'The Chantilly *Miroir de l'humaine salvation* and its Models'. In *Studies in Late Medieval and Renaissance Painting in Honor of Millard Meiss*. 2 vols. (text, plates). Ed. I. Lavin and J. Plummer. New York, 1977, pp.274-82.

Kirschbaum, E., ed. *Lexicon der christlichen Ikonographie*. 8 vols. Rome, 1968-1976.

Klapper, J. 'Spiegel der menschlichen Seligkeit'. In *Die deutsche Literatur des Mittelalters: Verfasserlexicon*. Gen. ed. K. Langosch. Vol. IV. Berlin, 1953, cols.237-44.

Kloss, E. *Speculum Humanae Salvationis: ein niederländisches Blockbuch*. Munich, 1925.

Koch, R. A. 'The Sculptures at the Church of Saint-Maurice at Vienne, the *Biblia Pauperum* and the *Speculum Humanae Salvationis*'. *Art Bulletin*, 32 (1950), 151-55.

Kolve, V. A. *The Play Called Corpus Christi*. London, 1966.

Körner, H. *Der früheste deutsche Einblattholzschnitt*. Studia Iconologica, 3. Mittenwald, 1979.

Korshin P. J. *Typologies in England 1650-1820*. Princeton, 1982.

Künstle, K. *Ikonographie der christlichen Kunst*. 2 vols. Freiburg, 1928, 1926 [sic].

Kunze, H. *Geschichte der Buchillustration in Deutschland das 15. Jahrhundert*. 2 vols. (text, plates). Leipzig, 1975.

Küppers, L., ed. *Die Gottesmutter: Marienbild in Rheinland und Westfalen*. 2 vols. Recklinghausen, 1974.

Lafond, J. *Un Livre d'heures rouennais, enluminée d'après le Speculum Humanae Salvationis: reproduction phototypique d'un manuscrit de la bibliothèque de Cherbourg*. Rouen, 1929.

Langland, W. *The Vision of William Concerning Piers the Plowman in Three Parallel Texts Together with Richard the Redeless*. Ed. W. W. Skeat. 2 vols. London, 1886.

Latham, R. E. *Revised Medieval Latin Wordlist from British and Irish Sources*. London, 1965.

Laȝamon: Brut. Edited from British Museum MS.Cotton Caligula A.IX and British Museum MS.Cotton Otto C.xiii. Ed. G. L. Brook and R. F. Leslie. 2 vols. EETS OS 250, 277. London, 1963, 1978.

Leclercq, J., H. Rochais and C. H. Talbot, eds. *Sermones super Cantica Canticorum*. Vol. I of *S. Bernardi Opera*. Rome, 1957.

Leclercq, J., and H. Rochais, eds. *Sermones I*. Vol. IV of *S. Bernardi Opera*. Rome, 1966.

Lehrs, M. *Geschichte und kritischer Katalog des deutschen niederländischen und französischen Kupferstichs im XV Jahrhundert*. 9 vols. Vienna, 1908-1934.

———. *Katalog der im germanischen Museum befindlichen deutschen Kupferstiche des XV. Jahrhunderts.* Anzeiger des germanischen Nationalmuseums, 2vii, viii, ix. Nuremberg, 1888.

———. *The Master of the Amsterdam Cabinet.* Berlin, 1893 and 1894.

Leiter, L. H. 'Typology, Paradigm, Metaphor and Image in the York *Creation of Adam and Eve*'. *Drama Survey*, 7 (1969), 113-32.

Le May, M. de L. *The Allegory of the Christ-Knight in English Literature.* Diss. Washington D.C. 1932. Washington, D. C., 1932.

Lewis, C. T., and C. Short. *A Latin Dictionary.* Oxford, 1879.

Ludolph of Saxony. *Vita Christi.* Lyons, 1510.

———. *La Grande Vie de Jésus-Christ.* Trans. M. P. Augustin. 6 vols. Paris, 1864-1865.

———. *The Hours of the Passion Taken from The Life of Christ.* Trans. H. J. C[oleridge] London, 1887.

Ludus Coventriae or The Plaie Called Corpus Christi. Ed. K. S. Block. EETS ES 70. London, 1922; repr. EETS ES 120, 1960.

Lutz, J., and P. Perdrizet, eds. *Speculum Humanae Salvationis: texte critique: traduction inédite de Jean Mielot (1448); les sources et l'influence iconographique principalement sur l'art alsacien du xive siècle: avec la reproduction, en 140 planches, du Manuscrit de Sèlestat, de la série complète des vitraux de Mulhouse, de vitraux de Colmar, de Wissembourge, etc.* 2 vols. Mulhouse and Leipzig, 1907, 1909. [Staatsbibliothek München clm 146].

Mâle, E. *L'Art religieux du XIIe siècle en France: étude sur les origines de l'iconographie du moyen âge.* 2nd edn. Paris, 1924.

———. *Religious Art in France: the Twelfth Century: a Study of the Origins of Medieval Iconography.* Bollingen Series, 90i. Princeton, 1978.

———. *L'Art religieux du XIIIe siècle en France: étude sur l'iconographie du moyen âge et sur ses sources d'inspiration.* 6th edn. Paris, 1925.

———. *Religious Art in France: the Thirteenth Century: a Study of Medieval Iconography and Its Sources.* Ed. H. Bober. Trans. M. Mathews. Bollingen Series, 90ii. Princeton, 1984.

———. *L'Art religieux de la fin du moyen âge: étude sur l'iconographie du moyen âge et sur ses sources d'inspiration.* 3rd edn. Paris, 1925.

———. *The Late Middle Ages: a Study of Medieval Iconography and Its Sources.* Ed. H. Bober. Trans. M. Mathews. Bollingen Series, 90iii. Princeton, 1986, forthcoming.

———. *The Gothic Image: Religious Art in France of the Thirteenth Century.* Trans. Dora Nussey from the 3rd edn. London, 1961.

Marrow, J. 'From Sacred Allegory to Descriptive Narrative: Transformations of Passion Iconography in the Late Middle Ages'. Diss. Columbia 1974.

McCulloch, F. *Mediaeval Latin and French Bestiaries.* University of South Carolina Studies in the Romance Languages and Literatures, 33. Rev. edn. Chapel Hill, 1962.

Mather, S. *The Figures or Types of the Old Testament, by which Christ and the Heavenly Things of the Gospel Were Preached and Shadowed to the People of God of Old, Explained and Improved, in Sundry Sermons.* London, 1683.

Meditations on the Life of Christ: an Illustrated Manuscript of the Fourteenth Century: Paris, Bibliothèque Nationale, MS.Ital. 115. Ed. I. Ragusa and R. B. Green. Trans. I. Ragusa. Princeton Monographs in Art and Archaeology, 35. Princeton, 1966; repr. 1977.

Mellinkoff, R. *The Horned Moses in Medieval Art and Thought.* California Studies in the History of Art. Berkeley, 1970.

The Metrical Life of Christ ed. from MS BM Add.39996. Ed. W. Sauer. MET, 5. Heidelberg, 1977.

The Metrical Version of Mandeville's Travels from the Unique Manuscript in the Coventry Corporation Record Office. Ed. M. C. Seymour. EETS OS 269 (1973).

Meyers, W. E. 'Typology and the Audience of the English Cycle Plays'. *Studies in the Literary Imagination,* 8i (1975), 145-48.

Michel, Dan. See Dan Michel.

Middle English Dictionary . Gen. eds. H. Kurath and S. M. Kuhn. Ann Arbor, 1954-.

The Middle English Harrowing of Hell and the Gospel of Nicodemus. Ed. W. H. Hulme. EETS ES 100. London, 1907.

Migne, J.-P., ed. *Patrologiae Cursus Completus ... Series Latinae.* 221 vols., Supplement 3 vols. Paris, 1878-1890 and 1958-1963.

———, ed. *Patrologiae Cursus Completus ... Series Graeca.* 162 vols. Turnholt, n.d.

The Miroure of Mans Saluacionne. See Huth.

Morgan, N. J. *The Medieval Painted Glass of Lincoln Cathedral.* London, 1983.

Morris, W. 'On the Artistic Qualities of the Woodcut Books of Ulm and Augsburg in the Fifteenth Century'. *Bibliographica,* 1 (1895), 437-55.

Munrow, D. *Instruments of the Middle Ages and Renaissance.* London, 1976.

Musper, H. Th., ed. *Der Antichrist und die fünfzehn Zeichen. Faksimile-Ausgabe des einzegen erhaltenen chiroxylographischen Blockbuches.* Munich, 1970.

———. *Der Holzschnitt in fünf Jahrhunderten.* Stuttgart, 1964.

———. *Die Urausgaben der holländischen Apokalypse und Biblia Pauperum.* Munich, 1961.

Muther, R. *German Book Illustration of the Gothic Period and Early Renaissance 1460-1530.* Trans. R. R. Shaw from the 1884 edn. Metuchen, New Jersey, 1972.

Naumann, Hans. *Die Holzschnitte des Meisters vom Amsterdamer Kabinett zum* Spiegel Menschlicher Behaltnis *(gedruckt zu Speier bei Peter Drach) mit einer Einleitung über ihre Vorgeschichte.* Studien zur deutschen Kunstgeschichte, 126. Strassburg, 1910.

Neumüller, W., ed. *Speculum Humanae Salvationis. Vollständige Faksimile- Ausgabe des Codex Cremifanensis 243 des Benediktinerstifts Kremsmünster.* Codices Selecti, 32. 2 vols. Graz, 1972.

New Catholic Encyclopedia. New York, 1967.

Niermeyer, J. *Mediae Latinitatis Lexicon Minus.* Leiden, 1976.

Opie, I. and P., eds. *The Oxford Dictionary of Nursery Rhymes.* Oxford, 1952.

The Orcherd of Syon. Ed. P. Hodgson and G. M. Liegey. Vol. I (text). EETS OS 258. London, 1966.

Owst, G. R. *Literature and Pulpit in Medieval England: a Neglected Chapter in the History of English Letters and of the English People.* Cambridge, 1933; repr. Oxford, 1966.

The Oxford Book of Medieval Latin Verse. Ed. F. J. E. Raby. Oxford, 1959.

The Oxford Dictionary of the Christian Church. Ed. F. L. Cross and E. A. Livingstone. 2nd edn. London, 1974.

Oxford English Dictionary Being a Corrected Re-issue with an Introduction, Supplement, and Bibliography of a New English Dictionary on Historical Principles Founded Mainly on the Materials Collected by the Philological Society. 13 vols. Oxford, 1933. See also *A Supplement.*

Parker, Elizabeth. 'The Descent from the Cross: its Relation to the Extra-Liturgical *Depositio* Drama'. Diss. New York 1975.

Passavant, J. D. *Le Peintre-Graveur: contenant l'histoire de la gravure sur bois, sur métal et au burin jusque vers la fin du xvie siècle. L'histoire du nielle avec complément de la partie descriptive de l'essai sur les nielles de Duchesne aîné. Et un catalogue supplémentaire aux estampes du XV. et XVI. siècle du Peintre-Graveur de Adam Bartsche.* 6 vols. Leipzig, 1860.

Perdrizet, P. *Etude sur le Speculum Humanae Salvationis.* Paris, 1908.

———. *La Vierge de Miséricorde: étude d'un thème iconographique.* Bibliothèque des écoles francaises d'Athènes et de Rome, 101. Paris, 1908.

Petrus Comestor. *Historia Scholastica. PL* CIXVIII 1053-1722.

Pfister, A. *Das deutsche Speculum Humanae Salvationis (Spiegel Menschlicher Behältnis) und der frühe Basler Inkunabelholzschnitt.* Diss. Basel 1937. Basel, 1937.

Plutarch's Lives. Trans. A. Stewart and G. Long. 4 vols. London, 1894.

Polain, M.-L. *Catalogue des livres imprimés au quinzième siècle des bibliothèques de Belgique.* 4 vols. Bruxelles, 1932.

Pollard, A. W. ed. *Checklist of Fifteenth-Century Printing in the Pierpont Morgan Library.* Compiled A. Thurston and C. P. Bühler. New York, 1939.

Poppe, P. *Über das Speculum Humanae Salvationis und eine mitteldeutsche Bearbeitung desselben.* Diss. Strassburg, 1887. Berlin, 1887.

Post, R. R. *The Modern Devotion: Confrontation with Reformation and Humanism.* Leiden, 1968.

Raby, F. J. B. *A History of Christian-Latin Poetry from the Beginnings to the Close of the Middle Ages.* 2nd edn. Oxford, 1953.

Reallexikon zur deutschen Kunst-geschichte. Ed. O. Schmidt, K-A. Wirth, et al. Vols I-VI-. Stuttgart, 1937-1973-.

Réau, L. *Iconographie de l'art chrétien.* 3 vols. Paris, 1955-1958; repr. Nendeln/Liechtenstein, 1974.

Robb, D. M. 'The Iconography of the Annunciation in the Fourteenth and Fifteenth Centuries'. *Art Bulletin,* 18iv (1936), 480-526.

Röhrig, F. *Der Verduner Altar.* Munich & Vienna, 1955.

Roques, M. 'Le Monetier (Hautes-Alpes) Chapelle Saint-Martin.' In *Les Peintures Murales du sud-est de la France XIIIe au XVIe siècle.* Paris, 1961, pp. 211-15, see also 31-32, Pl. XXXII. [Paintings showing influence of *SHS*]

Rorimer, J. J., and M. B. Freeman. 'The Glorification of Charles VIII'. *Bulletin of the Metropolitan Museum of Art,* 12x (1954), 281-301.

Rumpel, H. *Wood Engraving.* Trans. F. Jellinek. Geneva, 1972; London, 1974.

Sausseret, P. *Apparitions et révélations de la très Sainte Vierge depuis l'origine du christianisme jusqu'à nos jours.* Vol. I. Paris, 1854.

Schiller, Gertrud. *Iconography of Christian Art.* Vols. I and II. Trans. J. Seligman from the 2nd edn. London, 1971-1972.

———. *Ikonographie der christlichen Kunst.* Vols. III, IVi, IVii. Gütersloher, 1971-1980.

Schlosser, J. von. *Quellenbuch zur Kunstgeschichte des abendländischen Mittelalters.* Vienna, 1896; repr. Hildesheim, 1976, pp. 317-22. [Tituli of lost St Alban's glass; see also Dugdale]

Schmid, H. H. *Augsburger Einzelformschnitt und Buchillustration im 15. Jahrhunderts.* Studien zur deutschen Kunstgeschichte, 315. Baden-Baden, 1958.

Schmidt, G. *Die Armenbibeln des XIV. Jahrhunderts.* Veröffentlichungen des Instituts für Österreichische Geschichtsforschung, 19. Graz-Cologne, 1959.

——. 'Speculum Humanae Salvationis. Vollständige Faksimile-Ausgabe des Codex Cremifanensis des Benediktinerstifts Kremsmünster.' Review of W. Neumuller, *Speculum Humanae Salvationis. Kunstchronik*, 27 (1974), 152-66.

Schmidt-Wartenberg, H. 'Zum Speculum Humanae Salvationis.' *PMLA*, 14 (1899), 137-68.

Schramm, A. *Der Bilderschmuck der Frühdrucke, fortgeführt von der Kommission für den Gesamtkatalog der Wiegendrucke.* 23 vols. Leipzig, 1920-1943; repr. Stuttgart, 1981-1984.

Schreiber, W. L. *Manuel de l'amateur de la gravure sur bois et sur métal au XVe siècle.* 8 vols. 2nd edn. Leipzig, 1926-1930.

——. *Basels Bedeutung für die Geschichte der Blockbücher.* Strassburg, 1909.

Sentis, G. 'Les Peintures murales de la chapelle Saint-Martin au Monêtier- les-Bains (Hautes-Alpes)'. *Congrès Archéologique de la France*, 130 (1972), 222-27.

Shorr, D. 'The Iconographic Development of the Presentation at the Temple'. *Art Bulletin*, 28 (1946), 17-32.

Silber, E. A. 'The Reconstructed Toledo *Speculum Humanae Salvationis*: the Italian Connection in the Early Fourteenth Century'. *JWCI*, 43 (1980), 32-51, Pls. 2d-10b.

——. 'The Early Iconography of the *Speculum Humanae Salvationis*: the Italian Connection in the Fourteenth Century'. 2 parts. Diss. Cambridge 1982.

Smalley, B. *The Study of the Bible in the Middle Ages.* Oxford, 1941.

The South English Legendary Edited from Corpus Christi College Cambridge MS.145 and British Museum MS.Harley 277 with Variants from Bodley MS.Ashmole 43 and British Museum MS.Cotton Julius D.IX. Ed. C. D'Evelyn and A. J. Mill. 2 vols. EETS OS 235, 236. London, 1956.

The South English Nativity of Mary and Christ Ed. from MS BM Stowe 949. Ed. O. S. Pickering. MET, 1. Heidelberg, 1975.

Speculum Humanae Salvationis. n.p., c.1468. [1st Latin blockbook edn.]

(*Speculum Humanae Salvationis*) *Dat speghel onser behoudenisse.* n.p., c.1471. [1st Dutch blockbook edn.]

Speculum Humanae Salvationis. n.p., c.1474. [2nd Latin blockbook edn.]

(*Speculum Humanae Salvationis*) *Dat speghel onser behoudenisse.* n.p., c.1479. [2nd Dutch blockbook edn.]

Speculum Humanae Salvationis cum Speculo S. Maria Virginis. Augsburg: Gunther Zainer, c.1473.

(*Speculum Humanae Salvationis*) *Der Spiegel der menschen Behältnis mit den Evangelien und mit Episteln nach der Zyt des Jars.* Speier: Drach, c. 1476.

(*Speculum Humanae Salvationis*) *Spiegel menschlicher Behältnis.* Basel: Bernard Richel, 1476.

Stevenson, A. H. Introduction to Briquet (1968), q.v.

Stockmeyer, I., and B. Reber. *Beiträge zur Basler Buchdruckergeschichte.* Basel, 1840.

Storck, W. F., and H. Th. Bossert, eds. *Das mittlalterliche Hausbuch. Nach dem Originale im Besitze des Fürsten von Waldburg-Wolfegg-Waldsee.* Deutscher Verein für Kunstwissenschaft. Leipzig, 1912.

Suckale, R. 'Arma Christi: Überlegungen zur Zeichenhaftigkeit mittelalterlicher Andachtsbilder'. *Städel-Jahrbuch*, N.F. 6 (1977), 177-98.

A Supplement to the Oxford English Dictionary. Ed. R. W. Burchfield. 3 vols. [A-Scz], Oxford, 1972-1982.

Taylor, T. *Christ Revealed, or the Old Testament Explained: a Treatise of the Types and Shadowes of Our Saviovr Contained Throughout the Whole Scriptvre: All Opened and Made Usefull for the Benefit of Gods Church.* London, 1635.

Thomas, A. *Die Darstellung Christi in der Kelter: eine theologische und kulturhisorische Studie.* Dusseldorf, 1936.

———. 'Schutzmantelmaria'. In *Die Gottesmutter: Marienbild in Rheinland und Westfalen.* Ed. L. Küppers. 2 vols. Recklinghausen, 1974, pp. 227-42.

Thomas, H. M. 'Zur kulturgeschichtlichen Einordnung der Armenbibel mit *Speculum Humanae Salvationis* unter Berücksichtigung des *Liber Figurarum* in der Joachim de Fiore-Handschrift der Sächsichen Landesbibliothek Dresden (Mscr. Dresden A 121)'. *Archiv für Kulturgeschichte*, 52 (1970), 192-225.

———. 'Lo *Speculum Humanae Salvationis* e l'idea occidentale della Redenzione.' *Nuova Rivista Storica*, 58 (1974), 379-94.

———. 'Heilsspiegel und Gottesschau; Zur chronologisten Einordnung der Speculum Humanae Salvationis nach der historischen Kontroverse über der Visio Beatifica'. *Freiburger Zeitschrift fur Philosophie und Theologie*, 22 (1975), 204-33.

Tischendorff, C. von. *Evangelia Apocrypha: Adhibitis Plurimus Codicibus Graecis et Latinis Maximam Partem Nunce Primum Consultis atque Ineditorum Copia Insignibus.* Leipsig, 1876.

Trevisa, J., trans. *On the Properties of Things. John Trevisa's Translation of Bartholomaeus Anglicus De Proprietatibus Rerum: a Critical Text.* Gen. ed. M. C. Seymour. 2 vols. Oxford, 1975.

Tubach, F. C. *Index Exemplorum: a Handbook of Medieval Religious Tales.* FF Communications, 204. Helsinki, 1969.

Tuve, R. *A Reading of George Herbert.* London, 1952.

Ulbert-Schede, U. *Das Andachtsbild des kreuztragenden Christus in der deutschen Kunst von den Anfängen bis zum Beginn des 16. Jahrhunderts: eine ikonographische Untersuchung.* Munich, 1968.

Valerius Maximus. *Valerii Maximi Factorvm et Dictorvm Memorabilivm Libri Novem.* Ed. C. Halm. Teubner Classics. Leipzig, 1865.

Verougstraete-Marcq, H., and R. Van Schoute. 'Le Speculum Humanae Salvationis considéré dans ses rapports avec la Biblia Pauperum et Le Canticum Canticorum'. *De Gulden Passer*, 53 (1975), 363-79.

Vincent of Beauvais. *Bibliotheca Mundi sev Speculi Maioris.* 4 vols. Douai, 1524.

Von der Osten, G. 'Job and Christ.' *JWCI*, 16 (1953), 153-58.

Voragine, Jacobus de. *Legenda Aurea.* Ed. J. G. T. Graesse. Dresden, 1846.

———. *The Golden Legend or Lives of the Saints.* Trans. William Caxton. 7 vols. The Temple Classics. London, 1900; repr. New York, 1973.

Voullième, E. *Die deutschen Drucker des fünfzehnten Jahrhunderts.* 2nd edn. Berlin, 1922.

Vriend, J. *The Blessed England, with Additional Studies in Middle English Literature.* Diss. Amsterdam 1928. Purmerend, 1928.

Watson, A. *The Early Iconography of the Tree of Jesse.* London, 1934.

Wayment, H. G. *King's College Chapel.* Corpus Vitrearum Medii Aevi. Cambridge, 1972.

Weckwerth, A. 'Christus in der Kelter. Ursprung und Wandlungen eines Bildmotives'. In *Beiträge zur Kunstgeschichte, Festgabe Rosemann.* Munich, 1960, pp. 95-108.

Weisbach, W. *Die Baseler Buchillustration des XV. Jahrhunderts.* Studien zur deutschen Kunstgeschichte, 8. Strassburg, 1896.

White, T. H., trans. *The Book of Beasts: Being a Translation from a Latin Bestiary of the Twelfth Century.* London, 1954.

Whiting, B. J., and H. W. Whiting. *Proverbs, Sentences and Proverbial Phrases from English Writings Mainly Before 1500.* London and Cambridge, Mass., 1968.

Williams, A. 'Typology and the Cycle Plays: Some Criteria'. *Speculum*, 43 (1968), 677-84.

Wilmart, A. *Auteurs spirituels et textes dévots du moyen âge latin.* Paris, 1982.

Wilson, A., and J. L. Wilson. *A Medieval Mirror: Speculum Humanae Salvationis, 1324-1500.* Berkeley, 1985.

Winterfeld, L. von. 'Das Cleppingsche Speculum Humanae Salvationis in der Landesbibliothek zu Darmstadt (Hs. 2505)'. *Beiträge zur Geschichte Dortmunds und der Graffschaft Mark*, 26 (1919), 96-118.

Woolf, R. 'The Effect of Typology on the English Medieval Plays of Abraham and Isaac'. *Speculum*, 32iv (1957), 805-25.

———. 'The Theme of Christ the Lover-Knight in Medieval English Literature'. *RES*, N.S. 13 (1962), 1-16.

Worringer, W. *Die aldeutsche Buchillustration.* Munich, 1921.

The York Plays. York Medieval Texts, 2nd Ser. Ed. R. Beadle. London, 1982.

Zoege von Manteuffel, C. *Der deutsche Holzschnitte: sein Aufstieg im XV. Jahrhundert und seine grosse Blüte in der ersten Hälfte des XVI. Jahrhunderts.* Kunstgeschichte in Einzeldarstellungen, 1. Munich, 1921.

Zonghi, Aurelio, and Augusto Zonghi. *Zonghi's Watermarks.* Monumenta Chartae Papyraceae Historiam Illustrantia or Collection of Works and Documents Illustrating the History of Paper, 3. Gen. ed. E. J. Labarre. Hilversum, 1953.

INDEX OF PROPER NAMES

In the index of proper nouns which follows, identifications are given only where they are essential to the prevention of ambiguity within the index. The explanatory notes (pp.229-60) and the captions to the illustrations provide full identifications or give references which enable the reader to do so. Names of persons and places are given, but races and nations (eg. *Galilens*, *Jewes*) are not. Unlike the glossary, this index includes material from the modern English sections of the text. Only plurals and genitives are identified.

GLOSSARY

The glossary is highly selective, citing only words which may be unfamiliar, or are made to seem so by their spelling, or are seriously ambiguous. However, all line references for given meanings are listed. Thus examples of *spouse* meaning 'marriage partner' are omitted, but all those meaning 'marriage' are listed, and examples of *fest* meaning 'feast' are omitted while all those meaning 'landed, fixed' are listed. The result is that one or two entries intended to act as aids against ambiguity (such as *be*) are unconscionably long.

Words are in alphabetical order regardless of the function of their initial letters: so *vitaille* (in which *v* is consonantal) is followed by *vnbrosten* (in which *v* is vocalic). The scribe never begins a word with *u*. Thorn follows *t*, yogh follows *y*.

Sometimes the nearest Latin equivalent of the Middle English is given in square brackets after the meaning; the Latin is from Lutz and Perdrizet's edition.

Italicisation and warning of emendation which appear in the main text are ignored in the glossary.

Round brackets contain alternative elements in spellings: e.g. 'man(ne)' means that the word is 'man' or 'manne'. Italicised round brackets contain editorial comments.

Question marks precede the doubtful material: for example '**and** *adv. ?* also' shows that the meaning, not the grammatical definition, is in doubt. Line references with 'n.' suffixed refer the reader to an explanatory note. Reference has been made to *MED* up to *propugnacle*.

a *v. (for* **have***)* have 2076.

above *adv.* in ~ *kynde* supernaturally 4965.

absinthe *n.* bitterness *(from wormwood, the bitter artemisia absinthium)* 3592, 4452 *(MED cites only this example)*; **absinthy** 1842.

absurditee *n.* cacophany, lack of tunefulness 4449.

accepcioune *n.* approval, acceptance as valid 1615.

accide *n.* sloth 645; **acide** 3090.

accompted *pa.t.sg.* counted, regarded 3816.

acconpt *? n.* in *als to* ~ as far as (its) importance is concerned 4444n.

accordantly *adv.* suitably, fitly 3842.

accordis *intr.pr.3 sg.* in ~..*vnto* tally with 1358. **according** *pr.p.* agreeing 3428. **accordid** *tr.pa.t.sg.* reconciled 3982.

accusat *pp.* accused *[accusatus]* 3253.

acetable *n.* vinegar-vessel 3263 *(unrecorded in this sense)*.

acide see **accide**.

adiutorie *n.* aid *[adjutorium]* 3339 *(not in MED, OED's earliest example is of A.D.1504)*.

adiutrice *n.* (female) advocate *[adjutrix neque advocata]* 4246.

admirable *adj.* wonderful, awe-inspiring 3876.

admirably *adv.* in a marvellous manner 3506.

admyre *v.* wonder at 2219.

affluaunt *adj.* over-flowing *[affluens]* 3861.

affluence *n.* abundance 4421.

after *prep.* according to 1839, 1889, 4220; in accordance with 2387.

agayne *prep.* to meet 1683; **agein** in ~ *kynde* supernaturally, against the natural order 4963.

ageyns *prep.* in 1826; **ageins** over 1873.

aght *n.* property 1190.

aght see **eght**.

agilitee *n.* the ability, possessed by the unfallen or resurrected body, of traveling to any place without delay and without the need of a supporting medium 4334, 4341.

alder(e)-, **alther(e)-** *pron.gen.pl. as prefix, literally* of all *intensifying the adj. to which it is prefixed, as in the next four entries.*

alder-formast *sup.* first of all 1550.

alder-metest *sup.* most suitable 3490.

alder-most *sup.* most valuable of all 838; largest of all 1380; greatest of all 1810; **alder-moste** greatest of all 1393.

alder-piest *sup.* most merciful 4251.

alle *adj.absol.* in *at* ~ in every way 493, 2585, 3965; ~ *and som(m)e* one and all 1316, 1604; whole *[toto]* 4092, 4510.

alle *adv.* although 526; in ~ *one* alone 970, 2355; quite alone 4135; ~ *onely* only 2557, 3373, 4569; alone 4487; ~ *ware he* although he was 2671; ~ *be thay neuer so felle* however terrible they are 3040; ~ *so* altogether 4488.

allere *pron.gen.pl.* in *thaire allere* of them all 3166.

almandine *adj.* of almond wood 1071 *(neither OED nor MED records this example of a rare word).*

almouse *n.* alms 442, 2794; **almovse** 2778; **almus** 2042.

almuse-dede *n.* deed of charity 4267.

almuse-delyng *n.* giving of alms 3036.

almyght *n.* omnipotence 3452 *(OED does not record the word, nor MED this example).*

als *rel.pron.* (by) which 3747.

als *adv.* in ~ *when* when 29; ~ *be* in connection with, derived from 334; ~ *in sawle* as far as (his) soul was concerned 526; ~ *tite* at once 2681, 3007; ~ *in regarde of* in comparison with 3592; ~ *for fleghyng* for flying 3891; ~ *in dede* in the act 3921; ~ *outwards* as regards 3925; ~ *to accompt ?* as far as its importance is concerned 4444n; in *vnlike* ~ *to* see **vnlike**.

als *conj.* for instance 4942; in ~ *so* as if 4264.

alther(e)- see **alder(e)-**.

amayde *pp.* dismayed 3491.

ambidextere *adj.* capable of using both hands at once *[ambidexter]* 3171.

amend *v.* make amends 2830; **amende** improve 3558.

amendes *n.* retribution 2124.

amese *v.* reduce 2083. **amesid** *pa.t.sg.* pacified 253. **amesdid** *pp.* 3972.

amiable *adj.* worthy of love 4595.

amyssioune *n.* loss 2854.

an *conj.* and 5, 751.

ancilles *n.pl.* maid-servants 3669.

and *adv. ?* also 2931n.

angulere *adj.* in *stone...* ~ corner-stone 3485n. as *n.* corner-stone 3490, 3494, 3496, 3499.

anone *adv.* at once 1465, 1573, 1608, 2818, 3116, 3180, 3244, 3308, 3314, 3424, 3445, 3467, 3507, 3758, 4192, 4616, 4935, 4955, 5094.

anournyng *pr.p.* worshipping 5031. **anourned** *pa.t.sg.* worshipped 349; honoured 1180.

apercioune *n.* opening 1613, 4705.

apert *adj.* plain 521; in *in* ~ openly 2136; **aperte** manifest *[apertus]* 463.

apertly *adv.* clearly 169; **apertely** 357.

apocrisyng *vbl.n. ?* practising of hypocrisy 4270n.

appensioune *n.* weighing 277 *(MED cites only this example)*.

appliables *adj.* appropriate 24.

appropred *pp.* appropriate 3001.

approve *v.* endorse 827. **approved** *pa.t.sg.* accepted 4121. *pp.* confirmed 821, 831.

arace *v.* pull out 1798.

aray *n.* fashion 913; **arraye** manner 1771, clothing 3925; **arraie** garments 2680.

are *adv.* before 568, 940, 1419, 1424, 1463, 1472, 1767, 1845, 2590, 3582, 3596, 4360.

arely *adv.* early 2208, 3446.

argentyne *adj.* made of silver 1372.

armes *n.pl.* weapons, armour (coat of arms) *[armis, arma]* 3219, 4229, 4231.

aromatyze *n.pl.* aromatic spices *[aromatum et deliciarum]* 4985.

arraie, **arraye** see **aray**.

asay *v.* try 13; **assay** assess 4932.

aselle see **ayselle**.

aspyed *pp.* seen 274; **asspied** perceived, recognised 2689.

assay *n.* (the) test 3480n.

assay see **asay**.

assoigne *v.* offer an excuse 426, excuse 2417.

asspied see **aspyed**.

astoned *ppl.a.* astonished 2963.

at in ~ *a brayde*, ~ *alle*, ~ *devis*, ~ *disese*, ~ *drynke*, ~ *(his/oure) myght*, ~ *the fulle*, ~ *the large*, ~ *thi parte*: see **brayde**, **alle**, etc.

attigne *v.* in ~ *perto* achieve that 1898.

auantis *v.refl.* boasts 2756. **auauntid** *pa.t.sg.* 1579.

auarous *adj.* motivated by greed 1593; **auerous** 3916.

auntre *n.* in *in* ~ in case, lest 947.

auokette *n.* advocate 4112.

auoutrere see **avotrer**.

aurea in *vrna* ~ see **vrna**.

auricalke *n.* latten (alloy of copper and tin with other ingredients) 837.

autiere *n.* altar 1056, 2486, 2967. **autiers** *pl.* 3146.

aventour *v.refl.* risk 485.

avise *v.refl.* consider 2822.

avisee *adj.* prudent 641; **avysee** 324.

avision *n.* vision 250; **avisioune** 3941.

avotrer *n.* adulterer 96; **auoutrere** 1688.

avoutresse *n.* adulteress 810, 1697.

avysee see **avisee**.

awayte *n.* ambush 463; **awayt** 4095.

awayte *v.* lie in wait for 3279; ambush 4425.

awe *pr.3 sg.* owns 1234. **awe** *impers.pr.3 sg.* in ~ *noght* it is not right 451; *thaym* ~ they should 1834; *Hym* ~ he should 4510.

ayselle *n.* vinegary drink 2512, 2640, 3734, 4696; **aselle** 3263; **aysell** 2799; **aysile** 4452.

aywhare *adv.* everywhere 3440; **aywhere** 3911.

aȝayne *adv.* towards 1739.

aȝeinward *adv.* in return 2344, 2346; **aȝeinwarde** 2370.

baiske *adj.* bitter 669.

baiulacioune *n.* carrying of the Cross 2449 *(MED cites only this example)*.

bakhalve *n.* back 2763.

baldere *comp.* bolder 366.

bande *pa.t.sg.* bound 530, 5087. *pl.* 4566, 4639.

bandes *n.pl.* bonds 2414, 2632, 4579; **bandis** 2518, 4148.

banyoure *n.* leader 2061.

bare *pa.t.sg.* in ~ *thorgh* pierced 2696; ~...*in* thrust 3179. *pl.* in ~..*thorgh* pierced 2736. **borne** *pp.* in ~ *thurgh* 176.

barme *n.* bosom, arms 4988.

base *adj.* low 1926; **bas** 4881.

bavme *n.* balm, healing ointment 4981, 4982.

be *prep.* about 11; by 26, 26, 30, 39, 40, 47, 52, 53, 54, 55, 60, 61, 66, 68, 73, 78, 79, 79, 82, 83, 84, 125, 133, 142, 145, 159, 167, 204, 205, 209, 210, 215, 216, 216, 219, 228, 229, 230, 242, 243, 247, 248, 270, 277, 278, 288, 295, 311, 319, 322, 338, 356, 367, 380, 394, 419, 423, 429, 434, 457, 458, 467, 486, 490, 495, 496, 497, 501, 521, 532, 542, 543, 544, 580, 583, 585, 587, 592, 593, 594, 596, 598, 613, 616, 622, 646, 666, 690, 723, 731, 736, 760, 763, 791, 819, 851, 855, 864, 868, 872, 881, 890, 894, 939, 973, 978, 980, 991, 1029, 1032, 1067, 1068, 1072, 1115, 1129, 1136, 1194, 1232, 1234, 1257, 1257, 1272, 1284, 1288, 1300, 1301, 1307, 1342, 1353, 1370, 1418, 1423, 1418, 1427, 1434, 1452, 1459, 1461, 1462, 1473, 1490, 1503, 1507, 1512, 1535, 1543, 1548, 1550, 1554, 1564, 1565, 1566, 1572, 1579, 1590, 1610, 1610, 1613, 1616, 1625, 1626, 1628, 1655, 1676, 1677, 1679, 1680, 1682, 1687, 1708, 1715, 1734, 1734, 1736, 1742, 1744, 1775, 1783, 1865, 1866, 1879, 1899, 1900, 1941, 2042, 2099, 2129, 2135, 2156, 2162, 2170, 2190, 2202, 2229, 2230, 2232, 2243, 2253, 2254, 2256, 2264, 2274, 2347, 2369, 2429, 2430, 2432, 2433, 2434, 2436, 2444, 2447, 2452, 2455, 2472,

2485, 2486, 2497, 2501, 2502, 2514, 2521, 2530, 2551, 2555, 2587, 2588, 2589, 2631, 2661, 2672, 2693, 2703, 2732, 2784, 2808, 2871, 2877, 2879, 2880, 2881, 2883, 2884, 2907, 2939, 2946, 2996, 2997, 3030, 3035, 3036, 3036, 3036, 3037, 3037, 3037, 3038, 3044, 3048, 3056, 3077, 3082, 3087, 3088, 3095, 3116, 3126, 3127, 3130, 3131, 3132, 3136, 3137, 3138, 3141, 3142, 3143, 3144, 3150, 3153, 3155, 3189, 3190, 3193, 3194, 3194, 3205, 3206, 3208, 3210, 3214, 3216, 3217, 3218, 3221, 3234, 3240, 3250, 3251, 3252, 3271, 3280, 3303, 3324, 3329, 3331, 3336, 3345, 3345, 3393, 3399, 3402, 3413, 3415, 3442, 3452, 3461, 3469, 3475, 3484, 3487, 3492, 3500, 3510, 3512, 3525, 3530, 3539, 3542, 3580, 3596, 3645, 3646, 3660, 3668, 3682, 3686, 3693, 3694, 3695, 3729, 3732, 3744, 3756, 3761, 3784, 3786, 3826, 3842, 3908, 3920, 3939, 3942, 3951, 3952, 3954, 3955, 3957, 3972, 3975, 3985, 3985, 3988, 3995, 4001, 4023, 4025, 4028, 4034, 4039, 4041, 4045, 4047, 4047, 4051, 4051, 4078, 4083, 4083, 4085, 4085, 4087, 4093, 4123, 4125, 4164, 4187, 4197, 4198, 4255, 4267, 4277, 4283, 4284, 4289, 4322, 4325, 4345, 4374, 4384, 4389, 4399, 4412, 4466, 4497, 4498, 4537, 4577, 4578, 4587, 4592, 4598, 4629, 4676, 4680, 4681, 4682, 4708, 4733, 4747, 4863, 4889, 4915, 4957, 4958, 4964, 4967, 4973, 4993, 5006, 5019, 5028, 5045, 5071, 5083, 5097, 5109, 5123; from 202, 2626; as a result of 214, 334, 809; out of 468; by means of 604, 732; in accordance with 697, 4283, 4285, 4885; according to 3009; concerning 3029; in ~ *tresoune* treacherously 113; ~ *enuye* jealously 116; ~ *synne* sinfully 896; ~ *the ayre* through the air 1517; ~ *the mydward* down the middle 1632; ~ *dreme* in a dream 2424; ~ *discrecioune* wisely 3568; ~ *noumbre* total 3959; ~ *the morowe* the next day 4614; ~ *entaylle* see **entayle**; ~ *resoune* see **resoune**; ~ *right* see **right**; ~ *tale* see **tale**; **by** of 1788.

be see **bee**.

bedde see **bide**.

bede *n.* offering 2560.

bede see **bide**.

bedene *adv.* in *alle* ~ completely 695.

bedyng see **bide**.

bee *v.* in *told to* ~ foretold 1311. **bes** *pr.3 sg.* is 274, 2322, 4316, 4330, 4426, 4427, 4428, 4429, 4431, 4433, 4436. **nys** *neg.* (ne + ys) is not 424, 844, 1441, 2945, 3023, 3460, 4223, 4745; **nes** (ne + is) 4371. **ere** *pr.pl.* are 159, 439, 617, 619, 655, 819, 889, 1255, 1265, 1277, 1284, 1462, 1587, 1664, 2087, 2094, 2448, 2528, 2720, 2771, 2788, 2795, 3009, 3018, 3035, 3087, 3089, 3091, 3122, 3133, 3136, 3355, 3440, 3559, 3560, 3562, 3615, 3621, 3623, 3644, 3964, 3970, 4009, 4038, 4070, 4076, 4085, 4087, 4332, 4346, 4356, 4370, 4406, 4407, 4409, 4410, 4941; **erre** 615, 619, 1011, 1824, 3922, 3965; **ern** 1047. **ware** *subj.pr.3 sg.* might be (*or pa.t.sg.* was) 478. **warre** *pa.t.sg.* was *(or subj.pr.3 sg.* might be*)* 576; was 2738; **ware** *(or pl.* were *in error by attraction of* bordes*)* 1561; *(or pl.* were *in error by attraction of* thaire*)* 4590; **were** *(or pl. in error by attraction of* taknys*)* 2441; **ware** was 2663, 2851; might be 3051, 3596; would be 3312, 3320, 3602, 3969, 4441, 4442, 4443, 4449, 4481, 4483, 4483, 4887; in *alle* ~ although he was 2671; ~ *noght* might not be 3426; *ne* ~ *his wreth* if his anger were not 3972; **were** to be 807, would be 1318, in *alle* ~ *it* although 346; **war** in ~ *ne* had it not been (for the fact that) 1529; **werre** in *alle* although she was 895; **where** were 4185n. **be** *pp.* been 809.

beestisshe *adj.* bestial 2642.

befelle *pa.t.sg.* happened 2960, became 2989.

begile *v.* deceive 2774. **begilt** *pa.t.sg.* 322. *pp.* 2211.

beheste *n.* in *lande of* ~ promised land 1474, 3980.

beiaped *pp.* mocked 3726, 4613; **beiapid** 3724; **bejaped** 2176.

benedice *pr.pl.* bless 1753 *(MED cites only this example)*.

bere *v.* wear 449; in ~ *hym stout* behave haughtily/aggressively 628. **beres** *pr.3 sg.* in ~ *hym on hande...for to spitte* asserts that he spits 2761; **bers** in ~ *takenyng* signifies 3184. **beres** *pl.* in ~ *takenyng* signify 1870. **beryng** *pr.p.* showing 4940. **bering** *vbl.n.* birth 705; **beryng** carrying (of) 140.

bes see **bee**.

besauntes see **bezaunt**.

beseen *pp.* treated 2407.

beseke *v.* beseech 4968, 4994, 5020, 5046, 5072, 5098, 5124. *pr.1 sg.* 4653, 4681.

besemes *impers.* in *wham...~ no* it is not fitting for him whom 450.

besily, **besilye** see **bisyly**.

bestaille *n.* livestock 1476.

beswngen *pp.* flogged 2258.

betake *imp.* surrender 2286. **betakeing** *pr.p.* 2724; **betaking** giving 4343. **betaken** *pp.* granted 1060; entrusted 2780. **betakene** *refl.pp.* put 2360.

betaknes *pr.3 sg.* signifies 3997; **betaknys** 4069. **betaknyd** *pa.t.sg.* signified 2609, 3879. **betakened** *pl.* 1595, 1731. **betaknyd** *pp.* 4025. **betaknyng** *vbl.n.* a sign *[designari]* 3492; in *has...~* is signified 3469.

bezaunt *n.* coin 4217. **besauntes** *pl.* 4294; **bezauntes** 4211.

bide *v.* offer 2128. **bedyng** *pr.p.* offering 5014; **biding** commanding *[ad jussum]* 1457. **bede** *pa.t.sg.* ordered 163, 2307; **bedde** offered 4242. *ppl.a.* 3734.

bides *pr.pl.* wait 3318. **biding** *pr.p.* waiting 3309; waiting for 3447. **bode** *pa.t.sg.* engaged 4569.

biding see **bides**.

biggers *n.pl.* builders 3479, 3496, 3681.

bigging *pr.p.* building 3477.

biriales *n.* funeral 2969. **birialles** *pl.* 2941n.

birre *n.* encounter 110.

birthyn *n.* packet 2863, 3235; **birthin** 2865; **byrthyne** 3234.

bisily see **bisyly**.

bisis *refl.pr.pl.* hasten 2769.

bisy *adj.* diligent, careful 502; devout 852; active 2786; eager 4512; intent 4721; **bysy** anxious 4514.

bisy *pa.t.sg.* looked around to see 780.

bisyly *adv.* carefully 1243, 3392, 3425, 3674; constantly, readily 4098, 4240, 4432; **bisily** carefully 1214; earnestly, quickly 3797; **bysyly** carefully 3175, 3233; devoutly 4940; **bysily** carefully 3758; constantly 3769; **besily** carefully 454; **besilye** 764; **bisylye** constantly, devoutly 767; **bysylye** scrupulously, constantly 2240.

bisynesse *n.* in *with* ~ whole-heartedly 3538; *didde alle hire* ~ did her utmost 4018; **bysynesse** industry, effort 3480.

bla *adj.* bruised 4874.

blame *v.* in *to* ~ blameworthy 456. **blames** *pr.pl.* censure 3927. **blamyng** *pr.p.* censuring

2168, 2260. **blamed** *pa.t. 3 sg.* censured 120, 3572. *pl.* 1629. **blamyng** *vbl.n.* disparagement *[cruciat]* 1649.

bocchis *n.pl.* boils, sores 129.

bode *n.* annunciation, news *[annunciatio]* 563; announcement *[nunciationi]* 1000.

bode see **bides**.

bolnyng *ppl.a.* swelling 623. *vbl.n.* swelling, arrogance 621, 4039.

borde *n.* table, altar 45, 709, 717, 1337. **bordes** *pl.* tables 1561n, 1759.

borne see **bare**.

bot *conj.* unless 844, 1556, 3620; only, just 1778, 1818, 1846, 1852, 4138; except (by) 3619; in ~ *if* but 2280; unless 2674, 3196; in ~ *so be þat* unless 3639.

bote *n.* in *to* ~ in addition 4222.

botellere *n.* cup-bearer 65; **botlere** 1029; **bottellere** 1128; **buttellere** 1130.

bourgeys *gen.pl.* burgess' 1660; **burgeys** 1667.

brace *n.* arm 2963.

bracying *pr.p.* holding 2924.

brast *pa.t.sg.* broke 79, 1387, 3102; destroyed 3375, 4642, 4702; **braste** broke 2347. **brystyn** *pp.* destroyed 3377.

brayde *n.* in *at a* ~ at once 4700.

brede *n.* breadth 3411, 3417.

brenne, **brennyng** see **brynne**.

brent see **brynne**.

bridde *n.* bird 381; fledgling 3096, 3097, 3100. **briddes** *pl.* young 204; birds 474, 2613; **briddis** 2625.

brode *n.* race, brood 1449.

brode *adj.* great, uninhibited 2712.

brode *adv.* in ~ *waking* wide awake 2180.

broght *pa.t.sg.* in ~ *him inne* persuaded, enticed 358.

bronstone *n.* burning brimstone (sulphur) 3938, 4378.

brynne *v.* burn 1874, 2953, 4062, 4369; **brenne** 3626, 4222. **brent** *pa.t.sg.* burned 3291, 3775, 3791. **brent** *pp.* burnt 380, 3362. **brennyng** *ppl.a.* burning 61, 960; ardent 3821. **brennyng** *vbl.n.* burning 376, 3365; in ~ *to the* ardour 2289; **brynnyng** strong desire 1153.

brystyn see **brast**.

burgeys see **bourgeys**.

buttellere see **botellere**.

by *adv.* besides 4084.

by see **be**.

bygone *pp.* covered, adorned 1259.

byrle *v.* pour out 1131.

byrthyne see **birthyn.**

bysily, bysyly see **bisyly.**

bysy see **bisy.**

bysynesse see **bisynesse.**

castis *pr.3 sg.* plans 464. **kast** *pa.t.sg.* plotted 2080; **kest** 1362. **kest** *pl.* gave 3065. **casten** *ppl.a.* 3463.

causeynge *vbl.n.* in *for peece* ~ to make peace 2391.

cayre *v.* go 1510.

celestre *adj.* celestial 1128 *(unrecorded).*

celsitude *n.* sublimity 1639.

centisme *n.* a hundredfold 836.

centurio *n.* the centurion 951. **centurys** *gen.* 3268.

certayne *n.* exact time *[tempus]* 3811.

chace *v.* drive. **chaces** *pr.pl.* drive out 653. **chacinge** *pr.p.* routing 2353. **chaced** *pa.t.sg.* drove 98; **chacid** 2075. **chaced** *pl.* routed 2357. *pp.* driven out 3136; **chasidde** 2448; **chacid** driven 1405.

chace see **chesing.**

chalenginges *vbl.n.pl.* rebukes 2165.

charge *n.* burden 301, 374.

chase see **chesing.**

chasidde see **chace.**

chasty *v.* chastise 3383. **chastie** *subj.pr.2 sg.* 4655. **chastying** *pr.p.* 4526.

chaufed *pa.t.sg.* upbraided 2714. **chaufid** *ppl.a.* excited, kindled 4188.

chaunce *n.* in *for all* ~ come what may 1790; *for no* ~ for any reason 3394.

chaunging *vbl.n.* in *haf...*~ alter 2641.

chaze see **chesing.**

chere *n.* expression, manner 3944; in *with gude* ~ joyfully 4945; **cherre** 4936.

chere *adj.* valuable 2896.

chesing *pr.p.* choosing 3917. **chase** *pa.t.sg.* chose 2040, 3162, 4194, 4195, 5115; **chese** 566, 970; **chace** 319; **chaze** 996.

childing *pr.p.* giving birth *[pariens]* 1078; **childyng** bearing 5002, 5005. **childed** *pa.t.sg.* gave birth 4904; gave birth to 4910. **childede** *pp.* 1326. **childid** *ppl.a.* giving birth 4906. **childyng** *vbl.n.* 3631.

chokes *pr.3 sg.* makes suffocate 4041.

chyricynge *pr.p.* taking care of 1679.

cicatrices *n.pl.* scars 4113, 4120, 4130, 4166, 4173.

cisere *n.* cider 3560.

cisterne *n.* well 197, 1116, 1125, 1127, 1129, pit 207, 379, 3118; **cistern** pit 3119. **cisternys** *gen.* well's 2972.

clame *pa.t.sg.* ascended 1520.

clamouse *adj.* loud 1745.

claritee *n.* the quality (possessed by the unfallen or resurrected soul) of being surrounded by the divine light 4333, 4337.

claustrale *adj.* cloistered 1588.

clausure *n.* cloister, enclosure of the Temple 911.

clerke *n.* scholar 3808. **clerkes** *pl.* 200, 549, 3044; **clerks** 808, 2537, 3064.

closeur *n.* enclosure 2484.

coaccioune *n.* coercion 2784.

coccyn *n.* a scarlet garment 4645; **coccyne** 3228, 4162; **cokcyn** 2324.

cogniciounc *n.* knowledge, understanding 662.

cohabitacioune *n.* in ~*of* living in the same quarters as 953; **cohabitacione** in ~*of* living as man and wife with 954.

colaphizid *pp.* flogged with rods *[colophisatus]* 118 *(MED cites only this example)*; **colaphized** 2369; **collaphizidde** 3724.

colee *n.* blow on the neck (with the flat of a sword, in dubbing a knight) 4139, 4141.

collibies *n.pl.* gifts given as part of a bargain, premiums 1784, 1785.

collibistes *n.pl.* money-changers 1760; **collibists** usurers 1781.

colloved *pa.t.sg.* co-praised 5066 *(unrecorded; cf.* **laved***)*.

colys *n.pl.* coals 1353.

come *n.* arrival 1118, 1624.

comfortably *adv.* cheerfully 4927, 4936.

commixtioune *n.* in *mans* ~ sexual intercourse with a man 1076, 1210.

commvne *v.* receive communion 1871, 1874. **communing** *pr.p.* when receiving communion 3280.

compaciant *ppl.a.* in ~ *on* affected by 1712; **compacient** in *of...* ~ jointly affected by 2184.

compas *n.* in *in* ~ all round 888.

compassioune *n.* shared suffering (co-passion) 214, 216, 2806, 3206, 3208, 3210, 3214, 3216, 3218, 3231, 3234, 4888.

compleignyng see **compleyn**.

compleint *n.* lamentation 2847, 2919, 2936, 3740; **compleynt** 2949.

completorie *n.* Compline (the last of the canonical hours) 4559 *(MED cites only this example)*.

compleyn *v.* lament 3778. **compleynyd** *pa.t.pl.* 2850. **compleignyng** *vbl.n.* lamentation 2912.

con *v.* in *to* ~ *neuere hoo* never mind who (it is) 4053. **kan** *pr.3 sg.* knows 3959.

con *imp.* in ~*fest on it thyn eghe* fix your eyes on it *[contemplare oculis]* 599. **couthe** *pa.t.sg.* could 2715, 4355. **couth** *subj.pa.t.sg.* knew how 4542. *pa.t.pl.* could 2143; knew 2570. *subj.pa.t.pl.* in ~ *thay* if they knew 4448.

conclose *ppl.a.* enclosed 4985 *(MED cites only this example)*. **conclosid** *pp.* engulfed, covered *[conclusit]* 4400.

condampned *pp.* condemned, damned 2892.

condigne *adj.* worthy 3888.

condignely *adv.* appropriately 42, 3910 *(MED cites only 42).*

condole *v.* lament 3741; in ~ *(of)* be sorry for 4258. **condoelid** *pa.t.pl.* in ~ *on* shared the anguish of 4703. **condolent** *ppl.a.* in ~ *(of)* sympathetic over 2183 *(MED cites only 2183).*

confable *v.* talk, chat 3923 *(MED cites only this example).*

confoving *pr.p.* fostering 4988 *(MED cites only this example).*

coniettes *pr.3 sg.* surmises 1548.

conioignes *pr.3 sg.* in ~ *(to)* unites with 1169. **conioint** *pp.* joined in marriage 872.

coniured *pa.t.sg.* solemnly charged 2135.

conke *n.* shallow bowl *[concham]* 989.

connyng *n.* knowledge 4427.

consequent *adj.* in *is* ~ (it) follows 2406.

consequently *adv.* afterwards 4922.

consolatrice *n.* (female) comforter 4740, 4870, 4896 *(MED records no example, OED only one).*

consuffred *pa.t.sg.* suffered in sympathy with 2811.

consummatum Lat. *pp.* in ~ *est* it is finished 2726, 4699.

contempland *pr.p.* contemplating 50. **contemplyng** 1838 *(MED records only one example of the pr.p., c.A.D.1450).* **contemplid** *pa.t.sg.* contemplated 3064 *(OED records the verb only A.D.1502ff).* **contempling** *vbl.n.* 3356, 4480.

contemplant *adj.* engaged in contemplation *[contemplatione se dabat]* 768.

contenant *pr.p.* containing 4982.

contrariaunce *n.* animosity 4428.

contrenaturely *adv.* against the laws of nature 1073.

contrepledid *pa.t.sg.* made a counterplea against, counteracted, opposed *[contradictit]* 2074.

contumelye *n.* insult, abuse 4089, 4604, 4623, 4677; **contumely** 2440. **contumelies** *pl.* 3716; **contumelyes** 4629.

conueniently *adv.* appropriately 2615.

conuersacioune *n.* conduct 640; association 945; conduct, ? haunting of certain places 3805n.

convers *v.* live 923. **conuersed** *pa.t.sg.* lived 2469. **conuersyng** *vbl.n.* conduct *[conversatio(ne)]* 3706n, 3774, *(no equivalent in the Latin)* 4899.

corce *n.* corpse 428; **corse** body 1580.

corporaly *adv.* in the flesh 3779.

cosse *n.* kiss 111, 2915; **cusse** 3245, 3867.

countresay *v.* argue with 3969.

coupable *adj.* in *is* ~ *(of)* deserves 4594.

couth, couthe see **con**.

covenable *adj.* suitable 3479.

covettid *pa.t.sg.* in ~ *(to)* desired 915.

covetye *n.* covetousness 654n.

craft *n.* in ~ *to telle* it can be told 793n; *be* ~ as a result of (any) ingenuity 3487.

craftily *adv.* skilfully 1330; **craftyly** 2816.

cressid *pp.* increased 4675.

creved *pa.t.pl.* split 2957.

criste *n.* crest 4147.

croisid *pp.* crucified 4363.

crokes *pr.3 sg.* leads astray, perverts 1590.

crucifie *v.* in *made hymself* ~ caused himself to be crucified 3358.

cure *n.* care 386, 2880.

cusse see **cosse**.

custumably *adv.* traditionally 3887.

daffe *n.* fool 1669.

dalied *pa.t.sg.* flirted 914.

dalte see **dele**.

day-sterne *n.* day-star.

declare *v.* set down 1220; describe 2198, 2911; tell 4521. **declares** *pr.3 sg.* describes 305. **declared** *pa.t.sg.* 1105. *pp.* 3002.

decovrid *pa.t.sg.* opened up *[perforavit]* 3186n.

dede *n.* death 105, 164, 227, 1250, 1252, 2138, 2455. **dedes** *gen.* of death *[mortis]* 418.

dedeigne *n.* disdain 2166, in *has* ~ *to* is offended by 3999.

defensoure *n.* defender 4570.

deffensatrice *n.* (female) defender 4006, 4037, 4058, 4071, 4106.

defourmable *adj.* deformed, ugly 4318 *(MED cites only this example).*

degree *n.* rank 642, 2687; in *(more)...in*~more 816; *best... in*~best 834; *(superexcellis)...in*~far excels 1176.

deken *n.* deacon 4364, 4466; **dekene** 515; **dekne** 527.

dele *v.* distribute 446. **deles** *pr.p.* 2794. **dalte** *pa.t.sg.* distributed 2750.

delectable *adj.* spiritually delightful 4484.

delicable *adj.* pleasure-loving 3924; delightful 4947, 5022, 5077 *(MED cites only 3924, 5022).*

delicacye *n.* pleasure 4415.

delicat *adj.* fond of good food 1552; splendid 4468.

delice *n.* joy 330, 522, 5000; **delyce** 409, 3861. **delices** *pl.* 4452, admirable qualities 4469, 4974; delights 4986.

delitable *adj.* pleasing 667, 3563, 4416, 4599; **delytable** 2151.

deliurisoun *n.* deliverance 1030.

delvid *pa.t.pl.* pierced (with blunt points) 2522. **dolven** *pp.* buried 4912. *ppl.a.* buried 1498; dug 2749.

delyce see **delice**.

delytable see **delitable**.

delyvrenesse *n.* speed 4434.

delyvring *n.* release 2427, 2652.

deme *v.* judge 2214; regard as 4448. **demyng** *pr.p.* assuming 1317. **demed** *pa.t.sg.* inferred, concluded 1326, 2138; decreed 2553; **demyd** condemned 4666. **demed** *pl.* regarded 4593. *pp.* sentenced, condemned 810; judged to be 1212; thought 4068; regarded as 4454; **demyd** thought 2787. **demyng** *vbl.n.* judgement 3034, 4219.

depart *v.* in ~ *to* divide among 2771. **departid** *pa.t.sg.* cut in half 156; separated 3051. *pl.* divided 2567. *pp.* divided up 237, 4199; separated 2804. **departing** *vbl.n.* departure 3635; in ~ *with* parting from 3637; **departyng** departure 3745; separation 4284.

departement *n.* in *without* ~ without ceasing 1904 *(MED records only this example)*.

departisoune *n.* distribution 3258, division 4198.

descendant *pr.p.* descending 3349.

descriving *pr.p.* describing 3598. **descryvid** *pp.* described 3596. **discrived** signified 3087.

desesed see **disese**.

desiderable *adj.* longed-for 4900; desirable 5078.

designed *pp.* signified 2588.

desire *n.* in *has in* ~ long 2151; *at his* ~ at...will 2242.

despite *n.* contempt 670. **despits** *pl.* hostilities 2374.

desseueryd, **desseueryng** see **disseuer**.

determinacioune *n.* definition 3808.

dette *ppl.a.* in *be* ~ *to kepe* must be kept 455.

deuouratours *n.pl.* gluttons *[voratores (devoratores in 1574)]* 1575 *(unrecorded)*.

devis *n.* in *wele at* ~ well in obedience to the will (of the Father); *?* in accordance with his purpose *[fideliter]* 4163.

devise *v.* in *to* ~ to be understood as 4371. *pr.pl.* in *men may...*~ may be understood 4499. **devisyng** *vbl.n.* division 4299.

did, **didde**, **dide** see **do**.

diffame *v.* damage the reputation of *[infamare]* 2764. *subj.pr.3 sg.* shame 1916.

differences *pr.3 sg.* differs 3042.

dight *pa.t.pl.* in ~*...with... whippes* whipped 1772.

digne *adj.* worthy of respect 1615; worthy (of it) 1832; worthy 4542.

dignely *adv.* deservedly 3577.

dileccioune *n.* love 1199, 1793, 2601; divine love 2289, 4543, 4673.

diliciouse *adj.* epicurean 921.

discomfit *pa.t.pl.* defeated 1879.

discordant *adj.* inconsistent 2134.

discorde *v.* differ 1241.

discouer *v.* expose 1535; **discoure** disclose 1913. **discoueryd** *pa.t.sg.* made known 2733.

discrecioune *n.* in *be* ~ rationally, prudently 3568.

discrete *adj.* discerning *[discretus]* 789.

discrived see **descryving**.

disefully *adv.* *(? for* derisefully*)* derisively 2188 *(MED cites only this example)*.

disese *n.* misery, trouble 412, 461, 601, 631, 634, 2594, 4024, 4045; inconvenience 1238; suffering 1366, 3040, 4851, 4899; injury 2084, 2295; tribulation 3385, 3387, 3590, 3633, 3830, 3832, 3833, 4106, 4891, 5073; in *at* ~ suffering 1724; **disesse** suffering 2912. **diseses** *pl.* 3032.

disese *v.refl.* in *hym*...~ inconvenience himself 1936. *tr.* in ~ *nothing* no harm at all 2677. **diseses** *pr.3 sg.* troubles 465. **desesed** *pp.* harmed 382.

disespayre *v.* despair 396. **disespaire** *subj.pr.3 sg.* in *no wight* ~ let no-one despair 4167. *imp.* despair 597.

dishonested *pa.t.sg.* humiliated 2390.

dispence *n.* in *lyves* ~ conduct 4933.

dispendid *pa.t.pl.* spent 4288.

dispersioune *n.* the dispersion (of the Jews among the Gentiles after the Babylonian Captivity) 3657.

dispite *n.* injury 138; contempt 2166; spite 3726.

dispitefulle *adj.* terrible 2140.

dispitously *adv.* contemptuously 2767; **dispitusly** violently 141.

displacens *n.* dislike, dissatisfaction *[displicentiam]* 1446 *(MED cites only this example)*.

disposing *refl.pr.p.* in ~ *hymself to* preparing himself for 2694.

disseuer *v.* distinguish 1420. **desseueryd** *pa.t.pl.* separated 2568. **disseueryd** *pp.* isolated 3052. **desseueryng** *vbl.n.* in ~ *(of)* distinction 1242.

dissimuling *ppl.a.* dishonest 1780. **dissymuiling** *vbl.n.* deceit 2939.

do *v.* behave, proceed 4307. **dose** *pr.3 sg.* in ~ *he come inne* attracts 1678; ~...*do* makes 2436. **do** *imp.* put 2412; in ~ *grave* have buried 1268; **dose** do 1612. **done** *pr.p.* in ~ *almuse-dede* gave alms 1750; **doing** *?* saying, *?* singing 2713n. **didde** *pa.t.sg.* put 3226; in ~ *bringe* brought 2408; ~ *on(ne)* put on 3223, 3225; **did** in ~ *hym norisshid to be* had him cared for 1345; ~ *he dede* he had put to death 1629; ~...*be cleved* had split 1632; **dide** in *to...deth hire* ~ killed her 740. **done** *pp.* in *on Crosse to be* ~ crucified 2416; ~ *on the Crosse* 2618; **doine** done 1431. **doyng** *vbl.n.* act 1351; happenings 1805; behaviour 2186; **doing** actions, deeds 2082; **dowyng** gift 4347.

doel *n.* grief 241, 2806, 2808, 2826, 2839, 2842, 2844, 2846, 2852, 2856, 3743, 3787, 3799, 4722, 4747, 4862, 4863, 4871, 4883, 4888, 4889, 4897, 4899, 4915 lamentation 2919, 3745, 3781 pity 2936, 4851 mourning 2949 torment 4377 a torture *(? pr.pl.)* 4640n; **doele** grief 189, 2741, 2930, 3751, 3755, 3801.

doelfulle *adj.* terrible 2284, 4246, 4525; anguished 2722, 2847, 2876, 2911, 2921, 2947, 2986, 4691, 4879; **doelefull** sorrowful 244; **doelfull** sad 2941; **doellfulle** terrible 2409. **doelfullest** *sup.* 2909, 3247.

doelfully *adv.* terribly 2258, in anguish 2872, 3332, 4876.

doght *pa.t.pl.* in *noght ne* ~ were useless 2134.

doghty *adj.* brave 3947, 4125.

doine, doing see **do.**

dolven see **delvid.**

dome *n.* judgement 269, 277, 328, 2196, 2208, 2225, 2246, 3513, 4283, 4616, 4681 sentence 2250, 4255, law 2316; execution of a sentence 4664; in *to the same* ~ by the same token 3058.

dominatour *n.* ruler 1009 *(MED cites only this example).*

done, dose see **do.**

dotacioune *n.* endowment 4345.

doughtyly *adv.* well 2068.

doute *n.* in *This is no manere* ~ it is certain 388; *haf...* ~ be afraid 2480; *(is) no* ~ certainly 301, 3321.

doute *v.* in *nedes noght to* ~ there is no question 4185. **doute** *subj.pr.2 sg.* fear 599.

dowairs *n.pl.* gifts 4335.

dowyd *pp.* in ~ *with* granted 3772; **dowed** in ~ *be* provided with 4345.

dowyng, doyng see **do.**

draffe *n.* chaff 1670.

dramme *n.* drachma 243, 3756, 3759. **drammes** *pl.* 3757, 3762, 3765.

drede *n.* fear 408, 622, 647, 1540, 1756, 2048, 3241, 4377; awe 955; reverence 2288; **dred** in ~ *of hert* reverence 918.

drede *v.* fear 4937; in ~...*didde he* he made fear 2349. **dredes** *pr.3 sg.* in ~ *nothing* does not fear at all 1171. *pr.pl.* in ~ *the* hold in awe 676; ~ *noght* are not frightening 3820. **dreding** *pr.p.* fearing 1801. **dred** *pa.t.sg.* was afraid 949; **dredde** was worried by 953; feared 2432. *pl.* 1334, 1338; in ~ *thay nothing* they did not hesitate 2159. **dred** in ~ *noght* did not fear at all 1121; ~ *thai noght* they did not hesitate 2152. **dredeing** *ppl.a.* fearing 4061.

drenche *v.* drown 1360.

drery *adj.* melancholy 3770.

dreryly *adv.* sorrowfully 4913.

drerynesse *n.* grief 3241.

drewe *n.* drop 974.

duc *n.* general-in-chief 2254; **duce** leader ('Judge') 4391.

dulcoure *n.* pleasantness 153; sweetness 2549, 3868, 4552.

duryng *pr.p.* in *was...* ~ lasted 4491. **durid** *pa.t.pl.* lasted 2146.

dyrupcioune *n.* being torn 2979.

dyvelleres *n.pl.* evil spirits 2037.

eage *n.* age 1396, 4499. **eages** *pl.* 1178.

ee see **eghe.**

effluxioune *n.* flowing-out 3268.

eft *adv.* afterwards 312, 2438, 3614; then 515; again 1463, 1866, 2438, 3394, 3460, 3520.

eftsones *adv.* again 2286, 2746, 2752, 3851, 3978; afterwards 2714, 4210.

egale *adj. as n.* equal 1196.

eghe *n.* 430, 599, 797, 867; **ee** 1376, 2059, 2059; **egh** 4411. **eghen** *pl.* 378, 476, 799, 2139, 2149, 2157, 2769, 2928, 3258, 3497, 3723, 4595, 4601, 4860.

eght *adj.* eighth 63.

eght *pa.t.sg.* ought 4923. **aght** *impers.pa.t.sg.* in *vs ~ vs* we should 650, 1199, 3584; *~ hym* he should 652; *~ the* you should 3832. **eght** *pl.* in *~ vs* we should 3777. **aght** *tr.pp.* due 835, 4714.

eghtend *num.* eighth 825; **eghten** 1235.

eke *adv.* also 31, 52, 115, 127, 189, 217, 238, 1257, 1385, 1588, 2174, 2938, 2942, 3022, 3171, 3218, 3224, 3429, 3561, 3563, 3624, 3702, 3717, 3827, 3936, 4035, 4043, 4324, 4463.

eke *v.* increase 2336. **eked** *pa.t.sg.* added 355. *pp.* added 2322, 3141; increased 3137, 3142, 3198, 4862.

elles *adv.* in a different manner 534; otherwise 1797, 1802, 3920; **ellis** also 947.

ellis *adj.* else 1444.

embelissours *n.pl.* decorations *[decoraverunt]* 1181 *(unrecorded)*.

empris *n.* purpose 3934.

emprowyng *vbl.n.* increasing, making profitable use of 4211.

encloos *pp.* contained 497; **enclosid** 4399. **enclos** *ppl.a.* 702; shut away 930; **enclose** enclosed 571.

endelesly *adv.* for ever 215.

endityng *pr.p.* singing 4980.

endure *v.* suffer 2458. **endures** *pr.3 sg.* 3201.

enebried *pp.* intoxicated 1053 *(MED cites only this example)*.

enebriouse *adj.* health-giving *[saluberrima]* 1062.

enen *adj.* brass 1433, 1441.

enevy, enevye see **envye**.

enevyous *adj.* malicious, envious *[invidit]* 2087; **eneuyous** hostile *[impugnatione]* 3176.

enforces *pr.3 sg.* in *~...for to assaille* succeeds in attacking 2755; *~...to crucifye* succeeds in crucifying 3978. **enforce** *subj.pr.3 sg.* tries 2764. **enforcyng** *pr.p.* trying 2826. **enforcyng** *vbl.n.* achievement 4602.

engyne *n.* skill, method 2319.

enhauncid *pa.t.sg.* elevated, exalted 5111.

enke *n.* ink 3595.

ennournyd *pp.* embellished 696.

ensaumpling *pr.p.* setting an example 3776.

entaylle *n.* in *didde...make be ~* carved 1319.

entende *imp.* in *~ (in)* come to, turn your attention to 3339; *(~ to)* concentrate on 3396.

ententifly *adv.* with close attention 3906.

entercesing *vbl.n.* cessation between them 4382.

enterchaungable *adj.* exchanged between them 3015.

enterreconsiliacioune in *gadrid ~* see **gadere**.

entrant *pr.p.* entering 1122; **entrande** in *were...~* came into 1309.

entyced *pa.t.sg.* incited 2278.

envye *n.* malice, envy 383, 2814, 4854; **enevy** animosity *[invidia]* 2838; **enevye** in *for ~* out of malice 4588.

ere *n.* ear 2108, 2110, 2120, 3248, 4412.

ere, ern, erre see **bee.**

errys *n.pl.* scars 267; **erres** 4118.

erth-dynne *n.* earthquake 3269.

erthi *adj.* worldly 4269 *(the earliest example in MED).*

esnuyed *pa.t.sg.* distressed 1716.

est Lat. *pr.3 sg.* in *id* ~ that is 101, 3109, 3111; *consummatum* ~ it is finished 2726, 4699.

estate *n.* rank 452, 1098; high rank 479; **estat** state (of life) 924. **estates** *pl.* states (of life) 829.

estories *n.pl.* tales 12.

etand *pr.p.* eating 1861.

ethe *adv.* easily 14; **eth** 327.

euerilkone *pron.* everyone 2280; **euerylkone** 12.

even *n. as adv.* in the evening 2841.

even *adj.* ? straight 3603n; exact 3851; equal 4304 in *fulle* ~ exact 3546.

even *adv.* precisely 1129; exactly 1468; in *full* ~ indeed; *?* together 388; completely 616; indeed 2529, 3523; exact 3546; *the ~fulnesse* exactly the full amount 1850; *~forth* fluently 3670; **evene** exactly 306.

even-Cristen *n.* fellow Christian 1742.

evenly *adv.* exactly 2976.

evomed *pa.t.sg.* spewed 3468 *(MED cites only this example).*

evrydele *adv.* in every detail 3207.

exaltate *pp.* raised 1173.

excesse *n.* difference in amount 978, violent emotion 3710.

excited *pa.t.sg.* exhorted 3555; 2942. **excitid** *pp.* provoked 4027.

excusacioune *n.* plea 4121.

exourned *pa.t.pl.* decorated 1179.

expired *pa.t.sg.* breathed out 3307.

expounding in *touches noght in* ~ see **touche.** **expovned** *pp.* said 3789.

expresse *adv.* clearly 1876.

exultacioune *n.* in ~ *(of)* delight (in) 1135.

eye *n.* egg 4295.

eyghen *n.pl.* eyes 4603.

facounde *n.* skill (in the use of language) 3599.

faders *n.pl.* patriarchs 1008; ancestors 2160; ancestors, patriarchs 2431, 3072, 3083, 3105, 3310, 3325; Fathers of the Church 3310; **fadres** ancestors, patriarchs 200, 3328; **faderes** forefathers, patriarchs 3368.

faging *ppl.a.* coaxing, beguiling 358.

faille *n.* in *without* ~ without doubt 460, 2383, 2489, 3202, 3653; *sanz* ~ 1320, 2756.

failling *pr.p.* lacking 1172, 2584. *vbl.n.* lack 3929; deficiency, lack 4435.

faldes see **folde**.

falle *v.* in *vntil hym* ~ come to agree with him, give in to him 367; *to* ~ would fall 390. **fallen** *pp.* in ~ *of* happened to 1541. *ppl.a.* in *the cas* ~ what had happened 3436.

fame *n.* reputation 879, 4471, 4473, rumour 3438.

fande *pa.t.sg.* came to possess 691; made, took 748; found 752, 999; discovered, invented 2540, 2556; **fand** found 773, 911, 1766. **fande** *pl.* 1114, 1848, 4589; discovered 2552. **fanding** *vbl.n.* temptation 1528, 1586, 1598. **fandinges** *pl.* 1587.

fare *v.* in ~ *(with)* act (towards) 1951. **for** *pa.t.sg.* did 2496.

farest *sup.* fairest 3860.

fassicle *n.* small bundle *[fasciculum]* 3237 *(MED cites only this example).*

fast *adj.* certain 1386. **fastere** *comp.* more firmly 2400.

fast *adv.* firmly 124, 1790, 2412, 3178, 3445, 3871, 3871, 4402; securely 1634; **faste** firmly 2348.

favourably *adv.* benevolently 3900.

fayne *adj.* happy 1485, in *for* ~ for joy 773, 1684, 1740, 1776, 5011 *so MED: OED regards* fayne *as n. in this context).*

fayne *adv.* gladly 4541.

fayne *v.* be happy 423.

fedyng *pr.p.* being fed 4906. **feding** *vbl.n.* nourishment 3354.

feere *n.* in *alle in* ~ as a whole 3486.

feigne *v.* invent 2133; **feygne** falsify 2788. **feynyng** *vbl.n.* pretence 4184.

feint *adj.* deceitful 464.

feling *adj.* perceptible to the senses, visible 25.

feling *pr.p.* experiencing, sensing 1843.

felle *adj.* enraged, ferocious 649; formidable 1927; terrible 3040; fierce 5091.

felle *pa.t.sg.* came by chance 1660; came 1669; happened 1706; it happened 3993, 4517. *pl.* happened 1707. *pp.* 868. **felle** *ppl.a.* fallen 3933.

felly *adv.* brutally 2117.

fere *v.* frighten 3126, 3130, 3150.

ferefulle *adj.* fearsome 5085.

ferforthe *adv.* in *so* ~ to such an extent 1675.

ferme *adj.* in *for* ~ certainly 2650.

ferre *adj.* distant 271, 1657, 1663; far 1664; remote 4404.

ferre *adv.* far 891, 974, 1797, 2252, 2351; from a distance 2713n.

fervenst *sup.* most eager 4100.

fest *v.* in *con* ~ fix 599. *pa.t.sg.* landed 2378; **festte** planted 1769. **fest** *pp.* fixed 2743.

festined *pp.* fixed 800.

festiuable *adj.* suitable for singing on feast-days *[cantatur]* 3498 *(the unrecorded word is glossed in the MS:* id est songen festiually*).*

festivaly *adv.* with due ceremony 3840, 3856; **festivalye** 717; **festivaylye** 246.

festte see **fest**.

festyvale *adj.* befitting a feast-day 3223.

fetour *n.* stench 422.

fette *v.* fetch 2475.

feygne, feynyng see **feigne.**

fieblesse *n.* infirmity 1849.

fierstee *n.* severity 4255.

figuracioune *n.* a prefiguration 143; in *gaf* ~ prefigured 1381; *hadde...* ~ was prefigured 2497.

figure *n.* foreshadowing 501, 521, 543, 1147, 1471, 1821, 3686, 4114, 4279, 4467, 4485, 4493; symbol 1822; in *bare* ~ prefigured 3699; *be* ~ figuratively 4399. **figures** *pl.* foreshadowings 44, 60, 64, 186, 1020, 1708, 3275, 3954; designs, patterns 2816.

figure *v.* prefigure 291. **figures** *pr.3 sg.* prefigures 245, 1647. **figuring** *pr.p.* symbolising 2472. **figured** *pa.t.sg.* prefigured 101, 108, 113, 149, 175, 195, 206, 217, 253, 255, 259, 267, 270, 283, 1071, 1129, 1369, 1445, 1594, 1882, 1890, 2618, 3072, 3281, 5117; **figurid** 129, 171, 197, 4962; **figurede** 5041. **figured** *pl.* 32; **figurid** 189. **figured** *pp.* 48, 760, 1029, 1327, 1726, 1892, 2536, 2551, 2661, 2871, 3153, 3515, 3693, 4123; **figurid** 3782, 3837, 3894, 4958, 5109; **figurd** 1413. **figured** *ppl.a.* 38, 124, 242, 1064; in *the shette ȝate* ~ the image of the closed gate 5003. **figuring** *vbl.n.* in *hadde* ~ was prefigured 2170.

figurelly *adv.* in the form of a statue 77.

fikke *v.* struggle, twitch 1672.

files *pr.pl.* defile 447.

fille *v.* perform 1271; fulfil 4181. **fille** *pr.pl.* carry out, obey 3564. **fillid** *pa.t.sg.* in ~ *hym with* served him up 3302. **filled** *pp.* fulfilled 933; **fillid** in *be* ~ *to slee men* kill enough men 3292.

filthes *n.pl.* acts of impurity 3923.

firmitee *n.* strength, security 1864.

flatling *adv.* flat 2515.

flavme *n.* flame 1420, 1423, 3349, 3656; **flawme** 961.

flaying *vbl.n.* ? fear, ? flaying 3012n.

flee *n.* fly, flying insect *[culex]* 465.

flegh *n.* flea *[pulex]* 466n *(MED does not record exactly this form; the words in this and the previous entry are often indistinguishable).*

flese *n.* fleece 61.

flesshely *adj.* physical 2879, 3924, carnal 3923.

fleyng *vbl.n.* retreat 3016, flight 3248.

flom see **flvmme.**

florist *pa.t.sg.* blossomed 678; **florisshed** 1072, 1247, 4961. **floryshed** *pl.* 1063.

flvmme *n.* river 1408, 1420, 1421, 1431, 1457, 1481, 1485; **flvmne** 1429, 1466; **flom** 83; **flvme** 84.

foghil *n.* bird 1012.

folde *n.* in *so many a* ~ so, to such an extent 4847. **faldes** *pl.* in *be* ~ *sevene* seven times 4322.

fole *adj.* foolish 273, 4087, 4257, 4261; **foole** 3963.

folenesse *n.* foolishness 4445.

fole-wastoure *n. as adj.* prodigal 95; **fole-wastour** 1656 *(unrecorded).*

folkes *n.pl.* peoples, races 126, 2263, 2266, 2495, 2499; **folke** 145.

fondyng *vbl.n.* temptation 892. **fonden** *pp.* in ~ *vp* recovered 3759.

fonge *v.* seize 56.

fonn *n.* a dupe 366.

foole see **fole.**

for *prep.* on account of 649, 755, 756, *[propter]* 874, 1193, 1640, 2177, 2189, 4472; because 721, 2102, 2137, 2167, 2259, 2260, 2261, 2262, 2358, 3635; in 781, 1580, 2106, 2326, 3725, 4623; concerning, with 909; in order that 1088; since 1519, 1547, 1783, 2091, 2958, 3189, 4309, 4943; as a result of 3533; for the sake of 4244; in ~ *martirdome is tolde* is thought of as martyrdom 1164; ~ *þat* because 1182, 3186; ~ *soth* truly 3060; ~ *alle chaunce*, ~ *no chaunce* see **chaunce**; ~ *ferme* see **ferme**; ~ *freel* see **freel**; pleonastic in ~ *to* 25, 162, 166, 184, 276, 301, 316, 492, 504, 606, 708, 827, 906, 957, 996, 1007, 1026, 1088, 1120, 1204, 1346, 1408, 1416, 1430, 1480, 1684, 1743, 1778, 2037, 2051, 2070, 2200, 2203, 2219, 2315, 2320, 2331, 2385, 2386, 2464, 2475, 2480, 2493, 2510, 2556, 2574, 2628, 2659, 2666, 2676, 2750, 2755, 2761, 2772, 2774, 2791, 2797, 2896, 2904, 2942, 2955, 2959, 2982, 2995, 3080, 3128, 3191, 3245, 3340, 3343, 3386, 3450, 3464, 3554, 3555, 3558, 3628, 3634, 3646, 3741, 3776, 3806, 3833, 3895, 3919, 3948, 3966, 4014, 4049, 4053, 4210, 4224, 4235, 4262, 4308, 4440, 4482, 4520, 4527, 4528, 4540, 4564, 4599, 4600, 4860, 4968, 4994, 5000, 5020, 5032, 5046, 5048, 5056, 5072, 5072, 5098, 5114.

for see **fare.**

forbe *prep.* in preference to 4954.

forbere see **forebere.**

force *n.* power 427, 1579 fortitude 646, 1255 violence 850.

fordone *pp.* overcome, dispelled 3345.

forebere *v.* avoid, eschew 4223. **forbere** *subj.pr.3 sg.* may tolerate 4396.

forfastid *pp.* exhausted by fasting 1549.

forgetyng in *renne to* ~ see **renne.**

for-japed *ppl.a.* exhausted by mocking abuse 2507.

forlayne *pp.* in ~ *violently* raped 847.

forliknesse *n.* in *gaf* ~ prefigured 2971; **forlyknesse** in *gaf* ~ 2747.

forlorne *pp.* left 1332. **forlorne** *ppl.a.* gone 2223.

forlost *ppl.a.* forfeited, lost 298, 851.

forme *adj.* first 564.

forme-fadere *n.* male progenitor (Adam) 4028.

for-modere *n.* female progenitor (Eve) 586.

formouse *adj.* beautiful 4025.

forouten *prep.* without 2064.

forpassing *pr.p.* surpassing, exceeding 3040.

forschewed *pa.t.sg.* 137; **forshewed** foreshadowed 2606. *pp.* foreshadowed 501, 1148, 2264. *ppl.a.* 3275; **forshowed** 60.

forshope *refl.pa.t.sg.* mutilated, degraded 406.

forsoth *adv.* indeed, truly 577, 1423, 3060.

fortakened *pa.t.sg.* forshadowed 165; **fortakenyd** 2938; **fortakned** 77. **fortakned** *pp.* 1490, 3987; **fortaknyd** 2847, 2877; **fortakened** 186.

forth in *even* ~ see **even**; *having* ~ see **having**; ~ *laide* see **laide**; *tilled* ~ see **tillid**; **forthe** in *so* ~ see **so**.

forthemast *adj.* outermost 3409; **forthmast** first 617.

forthemast *adv.* first of all 22; **forthmast** first 2234.

forthere *adj.* former 1240, in ~ *fete* forefeet 1769.

forthering *pr.p.* improving 1396.

forthermore *adv.* also, afterwards 3306.

forthmast see **forthemast**.

forthy *conj.* for that reason 1557, 1901, 2332, 2508, 3114, 3197, 4111; on that acount 2054, 3612; therefore 2244, 2328, 2967, 3980; **forthi** therefore 344, 640; for that reason 538, 867, 1261, 3795; **forthye** therefore 350.

forto *adv.* even if 3591.

fortolde *pp.* described earlier 2120. *ppl.a.* 3071.

fortouchid *pp.* suggested earlier *[praetaxata]* 3475. *ppl.a.* touched upon before 3781.

forwarde *adv.* in what follows 3706.

forwardis *adv.* in what follows 1070.

forwhi *conj.* since 2875.

forwith *adv.* previously 3691.

foudre *n.* lightning 3433.

fourme *n.* manner 1914; shape 3417; body 4026.

fourtied *ord.num.* fortieth 1207.

fovrefolds *adv.* in four ways 4332 *(MED does not record the* -s *form)*.

free *adj.* handsome, noble 1339; in *hert* ~ generosity 3564.

freel *adj.* in *for* ~ on account of being weak 3389.

freendful *adj.* benevolent 1529.

freendfully *adv.* lovingly 2399; **freendfullye** 1810.

freetyng *pr.p.* gnawing 3013.

frere *n.* friar 4733; in ~ *Prechoure* Dominican 4719. **freres** *pl.* in ~ *Prechours* 3949; ~ *Menours* Franciscans 3950.

frist *adj.* first 11. *ord.num.* 187, 809; **fryst** 15.

fro *conj.* as soon as 413; from the time that 2245, 3979; when *[quando]* 3415.

frount *n.* forehead, face *[collum]* 798. **frontes** *pl.* foreheads 2446.

fructified *pa.t.sg.* grew 1075; was fruitful 4235.

fruycioune *n.* spiritual joy (of communion) 3772.

fryst see **frist**.

ful see **fulle**.

fulfille *v.* supply, make up 3780. **fullfillid** *pp.* in *be* ~ *of* have enough of 3300. *ppl.a.* sated 2249, 2409. **fullfillyng** *vbl.n.* performance 3038.

full *adv.* very 87, 102, 152, 179, 304, 321, 355, 440, 466, 478, 482, 525, 839, 918 most 415, 431, 433, 482, 582, 668, 724, 729, 1687; in ~*even* see **even** 388, 616, in all 615, fully 836; **ful** very 14, 977; most 782.

fusours *n.pl.* melters (of metals) *[artifices]* 1434 *(unrecorded).*

fyle *v.* defile 4600. *refl.* 3916, 3918.

fylowingly *adv.* in what follows 4107, 4406.

fynder *n.* inventor 149; **fyndere** 2551. **fynders** *pl.* 2538.

gadere *v.* collect together 1917; **gedire** collect 1847, 1849; **gedre** bring in 1266. **gadred** *pa.t.sg.* gathered 1478, 3233. *pl.* brought together 2355; gathered 2841; come together 2843; **gadrid** gathered 1929, 3654; in ~ *enterreconsilicaioune* formed a mutual agreement 4626. *pp.* gathered 4587; **gedrid** accumulated 977. **gadred** *ppl.a.* all together 3233. **gadering** *vbl.n.* gathering, amassing 4078; **gaderyng** meeting 2086.

gane *pa.t.sg.* began 1659. **gon** *pl.* in ...*telle* told 549.

garding *n.* in ~ *suspensil* hanging garden 49.

garnyst *pa.t.sg.* enriched 890. **garnist** *pp.* garrisoned 3093.

gastly *adj.* spiritual 2503.

gate *n.* way 685.

gavde *n.* trinket 416. **gavdes** *pl.* in *make*...~ perform tricks 174.

gayncome *v.* return 4212.

gayne-calle *v.* contradict 3966.

gedire, **gedre**, **gedrid** see **gadere**.

geme *v.* lament 3741. **gemyng** *vbl.n.* lamentation 2919, 3751, *[gemitus]* 4877; *(cf. OED* yeme, yomer*).*

generacioune *n.* conception (by her own mother) 606, 699; conception (by his mother) 1006, 1105; **generacione** conception (by her own mother) 508.

gentilst *sup.* most noble 5052.

gerdoune *n.* reward 4216 n; **gerdon** 4506; **gverdoune** 4306.

gert *pa.t.sg.* in ~ *calle* named 1345; ~...*pray* invited 4487.

gifs in ~ *to mene* see **mene**.

gildres *n.pl.* snares 258.

glade *v.* gladden 3070, 3746; **glad** 200. **glading** *pr.p.* gladdening 3556; **gladyng** rejoicing 4979. **gladid** *pa.t.sg.* 3326, 3645; **gladide** 3105. **glading** *vbl.n.* pleasure 3141.

glasse *n.* glass bottle 204.

glose *n.* commentary, explanation 1220, 3110.

gloses *pr.3 sg.* flatters 2774. **glosing** *ppl.a.* deceptive 2095; **gloosyng** smooth-talking 2435. **glosing** *vbl.n.* smooth talk 359; **glosinge** 356.

glozaunt *adj.* gracious, compliant *[blandiens]* 3862 *(MED cites only this example).*

glutterye *n.* gluttony 86, 661, 1553, 1556, 1557, 3090; **glutterie** 1551, 1576; **gluterie** 1544; **gluttery** 1550.

gnaisting *pr.p.* gnashing his teeth 1770. **gnaistid** *pa.t.pl.* in ~ *on* gnashed their teeth at 2411. **gnaysting** *vbl.n.* gnashing 4376.

gobettmale *adv.* piecemeal 4362.

gomor *n.* (a biblical measure of weight or volume, a vessel containing this weight or volume) 1846.

gon see **gane.**

graces *n.pl.* spiritual gifts 627, 1201, 4713; thanks 4242, 4557, 4583, 4609, 4635, 4661, 4687. **graces** *gen.pl. (? sg.)* of grace *[gratiarum]* 4733.

graciouse *adj.* full of spiritual grace 4034, 4480; **graycious** kind 478. **graciousest** *sup.* most full of spiritual grace 4976.

graciously *adv.* by means of grace 4528.

graue see **grave.**

grauidacioune *n.* pregnancy *[gravidationem]* 931 *(MED cites only this example).*

grave *v.* bury *[sepelire]* 2935; **graue** in *do* ~ have buried 1268. **graven** *pp.* buried, entombed 2906, 3425, 3735. **graving** *vbl.n.* burial 2937.

gravell *n.* sand 93, 1638.

gravely *adj.* sandy 721.

graycious see **graciouse.**

greces *n.pl.* steps 1173, 1177, 1179.

grete *adj.* pregnant 809, 958, 4984.

grette *pa.t.sg.* greted, saluted 4952.

gruche *pr.pl.* complain 3586. **gruch** *subj.pr.pl.* 3387.

gude *n.collective* possessions 271, 416, 423, 425, 427, 444, 481, 660, goods 1719, 2770; benefit 2762; benefits 2794; wealth 2796, 2800; profit 2819. **gudes** *n.pl.* possessions 457, 513, 656; benefits 523; good things 4421.

gude *adj.* in ~ *is* it is right that 4945.

gudely *adj.* good 993, 2918; handsome, good 4015. **gudeliest** *sup.* most beautiful 895; **gudliest** kindest 4975.

gudely *adv.* kindly 518, *[misericordier]* 1644, 1692, 2987; expertly 530, very *[prudenter]* 787; properly 1068; rightly 1169; gladly 1114; courteously 1921.

gudelynesse *n.* goodness 309, 638, 1814.

gudes see **gude.**

gudliest see **gudely.**

gulows *adj.* greedy 1575.

gulyards *n.pl.* gluttons 1847 *(MED cites only this example).*

guyse *n.* procedure 21; manner 505.

gverdoune see **gerdoune.**

gyloure *n.* deceiver 2210, 2380.

gynne *n.* contrivance 4388.

gyvyng *vbl.n.* grace 4963.

habite *n.* clothing 2682.

hailsen *pr.pl.* greet 2775. **hailesid** *pa.t.sg.* greeted 2055; **haylsid** 2350. **hailsing** *vbl.n.* greeting 792. **hailsynges** *pl.* supplications 4736.

halds see **holdis.**

half *n.* side 1477, 3416, 4684, 5118; **halfe** 248.

hals *v.* embrace 1684. **halsing** *pr.p.* 924, 1096; **halsyng** 4908. **halsed** *pa.t.sg.* 774; **halsid** 4876. **halsinges** *vbl.n.pl.* 2915, 3858.

ham *pron.pl.* them 1878.

hande-makeyng *n.* in *of* ~ made with hands 2235.

happily *adv.* fortunately 1525; **happyly** 3181.

harbergh *n.* shelter 1266.

hard *adj.* severe 2980; harsh 4654; **harde** severe 3607, 4721; implacable 4854, 4887; **herd** hard 1826, 1828; **herde** 4154.

hard see **heres.**

hardily *adv.* certainly 2715, 3664.

hardnesse *n.* severity 2807.

hare *n.* hair 1571.

harlot *n.* professional male entertainer, reprobate *[scurram]* 2717. **harlots** *pl.* 173, 2716.

has *pr.3 sg.* in ~ *liknyng* see **liknyng**; in ~..*betaknyng* see **betake.** **has** *pl.* have 3692; in ~ *in desire* see **desire**; ~ *curacioune* see; **curacioune.** **having** *pr.p.* in ~ *forth* attacking 2096. **nhad** *pa.t.sg.neg.* (ne + had) in ~ *noght be* would not be 809.

hatte *v.intr.* be called 191. *pr.3 sg.* is called 3729. **heght** *pa.t.sg.* was called 710, 1123, 3784. **hight** *tr.pp.* called 2509, 3095. **heght** *ppl.a.* called 2415.

haubergeoune *n.* coat of mail 4151.

haylsid see **hailsen.**

hayre *n.* hair-cloth 4704n.

hede *n.* in *taking*... ~ taking precedence over 1896.

heende *n.* noble 4679, 5121.

heght *n.* height 761, 3412, 3414, 3419.

heght see **hatte, heghts**

heghting see **heghts.**

heghtis *n.pl.* promises 417.

heghts *pr.3 sg.* promises 419, 421; **heghtis** 1020. **heghting** *pr.p.* promising 416. **heght** *pa.t.sg.* promised 3646; **hight** 2723. **hight** *ppl.a.* 2501.

hele *n.* health 419, 1456, 2281, 2982, 4429, 4641; spiritual well-being 442, 542, 560, 602, 738, 771, 1138, 1287, 1410, 1610, 1664, 1675, 2290, 2558, 2725,3540, 4104, 4702.

hele *n.* heel 3279.

helefulle *adj.* salutary 1060, 4403.

hely from Hebrew *n.*+ *pers.pron.* my God 2727n, 4692.

hent *subj.pr.3 sg.* receives 1426. *pa.t.sg.* put on 2680. *pp.* in *out* ~ drawn 2125.

herbes *n.pl.* plants 3597.

herd, herde see **hard**.

here *n.* hair 2732.

here *pron.* her 799.

here *subj.pr.3 sg.* may hear 4185. **heres** *imp.* hear 1406, 1706, 1806, 2306, 2506, 2806, 3206, 3306, 3506, 3906, 4120, 4306; **heris** 1306. **hard** *pa.t.pl.* heard 1505.

hereby *adv.* nearby 1818; by means of this 2899; **herebye** 1914.

herefore *adv.* in view of this 1335.

hereof *adv.* of this 612, 3117, 3811; **hireof** 496.

heres *n.pl.* ears 377.

heretofore *adv.* previously 1305.

heries *pr.pl.* praise 3148.

hertfully *adv.* sincerely 1724, 2067, 2902.

hertly *adj.* heartfelt 1446, 4418.

hertly *adv.* sincerely 3778; exceedingly 4925; carefully, devoutly 5132.

heryde *pa.t.sg.* despoiled, harrowed 3048.

hest *n.* promise 2776. **hestes** *pl.* 468.

hete *n.* strong desire 537.

heved *n.* head 219, 256, 338, 781, 1110, 1371, 2335, 2340, 2342, 2348, 2363, 2364, 2366, 2767, 3213, 3224, 3295, 3869; in *in the* ~ at the head *[in caput]* 3496 (see 3475n); **hevede** 3280. **heveds** *pl.* 1931, 3912; **hevedes** 3655.

hevedid *pa.t.sg.* beheaded 3290. *pl.* 4360.

hevenfull *adj.* holy, heavenly 265 *(MED does not cite this example, though it has only one)*.

heyre *n.* heir 141.

hight see **hatte, heghts**.

hile *v.* cover 428, protect 600; **hille** conceal 1536, 2954, cover 4850; **hil** 4602; **hils** *pr.3 sg.* protects 4009, 4072. **hilyng** *pr.p.* covering 2157. **hild** *pa.t.sg.* covered 4595; **hilde** 2149. **hild** *pp.* in ~ *about* covered 1442; **hiled** 1499. **hiling** *vbl.n.* covering 3258.

hilts *n.pl. (with sg. meaning)* hilt 3180.

hird *n.* shepherd 1585.

hire *pron.* its 308.

hired *pa.t.pl.* bribed 2308, 2310.

hireof see **hereof**.

hires *pron.* her 2914n.

hirnes *n.pl.* corners 2115.

his *pron.* his possessions 485; in ~ *strongere* one stronger than he 3111; *maugre/mavgre* ~ see **maugre**; *(this entry does not distinguish absolute uses of the pronoun, about which, in the case of* maugre his, *OED and MED disagree)*.

historiale *adj.* historical, literal 1039.

hoege *adj.* great 348, 427, 761, 866, 868, 955, 1813, 1950, 2109, 2147, 2219, 2371, 2517, 2534, 2581, 2595,

2695, 2851, 3025, 3142, 3573, 3662, 3749, 3818, 4533, 4611; 4901, very numerous 2583, 4408; huge 3186, 5092; **hoge** great 1016, 2342. **hoegest** *sup.* greatest 1732, 4547, 4673, 4679; **hogest** enormous 1478.

hoegely *adv.* greatly 830, 2893, 3331, 3463, 3481, 3683, 4028, 4390, 4663, 4675; exceedingly 1560, 3652, 3696; very 2585; **hogely** very 714.

holdis *pr.3 sg.* in ~ *the heght (als)* is as high (as) 3412; **halds** in *In lenght*......*feet eght* is eight feet long 3411. **holden** *pp.* held 2250; bound 3133; made 3818; **holdene** in *we be* ~ it is our duty *[tenemur]* 3129.

holpen *pp.* helped 301.

homely *adj.* gentle 641.

homely *adv.* intimately 914.

hondes *n.pl.* dogs 2411, 3124.

honest *adj.* respectable 449; honourable 878; decent 1416.

hope *v.* think 814. *pr.1 sg.* 296, 4494. *pl.* 2271, 2833; **hopes** 3309. **hoped** *pa.t.sg.* thought 1549, 2223. **hoped** *pl.* 2150. **hoped** *pp.* 809, 2428, expected 3058; **hopid** thought 4179.

horne *n.* arm (of the Cross), drinking cup 1050.

houre *n.* time 154, 2550; **hovre** 183, 1343; **howre** appointed time 418.

howseling *vbl.n.* giving communion 1914.

howsill *n.* communion 1915.

hulde *adj.* glorious 1109.

hy *v.* go quickly 3948.

hye *n.* haste 325.

hye *adj.* great 421, 3204.

hyeghnesse *n.* rank 693.

hyghly *adv.* greatly 1795, 4469; **hyeghly** deeply, greatly 1118; majestically 3899.

hym in ~ *awe* see **awe**; ~ *hapne* see **hapne**; ~ *lest* see **lest**; ~ *like(d)* see **like**; *nedes mot* ~ see **mot**; ~ *thinke*, ~ *thoght* ~ *shuld think* see **thinke**.

hyre *n.* reward 2202.

id see **est**.

if in *bot* ~ see **bot**.

ilk *adj. as pron.*[1] same 302, 3173, 3375, 3975, 4023; very 3060, 3444, 3601; in *in þat* ~ *one houre* at the same time 154; *pleonastic* in *this* ~ 2828.

ilk *adj. as pron.*[2] each 24; every 449, 453, 634, 827, 1058, 1131, 1218, 1473, 1561, 1846, 3400, 3482, 3625, 3658, 3661, 3825, 3939, 3976, 4676, 4923; **ilke** same 516, 2119.

ilka *adj.* each 21.

ilkonę *pron.* each one 107, 2411, 3400, 4400, 4568, 4590, 4908; each 1388, 1668, 1846, 1862, 1923, 3428, 3661, 4214, 4495; each one (of) 2138, 3491, 3655; each (of) 3883; in ~ *by one* one by one 1218; **ilkon** 3709.

illesioune see **illusioune**.

illuminacioune *n.* restoration of sight 3267.

illusioune *n.* mocking 2361, 4161, 4625; **illesioune** destruction in sport *(mistranslation)* 3081n. **illusiounes** *pl.* 2352.

immense see **inmense**.

impacience *n.* inability to bear adversity 3390.

impassibilitee *n.* the quality (possessed by the unfallen or resurrected body) of being incapable of feeling pain, or suffering disease or death 4333; **inpassibilitee** 4343.

impassible *adj.* exempt from illness, pain and death 4314.

importible *adj.* unbearable 4376.

imprivable *adj.* everlasting 3630 *(MED cites only this example).*

impugnacioune see **inpugnacioune**.

imputrible see **inputrible**.

in *prep.* ? by means of *[et]* 108, 4733; on 248, 709, 720, 773, 878, 1056, 1087, 1151, 1382, 1843, 2446, 2720, 3007, 3059, 3101, 3124, 3135, 3145, 3146, 3196, 3266, 3536, 3546, 3688, 3715, 3717, 3724, 3731, 3874, 4062, 4136, 4338, 4707, 4722, 4745, 4876, 4898, 5107, 5118, 5120; of 761; in the matter of 1557; with regard to 1688; among 3162; in ~ *apert* see **apert**; ~ *auntre* see **auntre**; ~ *descriving* see **descriving**; *has* ~ *desire* see **desire**; ~ *expounding* see **expounding**; ~ *feere* see **feere**; ~ *kynde* see **kynde**; ~ *oone* see **oone**; ~ *o soume, a sovme* see **soume**; ~ *twynne* see **twynne**; ~ *tyme* see **tyme**.

in *adv.* on to 1378; in *Broght* ~ *on* broght on 328; ~...*bryng* introduce 456.

inconsutyle *adj.* seamless *[inconsutili]* 3225 *(MED cites only this example).*

incredulitee *n.* lack of faith 4045.

increment *n.* addition, offspring 2995.

incurs *n.* attack 876.

indiscretly *adj.* ignorantly 47.

indomable *adj.* untameable 5086.

induccioune *n.* the act of bringing 1514.

indurable *adj.* impermanent 424.

indure *v.* harden 393. **indures** *pr.3 sg.* hardens (in heart) 404.

inenarrable *adj.* unspeakable 3014, 4353, 4380.

inenarrably *adv.* inexpressibly 5061.

influyng *pr.p.* in ~ *(vnto)* affecting 4417.

infusiounes *n.pl.* radiations of light 894.

ingent *adj.* mighty *(MED cites only this example).*

inmense *adj.* immense, immeasurable 1058, 1693, 5013, 5053; **immense** 4888.

inmensitee *n.* immeasurability 1398.

inmobles *n.pl.* non-portable property 1242.

inne in *broght him* ~ see **broght**.

inopynably *adv.* inconceivably 4951.

inpassibilitee see **impassibilitee**.

inprovise *adv.* suddenly 4935 *(unrecorded).*

inpugnacioune *n.* assault, temptation 4426; **impugnacioune** 3197. **inpugnaciounes** *pl.* 4036.

inpugne *v.* make war on 4039, 4233. **inpugnys** *pr.3 sg.* 4057. **inpungned** *pp.* attacked 467.

inputrible *adj.* rot-proof 1251, 1497; **imputrible** 3845.

insite *adj.* instituted 1806.

instaunce *n.* insistence 4619; in *at..~* at the request 240.

instode *pa.t.sg.* urged 347; pressed 2427.

instuyd *pa.t.sg.* instituted 1859.

integritee *n.* virginal entirety (of the hymen) 4340.

interfeccioune *n.* murder 2410.

invite *adv.* unwillingly *[invite]* 2664.

inwith *prep.* within 1540; inside 3407.

irrited *pp.* provoked 1641.

is *poss.pron.3 sg. (for gen.)* in *Encense ~* incense's 1195.

isshed *pa.t.sg.* left *[exivisti]* 5055.

jape *n.* joke 417. **japes** *pl.* mockery 2139, 2224, 4672.

jape *v.* trick 464; deceive 813; mock 4855. **japed** *pa.t.pl.* mocked 3228. *pp.* 118, 2407; **japid** 4586.

jentellenesse *n.* courtesy, nobility 2579.

jentil *adj.* noble, *?* gentile 2582; **jentyle** gentle, noble 3955.

jentillye *adv.* graciously 4199.

jobbe *n. ?* rough time 1777n.

jubilynge *ppl.a. ? vbl.n.* in *songe ~* song of rejoicing 769n. **jubilyng** *vbl.n.* rejoicing 4432, 5068; **jubylyng** 4978.

kaces *n.pl. ?* carcases 1562n.

kan see **con**.

kast see **castis**.

kavil *n.* lot (cast) 3259.

kepe *n.* in *takes ~* takes notice 1595.

kepe *v.* receive 2862; guard 3427; protect 4151. **kepes** *pr.3 sg.* retains, holds 3109; protects 4073; reserves 4201.

kepere *n.* protector 531, 533, 872, 875, 877. **kepers** *pl.* guards 3432, 3434, 3440.

kest see **castis**.

kinde see **kynde**.

knave *n.* boy 1109. *as adj.* 1239, 1331.

knawes *pr.3 sg.* understands, recognises 665. **knawyng** *vbl.n.* 666, 2655, 3676; **knawing** knowledge 622, 3029.

kynde *n.* nature, shape 319; in *man(ne)s* ~ mankind's 307, 3300; in *broght...forth in* ~ produced *[generaverunt]* 737; *freendes* ~ friends 4942; *agein* ~ unnaturally 4963; *above* ~ supernaturally 4964; **kinde** nature 2881, 2965.

laccere *comp.* in *Neuer the* ~ yet *[Tamen]* 2628 *(MED does not record the comp. before A.D.1459).*

lagh *n.* the Law 5229.

laide see **lay**.

lake *n.* pit 3078, 3079, 3085; in ~ *of lyouns* lion pit 202, 3077.

lakke *n.* in *gyves the* ~ *(of)* blames (for) 2760.

lamazabatany Hebrew *(for* lama sabachthani*)* 2727n.

land *n.* in ~ *of promissioune* 144, 1470. **lande** in ~ *of beheste* promised land 1474, 3980; ~ *of promissioune* 2498, 3984, 4451; *hight* ~ 2501

lane *n.* loan 1796.

langour *n.* sorrow 3818, 4899; **langoure** 3791.

langvisse *pr.1 sg.* suffer pain 3798. **langvised** *pa.t.sg.* suffered 4885; **langvyst** longed 1670. **langvist** *pl.* suffered pain 3794.

lare *n.* teaching 2238, 2622.

large *n.* in *at the* ~ without restraint 2096.

largely *adv.* widely 547.

last *sup.* worst 2148, in *at the* ~ finally 1347.

lastis *pr.3 sg.* remains 3881. **lasting** *pr.p.* remaining 4342.

lastyngly *adv.* continually 4914.

lat *imp. (exclamation)* in ~ *see* look, now 222, 4266, 4597; **late** let 452; in ~ *see* let us see 300. **laten** *pp.* let 1951. **laten** *ppl.a.* let 1934.

late *adv.* in *of now* ~ very recent 9.

latsomest *sup.* most valuable *[carissima]* 1154.

lauacre *n.* in *baptesmes* ~ baptismal font 1473.

lauatorie *n.* ritual cleansing font 1433.

laude *n.* praise 1201, 1725; **lavde** 1590, 2778.

laude *n.* ? burden, ? praise *(perhaps belonging in the previous entry)* 3037n.

laved *pa.t.pl.* praised *[laudebant]* *(MED* lauden *cites only this example).*

lawe *adj.* low 789.

lay *v.* in *forth* ~ offer 1538. **laide** *pa.t.sg.* in *on...*~ attacked 136; ~ *for* aimed at 2072, *forth* ~ produced 3677. **laide** *pl.* in *forth* ~ 2233.

layned *pa.t.sg.* concealed 2057.

ledde *n.* ? control, direction *[stimulum]* 2434n.

ledere *n.* guide 590.

leef *adv.* willingly 2093.

leel see **lele**.

leeme *n.* brilliance, ? tail of a comet 1108.

lefe *adj.* in *ere* ~ prefer, are disposed 2788

lefe *subj.pr.pl.* release *[dimittimus eum]* 2092.

leghe *adj.* false 2134.

leghes *n.pl.* lies 1236.

lele *adj.* noble 998, loyal 1019; **leel** noble 3390.

leonceux *n.pl.* statues of young lions 1179, 1181.

lepre *n.* leprosy 1458, 1461.

lere *v.* learn about 308; learn 708; in ~...*(in)* learn (from) 503. **leryng** *ppl.a.* learning from 2271.

lerned *pa.t.sg.* taught 3737.

leses *pr.3 sg.* loses 848. **lesyng** *pr.p.* losing 3533, 4984. **lesing** *ppl.a.* missing, lost *[amisisse]* 3763.

lesse *comp.* in *neuer the* ~ not reduced at all 2054; **lessen** in ~ *nor more* neither more nor less 1848.

lest *impers.pr.3 sg.* in *hym* ~ he pleases 404[1,2]; ~ *the* you please 2575.

lette *v.* stop 2419; prevent 2425, 2426, 2429, 2433. **lettis** *pr.pl.* hinder 3088; in ~ *noght* do not hesitate 3916. **lettid** *pa.t.sg.* prevented 2382. *pp.* 2381. **lettyng** *vbl.n.* hindrance 1464; **letting** in *turn...to* ~ see **turne**.

lettrure *n.* holy scripture 708.

leve *pr.1 sg.* believe 190.

leve *v.* remain 749, 2628.

levefulle *adj.* permissible, honourable 2060, 3898.

levere *comp.* better 1336; **levre** in *wele* ~ far rather 2199; ~ *hadde sho* she preferred 3741.

lewed *adj.* foolish, worthless 410, 1669.

lewedly *adv.* in an ignorant manner 2716.

lewednesse *n.* ignorance 4446.

liberale *adj.* freely available 1613.

lif-while *n.* life-time 759.

ligges *pr.3 sg.* lies, remains 1651. **ligging** *pr.p.* lying 3410.

lightned *pa.t.sg.* enlightened *[inspiravit]* 397; lit 2158. **lightned** *pp.* illuminated 1288.

lik *impers.pr.3 sg.* in ~ *thaym* let them 3780. **like** *subj.pr.3 sg.* may it please 3867; in *if it ȝow* ~ if you will 1040; ~ *the* may it please you 3339, 5124; ~ *ȝow* may it please you 3706, 4521; *hire* ~ she may be pleased 4101; **lyke** in *hym* ~ he may be pleased 5021. **likyng** *pers.pr.p.* wishing 937; **lyking** being willing 8. **liked** *pa.t.sg.* wished 29, 1028, 2703, 2891, 4953; **lyked** pleased 4725. **liked** *impers.* in ~ *hym*, *hym* ~ he wished 3450, 3520. *pers.pp.* wished 387.

likely *adv.* in the same way 3368.

likest *sup.* in *was* ~ *for to be* was inevitably 1480.

liklynesse *n.* in *in* ~ so to speak *[tanquam]* 3700

liknyng *n.* in *has* ~ is like 3231.

likyng see **lik**.

list *n.* desire 727; in *to thi* ~ to satisfy you 3298; **lyst** wish 13.

list *pr.3 sg.* wishes 4307. *impers.pr.3 sg.* in *hym* ~ he pleases 2657. *pers.subj.pr.3 sg.* wishes 1777. **lyst** *pa.t.sg.* wanted 2480, 5064; **list** wished 777.

logh *pa.t.sg.* laughed 171. **loght** *pl.* 122.

loke *v.* in *eft* ~ look back to 3394. *imp.* see 93, 417; look at 3827[1,2], 3829[1,2], 3830; **luke** look at 2127.

lontaigne *adv.* distant 4209.

loos *pp.* praised 5001.

lore *n.* teachings 4573.

lorne *pp.* lost 233, 534.

louse *v.* break (a siege) 4012, 4032.

lovyng *vbl.n.* praise 1133; in *als for* ~ in thanksgiving 753. **lovinges** *pl.* praise 1745.

luf-brennyng *ppl.a.* ardent 1828.

luke see **loke**.

lusaunt *adj.* bright 3886 *(MED* lucent *cites only one example of 1449).*

lust *n.* pleasure 672, 3026, 4272; desire 674, 1590, 3926; in ~ *of* passion for 3291. **lustes** *pl.* 4078; **lustis** 670.

lustfulle *adj.* pleasant 4413.

luxouriously *adv.* sumptuously 1658 *(OED's earliest example is A.D.1540; not in MED).*

luxuree *n.* lust 3920, 3937, 4085; **luxure** 669, 3912; **luxurie** 3931. **luxures** *pl.* 900.

luxuryouse *adj.* lustful, dirty 3922.

lyes *intr.pr.3 sg.* it is relevant, fitting 554.

lyke, lyked, lyking see **lik**.

lymbe *n.* limbo 2431, 3053, 3055, 3063, 3074, 3076, 3083, 3328, 3373, in *helles* ~ limbo 498.

lymbus *n.* limbo 3044, 3109

lymme *n.* in *thevis* ~ a member of the thieving fraternity 2779.

lyst *conj.* in ~ *they...wald haf shame* (to see) if they would be ashamed *[si forte vererentur]* 2480.

lyst see **list**.

lyueraunce *n.* release 3261.

lyve *n.* in *of* ~ alive 342, 928, 2993, 5032.

lyvrisoune *n.* in *made* ~ caused to be released 3336.

made in ~ *hymself crucifie* see **crucifie**; ~ *lyvrisoune* see **lyvrisoune**; ~ *mynde* see **mynde**.

magnifiant *pr.p.* giving glory *[magnificebant]* 5067. **magnified** *pa.t.sg.* gave praise to 2261.

magnificat Lat. *pr.3 sg.* gives glory to 4992n.

magnyfy *? n.* in *made...a* ~ made a song of praise 4978n *(unrecorded).*

maide *? ppl.a.* created 459

maistry *n.* authority 3288.

maiestyfly *adv.* majestically 3510 *(unrecorded).*

make *v.* in *Crist to be scourged* ~ to have Christ scourged 2248, ~ *fonn* 366 see **fonne**; ~*...gavdes* see **gavdes**; ~*...to be shent* see **sheend**.

malison *n.* cursing 586; **malicioune** being cursed 3015; **malyson** condemnation, being cursed 2441.

malliacioune *n.* nailing (of Christ to the Cross) 2542 *(MED cites only this example).*

mane from Aramaic *n.* mina (a measure of money) 275, 4281n.

manhede *n.* human nature 1006, 3355; **manhode** 3618, 3767; **mannhed** 2641.

manifestour *n.* one known to all *[ad notitiam omnium]* 2653 *(OED records this only A.D.1612ff, and not in this sense).*

mannes *gen.sg.* in ~ *kynde* mankind's 307.

manquhellere *n.* murderer 2379; **manwhellere** 96.

man-sawle *n.* (man *gen.* + sawle) the soul of man 2464.

man-sleere *n.* killer of man 3299.

mansuet *adj.* gentle 5085.

mansuetude *n.* humility 4563, 4575.

manswetely *adv.* humbly 2122.

manwhellere see **manquhellere**.

manyfaldly *adv.* in various ways 3338.

mare *n.* sea; in ~ *enen* the bronze laver in the Temple 1433, 1441.

mare see **more**.

maritales *adj.* conjugal 5008 *(MED cites only this example).*

maters *n.pl.* subject-matter 12; ideas (in what has been said) 1389.

mates *refl.pr.3 sg.* in ~ *hym* controls himself 624. **matid** *tr.pa.t.sg.* overcame 3301.

matiers *n.pl.* elements 1284; (harmful) bodily fluids, humours 3193; **matieres** substances 1374.

maugre *prep.* in spite of 498, 3166, 3430; in ~ *his* in spite of himself 346; **mavgre** in ~ *his* against his will 2509; **mawgree** in ~ *wham þat it awe* no matter whose it is 1234; **mavgree** in *thaire* ~ against their will 850.

maundement *n.* commandment 17, 3544, 4182. **maundements** *pl.* 3564.

mavfesours *n.pl.* enemies 1721.

mavmetrye *n.* idols, idolatry 349; **mawmetry** 1310.

mawmet *n.* idol 1378, 1559. **mawmets** *pl.* idols 1387; **mawments** 1349.

mawmetiers *n.pl.* idolaters 119.

maydenhede *n.* virginity 748, 834, 845, 846, 856, 1169, 3350; **maydenhode** 1172, 4984, 4990, 5010; **maydenhed** 843; **maydenhod** 5005.

maze *n.* state of confusion; *?* heap of rubble 1388.

mede *n.* benefit 7; compensation 850; reward 3200, 3202, 3428; payment 4216.

mediatrice *n.* (female) mediator, intercessor 3906, 3940, 3945, 3952, 3953, 3986, 3987, 4000, 4005, 4092, 4100, 4105.

medled *pp.* mingled 3263; **medlid** 4696.

meignee *n.* household 1564.

meked *pa.t.sg.* subdued 5091.

melle *v. ?* cause 2386n; mingle 2903. **mellid** *pa.t.sg.* mingled 1571.

melliflewe *adj.* sweet 4554, 5014; **melliflowe** 4886; **melliflwe** 3712.

membratly *adv.* limb by limb *[membratim]* 4386 *(MED cites only this example).*

mene *v.* in *gifs to* ~ means *[interpretatur]* 4282.

menge *pr.pl.* mix 2799. **mengid** *pa.t.pl.* 2513. **mengid** *pp.* 2512.

menours in *Freres* ~ see **freres.**

mensurid *pp.* measured *[mensurari]* 4408 *(unrecorded).*

menyng *pr.p.* in ~ *of* referring to 786, 3960. *vbl.n.* in *makes..*~ speaks of 3795.

mercyable *adj.* merciful 4168.

meroure *n.* mourning *[moerore]* 3792 *(MED cites only this example).*

merueile *n.* in *to* ~ amazingly 1073 *(OED records this only A.D.1500ff).*

mes *n.* courses of food 3565, food 3567.

meschef *n.* affliction, misfortune 412; **meschief** 1712; **myscheif** evil-doing 507.

mesel *adj.* in ~ *man* leper 4652.

message *n.* messenger 1001, *[nuntio]* 4955, 4975. **messages** *pl.* 2389.

mesure *n.* moderation 455, 458; in *ouere* ~ too great 4951.

mete *n.* food 202, 447, 673, 736, 921, 1265, 1569, 1835, 1848, 1867, 2584, 3078.

mete *adj.* equal 3418.

mette *pa.t.sg.* welcomed *[honoravit]* 5119.

mikelle see **mykel.**

ministrant *pr.p.* giving 1228.

mirable *adj.* wonderful, miraculous *[mirabilem]* 906, 959, 1825, 3497, 4550; wonderful 5004.

mirre *n.* myrrh 1146, 1197, 1202, 2863, 2865, 3231, 3234, 3237, 5030, 5035.

mirred, mirrid see **myrred.**

misdoars, misdoere, misdoers see **mysdoere.**

miseracioune *n.* compassion 1673.

misericordous *adj. as n.* compassionate person 632.

missaide *pa.t.sg.* abused 135.

mo *adj.* more 2364, 2477.

mobles *n.pl.* movable things 1242.

mode *n.* mind, heart 1450; manner 1922.

moderfull *adj.* maternal 214; **modrefulle** 3218. **moderstfulle** *sup.* most mother-like 2932.

moderfulli *adv.* in the manner of a mother *[more matris]* 4860 *(unrecorded)*

moght see **mow.**

monstrable *adj.* capable of being revealed *[praemonstrata]* 1708.

more *n.* more, *? (conj.* moreover*) [addidit etiam]* 2621, *[addiditque]* 2627, *[adjecitque]* 2647, *[adjecit quoque]* 3667

more *comp.* greater 2440

mare *adv.* more 1172.

most *sup.* greatest 2370.

mot *pr.3 sg.* must 508, 1473; in *nede* ~ *it be* it must 456; *nedes* ~ *hym* he must 1468; **most** must 4, 30, 3583. **mot** *pl.* must 4224. **mote** *impers.pa.t.sg.* in *vs* ~ we should 3192.

mot, mote see **mow**.

motes *n.pl.* dust particles 1531.

mot-halle *n.* court-room 3727.

moving *vbl.n.* prompting 1508. **movinges** *pl.* actions 4287.

movth-sede *n.* mouth-seed, preaching (spiritually nourishing instruction) 4226 *(unrecorded)*.

mow *v.* be able 4183; **mowe** 4252, 4409. *pr.pl.* may 604, 1404, 2504, 2530, 2604, 3304, 3704. **mot** *subj.pr.1 sg.* 4709. *2 sg.* 675, 700. *3 sg.* 2110, 2822, 3869. **mowing** *indic.pr.p.* being able 2688. **moght** *pa.t.sg.* could 291, 527, 696, 750, 762, 857, 864, 881, 886, 896, 902, 1144, 1257, 1291, 1341, 1945, 1947, 1949, 1951, 2093, 2419, 2508, 2668, 2670, 2911, 3376, 4467. **mote** *subj.pa.t.sg.* might 1321; may 2180. **moght** *indic.pa.t.pl.* could 56, 1849, 1898, 2133, 2232, 2313, 2592.

mowe *n.* grimace 4648. **mowes** *pl.* 4672.

murmure *n.* grumbling 3389.

murmure *v.* grumble 2295.

must *n.* new wine 3664.

musyd *pa.t.sg.* wondered at 3859.

myght *n.* in *at oure* ~ as far as we can 1536; *at his* ~ as far as he can 4928.

mykel *n.* much 4215.

mykel *adj.* much 3437, 3576, 3622, 4215, 4293, 4883, 4940, great 4879; **mikelle** much 3799; **mykell** 581.

mykel *adv.* much 2846, 3549, 3800; in *how* ~*...the more* the more 2283; *in so* ~ so 4017; *so* ~ the more, to the same extent 4318, 4320; **mikelle** much 3584; **mykelle** 2423, 2833, 3133; **mykell** 581, 2585; **mykil** 1117.

mynde *n.* intention 540, 738; memory 1808; attitude 2188; in *Haf...* ~ remember 1017, 1225; *made* ~ recorded 1247; ~ *makes* makes mention 1656; *toke...in* ~ intended 3348.

myrily *adv.* cheerfully 4261.

myrred *ppl.a.* mixed with myrrh 2797 *(MED cites only this text)*; **mirred** 4695; **mirrid** 2512; **myrrid** 3264.

myrye *adj.* happy 3759.

mysbegetyn *ppl.a.* ill-gotten 2800.

myschaunce *n.* evil 1666.

myscheif see **meschef**.

myscoveyting *vbl.n.* sinful craving 3920.

mysdid *pa.t.pl.* in ~ *(to)* sinned against 4028. **mysdoing** *ppl.a.* wicked 2945.

mysdoere *n.* criminal 2210, 2380; **misdoere** 4639. **misdoars** *pl.* criminals 2315; **misdoers** 2447.

mysese *n.* suffering 3581, 3835.

mysse *subj.pr.1 sg.* lack 4865.

mys-sittying *pr.p.* in ~ *(on)* defiling 1444.

mysvsing *pr.p.* deceiving 1234.

myte *n.* mite (a coin of very small value) 4293.

naknes *refl.pr.pl.* in ~ *thaym* show themselves naked 174. **naknyng** *pr.p.* in ~ *hym* showing himself naked 2716. **naknedde** *tr.pa.t.sg.* stripped naked 2394.

namely *adv.* particularly 4746.

natures *gen.* in *of* ~ *ordre* according to the laws of nature 1074; *above* ~ *vsage* supernaturally 1294.

nay *n.* in *this is no* ~ undoubtedly 2528; **naye** in *this is no* ~ 2216.

neckyng *vbl.n.* beating on the neck *[colaphorum]* 4604. **neckings** *pl. [colaphi]* 3257.

neddre *gen.* in ~ *brode* offspring of vipers 1449.

nedefulle *adj.* in need 3638; necessary 4037.

nedes *adv.* in ~...*most* must 30; ~ *mot hym* he must of necessity 1468.

nedes *impers.pr.3 sg.* in *hym* ~ it is necessary 454; he must 1418; *me* ~; I must 948; ~ *noght to doute (where)* there is no doubt about (whether or not) 4185.

nedesly *adv.* necessarily 508.

neeing *pr.p.* neighing *[fremebundus]* 1770.

negh *adj.* close, attentive 4157; close 4158.

negh *adv.* near 517, 1599, 2862, 2909, 3607, 4859; nearly 1612, 2584, 2920, 3419, 3937; nearby 2117, 5057; thoroughly, closely 4227.

neghande *adv.* almost 1942.

nemne *v.* name, give 2231.

nes see **bee**.

neuer *adv.* in ~ *the rathere* not at all 1516, 2842; ~ *the laccere* yet 2628; *to con* ~ *hoo* see **con**; **nevre** in ~ *the more* not at all 2664.

neven *v.* explain 232; describe 3604, 5104. **nevens** *pr.pl.* use, mention 3578.

newe *adv.* in ~ *and* ~ continually 595, 704, 2336, 4508; **new** in ~ *and* ~ again and again 179.

nhad see **has**.

ni *adv.* no 2626.

nice see **nyce**.

noblay *n.* dignity, ceremony 3686.

nones *n.* in *for the* ~ for the occasion 1482; expressly 2440; appropriately 2521.

norist *pa.t.sg.* nourished, nurtured 4989. **norisshid** *pp.* brought up, nurtured 1345. **norisshing** *vbl.n.* nourishment 2614.

Noster in *Pater* ~ see **Pater**.

nota Lat. *imp.* take note 329, 1419, 1543, 2263, 3441.

note *n.* sign, token 4279.

notes *pr.pl.* denote 3892. **notid** *pa.t.sg.* indicated 4207; **notide** denoted, indicated 1625. **noted** *pp.* 3755, 4255; **notid** denoted 4957.

nothing *adv.* not at all 364, 987, 1121, 1170, 1171, 1455, 1936, 2056, 2159, 2338, 2368, 2677, 3910, 4223, 4258; in no way 1209.

notyfied *pa.t.sg.* proclaimed 2262.

nuclee *n.* kernel 1079.

numelariens *n.pl.* money-changers 1759.

numularies *n.pl.* money-changers 1781n *(MED cites only this example)*.

nuyed *pa.t.sg.* in *to deth* ~ fatally injured 167.

nwold see **wold**.

nyce *adj.* foolish 2436, 3957; ingenious *[multa et raria]* 4038; **nice** foolish, frivolous 258, 410.

nygromancere *n.* sorcerer 4618.

nying *vbl.n.* denial 3252 *(MED cites only this example)*.

nys see **bee**.

o *num.* one *(often hard to distinguish from indef.art.)* 2, 207, 398, 425, 426, 478, 892, 952, 1033, 1527, 1846, 1930, 1934, 2294, 2356, 2580, 2603, 2879, 2895, 2931, 2935, 2993, 3115, 3500, 3543, 3678, 3732, 4136, 4141, 4160, 4254, 4297, 4355, 4359, 4868.

o *prep.* of 166; on 2148; in 2195.

o *indef.art. (often hard to distinguish from num.)* a 1122, 2117, 2181, 3867, 4286; a (certain) 2191, 2193

obeiant *adj.* obedient 1227.

obsessioune *n.* siege 2667.

obsidioune *n.* being besieged 2594, 2602, 4012, 4032 *(MED cites only this text)*.

obumbre *v.* cover 4602. **obumbred** *pa.t.sg.* cast shadow over 548.

occisioune *n.* in *tholid* ~ was slaughtered 2951.

occoours *n.* meeting 5259n.

of *prep.* by 1577, 1607, 2409, 2848, 2902, 2905, 3080, 3476, 3756, 4043, 4065, 5084; by means of 2069; over 2839, from 2857, 3092, 3286; for 2859, 4351; ? for the sake of 2931; on 3167; because of 3663; by (the hand of) 4068; in *condole (~)* see **condole**; *gyves the lakke (~)* see **lakke**; **off** by 2107.

of *adv.* off 2108, 3295, 3625, 3995, 4001.

of *prep.* because of 3663.

ofbraide *pa.t.sg.* cut off 219 *(MED cites only this example)*.

off see **of**.

oftsith *adv.* often 134, 179, 476, 543, 2045, 3508, 3711, 3972, 4524, 4907; **oftsithe** 1541, 1589, 1680, 2077, 3747; **oftsyth** 179.

olyve *adj.* living 342, 352, 495, 2469; alive 514, 2993.

on see **one**.

on *indef.art.* a(n) 867, 4172.

on *pron.* one (who was) 3989.

on *prep.* in the matter of 283; in 1896, 2092, 2745, 3059, 4243; at 2646; in (the lifetime of) 2647n; over 3288, 3989, into 4061; against 2419, 3288, 4234, 4681; in ~ *tyme* once 1899.

one *num.* only 304, 2576; alone 1935; in *alle* ~ 970, 2355, 4135; **on** one 131, 1899; **oone** only 2393, 2491, 2881, 2900; in *in* ~ constant 3881; **oon** only 2479; alone 3243.

onene *adv.* in ~ *þat* as soon as 1049 *(MED cites only this example)*.

onone *adv.* at once 80, 1144, 1308, 1464, 1937, 2109, 2233

open *adj.* plain 3801.

openly *adv.* plainly 186, 2521, 3002, 3509, 3670, 3684, 3736, 3756, 4019.

or *adv.*[1] now 1177, 1181

or *adv.*[2] before 3446, 3609.

ostendid *pa.t.sg.* showed 4166. **ostendit** *refl.* 3508. **ostendid** *tr.pp.* 3516.

other, othere, oȝer see **ovthere**.

othere *adv.* either 1592.

othire see **ovthere**.

ouer *prep.* more than 178, 1222; moreover *[ultra]* 793; in addition 850; surpassing 1098; beyond 1840, 2252, 2308, 2358, 3753, 4484, 4675; above 2813, 3578; in excess of 3928; in ~ *the gravell* more often than (there are grains in) the sand 93; *? prep.* in *for ~fayne* on account of (his) extreme happiness 1684; **ovre** in addition 1220, 2744; in ~ *and ouer* over and again 548; *bright* ~ brighter than 588; **ouere** above 970, 1615; in ~ *mesure* too long 4951.

ouer- *prefix* too.

ouergone *pp.* run over 282.

ouerlyve *subj.pr.3 sg.* should survive 1425. **ouerlyved** *pa.t.sg.* survived 3807.

ouertake *v.* overcome 2247.

ouertrw *intr.pa.t.pl.* collapsed 75.

oute *interj.* a curse on 1909; **out** in ~ *o* curse 2148.

outrage *n.* violence 1649.

outrageously *adv.* excessively 3173.

over *adj.* in ~ *half* upstream of 1477.

ovre see **ouer**.

ovthere *pron.sg.* either 2570; **oythere** each (side) 3411. **othere** *pl.* others 20, 401, 477, 588, 891, 894, 1739, 2492, 2942, 4041, 4194, 4470, 4746, 4948; **oþer** 796, 978, 999, 1096, 1388, 3022; **other** 282, 4469; **oythere** 2869; all 4184; **othire** others 816.

paas see **pas**.

pairatour *n.* attendant 2039.

palle *n.* robe 3226, 3229.

parcelles *n.pl.* separate parts 4332.

parcenere *n.* sharer 1004.

part *v.* share 660; settle (an argument) 1353.

parte *n.* side 1187; in *ware at thi* ~ make it your responsibility to be on your guard 364n.

partye *n.* part 1720; side, section 4683; **party** 3270.

pas *n.* section 1005, 1306; **paas** 360.

passage *n.* crossing 1469.

passible *adj.* capable of suffering 4313.

passis *imp.pl.* come 4490. **passing** *ppl.a.* surpassing 2581.

Pater Lat. *n.* in ~ *Noster* Our Father 4297.

patible *n.* cross-bar 4149.

patrine *n. (? form of* **patroun***)* founder *[pater]* 3950.

payed *pa.t.sg.* pleased 4017. *pp.* satisfied 4218.

payen *n.* pagan 1455; **payens** *pl.* 127, 1086, 2397, 2401, 3500, 4226. *gen.pl.* pagans' 1136, 3981.

payen *adj.* pagan *[paganus]* 2671, 3427

payentee *n.* paganism 2266, 2268, 2269 *(MED cites only this example).*

pees *v.* appease 4032. **peesid** *pa.t.sg.* appeased 4034; **pesid** 3956.

peple *n.* in *hoege* ~ a vast number of people 1950.

per Lat. *prep.* by means of 3825.

perauntre *adv.* perhaps 933.

perdurable *adj.* everlasting 4377, 4410.

perexcellently *adv.* very greatly 2675 *(MED cites only this example).*

perre *n.* jewellery 1329.

pesid see **pees**.

phares from Aramaic *n.* half-mina (a measure of money) 275, 4281n, 4299.

pie *adj.* merciful 703, *(according to the gloss)* 793, 1690, 1910, 3390, 4869, 4895, 4947, 5077; compassionate 4725 *(MED cites only 793, 1690)*; **pye** compassionate 2986; merciful 3379. **piest** *sup.* most merciful 4247, 4551, 5103; **pyest** 95.

piely *adv.* mercifully 2594; compassionately 3712; **pyely** mercifully 2602.

pierd *pa.t.sg.* appeared 3875.

pike *v.* in ~ *out (pride)* build up...pride 627.

pikke *n.* pitch 1571.

placable *adj.* pleasing 730, 2091.

planed *pa.t.sg.* levelled 2339.

plantacioune *n.* planting 1075.

pleigne see **pleygne**.

plener *adj.* complete 1452. **plenere** *comp.* 27.

plenerly *adv.* in entirety 1269.

plesance see **plesaunce**.

plesantlye *adv.* in a manner pleasing (to him) 1751; **plesantly** in a manner pleasing (to me) *[mihi gratius et acceptius]* 4519; **plesauntly** 4991.

plesaunce *n.* pleasure 3557, 4270; **plesance** 5, in *to thi* ~ at your will 4553.

pleses *intr.pr.3 sg.* is agreeable 1170, 4717. **plesed** *tr.pa.t.sg.* made agreeable 254.

pleygne *v.* complain 4237; in ~*...on* complain against 2209; **pleyne** complain of 4851; in ~ *(on)* complain against 4234. **pleigne** *imp.* 2969. **pleygnyng** *pr.p.* lamenting 4523. **pleyned** *pa.t.sg.* lamented 2521, 2940. **pleynyng** *vbl.n.* lamentation 4879.

pleyne *adj.* full. **pleynere** *comp.* more fully 232.

plight *n.* guilt 4605; **plite** situation 3181.

poaire *n.* power *[potentiam]* 2960.

point *n.* moment 426, 4439[1,2]; in *no* ~ not at all 418; *to no* ~ in no way 2294; *to* ~ suitably, fittingly *[digne]* 4548; **poynt** moment 372; in *o* ~ even one small part 2580.

polyt *ppl.a.* burnished 1499.

pooretee *n.* poverty 3927.

posteritee *n.* descendants 750.

postle *n.* the apostle 4363. **posteles** *pl.* apostles 1175.

potenciale *adj.* potential 5038.

pourge see **purge**.

pourpre see **purpre**.

poustee *n.* power 558, 864, 1018, 1048, 1895, 2360; authority 1099, 2038.

poynt see **point**.

prechoure, **prechours** see **frere**.

preciously *adv.* richly 734; as a thing of value 4959; **preciouselye** at great cost 724.

predicacioune *n.* preaching 1678.

prefiguraunce *n.* prefiguration 2253 *(MED cites only this example)*.

premonstracioune *n.* foreshadowing 44.

prenuncyd *pa.t.sg.* foretold 936 *(OED records only one example, A.D.1580)*.

preostende *v.* reveal beforehand 543. **preostendid** *pa.t.sg.* 3359, 3369, 4961. *pp.* 4114.

presenting *n.* presentation 1206.

presently *adv.* in person 2766.

presseur *n.* wine-press 2474, 2486; **pressoure** 4135.

prest *adj.* ready *[praesto]* 1622, 1743.

pretendid *pa.t.sg.* foreshadowed 4987; proclaimed in advance 5034.

preuaricatrice *n.* female transgressor 1212 *(OED cites only this example)*.

prevenant *adj.* preceding (human action) *[praevenientem]* 1685 *(MED, OED do not record this example)*.

price *n.* value 2531.

pricked *pa.t.sg.* urged 2434.

prikke *n.* goad, stimulus 2435; in *to the* ~ exactly 4292.

primogenit *n.* first-born 3457.

prince *n.* leader 3283, 4020. **princes** *pl.* 4587.

pris *n.* reward 3195, 3926; proceeds, payment 3428; in *for* ~ *of witte* to show off intelligence 389; **prise** praise 801, 2778.

prisefulle *adj.* brave 4059.

priuest *sup.* most private 4249.

priuytee *n.* in *in* ~ covertly 2764; **pryuitee** 2115.

prively *adv.* unobtrusively 948, secretly 1340.

processe *n.* in *be* ~ in turn 1032; ~ *of tyme* in the course of time 2991.

prodegate *adj.* prodigal 1661.

profited *intr.pa.t.sg.* improved, benefited from 778.

promissioune in *land(e) of* ~ see **land**.

prophetic *adj.* prophetic (carried out in order to make Christ identify his tormentors by 'prophecy') 3258 *(unrecorded in this sense)*.

propice *adj.* well-disposed 3951, 4245.

proponyng *pr.p.* setting forth 4207.

propre *adj.* inherent 3147; particular, distinctive 3484.

propugnatoure *n.* champion 1297.

propugnatrice *n.* female champion 3274, 4100.

propugnys *pr.3 sg.* fights (on behalf of) 4058.

protestacioune *n.* affirmation 3268.

provde *adj.* proud 4069.

prove *n.* proof 25.

prove *v.* 4119. **proves** *pr.3 sg.* 658, 2783, 3941. *pr.pl.* 2791. **proues** *intr. for refl.pr.3 sg.* shows itself 3801. **prove** *pr.pl.* 2789. **proved** *pp.* found 829, 2781, 2785, 2795, 2867.

pryuitee see **priuytee**.

pryvid *pp.* deprived 2878.

puerpure *adj.* fruitful, child-bearing 5002 *(OED cites only this example)*.

purge *v.* purify 3380; **pourge** 1758. **purged** *pp.* 3076.

purpre *n.* purple garment 2437; **pourpre** a purple robe 2314, purple 2325.

purveide *pa.t.sg.* arranged beforehand 2658.

putte *v.* in ~ *it in delay* 3312. *pa.t.sg.* in ~ *hire azeinst* resisted 3222 in ~ *it...til assay* 3480.

pye, pyest see **pie**.

pyely see **piely**.

pyment *n.* a drink (composed of wine sweetened with honey and flavoured with spices) 2049.

pynously *adv.* painfully 2900, 3728, 4650, 4728.

quadragenaries *n.pl.* sets of forty (lashes) 4360n.

quod *pa.t.sg.* said 2467, 2874, 3613, 4067, 4135, 4522, 4931; **qvodh** 2209.

qvhikke see **qwhikke**.

qvite see **qwite**.

qwall *n.* whale 229.

qwelle *v.* kill 2385.

qwellere *n.* killer 3290.

qweme *adj.* beautiful 2908.

qwhikke *adj.* alive 744, 1938, 4363; living 2534, 5059; **qvhikke** live 1353; alive 1500.

qwite *n.* white 4623.

qwite *v.* release 1366, 3472; **qvite** 2686; **qwyte** cease to enjoy 4550; **qwiit** release 2414; **qwhite** rid 3176; **qwhitte** release 2638. **qwitte** *pa.t.sg.* liberated 3996; delivered 4095; **qwhit** 2418. *pp.* 3306; **qwite** freed 1048.

qwitte *adj.* free 1525, 4737; in *be* ~ get off 4141; **qwite** released 1038, 1052; **qwhit** 3102; **qwhite** in *gyven out of synne dedely ~ [sine mortalibus largitum]* as long as you are free of mortal sin 4295.

radyouse *adj.* radiant 1276 *(OED records this only A.D.1500ff)*; **radiouse** 5026.

raft see **ref**.

raght *pa.t.sg.* received 3576.

ransoune *n.* in *make my*~ransom me 3343; **reaunceoune** in *mans*~*for to make* to ransom man 2574.

rathere *adj.* earlier 4214.

rathere *adv.* more quickly 1552; in *neuer the*~not in any way by this 1516, 2842; **rather** more quickly 326.

ravist *ppl.a.* enraptured 4472.

ravynne *n.* voracity 1596. **ravynes** *pl.* robberies 2768.

real *adj.* royal 1193, 1893, 4645; **realle** 1891, 2680, 2688; **reale** 5037, 5052.

reaunceoune see **ransoune**.

reclamed *pa.t.sg.* tamed (as a flying bird of prey is recalled by a lure) 5086.

recoreding *vbl.n.* repetition, recollection *[recordationem]* 1202.

recounsaille *v.* reunite in harmony 2464; **recounseil** absolve 4170.

rede *n.* advice 4001.

rede *pr.1 sg.* advise 2301, 3401.

rede *pr.pl.* read *[legamus]* 4735.

redoling *ppl.a.* fragrant 562 *(OED cites only this example)*.

ref *v.* plunder 2772; take away 3112; **refe** 1018. **reving** *pr.p.* carrying off 1596. **raft** *pa.t.sg.* took away 2366. **reft** *pp.* taken 558.

refeccioune *n.* refreshment 3082, 3084.

refourmed *pa.t.sg.* restored 312; made good 3530. **refourmyng** *vbl.n.* re-establishing 2397.

refourmour *n.* restorer 3522.

refrigery *n.* cooling, consolation 3069.

reft see **ref**.

refuse *v.* reject 1694. **refused** *pp.* 1299.

regalye *n.* royalty, kingship 2314, 2325, 2327; **regalie** 5039.

regarde *n.* in *in*~*of* with a view to 3588; in comparison with 3592.

regne *n.* rule, kingdom 272, 1584, 1612, 1646, 1885, 3586, 3616, 4199, 4453, 4684, 5108, 5126.

reherce *v.* recite 778. *pr.pl.* enumerate 1746.; **reherced** *pp.* described 22, 1761.

rehersaillies *n.pl.* re-statements 4250.

rekken *v.* work out 820. **rekkes** *pr.3 sg.* cares 1648. **reknyd** *pa.t.sg.* valued 3753. **reknyng** *vbl.n.* in *in*~when counted 2851; an account 4214, 4933.

roght *intr.pa.t.sg.* thought 3549.

relese *v.* forgive 1054, 1622. *imp.* 1022. **relessant** *pr.p.* forgiving 1686. **relesed** *pa.t.sg.* forgave 2987.

religious *adj.* belonging to the Order *[in ordine]* 4719.

remembre *pr.pl.* recall 289. **remembrid** *pp.* 3329.

remnaunt *adj.* remaining *(? n.* the remainder*)* 3764.

remocioune *n.* departure, separation 278.

remyttyng *pr.p.* in ~ *the* referring back your case 4625.

renne *v.* in ~ *to forgetyng* be forgotten 3634.

repaire *n.* in *have* ~ have resort 732.

repaire *v.* return 1702; **repare** in *make* ~ cause to return *[reduxerunt]* 528; **repayre** return 395. **repaired** *pa.t.sg.* returned 1395, 2684; **repayrid** 3451.

reparing *vbl.n.* rectification 308.

repentantz *n.pl.* penitents 1622, 1623.

replecioune *n.* habit of excess 661.

reproef *n.* insult 2130; **reprove** 4572; disgrace 4668. **reproves** *pl.* insults 2145, 2376, 3257; **reprowes** 128.

reproves *pr.pl.* condemn 745. **reproved** *pa.t.sg.* condemned 2167; rejected 3496. *pp.* found fault with *[incusandum]* 822; rejected 3489;. **reprovid** rejected 3476. **reproved** *ppl.a.* 230, 3484, 3493.

rescoving *pr.p.* rescuing 1597. **rescowde** *pp.* having been rescued 3367.

resed *pp.* in *on...*~ attacked 381.

residiving see **resydiving**.

resonably *adv.* with good reason 1244, 3001, 3889, 4175, 5117.

resoune *n.* a reckoning 272; intelligence 492; point, argument 1664; in *be* ~ properly; in accordance with rational behaviour 2171; logically 2853, 3767; with reason 2877; properly 4031; indeed 4887; in *gives* ~ demonstrates 3679; *open* ~ obviously 3801.

responsioune *n.* reply 4621.

restid *pa.t.sg.* remained 4995.

restoraunce *n.* restoration 2652n.

restore *v.* make up for 316; make amends for 507. **restorid** *pp.* restored 1068n.

resydiving *vbl.n.* relapsing 3399; **residiving** 3402.

resydyuaunt *adj.* relapsing into sin 2746.

retribucioune *n.* recompense 3198.

rette *pp.* seen, appraised *[aestimari]* 943.

reuthfulle *adj.* lamentable 1042.

reving see **ref**.

revme *n.* realm 548, 2241, 3754; **rewme** 3934, 4210, 4213. **revmes** *pl.* 3754.

revokes *pr.3 sg.* recalls 1623. **revokide** *pp.* 1626.

revthfulle see **rewthfulle**.

rewe *v.* pity, show compassion 194, 536, 1267, 1719, 1724, 2056; lament 2934; in ~*(on)*, ~*(ouer)* take pity on 536, 1267, 1721. **rewes** *pr.3 sg.* 632. **rewed** *pa.t.sg.* 529. *pl.* 2916.

rewfulle *adj.* pitiful 4653.

rewme see **revme**.

rewthfulle *adj.* full of pity 2806, 2924; **revthfulle** pitiful, compassionate 2926.

rewthlesse *adj.* without pity 2930.

ribavdes *n.pl.* licentious entertainers 173.

right *n.* in *be* ~ rightly 429, 467; justly 2320; **ryȝt** in *be* ~ with reason 30.

right *adj.* righteous 1015; true 1864.

right *adv.* exactly *[tag]* 580; appropriately 1687; in ~ *so* in just the same way 1164, 1473, 2173, 2195, 2717, 3164, 3299, 3337, 3384, 3620, 3689, 3852; in such a way *[ita]* 2803; *anone* ~ at once 2233; ~ *nouht/nothing* at all, whatever 1628, 3587, 3822; **ryght** true 36; just, exactly 216; in ~ *so* in just the same way 1121, 1138, 2282, 4263; *be* ~ justly 2232.

rist *n.* rest 4882, 4996.

rist *v.* rest 611.

rode *n.* Cross 2799, 2984, 3502; in ~ *tree* Cross 147; cross 2412; **rude** Cross 2836. **rodes** *gen.* in ~ *tree* the Cross 488.

roght see **rekkes**.

rounde *n.* in *to the* ~ fully 3600.

rounde *adj.* sound 486.

rout *n.* gathering 4568; **rovte** group 4598; **rowte** troop 1929.

rude see **rode**.

ruggid *pa.t.pl.* forcibly pulled 2519.

ruthfully *adv.* piteously 151.

ruyde *adj.* rough 5129.

rynne *v.intr.* run from 1672.

ryst *n.* peace 642.

sacles see **sakles**.

sacre *v.* consecrate 1902; sanctify 3134. **sacred** *ppl.a.* consecrated, sacred 2047, 3569.

sadde *adj.* steadfast 956.

sakles *adj.* undeserved 2078; innocent 2454, 4847; **sacles** undeserved 2946; **sakkelesse** innocent 2086; **saklesse** 2050. **saklest** *sup.* most innocent 1300.

salutere *n.* (agent of) salvation 1402, 4979.

salutere *adj.* beneficial, health-giving *[salubris]* 736n; salutary 4228, 4546; **saluter** beneficial, salutary 1248 *(OED cites this as the earliest example)*.

samne *adv.* together (with them) 1337; together 3486; **samen** 3237.

sangvinolent *adj.* blood-stained 4131.

sanz in ~ *faille* see **faille**.

sapience *n.* wisdom 670.

sat see **sittyng**.

satisfaccioune *n.* atonement for sin 1748, 3075, 3396.

satisfye *v.* atone 2790.

sauf *quasi-prep.* except 740.

sauf *adj.* safe 1011, 1088, 3401, 4988; in *vouching* ~ deigning 3066; *vouche(d)/vouchid* ~ deign(ed) 2047, 2103, 3134; *vouche* ~ deign 3380; **saufe** in *vouche* ~ deign 3103.

sauf *v.* save 2069.

sauourde see **sauoured**.

sauoure *n.* delight 1843; **savour** scent 617; taste 3567.

sauoured *pa.t.sg.* was of interest 912; **sauourde** tasted 1839. **sauouryng** *vbl.n.* delight 1840.

sauvable *adj.* conducive to salvation 826 *(OED cites only a doubtful example of A.D.1708)*.

savtere *n.* volume of psalms 4298.

sawe *n.*[1] in ~ *of tree* tree-saw 156, 1632, 2565. **sawes** *pl.* 281, 4386.

sawe *n.*[2] account 3009. **sawes** *pl.* sayings 3276.

sawe *v.* sow 2786.

sawen see **suwe**.

say *imp.* say *[dicendum est]* 1142.

science *n.* knowledge 638, 641; **sciens** 236; **scionce** 4446.

scorne *n.* mockery 2106, 2169, 2174, 2183, 2192, 2224, 2326, 2332, 2350, 4623, 4648; **scorn** 3725. **scornes** *pl.* 283, 2712.

scorne *v.* mock 2713, 2729, 2730, 4855. **scorneyng** *pr.pl.* 2708. **scornyng** *pr.p.* 4393, 4624. **scornyd** *pa.t.sg.* 2175, 2177, 2179, 2710, 4391; **scorned** 121, 170. *pl.* 2185, 2188, 2706, 2717, 4261, 4672. *pp.* 118, 132, 2181, 2205, 2207, 3227, 4612; **scornyd** 2175, 2177, 2179, 4911. **scornyng** *vbl.n.* 2139, 3226. **scornyngs** *pl.* 4697.

scorners *n.pl.* mockers 4393, 4395.

scoure *v.* flog, scourge 1800.

scournfully *adv.* in mockery 2324.

scovrynge *vbl.n.* beating 1680.

scripsione *n.* the writing 275.

scripture *n.* writing 2198, 4279.

seghen *pp.* (having been) seen 649, 650; seen 1370; **seighen** (having been) seen 2733.

seint *adj.* holy 831, 920, 1006, 1824, 1827, 2563, 3133, 3217, 3404, 3774, 3844, 4097.

seke *adj.* sick 2036, 2085, 4652. *adj. as n.* the sick 1267.

sekerly *adv.* truly 3847.

sekke *n.* sackcloth 450.

seled *ppl.a.* closed with a cover and sealed (against unauthorised use) 31, *[signato id est sigillato]* 572.

self *pron.adj.* in *vs* ~ ourselves 1540; ~ *fire* fire itself 3041.

sely *adj.* blessed 752, 5082, 5108. **selyere** *comp.* more blessed 752.

semblable *adj.* similar 2398.

semblably *adv.* similarly 2519, 4176.

sempiterne *adj.* everlasting 4501.

sempiternely *adv.* everlastingly 4302.

semyng *vbl.n.* seaming 3225.

sen *conj.* since 363, 929, 1270.

sensuel *adj.* sensory 3366 *(the earliest example in OED)*; **sensuele** 3023.

sentence *n.* opinion 2649.

sepulture *n.* entombment 193, 2971, 2997, 3003; tomb 3407.

sere *adj.* various 2816, 3044; separate 2849, 3655.

sergeantz *n.pl.* officers 4095.

seruage *n.* servitude 1356.

sese *v.* in *vs of the* ~ give you to us *[te nobis destinavit]* 565.

sethim *n.* shittah-tree, acacia 1251; **sethym** 4957, in *tree of* ~ shittah-tree, acacia 497. *as adj.* 3845.

sett *v.* in ~ *at noght* disregard 2624. *intr.* in *to* ~ to be set 3485. **settyng** *tr.pr.p.* in *at right noght* ~ setting no store by 1628, 4644. **sett** *pa.t.sg.* in ~*...at noght/nothing* disregarded 411, 3822; **sette** in ~ *bot shorte* thought very little of 2246. *pp.* determined, estimated 2124; devoted 3909.

seur *adj.* safe 3028.

seven *adj.* seventh 4499.

sewe *pa.t.sg.* sowed 4225, 4226n.

shape *subj.pr.pl.* let us endeavour 458. **shope** *pa.t.sg.* made 405. *refl.* in *hire* ~ prepared, set herself 759.

shappe *n.* excellence of form *[decor]* 4433.

share see **shere**.

shedde *pa.t.sg.* spilled 1759.

sheende *v.* destroy 4070. **shent** *pp.* destroyed 379; defiled 2394; in *make...to be* ~ destroy 317.

shene *adj.* beautiful, bright 802, 1152.

shere *imp.* cut, slash 2949. **share** *pa.t.sg.* cut, slashed 2839, 2840.

sherers *n.pl.* reapers 3078.

shete *n.* winding-sheet 428.

shoce *n.pl.* shoes 2341.

shope see **shape**.

shorne *pp.* cut 1383, 5007.

short *adj.* in *toke bot* ~ *hede by* paid little attention to 1788.

shorte in *sette bot* ~ see **sett**.

shortly *adv.* briefly 403; **shorttely** 710.

shourging *vbl.n.* scourging 1761.

showed *pa.t.sg.* thrust 3178.

shrewe *n.* wicked man 3963.

shrewed *adj.* depraved, evil 1663; sharp, rough 1777n.

shrift *n.* confession 1746, 3561.

shrikyng *vbl.n.* outcry 4881.

shroude *n.* clothing 1592.

shroude *v.* clothe 1752.

shwed *pp.* revealed 250.

signed see **signyng**.

signifiant *pr.p.* signifying 1258. **signifying** *vbl.n.* signification 1513, 2608.

signyng *pr.p.* signifying 1832. **signed** *pa.t.sg.* signified 46, 981, 1136.

singulere *adj.* sole 590; unique *(?* + solitary*)* 879; *[singularis]* 5017.

sith *conj.* since 625, 1523, 2094, 2374, 2845, 2931,.

sithe *n.pl.* many times 1457; **sithes** times 4606.

sithen *conj.* since 412, 457, 1200, 2888, 4360

sittingly *adv.* rightly, correctly, 3499.

sittyng *ppl.a.* suitable 1192. **sat** *impers.pa.t.sg.* in *hire* ~ *noght* it was not fitting that she 812. *intr.pa.t.pl.* knelt 4647.

skeppette *n.* basket 1342 *(the earliest example in OED).*

skille *n.* cause 2973, 4849; in *no* ~ unjust 846; *be the same* ~ by the same token 1272, 1418, 1427; *be* ~ justly, logically 1353; by rights 1535.

skippe *n.* leap 5094.

slade see **slide**.

slathe see **slithing**.

sleghly *adv.* cunningly, secretly 1787, 1792, 2774, 3163; **slely** 322.

sleght *n.* cunning, strategy 318. **sleghtes** *pl.* 1234; **sleghtis** 1236, 1931, 4036.

sleuth *n.* in *with* ~ idly 4298.

slew *pa.t.sg.* struck 3294.

slide *v.* in *to* ~ *ouer* to be ignored 1441. **slade** *pa.t.sg.* fell 1252, 1498, 3846.

slike *adj.* such 1155.

slithing *ppl.a.* (sliding) transient, unstable 457. **slathe** *pa.t.sg.* in *doun* ~ crashed down [*est illisus*] 1378n.

slwe *pa.t.sg.* killed 90.

smalle *adj.* fine 1390, 1757; little 2044.

smelle *n.* scent, aroma 633, 899, 2503; the sense of smell 4415.

smert *n.* pain 2275, 4724.

smert *adj.* painful 2927.

smertid *impers.pa.t.sg.* in *hyn* ~ he was in pain 1681.

smyte *v.* strike 892.

so *adv.* in ~ *forth* next 368; in *als* ~ see **als**; *what* ~ see **what**.

soeffrance *n.* forbearance, suffering 1910.

soeffre *v.refl.* allow 2674. **soeffre** *tr.* 2890. **soeffres** *pr.3 sg.* allows 3199. **suffring** *pr.p.* tolerating 1232. **suffred** *pa.t.sg.* allowed 2597, 3823; **soeffred** 2672, 2900; **soeffrid** 1952. **soeffred** *refl.* 2191. **suffred** *tr.pp.* 4858.

soelle *adj.* alone, solitary 326.

softnesse *n.* comfort 1679.

soght *pa.t.sg.* searched 3758; in ~ *to* sought out 5090.

sokke *n.* share (of a plough) 109.

some in *alle and* ~ see **alle**.

sometyme *adv.* once 45, 78, 250, 423, 470, 471, 510, 511, 569, 760, 783, 936, 960, 1027, 1290, 1453, 1514, 1578, 1618, 1625, 1687, 1713, 1726, 1762, 1948, 2158, 2186, 2272, 2362, 2582, 2747, 2847, 2871, 2938, 3095, 3135, 3143, 3171, 3275, 3281, 3330, 3476, 3570, 3668, 3686, 3744, 3837, 3973, 4187, 4336, 4513, 5037, 5109, 5113; **somtyme** 203, 2170; **sometym** 3516.

sometymes *adv.* at one time 2537, 3141, 3153, 3675, 3988, 4719.

somme in *alle and* ~ see **alle**.

somwhatte *adv.* to some extent 334.

sonde *n.* messenger 1337.

sonne *n.* sun *[soli]* 724, *[solis]* 726.

sonnysshe *adj.* radiant 3877.

sonovse *adj.* sonorous *[sonora]* 3652 *(OED cites only this example)*.

sore *n.* pain 3389.

sore *adj.* serious, painful 516, 524, 2118, 2274, 2284, 2703, 2986, 3317. **sorest** *sup.* most severe 3263.

sore *adv.* painfully 102, 125, 126, 1681, 2153, 2206, 4566; seriously 513, 516; intensely 751, 1546, 2274, 2346, 2916, 2934, 3483; hard 3547, 3731; strongly 4012; severely 3794, 4393, 4396.

soth *n.* truth 345 *(? adj.* true*)*, 719, 1524, 2257, 2258, 3851; **sothe** 22, 23, 2510, 3546.

soth *adj.* true 345 *(? n.* truth*)*, 2094.

sothen *pp.* boiled 1562, 1873.

sothfast *adj.* true 2671; truthful 4592.

sothfastly *adv.* truly 1817, 2547, 3587, 4532, 4960.

sothfastnesse *n.* truth 1010, 1617, 1822, 3346, 3575, 3641, 3692, 3699, 3911; **sothfastnes** 25, 2081.

sothly *adv.* truly, indeed 895, 934, 1652, 1737, 2610, 2837, 2844, 3074, 3214, 3278, 3374, 3426, 3812, 3854, 4254, 4276, 4431, 4476, 4558, 4584, 4610, 4662, 4688, 4939; **sothlye** 3824.

sothnesse *n.* truth 1698.

souereyn *adj.* supreme, powerful 875, 4583, 4609, 4661, 5082; **souerayne** 561, 1274, 3814, 5012; **souereyne** 3, 5027, 5105, 5127; **souerayn** 3582; **souerein** 1078.

souereynes *gen.* in ~ *bisshops* Lord Bishop's *[summo pontifice]* 1775n.

souereynly *adv.* supremely 3790, 4194.

souleyn *adj.* modest 789; **souleine** unique, singular 1072.

soume *n.* total 2307, 3959, 4332; in *in o* ~ all together 4355; **sovme** in *in a* ~ all together 4365; **sovmme** 2866.

soune *n.* sound 2540, 2541, 2958; **sovne** 1611.

souping *vbl.n.* supper 1806.

sovme, sovmme see **soume**.

sovre *adj.* sore 378.

soure *adj.* bitter 2738; **sovre** sour 430.

space *n.* time 1139.

spare *imp.* stint, be frugal 222.

speciouse *adj.* beautiful 714; **specious** pleasing, attractive 4026.

spede *v.* give success 8.

spedefulle *adj.* expedient 2248; beneficial 3637.

spedy *adj.* helpful *[expedire]* 3324.

spered *ppl.a.* locked, barred 686.

sperid *pa.t.sg.* asked 549. **spird** *pl.* 1321; **spired** 1314.

spices *n.pl.* kinds, attributes 1801n.

spoillid *pp.* having been despoiled (of the souls of those in Limbo) 3451. **spoilled** *ppl.a.* robbed, deprived 523, 2438. **spoilling** *vbl.n.* robbing 1779.

sporne *ppl.a.* shut 678.

sposailles *gen.* marriage's 946.

spouse *n.* marriage 907, 996.

spousing *vbl.n.* marriage 806; **spovsing** 855.

spye *v.* observe stealthily 913.

stede *n.* place 413, 1773, 1918, 2137, 2456, 2699, 3031, 3043, 3416, 3479, 3487, 3501, 3613, 3713, 3715, 3729, 4561, 4644. **stedes** *pl.* places 3708, 3738, 3777, 4907, 4913; **stedis** 3009.

stede *n.* mount 4143.

stegh *v.* ascend 231. **stegh** *pa.t.sg.* ascended 3514, 3556, 3736.

stends *refl.pr.3 sg.* in ~ *it* takes its course, extends 3826. **stendid** *tr.pp.* extended, stretched 2720.

stereneste *sup.* most fierce 5084.

sterevid *pa.t.sg.* died 757.

sterne *n.* star 581, 588, 593, 595, 598, 601, 603, 936, 1108, 1109, 5025. **sternes** *pl.* 1277, 3591.

sterre *n.* star 32, 35, 68. **sterres** *pl.* stars 3889; **sterris** 3886

stifly *adv.* strongly 2539, 4231.

stikt see **styked**.

stil *adv.* always 776; **stille** in *dwelt* ~ remained 1570.

stokke *n.* vertical beam 3552. **stokkes** *pl.* sticks, lumps of wood 136, 2377.

stole *n.* robe 986.

stone *n.* rock 3422. **stones** *n.pl.* rocks 2958, 3269. **stone** *n. as adv.* in ~ *naked* stark naked 2344, 4117.

storke *pa.t.sg.* struck 208.

stoure *n.* battle 4118, 4569.

stout in *bere hym* ~ see **bere**.

strainege *adj.* in ~ *man* stranger 2821.

strange see **straunge**.

strangely *adv.* severely 4385; greatly 4470.

strangled *pp.* suppressed, destroyed 2448; **stranglid** 3136.

straunge *adj.* remarkable 2219; in ~ *(to)* removed from 4251; **strahge** great *[grande]* 3684n, 4977n.

streit *adv.* strict 4206, 4255, *(? adv.* closely*)* 2668.

streitestly *adv.* as tightly as possible 4727.

streitly *adv.* strictly 4227; **streytly** 4291.

strenghfulle *adj.* powerful 2561.

streynyng *pr.p.* clasping 5015.

stronge-armed *adj. as n.* the strongly-armed one *[fortis armatus]* 3109.

strongere *comp.absol.* in *his* ~ his superior in strength 3111.

struccioune *n.* ostrich 3095, 3097, 3100; **struttioune** 203; **strucioune** 5295.

struyed *pa.t.sg.* destroyed 228.

study *v.* try 446. **studies** *pr.3 sg.* 889, 2319. **studie** *subj.pr.3 sg.* in ~ *he* let him learn 3558. **studied** *pa.t.sg.* considered, thought 3175.

stulth *n.* theft 4083n.

stupour *n.* admiring wonder 3662.

sturdy *adj.* intractable, ruthless 4088.

sturdynesse *n.* rebelliousness 3957.

styked *pa.t.sg.* transfixed 210. **stikt** *ppl.a.* 4364.

suave *adj.* pleasing 5017 *(OED records no example earlier than A.D.1501).* **suavest** *sup.* 4897.

suavitee *n.* pleasurableness 4416.

subiugat *ppl.a.* subject, submissive 5096.

subostending *pr.p.* secretly revealing (to those who understand) 2228 *(not in OED).*

substanciel *adj.* having a real existence (by virtue of its divine 'substance' as opposed to its material 'accidents' of appearance) 1816.

substaunce *n.* divine nature 2, 4304; means 1658, 1665, 4868.

subuersioune *n.* overthrow, destruction 3370.

subvencioune *n.* relief *[subventionem]* 2668 *(OED records no example before A.D.1535).*

succedent *adj.* following, succeeding 1034 *(the earliest example in OED).*

succincte *ppl.a.* girded (ready to travel) 1862 *(OED records no example before A.D.1604).*

succurable *adj.* affording succour 3946.

sucrish *adj.* sweet 265, 2053 *(OED records only these two examples and one of A.D.1857).*

sufferane *adj.* supreme 180.

suffice *v.intr.* be adequate 4547; **suffise** 2198; **suffize** 3376, 4542. **suffices** *pr.3 sg.* 3030; **suffises** 1023. **suffizes** *impers.pr.3 sg.* in *hym* ~ *noght* is not enough 1425. **suffize** *intr.subj.pr.3 sg.* may be adequate 4949. **suffized** *pa.t.sg.* was adequate 492, 3750; **sufficed** 2580. **suffized** *impers.* in ~ *(...) noght* was not enough for 2279, 2311, 2707, 2713. *intr.pa.t.pl.* in *Thai* ~ *noght of* they would not have been adequate for 3598.

suffrages *n.pl.* prayers (for the dead) 3316, 3322.

suffred, **suffring** see **soeffre**.

sugits *n.pl.* subjects 2675.

superne *adj.* celestial 1274.

supersuffrable *adj.* long-suffering in the highest degree 4627.

suppetyng *ppl.a.* satisfying *[suffiens]* 4415n *(not in OED).*

suspensil *adj.* hanging, on a roof *(perhaps with connotations of contemplation, cf. OED* suspense *adj.)* 49; **suspensile** *[suspensus]* 760.

sutiltee *n.* the capacity (possessed by the unfallen or resurrected body) of passing through matter like a spirit 4339; **sutyltee** 4334.

suwe *pa.t.sg.* sawed 281; sawed in half 2489. **sawen** *pp.* sawn (in half) 4357.

suwyngly *adv.* in succession 23.

suy *v.* follow *[imitari]* 643. **suys** *pr.3 sg.* follows 806. **suyde** *subj.pa.t.sg.* followed 2093.

swages *pr.3 sg.* reduces 621.

sweght *n.* force of impact 2698.

swetlynesse *n.* graciousness, kindness 676 *(not in OED).*

swilk *dem.pron.* those 2747.

swilk *dem.adj.* such 401, 403, 414, 435, 452, 659, 660, 721, 897, 1037, 1190, 1191, 1232, 1284, 1322, 1547, 1614, 1659, 1663, 1665, 1669, 1792, 1795, 1850, 2123, 2287, 2288, 2303, 2375, 2388, 2503, 2556, 2579, 2579, 2599, 2876, 3176, 3291, 3297, 3317, 3527, 3550, 3791, 3969, 3971, 4081, 4182, 4315, 4347, 4372, 4448, 4486, 4733, 4883, 5017, 5063, 5070; **swylk** 2290, 2326; **swilke** 1929. **swilk** *absol.* of that kind 364n, 1786.

swith *adv.* instantly 3111; constantly 3597; **swithe** instantly 1458.

swongyn *pp.* flogged 123.

swte *adj.* sweet, gentle 4577.

swylk see **swilk.**

swynke *v.* labour, struggle 2798.

synagoga *n.* Jewry 2266.

syndene *n.* fine linen 2907; **syndone** linen garment 3249.

syrope *n.* medicinal syrup 2297.

tabernacle *n.* tent 2177. **tabernacles** *pl.* dwellings 1844.

table *n.* board, tablet 3256, 4147. **tables** *pl.* tablets 1184, 1217.

taillies *n.pl.* accounts, records 4249.

take *v.* understand 683[2]; receive 1411, 4220; in ~ *eende* end 4410. **takes** *pr.3 sg.* suffers 1595, *(? pl.)* 4300. *refl.pr.pl.* in ~ *thaym to* embrace 3927. **take** *imp.* understand 683[1] 710; **takes** in ~ *kepe* note 1595. **taking** *pr.p.* in ~...*hede* taking precedence over, excelling 1896. **toke** *pa.t.sg.* gave 184, 1347, 2474, 3501, 4211; received 987, 4361; in ~ *exultacioune* rejoiced *[gaudebat et exultabat]* 1135; ~...*in mynde* remembered, acted in accordance with 3348; ~ *on boldnesse* had the audacity 3979. **take** *pa.t.sg.* took *[assumpsit]* 1025. **toke** *subj.pa.t.sg.* surrendered 4549. *indic.pa.t.pl.* gave 2314, received 3143. **taken** *pp.* undertaken *[inchoaverunt]* 1865; given 2642 *[dari]*, 4162, 4198, 4216, 4288, 4545; deduced, ? observed *[demonstravit]* 4341; understood 4493; **takin** given 411; **takne** 3128.

takenes *pr.3 sg.* signifies 1162, 1166. **takenyng** *pr.p.* signifying, typefying 1528, 2620, 2622, 2624, 3086, 3846; **taknyng** 3882, 3888. **takned** *pa.t.sg.* signified 232, 237, 275, 593, 982, 2737, 3169; **takened** 1435, showed 2659; **takenid** 1586; **takenyd** 500; **taknyd** 3889. **takened** *pp.* represented 616; signified 690, 1465; **takenyd** 731, 2485, 3539. **taknyd** *pp.* 3155, 3842, 4973; **takenid** 763. **takenyng** *vbl.n.* sign 496; in *ber(e)s* ~ signifies 1870, 3184; *bare* ~ signified 2483.

taknys *n.pl.* symbols 2441.

tale *n.* fiction 4745; in *be* ~ all told 1253, 4949; *after* ~ according to the story 4361.

targe *n.* shield 3183; buckler (a light shield) 4149.

tary *v.* delay 1021.

tast *v.* try, test 1550.

techel from Aramaic *n.* shekel 275; **thechel** 4281n.

telle *v.* announce 539; in *craft to* ~ *?* it can be said 793n; witness 2959; describe 3039, 3600, 4547, 4903, 4951; enumerate 4355, 4365. **telles** *pr.3 sg.* says 3810. **tellyng** *pr.p.* representing; *?* telling 3756n. **tolde** *pp.* described 4409; in ~ *(for)* counted as 1164; *wele* ~ exactly 4326.

told *pp.* in ~ *to bee* see **bee.**

tempestuouses *adj. (? + French pl. ending)* 590n.

tendre *adj.* in ~ *of* sensitive to 1203.

termyne *v.* determine 3030.

terremote *n.* earthquake 4705.

terrestre *adj.* earthly 1127, 3061.

testimoniales *adj.* associated with the ark of the testimony (covenant) *(? + French pl. ending)* 1501.

tha *dem.adj.* those 3122.

thaire *poss.adj.* of them 3931; in ~ *allere ire* the anger of them both 3166; ~ *mavgree* see **mavgre.** **thanking** *vbl.n.* thanks 1201, 1754.

thare *impers.pr.3 sg.* in *the* ~ *neuer* you need never 4937.

thareon *adv.* at that 4576.

thareto *adv.* in addition to that 130.

tharewith *adv.* in addition to that 2291.

thassautis *def.art.+ n.pl.* the assaults 4038.

that *dem.pron.* that one 438n. **thays** *pl.* those 1113.

thechel see **techel.**

then *conj.* than 366, 1552, 2754.

then *? dem.pron.dat.pl.* those 499n.

thenk *pr.1 sg.* intend 8. **thenking** *vbl.n.* pondering 1838.

there *dem.adj.* these 655, 1159, 2111, 2114.

thereby *adv.* in *thoght noght enogh* ~ did not think that enough 2735.

thereto *adv.* there 2466; **thereto** of that (place) 4966. **þerto** for that purpose 976, in addition 1886, *[insuper]* 3427

thi *pers.pron.* they 1114, 1787.

thilk *dem.pron.* that (which is) 3042.

thilk *dem.adj.* that 70, 95, 270, 520, 678, 715, 717, 721, 865, 939, 959, 973, 1033, 1094, 1097, 1107, 1338, 1413, 1573, 1656, 1716, 1813, 1847, 2363, 2371, 2525, 2550, 2552, 2783, 2961, 3025, 3120, 3128, 3472, 3667, 3839, 4733, 4959, 5041, 5043.

thing *n.* anything 680; property 1233; experience 1852. *pl.* things 556, 652, 656, 665, 2656, 2769, 3691, 3803, 3882, 4484, 4601; **thinge** 402, 2150, 2153, 2217, 3643; **thinges** events 2391; in ~ *of* matters concerning 909.

thinke *v.impers.* in *hym* ~ seem to him 672; **think** in *hym shuld* ~ seem to him 1842. **thoght** *pa.t.sg.* in *him* ~ it seemed to him 162, 1031, 4727, 4731.

think *v.tr.* imagine 2912, 2930, 4881, 5104. *intr.* intend 299. **thynk** *pr.1 sg.* 1220. **thinkyng** *pr.p.* in *after...* ~ longing for 4905. **thoght** *pa.t.sg.* intended 1860, 2036. *tr.pp.* imagined 4412.

thire *dem.pron.* these 617, 1089, 1145, 1389, 1761, 1790, 2145, 2887, 3089, 3091, 3914, 4290, 4332.

thire *dem.adj.* these 619, 829, 832, 1047, 1115, 1117, 1118, 1121, 1136, 1241, 2144, 2851, 2917, 3035, 3273, 3603, 3635, 3662, 3739, 3832, 3859, 3913, 3931, 3939, 3964, 4057, 4082, 4120, 4163, 4291, 4335, 4548, 4629, 4913, 4946, 4950, 5031; **thyre** 2537.

thirlid *pa.t.pl.* fixed 2520; pierced 3209.

this *dem.pron.pl.* these 1265.

this *dem.adj.* these 1129, 1285, 1575, 1803, 2719, 3803.

tho *def.art.* in ~ *whilk* which 3045n.

thoght *n.* anxiety 412.

thoght see **think**.

thole *v.* tolerate 625, 626; endure 652; suffer 1519, 1807, 2290, 2295, 2318, 2629, 2726, 3583, 3584, 3633, 4247; allow 4859. **tholes** *pr.pl.* suffer 1422. **thole** *subj.pr.2 sg.* 2298. **tholing** *pr.p.* suffering 2523, 4576, 4664. **tholid** *pa.t.sg.* suffered 1659, 2142, 2807, 2937, 2951, 2980, 3101, 3208, 3470, 3573, 3581, 3850, 4135, 4627, 4742; allowed 4854; in ~ *to dye* accepted death 3471; **tholed** suffered 214, 2192, 2275, 2457, 2887; tolerated 2372. *pp.* endured 3835.

tholemode *adj.* patient 4631.

tholemodely *adv.* patiently 3215.

thonwonges *n.pl.* temples 3285.

thorgh *prep.* all over 3653.

thorgh *adv.* thoroughly, totally 1461, 3595; in *bare (...)* ~ see **bare**.

thorghby *adv.* ? in addition, as a result 3269n.

thorghout *adv.* through 2734, 2810, 4732; in ~ *and out* wholly and completely 2591.

thovzandly *adv.* in *innoumbrable* ~ innumerable thousands of times 4944 *(OED cites only this example)*.

thraldome *n.* slavery, captivity 1104, 2418, 2638, 3330; **thralledome** 1014.

thrallid *pa.t.sg.* held captive 3337. **thralde** *pp.* enslaved 3331.

thrange *pa.t.pl.* thrust 2348.

thrast *pa.t.sg.* pierced 4747.

threfaldelye *adv.* three times 1605.

threpe *n.* argument 1353.

threttisme *num. as adj.* thirtyfold *[trigesimus]* 835n.

thrist *n.* thirst 654, 3263, 3297, 4851; **thrust** 221, 4376.

thrist *intr.pr.1 sg.* thirst 4695. **thristis** *impers.pr.3 sg.* in *Me* ~ I thirst 2725. **thrustyng** *tr.pr.p.* striving after, pursuing *[anhelavit]* 3884. **thristing** *intr.* thirsting 1265. **thristed** *tr.pa.t.sg.* 1138. *pp.* thirsted for 1137.

thrysty *adj.* thirsty 1131.

thusgates *adv.* thus 3483.

thwynne *v.* separate 2570.

thynk see **think**.

thyre see **thire**.

til *prep.* to 62, 106, 254, 429, 477, 491, 492, 500, 594, 704, 714, 788, 799, 827, 906, 918, 922, 994, 1000, 1015, 1023, 1066, 1103, 1106, 1114, 1131, 1138, 1189, 1238, 1306, 1308, 1318, 1368, 1388, 1405, 1412, 1521, 1538, 1554, 1561, 1624, 1646, 1660, 1667, 1671, 1676, 1682, 1745, 1751, 1772, 1776, 1814, 1839, 1844, 2042, 2083, 2088, 2089, 2098, 2130, 2141, 2159, 2219, 2254, 2294, 2300, 2304, 2307, 2336, 2393, 2440, 2461, 2526, 2576, 2596, 2633, 2652, 2653, 2661, 2776, 2790, 2808, 2817, 2819, 2825, 2829, 2831, 2864, 2869, 2890, 2914, 2915, 2967, 2981, 3085, 3088, 3107, 3128, 3129, 3142, 3151, 3231, 3304, 3315, 3323, 3340, 3354, 3368, 3391, 3395, 3397, 3403, 3408, 3480, 3506, 3514, 3525, 3526, 3531, 3536, 3554, 3558, 3563, 3565, 3582, 3583, 3630, 3676, 3749, 3764, 3776, 3784, 3788, 3802, 3814, 3819, 3826, 3836, 3840, 3848, 3852, 3856, 3876, 3888, 3898, 3902, 3932, 3947, 3951, 3967, 3974, 4018, 4037, 4066, 4097, 4127, 4172, 4174, 4200, 4201, 4201, 4211, 4233, 4264, 4282, 4288, 4344, 4344, 4414, 4438, 4527, 4540, 4540, 4572, 4599, 4616, 4616, 4639, 4670, 4714, 4716, 4857, 4898, 4926, 4936, 4938, 4981, 5003, 5044, 5056, 5074, 5106, as 1484, for 2078; **till** 20, 33, 95, 134, 173, 184, 207, 268, 340, 346, 383, 406, 475, 484, 528, 544, 555, 572, 602, 1002, 1293, 1317, 1622, 1623, 1684, 3333; **tille** 1344, 1548, 1569, 3712; **tylle** against 3293; to 3316.

til *conj.* until 781, 3631, 3982.

tillid *pa.t.sg.* in *~ forth* persuaded 2095

tilman *n.* labourer 3624. **tilmen** *pl.* 2474, 2478, 2481; **tylmen** 142.

tirved *pa.t.sg.* stripped 2344; **tirvid** rolled 3432; **tyrved** stripped 4117.

tite *adv.* in *als ~* immediately 2681, 3007.

to *prep.* in *nede ~* need of 878; pleonastic in *forgive ~* 2545.

to *adv.* too 914.

to-breke *v.* crush 3280. **to-brokene** *pp.* 1391.

to-bristing *pr.p.* shattering 1328. **to-brast** *pa.t.sg.* shattered 1348, 1367, 1368, 1379, 1385, 1573, 3094, 3099, 3152.

to-drawe *pp.* torn apart 4388.

tofore *prep.* before 754, 1031, 1614, 1624, 1729, 1856, 1928, 2234, 2354, 2711, 2716, 3075, 3253, 3294, 3327, 3329, 3426, 3746, 3839, 3853, 4292, 4619, 4647, 4932; above 4026; **tofor** before 107, 174, 290, 1396, 4124.

tofore *adv.* in times past 101; earlier 508; first 538, 3457; before 805; previously 905, 1005, 1029, 1156, 1301, 1312, 1413, 1605, 1761, 1811, 1866, 2074, 2216, 2396, 2405, 2505, 2536, 2559, 2663, 2705, 2805, 2905, 3005, 3442, 3505, 3527, 3678, 3805, 4335, 4405, 4505, 4713, 4882; in *longe/lange ~* long ago 87, 608, 1369, 3954; in *~ lange* 4114; **tofor** in times past 195, 206; previously 3452. **tofore** *as adj.* previous 1205, 2205, 3305, 3605, 3705.

tofore *conj.* before 3985; in *~ that/þat* before 1041, 3113, 3137.

toforesaide see **toforsaide**.

toforhande *adv.* before 1036.

toforne *prep.* before 30.

toforne *adv.* before 684, 1177, 1384, 2105, 2305, 2325; in *lange/longe ~* long ago 64, 121, 567, 937; **toforn** in *last ~* before 705. **toforne** *as adj.* previous 2391.

toforsaide *adj.* aforesaid 3539, 4383; **toforesaide** 4504.

toke see **take.**

to-kytt *pp.* cut to pieces 4362.

told, tolde see **telle.**

too *n.* toe 2281, 2982.

to-racyng *pr.p.* slashing to pieces 4394.

to-rent *pa.t.sg.* tore to pieces 3154. *pp.* torn to pieces 2820; torn to tatters 4152; **to-rentt** torn to pieces 470; **to-rentte** 209.

to-thrast *pa.t.sg.* pierced through 4871.

to-torne *pp.* torn to shreds 2834.

to-trede *v.* tread to pieces 3278.

touche *v.* mention, touch *[tangere]* 3147. **touches** *pr.3 sg.* in ~ *noght* does not relate to 3061; **tovches** in ~ *till* describes 20. **touchyng** *pr.p.* striking 4064. **touchid** *pa.t.sg.* related to 2709. **touched** *pp.* struck *[tactus]* 623. **touchyngs** *vbl.n.pl.* intercourse 5008.

towards *adv.* in *in* ~ entering 1443.

to-whils *conj.* until 3309, 3788, 4033, 4641; as long as 3698, 4000, 4886; **to-whiles** whilst 1652; **to-whills** until 493.

trace *n.* footprints 1565.

translacioune *n.* removal from earth to heaven (without death) 3570, 3574, 5129.

translatid *pa.t.sg.* transferred 330. *pp.* in ~ *(in)* transferred to 3838.

transsubstanciate *pp.* transubstantiated 1900.

traysed *pa.t.sg.* betrayed 2038, 2050, 2052; **traysid** 2105.

traytourye *n.* betrayal 111.

tredde *adj.* third 2329.

tree *n.* wood 1497; cross (the Cross) 4150, 4664, 4670; in *rodes* ~ the Cross 488.

trehttith *adj.* thirtieth 1407.

trest *adj.* sure 612.

trete *v.* induce 356. **treted** *pa.t.pl.* discussed 1318. *pp.* arranged 277; **tretid** 4283.

tretee *n.* entreaty 3994 *(the earliest example with this sense in OED).*

trowe *v.* believe 3847, 3849; in *to* ~ to be believed 816, 3855; **trow** *pr.1 sg.* believe 2125. **trowes** *3 sg.* 2092. *pl.* believe 2792. **trow** *imp.* 911. **trowing** *pr.p.* believing 350, 826; **trowinge** 343. **trowed** *pa.t.sg.* believed 345. *pl.* 2992. *pp.* 2119.

truferye *n.* mockery, trifle 2239 *(the earliest example in OED).*

turmes *n.pl.* troops, squadrons 3518.

turne *v.* return 4210; reverse 4352; **turn** in ~ *hire to letting* cause her difficulty 886n. **turned** *pp.* turned sour 2868. **turnyng** *vbl.n.* return 1138.

turtyle *n.* turtle-dove 5043.

tuyllyd *pp.* harassed 459.

twynne *n.* in *in* ~ apart 1335.

twynned *pp.* separated 2571; **twynnyd** 4694. **twynnyng** *vbl.n.* division 4282; separation 4300.

tylle see **til.**

tylmen see **tilman.**

tyrved see **tirved.**

þerto see **thereto.**

vacant *adj.* being absent 5008.

vale *n.* valley 410.

valour *n.* value 4293; **valoure** 1165.

vanitee *n.* futile things 4081.

varie *adj.* varied 4076.

vayne *adj.* worthless, empty 424, 1827, 2796, 3918, 3926, 4265; in *in* ~ lightly, irresponsibly 1223.

vaynglorie *n.* selfish pride 1590, 4081.

veel *n.* calf 2162.

veigne *n.* vine 65.

venerable *adj.* worthy of respect 4649.

vengeable *adj.* inclined to vengeance 2200.

venkust *pp.* vanquished 1599.

verraly *adv.* indeed 2868.

verray *adj.* true 72, 724, 875, 1019, 1157 *[veri]*, 1158, 1189, 1194, 1273, 1286, 1474, 1703, 1733, 1819, 2608, 2615, 2656, 2881, 3055, 3064, 3334, 3621, 3623, 3971, 4351, 4539, 4863; actual 2883; very 3725; real 5059; **verraye** 3863, 5032. **verraiest** *sup.* most true 1886.

verray *adv.* truly, very 55.

verrayde *pa.t.sg.* made war on 3174.

verrayly *adv.* indeed 1323, 1824, 3843, 3932, 3971; truly 4531.

vertue *n.* power 897, 1072, 1137, 1411, 1666, 2156, 3138, 3514; virtue 3395, 4540. **vertues** *pl.* virtues 885, 1166, 1254, 1256, 1260, 1752, 1896, 3775, 4500; **vertuz** 3194, 3401; **vertus** 58; **vertuse** 3192.

vif *adj.* living *[vivus]* 1819.

vignour *n.* vineyard owner 3624.

viletee *n.* vileness, abhorrent associations 3145.

virone *n.* in *in* ~ in a circle 3886.

vitaille *n.* supply 1563.

vnbrosten *ppl.a.* unforced 5006.

vnbrynnyng *ppl.a.* unignited 1171.

vncledde *pa.t.pl.* stripped 2437.

vnconnyng *n.* in *of* ~ in ignorance, innocently 1352.

vnderȝede *pa.t.sg.* underwent 1410.

vnderloute *adj.* submissive 794.

vnderstandinglye *adv.* unmistakeably 2789.

vndestressid *ppl.a.* not under compulsion *[sponte]* 4561.

vndigne *adj.* unworthy 945, 1639.

vndiscrete *adj.* injudicious 447.

vndiscretly *adv.* ill-advisedly 741.

vndos *pr.3 sg.* cures 637. **vndone** *ppl.a.* destroyed, ruined 3992. **vndoing** *vbl.n.* taking, destroying 3291.

vneged *ppl.a.* blunted, dead *[obstupescerent]* 377 *(? OED unedge v. A.D.1614ff).*

vnhande-made *adj.* not made by hand 2236.

vnhappy *adj.* unfortunate, unhappy 751.

vnherd *adj.* unheard-of 2320, 4543.

vnherthid *pa.t.sg.* cut out the heart (of) 182 *(OED* unheart *v. A.D.1593ff).*

vnhonestely *adv.* improperly 2175.

vnhopfulle *adj.* unpromising 2887 *(the earliest example in OED).*

vnite *ppl.a.* united 3053, 3308.

vnknawes *pr.3 sg.* does not understand 665. **vnknawing** *pr.p.* not recognising 2150, 2227.

vnkonnyng *adj.* unskilled 4448.

vnkynde *adj.* unnatural, unkind 2043.

vnkyndely *adv.* unnaturally, unkindly 2350.

vnleffulle *adj.* forbidden 1226.

vnlesing *pr.p.* not losing *[sine...amissione]* 3350 *(not in OED).*

vnlike *? adv.* in ~ *with* in contrast 2176n; on the contrary 2678n; ~ *als to* not comparable with 3589.

vnneths *adv.* scarcely 428; **vnnethes** barely 514; **vnnethis** hardly 2914.

vnrewth *n.* cruelty 4051.

vnselye *adj.* evil 4678.

vnshaply *adj.* deformed 4313.

vnsheendyng *pr.p.* destroying 5010.

vnsoundid *pa.t.pl.* tore 2977.

vntacte *adj.* virgin 5053 *(not in OED).*

vntholefulle *adj.* intolerable 3318.

vnthralle *v.* release from bondage 1023 *(OED c.A.D.1586ff.).*

vnthreft *n.* failure 412.

vnthrefty *adj.* useless 3968.

vntil *prep.* to 246, 367, 807, 908, 1111, 1616, 1754, 1816, 2206, 2214, 2329, 2524, 3191, 4102, 4165; **vntill** 124, 231; in (accordance with) 310; **vntille** to 1464.

vnto *prep.* to 53, 69, 119, 266, 273, 314, 387, 410, 415, 419, 433, 614, 620, 718, 725, 726, 744, 758, 855, 880, 1057, 1085, 1312, 1346, 1358, 1483, 1515, 1666, 1784, 1880, 2087, 2281, 2333, 2525, 2546, 2598, 2724, 2728, 2793, 2829, 3000, 3008, 3076, 3308, 3335, 3438, 3793, 3874, 3908, 4116, 4366, 4415, 4417, 4474, 4544; for 1077; until 2146, 3050, 3648; into 2998, 3098, 3583; in ~..*able* capable of 1694; **vntoo** to 571.

vntrest *n.* mistrust 4045.

vntwynned *adj.* undivided 2.

vnwasting *ppl.a.* not consuming 3349.

vnwemmyd *adj.* unblemished 862.

vnwithsayable *adj.* irresistible, ungainsayable 3952 *(OED cites only this example)*.

vnwitting *ppl.a.* without knowledge 910.

vnyt *ppl.a.* united 1500; **vnyte** 3008.

voide *adj.* empty 240.

voides *pr.3 sg.* removes, drives out 661, 673. **voiding** *pr.p.* 893. **voided** *pa.t.sg.* 1619.

vouche *imp.* in ~*sauf(e)* deign 3103, 3380. **vouching** *pr.p.* in ~*sauf* 3066. **vouched** *pa.t.sg.* in ~ *sauf* 2047, 3134; **vouchid** in ~ *sauf* 2103.

vovtours *n.pl.* vultures 184.

vp *adv.* in *(both) ~and doune* everywhere 4151, 4589; **vppe** in ~*nor doune* in any way 766; *both ~and doune* from top to bottom 2957.

vppere *comp.* higher 3395.

vrna Lat. *n.* in ~ *aurea* the golden vessel 1249.

vse *n.* behaviour of things 1293; normal practice 2308; custom 4140, 4860.

vses *pr.3 sg.* commits 2756; in ~*he to tempt* he tempts 4047. **vses** *pl.* do 2716; in ~*noght...to* do not 819; practice 3921.

vsure *n.* usury 1780, 1783, 1787, 1792, 1801; excessive interest 1789; interest 4217.

vtilitee *n.* benefit 1066; advantageousness 1069.

vtterly *adv.* absolutely 4861.

waa *n.* woe 3967.

wagrand *ppl.a.* in *soule*~wandering alone *[solivaga]* 812 *(not in OED)*; **wagring** homeless, itinerant *[hospitium non habentem]* 1266.

waike *adj.* weak 371. **waikest** *sup.* absolutely powerless 4881.

wakely *adv.* in an enfeebled condition 3911.

wakes *pr.3 sg.* is awake 786. **waking** *ppl.a.* awake 2180.

wandes *n.pl.* rods 2269, 3255.

wanhope see **wannhope**.

wanne *pa.t.sg.* won 4216.

wannhope *n.* despair 825; **wanhope** 4111; **wannehope** 3272.

want *v.* lack 1723. **wantyng** *pr.p.* lacking 3800, 4900. **wantid** *pa.t.sg.* 1782. **wanting** *ppl.a.* absent 4886. *vbl.n.* absence (of God) 3023; **wantyng** deficiency 3780.

wapeins *n.pl.* weapons 1933; **wapenes** 3091.

wapped *pa.t.sg.* wrapped 2324.

war see **bee**.

warde *n.* guardianship 873.

ware *adj.* cautious 324; informed 359; aware 1767; in *to be* ~ avoid 454.

ware *imp.* be on your guard 364.

warefore *adv.* for this reason 4527.

waried *ppl.a.* cursed 2443.

warne *v.* refuse 4183. **warnyd** *pa.t.sg.* 4564.

warnsture *? n.* fortifications *[muniunt castra]* 3092 *(OED warnestore).*

warre see **bee**.

wast *v.* lay waste 1716; **waste** destroy 1940. **wastes** *tr.pr.3 sg.* reduces 475. **wasting** *pr.p.* ravaging 3284. **wastyng** *intr.pr.p.* being consumed 4983. **waystid** *tr.pa.t.pl.* devastated 1877. **wast** *pp.* enfeebled 1549; **wastid** used up 3595. **wastyng** *intr.vbl.n.* waning 3881.

wawishe *adj.* turbulent 591 *(OED cites only this example).*

waxis *pr.p.* grows 649, 1828. **wax** *pa.t.sg.* developed into 1380; grew 1826, 2954; **wex** 4878. **waxen** *pp.* become 2591.

way *n.* road 914, 3158, 3731; **waye** path 1749; journey 3124; in *diuers* ~ many ways 1734. **wayes** *pl.* routes 3752; in ~ *even* ? direct route 3603n.

waymentid *pa.t.pl.* lamented 2872.

waystid see **wast**.

weeld *v.* command 445.

weende *v.* go 3304, 3639, 5106. **weending** *pr.p.* going 3157, 4209; **weendyng** 3435. **went** *pa.t.sg.* walked 4342. *pp.* in *was* ~ had been 4213.

weke *n.* wick 1285.

weking *vbl.n.* soaking *[repletio]* 981 *(OED weak v. only A.D.1559ff).*

wel see **wele**.

wele *n.* in *if* ~ *shall bene* if all goes well 4.

wele *adj.* blessed 700.

wele *adv.* beneficially 1062; very 1131, 2715; properly, truly 2101; much 2199, 2322, 2373, 2889, 2985, 3070; appropriately 3229; easily 3779; dearly 4094; in ~ *werre* exceedingly 2714; *a hondrethfald* ~ *tolde* fully a hundredfold 4326; **wel** in ~ *negh* nearly 2584, 2920.

welknyng *vbl.n.* withering, fading 4437 *(OED cites only this example of vbl.n.).*

welkyn *n.* sky 3593.

welle-strondys *n.pl.* small streams (flowing from a spring) 4642.

welth *n.* prosperity, wealth 421, 437; **weltth** 1679.

wend see **wene**.

wene *n.* doubt 520.

wene *pr.1 sg.* think, believe 4185. **wend** *pa.t.pl.* meant 2157.

went see **weende**.

wepfulle *adj.* tearful 4908.

wepynly *adv.* tearfully 2823.

werde *n.* world; in *in alle the* ~ at all 4275.

werdely *adj.* worldly 656; **werdly** 3960.

were *n.* war 1933, 3236; battle 4146; in *make hym* ~ make war on him 4234.

were see **bee**.

werraye *v.* make war on 4003. **werying** *pr.p.* warring 583. **werraying** *ppl.a.* 3279.

werre *n.* war 3293, 3990.

werre *adv.* in *wele* ~ 2714.

werre see **bee**.

wethin *adv.* whence 677.

wethire *n.* ram 2456, 2457.

wex see **waxis**.

wharefore *adv.rel.* for which reason 317, 535, 593, 879, 887, 917, 946, 1090, 1191, 1244, 1326, 1333, 1467, 1549, 1553, 1701, 1871, 2165, 2251, 2326, 2424, 2566, 814, 2856, 2871, 2886, 3377, 3471, 3521, 3524, 3557, 3573, 3616, 3991, 4029, 4059, 4095, 4127, 4133, 4352, 4735, 4945, 5034. *interr.* why 2337. **wharefor** *rel.* 944, 1292, 2969, 3313, 3835.

whareof *adv.rel.* about which 628; for which 3297, 4240. *interr.* from what source 931; to what purpose 2209, 3679.

whareon *adv.* on which 2447.

wharethorgh *adv.* for which 2232; as a result of which 4632.

wharewith *adv.rel.* by means of which 4224.

wharto *adv.interr.* why 1929.

what *pron.* in ~ *so* whatever 4511.

what *adj.* any 657, 1777.

what *adv.* how much 3129.

whene *n.* queen 1155.

where *conj.* whether 417, 980, 1092, 1386, 1648, 2136, 2944, 2950, 4591, 4655.

where see **bee**.

where *conj.* when 2039, 4941.

whightlake see **wightlayke**.

whilk *pron.* which 52, 55, 80, 144, 159, 162, 194, 224, 306, 308, 320, 402, 430, 432,492, 509, 547, 564, 620, 627, 688, 690, 692, 701, 710, 716, 718, 745, 754, 761, 762, 763, 888, 890, 972, 984, 1032, 1060, 1066, 1158, 1170, 1194, 1216, 1218, 1247, 1254, 1257, 1262, 1263, 1288, 1338, 1350, 1414, 1415, 1434, 14451487, 1489, 1502, 1619, 1742, 1743, 1768, 1812, 1824, 1836, 1856, 2042, 2151, 2161, 2263, 2328, 2334, 2452, 2454, 2465, 2633, 2658, 2823, 2922, 2937, 2960, 3026, 3031, 3088, 3092, 3126, 3130, 3134, 3185, 3209, 3226, 3227, 3228, 3235, 3236, 3240, 3271, 3345, 3417, 3440, 3464, 3470, 3476, 3489, 3496, 3517, 3525, 3530, 3535, 3542, 3559, 3634, 3652, 3656, 3668, 3685, 3697, 3721, 3729, 3732, 3733, 3757, 3763, 3766, 3768, 3775, 3868, 3879, 3883, 3886, 3892, 3897, 4151, 4239, 4335, 4601, 4642, 4702, 4961, 4986, 5036, 5042, 5105, 5110, who 122, 166, 254, 348, 551, 737, 915, 1030, 1048, 1131, 1332, 1421, 1472, 1474, 1575, 1584, 1585, 1631, 1657, 1662, 1689, 1715, 1726, 1732, 1793, 2088, 2117, 2169, 2171, 2602, 2758, 2760, 2762, 2786, 2794, 2900, 3152, 3154, 3170, 3172, 3290, 3291, 3338, 3377, 3462, 3513, 3700, 3745, 3890, 3928, 3948, 3956, 3966, 3967, 3970, 3974, 3994, 4028, 4034, 4060, 4069, 4188, 4211, 4615, 4920, 4927, 4936, 4995, 5029, 5081, 5132; whom 201, 1892, 2478, 2499, 2741; in ~*þat*, *the* ~ who 135, 525, 2872, 3435, 3540, 4156; which 619, 1007, 1152, 1219, 1282, 1433, 1570, 1708, 1820, 2519, 2608, 3424, 3459, 3692, 4303, 4346; by which 4606; **whilke** which 746.

whilk *adj.* which 23, 82, 206, 881, 1046, 1091, 1109, 1311, 1379, 1837, 1857, 1882, 2229, 2330, 2618, 2893, 3089, 3191, 3488, 3491, 3757, 4478, 4487, 4497, 4555, 4581, 4607, 4633, 4659, 4685, 4711, 4867, 4893, 4971, 4997, 5023, 5038, 5049, 5075, 5101, 5127; in *tho*/*the* ~ which 3045, 3181.

whilom *adv.* at times 469.

white *adj.* specious 358.

whitte *n.* in *evry* ~ whole 4287.

who *pron.* anyone 13, 623, 633, 643, 651, 671, 832, 845, 847, 853, 1141, 1417, 1428, 1430, 1525, 1782, 1834, 1852, 1853, 3557, 4215, 4216, 4221, 4509, those who 3075.

whoke *pa.t.sg.* quaked 2955.

whoso *pron.* whoever 1467, 1601, 2968.

wight *n.* creature, person 1624, 1694, 2090, 4167. **wightis** *pl.* 2255, 2916; **wightes** people 4640; **wyghts** 2201.

wightlayke *adj.* swift, immediate 4434. **whightlake** *as n.* speed *[velocitas]* 4441 *(the ME noun is unrecorded)*.

wilne *v.* desire 1237. **wilnes** *pr.3 sg.* wishes 1430, 4509. **wilne** *imp.* 1239. **wilnyng** *pr.p.* hoping 2425; wishing 3357, 3362. *vbl.n.* desire 1839.

wirshippe *v.* honour, respect 1903. **worships** *pr.3 sg.* honours 3685. **wyrshipt** *pp.* honoured 2171, 2331.

wise *n.* manner, way 937, 949, 982, 1487, 1681, 2535, 2700, 2745, 2930, 3059, 3194, 3347, 3623, 3672, 4219, 4361, 4372, 4408, 4522, 4541; fashion 1320; normal practice 4099. **wyse** way 3849. **wise** *pl.* ways 842, 1676, 1896, 4855

wist, wit see **witt**.

wites *pr.3 sg.* vanishes 1827.

with *prep.* until like 3591; like 3599; in *vnlike* ~ see **vnlike**.

withalle *adv.* along with the rest 368; as well 3264, 3733.

without *prep.* apart from 912; in *go* ~ be without 1524; ~ *noumbre* immesurably 3184; ~ *mesure* exceedingly 3488; **withouten** in ~ *meseur* exceedingly 3859.

without *adv.* outside 911, 2481; **withoute** 1259, 1260.

withseide *pp.* refused 266.

witte *n.* intelligence 389, 4427; reason 402; mind 1825, 2223; ingenuity 2317; skill 2668; wisdom 4444; **witt** understanding 578. **wittes** *pl.* mind 1666.

witte *v.* know 505; **witt** in *it is to* ~ it should be known 2189; *ȝe may wele* ~ you ought to know 3683; **wit** know 1512. *imp.* in ~ *wele* you can be sure 1409; ~ *ye* let me tell you 3023, 3045, 3407; **witte** in ~ *ȝe* mark you 608, 2945; **witt** in ~ *ȝe/thowe* you should know 1161, 4459. **witting** *pr.p.* knowing 3786. **wist** *pa.t.sg.* knew 2179. **witten** *pp.* known 2058.

wode *adj.* mad 2411; insane, furious 2492, 3250, 4602, 4678. **wodeest** *sup.* 2152.

wodely *adv.* insanely 2543, 2751.

wodenesse *n.* fury 596; savagery, cruelty 1909, 1929, 2074, 2148, 2247, 2748, 4597; **woodnesse** fury 637.

woke *pa.t.sg.* was awake 784.

wold *pa.t.sg.* wished 807, 1211; willed 2819; **wolde** wanted 2045; wished 3107, 5095; in *Godde* ~ by God's will 3658; **nwold** *pl.neg.* (ne + wold) would not 2690.

wombe *n.* stomach 229, 1670, 3462; belly 1373, 3180, 3183, 3186, 3187. **wombes** *gen.* in ~ *brothere* uterine brother 384, 2099.

wondere *n.* in *no* ~ it is not surprising that 685.

wondere *adj.* in ~ *thing* marvel 70.

wondere *adv.* marvellously 431.

wonderfullie *adv.* 1044; **wonderfully** 3078.

wondring *pr.p.* surprising 3482.

wonne *n.* custom 5035.

wonne *pp.* gained 4215.

wont *pp.* accustomed 922; established 2252; in *ware* ~ used 2397; *is* ~ *pertene* normally pertains 5033; **wonte** in *ware* ~ used 2333; *ere* ~ *be* are often 3087.

woodnesse see **wodenesse**.

worde *n.* report, talk *[sermo]* 2650.

worships see **wirshippe**.

worst *sup.* most vicious 2824.

worthily *adv.* fittingly 2071; **worthilye** suitably 2599.

wote *pr.3 sg.* knows 2150. **wote** *pr.pl.* know 722, 1195, 2537, 2545.

wounde *pr.pl.* pierce *[clavis configere et vulnerare]* 2793.

woune *v.* live, dwell 1304.

wrange *adj.* wrongful 740.

wreche *n.* a despicable person (? adj. despicable*)* 4119.

wrethid see **wrethis**.

wrething *pr.p.* hurting by twisting the limbs, torturing *[offendunt]* 2753 *(OED* writhe*)*.

wrethis *pr.pl.* anger 3970. **wrethid** *pp.* angered 1627.

wricchedly *adv.* despicably 2785.

wright *n.* craftsman 321.

wroght *pa.t.sg.* brought about 311, 2228, 2421, 2425. **wroght** *pl.* performed 2342. **wroght** *pp.* made 1330, 2816.

wronge *adv.* unsuitably 2588.

wronge *pa.t.sg.* wrung 989, 2926.

wrongwis *adj.* ill-gotten 3934; **wrongwys** unjust 4578.

wroth *adj.* angry 2368, 3387, 3663, 3944; in ~ *to* angry with 3939; **wrothe** 1648.

wrothly *adv.* angrily 251.

wrthyest *sup.* most noble 3238.

wryed *pp.* denounced 4115.

wyche *n.* sorcerer 2380.

wyde-whare *adv.* far and wide 1587; **wyde-where** 2996.

wyghts see **wight**.

wynne *v.* earn 598, 3708, 4170, 4224, 4273, 4508; **wyn** earn 442, succeed 2914. **wynnyng** *vbl.n.* profit 4212, reward 4220.

wyried *pa.t.sg.* choked, devoured 1575.

wyrshipfully *adv.* with honour, ceremoniously 3841.

wyrshipt see **wirshippe**.

wyse see **wise**.

ydropicye *n.* dropsy (bloating disease) 653.

yette *pa.t.sg.* poured out 574. **ȝettid** *pl.* 2398. **ȝett** *pp.* poured 1434. **ȝette** *ppl.a.* cast (in metal), man-made 119.

yfere *adv.* together 4310.

yhit see **ȝit**.

ylike *adv.* in *euer* ~ constantly 3054.

ymagyned *pa.t.sg.* planned 2068.

ympnis *n.pl.* hymns 769.

ynowe *adj.pl.* enough, plenty of 480.

yrnysshe *adj.* iron-like 1374.

ysope *n.* hyssop 3264.

yvel *n.* harm 3092.

yvel *adj.* damaging, immoral 3083, 3312.

yvel *adv.* wickedly 142.

yvoriene *adj.* made of ivory 5041.

ywisse *adv.* indeed 3584; **ywys** 4563.

ȝaf *pa.t.sg.* gave 1529.

ȝalde see **ȝelde**.

ȝarde *n.* field 3735.

ȝede *pa.t.sg.* went, walked 320, 2079; visited 4913. *pl.* went, walked 514. **ȝode** *pl.* went 1476, 1912, 1921.

ȝelde *v.* return 2060; give (in return) to 2599, 4548. **ȝalde** *pa.t.sg.* yielded up 2728; repaid 4217, 4700. *pl.* returned 2063; repaid 4230. **ȝolden** *pp.* given in return 2292; given up 2730, 3007.

ȝerde *n.* rod, staff 65, 677, 678, 939, 1071, 1073, 1075, 1081, 1247, 1489, 3118, 3120, 3122, 3123, 3126, 4961, 4963, 4999 **ȝerd** rod 38, stem 609, 613. **ȝerdes** *gen.* 1077. **ȝerdes** *pl.* 127, 4640 **ȝerdis** 4359;

ȝerde *n.* vineyard 142.

ȝerne *adv.* rapidly, thoroughly *(? adj.* active*)* 4039.

ȝernes *pr.p.* desire 3928. **ȝerned** *ppl.a.* desired 382.

ȝett, ȝettid see **yette**.

ȝit *adv.* moreover 1387; also 3440; eventually 3513; **yhit** 921.

ȝode see **ȝede**.

ȝolden see **ȝelde**.

ȝouthede *n.* youth 4437.

ȝynge *adj.* young 959.

zucrish *adj.* sugary 790; **zucrys** sweet 3858.

The Middle Ages

Edward Peters, *General Editor*

Christian Society and the Crusades, 1198–1229. Sources in Translation, including The Capture of Damietta by Oliver of Paderborn. Edited by Edward Peters

The First Crusade: The Chronicle of Fulcher of Chartres and Other Source Materials. Edited by Edward Peters

Love in Twelfth-Century France. John C. Moore

The Burgundian Code: The Book of Constitutions or Law of Gundobad and Additional Enactments. Translated by Katherine Fischer Drew

The Lombard Laws. Translated, with an Introduction, by Katherine Fischer Drew

From St. Francis to Dante: Translations from the Chronicle of the Franciscan Salimbene (1221–1288). G. G. Coulton

The Duel and the Oath. Parts I and II of Superstition and Force. Henry Charles Lea. Introduction by Edward Peters

The Ordeal. Part III of Superstition and Force. Henry Charles Lea

Torture. Part IV of Superstition and Force. Henry Charles Lea

Witchcraft in Europe, 1110–1700: A Documentary History. Edited by Alan C. Kors and Edward Peters

The Scientific Achievement of the Middle Ages. Richard C. Dales

History of the Lombards. Paul the Deacon. Translated by William Dudley Foulke

Monks, Bishops, and Pagans: Christian Culture in Gaul and Italy, 500–700. Edited, with an Introduction, by Edward Peters

The World of Piers Plowman. Edited and translated by Jeanne Krochalis and Edward Peters

Felony and Misdemeanor: A Study in the History of Criminal Law. Julius Goebel, Jr

Women in Medieval Society. Edited by Susan Mosher Stuard

The Expansion of Europe: The First Phase. Edited by James Muldoon

Laws of the Alamans and Bavarians. Translated, with an Introduction, by Theodore John Rivers

Law, Church, and Society: Essays in Honor of Stephan Kuttner. Edited by Robert Somerville and Kenneth Pennington

The Fourth Crusade: The Conquest of Constantinople, 1201–1204. Donald E. Queller

The Magician, the Witch, and the Law. Edward Peters

Daily Life in the World of Charlemagne. Pierre Riché. Translated, with an Introduction, by Jo Ann McNamara

Repression of Heresy in Medieval Germany. Richard Kieckhefer

The Royal Forests of Medieval England. Charles R. Young

Popes, Lawyers, and Infidels: The Church and the Non-Christian World, 1250–1550. James Muldoon

Heresy and Authority in Medieval Europe. Edited, with an Introduction, by Edward Peters

Women in Frankish Society: Marriage and the Cloister, 500 to 900. Suzanne Fonay Wemple

The English Parliament in the Middle Ages. Edited by R. G. Davies and J. H. Denton

Rhinoceros Bound: Cluny in the Tenth Century. Barbara H. Rosenwein

On the Threshold of Exact Science: Selected Writings of Anneliese Maier on Late Medieval Natural Philosophy. Edited and translated by Steven D. Sargent

Miracles and the Medieval Mind: Theory, Record, and Event, 1000–1215. Benedicta Ward

The Chronicle of Theophanes: An English Translation of anni mundi *6095–6305 (A.D. 602–812)*. Translated, with an Introduction, by Harry Turtledove

The English Medieval Landscape. Edited by Leonard Cantor

Dante's Italy and Other Essays. Charles T. Davis

Maurice's Strategikon: Handbook of Byzantine Military Strategy. Translated by George T. Dennis

The Republic of St. Peter: The Birth of the Papal State, 680–825. Thomas F. X. Noble

Pope and Bishops: The Papal Monarchy in the Twelfth and Thirteenth Centuries. Kenneth Pennington

The Origins of Courtliness: Civilizing Trends and the Formation of Courtly Ideals, 939–1210. C. Stephen Jaeger

The Conversion of Western Europe, 350–750. Edited by J. N. Hillgarth

From Servitude to Freedom: Manumission in the Sénonais in the Thirteenth Century. William Chester Jordan

Ransoming Captives in Crusader Spain: The Order of Merced on the Christian–Islamic Frontier. James William Brodman

Aristocracy in Provence: The Rhône Basin at the Dawn of the Carolingian Age. Patrick J. Geary

Meister Eckhart: Thought and Language. Frank Tobin

Dino Compagni's Chronicle of Florence. Translated, with an Introduction by Daniel Bornstein

Anatomy of A Crusade, 1213–1221. James M. Powell

The First Crusade and the Idea of Crusading. Jonathan Riley-Smith

Women in Medieval History and Historiography. Edited by Susan Mosher Stuard

The Mirour of Mans Saluacioune. Edited by Avril Henry